THE SEA OTTER
IN THE
EASTERN PACIFIC OCEAN

THE SEA OTTER

IN THE

EASTERN PACIFIC OCEAN

By Karl W. Kenyon, *Wildlife Biologist*

Formerly of the Division of Wildlife Research

UNITED STATES FISH AND WILDLIFE SERVICE

DOVER PUBLICATIONS, INC.
NEW YORK

Published in Canada by General Publishing Company, Ltd., 30 Lesmill Road, Don Mills, Toronto, Ontario.

Published in the United Kingdom by Constable and Company, Ltd., 10 Orange Street, London WC 2.

This Dover edition, first published in 1975, is an unabridged and corrected republication of the work originally published in 1969 by the Bureau of Sport Fisheries and Wildlife at the U.S. Government Printing Office, Washington, D.C. as Number 68 in the North American Fauna Series.

International Standard Book Number: 0-486-21346-3
Library of Congress Catalog Card Number: 74-18668

Manufactured in the United States of America
Dover Publications, Inc.
180 Varick Street
New York, N.Y. 10014

PREFACE

This report is the result of studies conducted from 1955 to 1967 by the Division of Wildlife Research of the Bureau of Sport Fisheries and Wildlife. In addition to field data gathered primarily in the Aleutian Islands, many unpublished reports, letters, and memorandums in U.S. Fish and Wildlife Service files were used. As a biologist working on studies of the Pribilof Islands population of northern fur seals from 1947 to 1955, I developed an interest in the sea otters of the Aleutian Islands. I was therefore pleased to be assigned as project leader of sea otter studies.

Many people contributed help in the field and laboratory. The following undertook special studies and have kindly permitted me to include their results. Dr. D. G. Chapman (statistical studies of phases of population dynamics); Dr. F. H. Fay (parasitism); Miss Neva Karrick (nutritional values of foods); Dr. J. K. Ling (skin structure); Dr. R. L. Rausch (parasitism); Dr. E. C. Roosen-Runge (reproduction in the male); Dr. R. P. Scapino (jaw muscles and joints); Dr. V. B. Scheffer (pelage and dentition); and Dr. D. B. Scott (dental attrition).

J. E. Burdick collected specimens and analyzed stomach contents. It would be impossible to list all those who assisted in other ways, but the following have been notably helpful: J. J. Alles, G. Baines, A. W. F. Banfield, V. D. Berns, A. Bezezekoff, F. Bezezekoff, K. L. Binkley, E. L. Boeker, R. A. Boolootian, J. W. Brooks, C. A. Brosseau, D. V. Brown, J. J. Burns, J. G. Carlisle, C. E. Carlson, C. H. Conaway, I. McT. Cowan, K. W. Cox, L. W. Croxton, S. V. Dorofeev (deceased), Y. E. Dawson (deceased), M. A. Edwards, C. H. Fiscus, R. M. Gilmore, I. Golodoff, C. J. Guiguet, E. Gunther, W. J. Hamilton, Jr., G. D. Hanna, S. J. Harbo, A. C. Hartt, L. G. Hertlein, C. L. Hubbs, A. Jensen, A. M. Johnson, E. J. Johnson, M. L. Johnson, R. D. Jones, Jr., M. C. Keyes, J. G. King, C. M. Kirkpatrick, D. R. Klein, E. G. Klinkhart, H. R. Krear, W. S. Laughlin, D. L. Leedy, C. J. Lensink, P. T. Macy, E. G. Magee, L. Margolis, V. F. Martin, P. A. McLaughlin, E. D. Mitchell, H. W. Mossman, K. A. Neiland, U. C. Nelson, I. M. Newell, T. P. O'Brien (deceased), R. T. Orr, R. L. Peterson, R. G. Prasil, J. Radovich, J. Rankin, C. A. Repenning, F. Richardson, A. Y. Roppel, L. V. Sagen, E. Sczuck, A. H. Seymour, A. A. Sinha, A. G. Smith, T. A. Smith,

D. L. Spencer, R. Thomas, J. S. Vania, F. Vincenzi, A. D. Welander, N. J. Wilimovsky, L. Williams, V. L. Yadon, C. E. Yunker, and M. Zhan.

The cooperation of Game Biologists of the Alaska Department of Fish and Game was of particular value. Reproductive tracts, stomachs, other specimens, and information contributed by them furnished much of the material upon which this report is based.

The Woodland Park Zoo, Seattle, and the Point Defiance Aquarium, Tacoma, generously furnished facilities and care for captive otters and routinely recorded certain observations on behavior, molt, and food consumption.

The help of Mrs. Ethel I. Todd, not only in typing the manuscript but in assisting in many other phases of its preparation, was indispensable.

All or a substantial part of the manuscript was read and editorial assistance was given by P. A. DuMont, C. Larson, R. H. Manville, D. W. Rice, V. B. Scheffer, K. Schneider, D. W. Slater, and F. Wilke.

Weights and linear measurements of animals were taken in either the metric or the English systems. The original measurement is shown first, followed by the conversion in parentheses.

Nautical charts show distances in nautical miles (1 nautical mile equals 1.15 statute or land mile). In the present report, "miles" means nautical miles unless otherwise specified. Depths are usually given in fathoms (1 fathom equals 6 feet) because of their use on nautical charts. Depths are given in meters when depth bears no particular relation to nautical charts. Maps are adaptations from U. S. Coast and Geodetic Survey charts.

Trade names referred to in this publication do not imply endorsement of commercial products.

Much work on the biology of the sea otter remains to be done. Many of the studies included in this report are preliminary approaches to subjects that will require years of future study.

CONTENTS

ILLUSTRATIONS

TABLES

THE SEA OTTER
IN THE
EASTERN PACIFIC OCEAN

INTRODUCTION

As early as 1733, Spanish missionaries and explorers bartered for sea otter (*Enhydra lutris*) pelts with the Indians of Upper and Lower California (Ogden, 1941). Apparently the high value of the skins in the Orient was unknown to them.

In 1741 Georg Wilhelm Steller was shipwrecked with the Bering expedition on Bering Island of the Commander Islands. Here he observed the sea otter and gave the western world its first scientific description of the animal and its habits. After the remnant of Bering's expedition returned with valuable furs and news of abundant otters and seals on the islands to the east, fur hunters from Siberia, the Promyshlenniki, soon began exploiting Aleutian sea otter populations.

In 1779, members of Captain James Cook's expedition to the North Pacific sold in Canton otter pelts that they had obtained at Vancouver Island. The high value of the pelts on the Oriental market soon precipitated a flood of fur hunters from America and Europe. Thus began intensive exploitation of otters along the west coast of the United States and Canada. Unregulated hunting throughout the sea otter's range was incessant, and by the end of the 19th century the sea otter was extinct commercially and nearly extinct as a species. Highlights of this period are recounted in context by Miller and Miller (1967).

Management of the sea otter as a valuable natural resource began in 1911 when the remnant population was given Federal protection. It was feared that after nearly 170 years of unregulated exploitation the species might not survive. The initial phase of Government control was one of complete protection.

In 1935, men of the U.S. Coast Guard saw many sea otters at Amchitka Island, and in 1936, U.S. Bureau of Fisheries agents were stationed there to guard against poaching.

In 1936 and 1937, expeditions under Olaus J. Murie of the U.S. Bureau of Biological Survey conducted the first comprehensive biological inventory of what had become, in 1913, the Aleutian Islands Wildlife Refuge (now a National Wildlife Refuge).

These expeditions were the first to reveal that otter populations at a number of islands were growing. During World War II, additional population growth was observed.

On my first brief visit to Amchitka in the late fall of 1947, Dr. V. B. Scheffer and I found dead otters on the beaches. Elmer Hansen, who was stationed there, found and sent us additional specimens. These were mailed wrapped, without preservative, inside weather balloons and, as the assistant who cleaned the bones, I had a strong and unforgettable introduction to the sea otter.

In the 1949–53 period, R. D. Jones, Aleutian National Wildlife Refuge Manager, observed winter "die-offs" at Amchitka. In 1950–51 he led an expedition there to capture and transplant otters to other areas. All captive otters soon died, and it became evident to him that the sea otter adapted poorly to captivity under field conditions. This experience demonstrated that until further knowledge of the animals' biological needs was gained, transplanting attempts would be futile.

As a first step toward a better understanding of sea otter biology, Dr. Robert L. Rausch went to Amchitka to study stranded animals, dead or dying, and Drs. C. M. Kirkpatrick and D. E. Stullken, with the aid of R. D. Jones, F. Wilke, C. J. Lensink, and D. Hooper went there in the winter of 1954 to study sea otter physiology and the responses of otters to captive conditions. Much useful knowledge was gained through these studies, but failure of a further effort to transplant otters from Amchitka to the Pribilof Islands in March and April of 1955 showed that still more knowledge was necessary.

It was now clear that the species was no longer endangered. Anticipating a public request that the resource be utilized, the second or long-term study phase of management was begun by the U.S. Fish and Wildlife Service in 1954 and 1955. An annotated account of field studies is in appendix I. Early in this period it became apparent that several island populations were at or near maximum size and that experimental harvests could be made.

When Alaska became a State in 1959, the statehood act provided that jurisdiction over the exploitation of game and fur-bearing mammals, including the sea otter, should pass to the State.[1] Soon State officials decided to harvest sea otter pelts. The third phase of management began at Amchitka in the winter of 1962 when an experimental harvest was taken by Alaska Department of Game and U.S. Fish and Wildlife Service biologists. Subsequent harvests were taken by State biologists at Amchitka in 1963 and

---

[1] Federal regulations govern the exploitation of these animals on National Wildlife Refuge lands but not in State waters adjacent to them. Thus, the sea otter is under Federal jurisdiction when it comes on shore on a National Wildlife Refuge and when it goes to sea beyond territorial boundaries.

1967, and at Adak in 1967. One thousand pelts were available for the first public auction (since 1911) on 30 January 1968, at Seattle, Wash.

The harvesting of otters served the dual purpose of furnishing a financial return to the public and making specimens available for biological research. Many of the facts thus obtained are presented in this report.

Biologists of the State of Alaska, particularly K. Schneider, under the direction of J. Vania are progressing in management studies, especially in transplanting otters from areas of abundance to vacant parts of their former range. Concurrently, biologists of the State of California are studying the population there. In the Soviet Union, long continued sea otter studies, principally in the Commander and Kuril Islands, have added much to our knowledge. A comprehensive review of published information on the sea otter is given by Harris (1968).

Wise conservation practices based on biological knowledge will assure not only that the sea otter will once again be an article of commerce, but also that this interesting member of our wildlife community will flourish as an esthetically and scientifically valuable part of our environmental heritage.

SYSTEMATICS

Evolution

It has been supposed that the sea otter derived from an Atlantic Ocean early Pleistocene ancestor *Lutra reevei* (Newton) (Thenius and Hofer, 1960, p. 166). Recent findings in California of sea otter remains from the early and late Pleistocene demonstrate that this supposition is incorrect. Mitchell (1966, p. 1908) studied all available paleontological material. In his exhaustive review of the fossils and literature he stated:

> Because these older North Pacific fossils are considered to be conspecific with the living sea otter, it is obvious that the *Lutra reevei* tooth cannot represent a direct ancestor of *E. lutris*. . . . The sea otter may probably be considered as a strict North Pacific endemic autochthon, just as McLaren (1960) has assumed it to be.

Taylor (1914) studied the osteology and aquatic adaptations of the sea otter and the river otter and concluded that the two otters are fundamentally alike and probably descended from a common ancestral form. Because the fossil record is incomplete, it is possible only to speculate where the sea otter originated. Dr. Charles A. Repenning suggests (letter, 3 March 1965):

> I would guess that *Enhydra* developed from the otters of the Pliocene of India and eastern Asia and moved northward along the western shore of the North Pacific with the accentuation of global climatic zonality. All of the otters of North America (including *Enhydriodon*) seem to be derived from Asiatic stock and seem to have arrived in North America in the Pliocene and early Pleistocene.

Taxonomy

The sea otter is the only member of the genus *Enhydra*. It is the largest (to 100 lb. [45 kg.]) member of the family Mustelidae, which includes nearly 70 species—river otters, skunks, weasels, and badgers, among others. Unlike other mustelids, it has no functional anal scent glands. The sea otter is the most specialized of the group, being adapted to a narrow ecological zone in the marine environment. Besides being the smallest marine mammal, it is the only one in the order Carnivora. Among mammals it shares the marine environment with the pinnipeds (seals), cetaceans (whales and porpoises), and sirenians (manatees and dugongs).

Miller and Kellogg (1955) and Hall and Kelson (1959) recognize a northern race, *Enhydra lutris lutris* Linn., formerly ranging from Vancouver Island to the end of the Aleutian Islands chain, and a southern race, *E. l. nereis* Merriam, ranging from the Strait of Juan de Fuca southward, formerly into Baja California, Mexico. The southern race was described on the basis of one skull. Barabash-Nikiforov (1947) reviewed available data and says "we are justified in drawing conclusions on the sea otter based on the slight amount of material we succeeded in collecting." He recognized three races: *E. l. lutris* Linn., "the Commander-Aleutian North American sea otter"; *E. l. gracilis* Bechstein, "The Kuril-Kamchatka sea otter"; and *E. l. nereis* Merriam, "southern California sea otter."

After superficial examination of several hundred sea otters taken at Amchitka Island (as mentioned elsewhere), and after observing the variation in color and body size among animals of this local population, I agree with Scheffer and Wilke (1950). They studied specimens from California and the Aleutian Islands and reviewed the basis for establishing a racial division. They concluded that "Neither on the basis of demonstrable variation nor on the grounds of geographical isolation is there support for a southern subspecies of the sea otter."

A careful study of specimens from the several geographical areas occupied by sea otters is now required before any racial differences in these populations can be recognized. Because of the variation among animals I have seen, the meager specimen material used to date in defining races, and the similarity of habitats occupied by the sea otter throughout its geographic range, it is not possible, without further study, to distinguish racially distinct populations which might exist.

PHYSICAL CHARACTERISTICS

The sea otter's characteristics include the following: (1) A coat of sparse guard hair and dense insulating fur which protects it from cold as blubber insulates other marine mammals. A blanket of air remains trapped at all times among the fur fibers of the sea otter so that the skin is never touched by the water of its chilly environment (fig. 1). (2) Flattened hind feet or flippers for propulsion. (3) Retractile claws on the front feet (fig. 2) (but not on the hind feet), the only member of its family so adapted. The forepaws are used to groom the fur, to gather and grasp food, to break the shells of mollusks and crustaceans against a rock held on the chest, and to pass food to the mouth. (4) A loose flap or pouch of skin under each foreleg, extending partially across the chest, is used to hold food organisms after they are gathered from the bottom until they are consumed while the otter floats on its back at the surface. In the wild it never voluntarily consumes food on land. (5) Flattened and rounded molar teeth having no cutting cusps. These are used to crush the shells, external skeletons, and flesh of food organisms. (6) A horizontally flattened tail aids propulsion. (7) A manner of swimming under water, similar to cetaceans, by means of vertical undulations of the hind flippers and tail. (8) An external ear (fig. 3) that resembles the ear of an otariid or eared seal more than it does the ear of a land carnivore or of its closest relative, the river otter.

The body of the sea otter is relatively long and heavy, making progress on land clumsy and slow. Although highly adapted to the marine environment, the sea otter is specialized to occupy the narrow zone of shallow water near shore. Apparently it cannot (or at least is not known to) obtain pelagic food where the sea is deep. It does not undertake seasonal migrations. If removed from its natural environment, i.e., water, and kept in a dry pen, it shows great distress, perhaps because it instinctively senses that its fur may become soiled and through eventual wetting cause chilling and death. Also, in captivity when water is not available, heat prostration and death may occur unless environmental temperatures are carefully controlled.

At birth the sea otter is covered with dense brownish fur and long silky yellowish-tipped guard hair. The head is a light buff

FIGURE 1.—Pelage appearance shortly after a sea otter emerged from the water and shook himself. Only the tips of the fur are wet and thus stick together to form points. Beneath, the underfur is dry, insulating the otter's skin and enabling it to maintain its body temperature. (KWK 59-8-1)

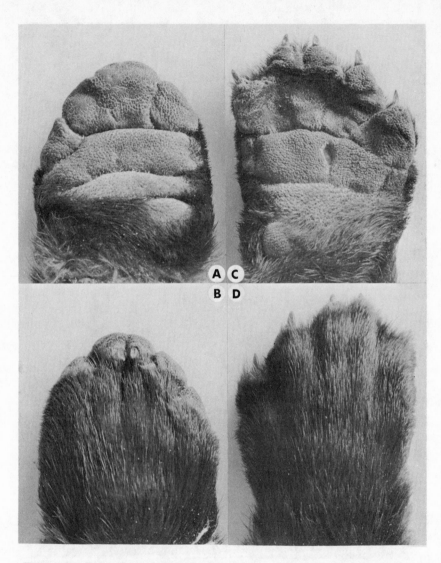

FIGURE 2.—Front feet of the sea otter. In the relaxed position the claws are retracted (*A* and *B*). The claws are extended (*C* and *D*) during feeding when food is grasped and, with the help of the teeth, torn into small bite-sized chunks. Much grooming is done with the claws retracted, but occasionally during this activity they may be extended. Note that the third and fourth digits are closely joined. The paws are highly sensitive. When an otter grasps a human finger between its forepaws, the mobile digits can be felt moving like fingers inside a mitten. (KWK 64–1–8)

FIGURE 3.—The external ear of the sea otter resembles the ear of an otariid seal. It is cartilaginous and thickened but not as pointed at the tip or as tightly rolled and "valvelike" as the ear of a seal. The ear length (from notch) of an adult male was 32 mm. and of a subadult female 30 mm. While the otter is beneath the water the ears are pointed sharply downward. When the head is above the surface the ears are usually held erect. (KWK 61–42–0)

color (fig. 4). Over a period of several weeks the guard hair grows out, often giving the pup a distinctly yellowish appearance.

The late juvenile pelage is similar to that of the adult, which is typically dark bodied and buffy to light gray headed. The head tends to become whiter with age, and grizzling may appear on other parts of the body. Body color varies from light buff (rare) through shades of brown to nearly black. The sparse guard hair may be dark or silvery white.

IDENTIFICATION OF THE RIVER OTTER AND THE SEA OTTER

The river otter *(Lutra canadensis)* is often seen swimming in salt water in coastal areas of the Pacific Northwest and Alaska.

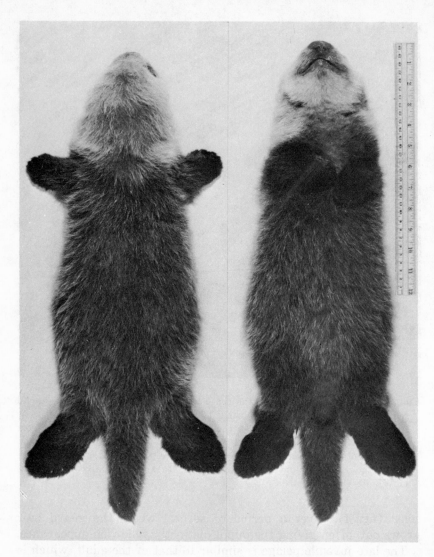

FIGURE 4.—Dorsal (left) and ventral (right) views of a newly born female sea otter taken on 6 April 1949 on Amchitka Island; weight 1,950 g. (4 lb. 6 oz.), length 560 mm. (22 in.); specimen BDM 378. The long, silky, yellowish-tipped natal pelage of the body and typical light buffy head and neck are demonstrated. The nearly black fur of the feet is soft and wooly. (KWK 500 and 501)

For this reason, observers often report the presence of sea otters when they have actually seen river otters. To help in correct identification of these two species, the following comparison of diagnostic physical and behavioral characteristics is presented (see also figs. 5 and 6):

Field observation

Sea Otter

1. Occurs in Alaska from Prince William Sound, along the Alaska Peninsula, in the Aleutians, and near Monterey, Calif. Is currently extending its range and should be looked for in Pacific coastal areas.
2. Found along open-sea coast in salt water only.
3. On surface usually swims belly up, forepaws on chest while paddling with hind flippers. Floats high in water.
4. Clumsy on land, seldom seen on shore except in isolated Alaskan areas.
5. Eats while floating on back, never eats on shore.
6. Sleeps (usually) in kelp beds or calm water while floating on its back (fig. 7).
7. Bears single young which is carried on the mother's chest as she swims on her back.

River Otter

1. Occurs on rivers and along seacoasts in the United States, Canada, and Alaska. Often swims several miles in salt water between islands.
2. Found in salt or fresh water.
3. On surface usually swims belly down, back nearly submerged.
4. Agile and graceful on land, often seen on land.
5. Brings food ashore to eat.
6. Sleeps on land, usually, in dens, never while floating on its back.
7. May have up to four young, does not carry them on chest while swimming.

Specimen Observation

Sea Otter

1. Maximum weight 100 lb.
2. Maximum length 58.25 in.
3. Fur long and soft, guard hair delicate and sparse.
4. Claws of forepaws short and retractile.
5. Hind feet decidedly flipperlike and webbed to tips of toes. Pads visible only at tips of toes (fig. 8) The fifth or outer digit is longest (fig. 9).
6. Tail somewhat flattened and does not thicken markedly at base, less than ⅓ of body length.
7. Eyes are open at birth.
8. Last upper molariform tooth broad and flattened, about ¾ inch or more in greatest width.
9. Baculum of adult about 6 inches in length (fig. 10).

River Otter

1. Maximum weight 30 lb.
2. Maximum length 50 in.
3. Guard hair coarse and dense, covering fur completely.
4. Foreclaws long and not retractile.
5. Hind feet webbed but not flipperlike. Pads cover much of palm and digits. The fifth digit is not elongated.
6. Tail nearly round in cross section and heavily thickened at base, more than ½ of body length.

FIGURE 5.—Adult male river otter. When compared with the sea otter, the river otter's tail is long, heavy at its base, and tapered. The hind feet, although webbed, are relatively small, and the body is less elongate than that of the sea otter. (Specimen VBS 1322, length 122 cm. [48 in.], weight 23.25 lb. [10.5 kg.], taken 8 December 1945 near Forks, Wash.) (VBS 1940)

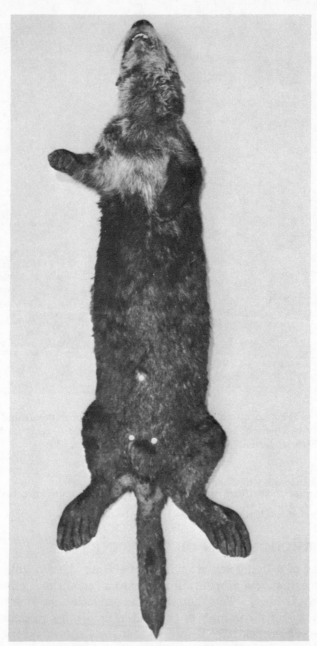

FIGURE 6.—A small adult female sea otter. White dots mark the umbilicus and mammae. The relatively short, flattened tail of nearly uniform width throughout its length, broadly flattened and webbed hind feet, and elongate body are obvious characteristics which differentiate the sea otter from the river otter. (Specimen KWK 61–2 [Susie], weight in life 40 lb. [18. 1 kg.], length 127 cm. [50 in.]. Captured 4 September 1955, Amchitka Island, died 27 October 1961 in Seattle zoo.) (KWK 61–42–16)

FIGURE 7.—Eight sea otters asleep in a kelp bed at Amchitka Island during a midday rest period. In the foreground a large juvenile rests its head on its mother's abdomen. (KWK 55–18–18)

7. Eyes do not open until age 25-35 days.
8. Last upper molariform tooth not broadly flattened and greatest width less than ½ inch.
9. Baculum of adult about 4 inches in length.

FIELD RECOGNITION OF THE SEXES

The sex of a living sea otter in the field may be recognized at a reasonable distance if prevailing weather conditions offer good light and visibility. The fact that the sea otter habitually rests on its back and floats high in the water facilitates recognition of the sexes. If the sea otter is wet, so that the fur is slick, the penial bulge of the male (fig. 11) and the two abdominal mammae of the female (fig. 12) may be visible with binoculars up to a distance of about 100 yards. When the fur is dry and fluffy, these definitive characters are less distinct but are visible at close range.

No instance is known of a male otter carrying a pup on its chest

FIGURE 8.—Plantar surface of the left hind foot of an adult male sea otter. The outer (fifth) digit is longest, a condition not found in other mammals. This adaptation increases efficiency of propulsion by the foot when the otter swims on its back. Pad development at the tips of the toes is minimal. The vestigial pads near the center of the foot are not visible on some individuals. (KWK 62–23–26)

or abdomen. Thus, all animals carrying young are recognized as females. Large juveniles, still with their mothers, may approach an adult male and romp with him. Thus care is necessary during observation to differentiate between the mother and a "visiting" male.

It was shown that the adult male averages larger than the female (see Body Measurements) but because of overlap, size alone is not useful in recognition of the sexes.

The head and neck are heavier and more muscular in appearance in the adult male than in the female. If a mated pair is observed, this difference is apparent. Because of individual variation, however, much observation and field experience is necessary before this relatively slight difference becomes a useful character in the recognition of sex.

In its behavior, the male sea otter is relatively bold. If a human approaches a group of males and females hauled out near each

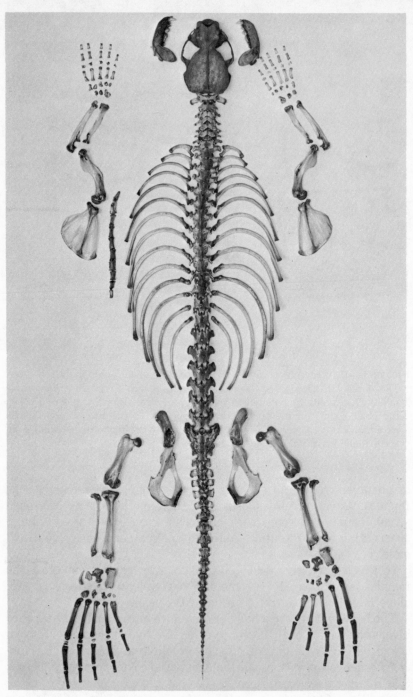

FIGURE 9.—The skeleton of an adult female sea otter (No. KWK 61–2) shows
the general location and shape of the bones. The last joint of each digit
was removed with the skin and is missing. The elongate fifth digit of the
hind foot is demonstrated. (VBS 4954)

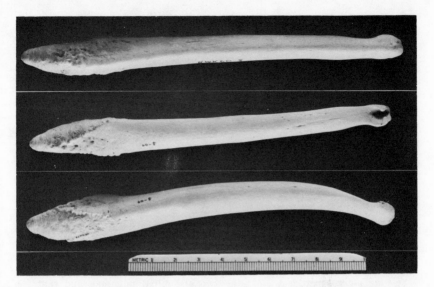

FIGURE 10.—The baculum of an adult male sea otter (No. KWK 60–8). Above, dorsal view; middle, ventral view; below, side view. The baculum is attached to the ischium by a ligament, composed of the ischiocavernosus and bulbocavernosus muscles, which inserts on the left. (KWK 66–15)

FIGURE 11.—Adult male sea otter. The penial and testicular bulges are evident when the outer pelage is wet and slick. They are less apparent when the pelage is dry and fluffy, making identification of sex difficult in the field. Note loose skin pouches beneath each foreleg. These are used to store food organisms as they are gathered from the bottom, until they are eaten at the surface. (KWK 56–29–11)

FIGURE 12.—Adult female sea otter eating the head of a large codfish (*Gadus macrocephalus*). Note the two abdominal mammae and that the head and neck are relatively of lighter structure when compared with the male. Also, females float somewhat higher in the water than do males. This is an unusually light-colored animal (albinistic), but the extremities and eyes were normally pigmented. (KWK 59-13-2)

other, the females usually take alarm and depart before the males do.

On several occasions we pursued sea otters in an outboard-powered dory in order to capture them in a dip net. Females attempted to leave the vicinity by making long dives. The relatively fearless males often tried only to avoid the immediate vicinity of the boat. One individual surfaced repeatedly in the same general area. After about an hour of fruitless pursuit, we abandoned the chase and the otter began diving for food near the place we first saw him.

The difference in color between adult males and females was not quantitatively determined. In general, females appear quite black when their fur is dry and fluffy. Males, in general, appear brownish under the same conditions. Black males and brownish females, however, are seen. Both sexes tend to become white headed with age. Dark-headed individuals, however, were examined which had worn teeth, indicating advanced age. Among a group of 10 captive juvenile otters, the animals having the lightest colored heads were males. In general, this difference tends to prevail also in older animals.

Examination of the photographs and this discussion of diagnostic characteristics, indicate that the sex of many otters may be recognized in the natural environment. Seldom, however, may the sex of all adult or subadult otters seen during a period of observation be positively identified.

During hunting it was demonstrated that recognition of sex in the field is impractical when obtaining skins is the primary objective. Between 31 July and 3 August 1963, officials of the Alaska Department of Game shot 20 sea otters of adult size. Mothers accompanied by pups were omitted from the kill in the hope that a high proportion of males would be obtained. Only one male (5 percent of the kill) was taken in the "female areas" where this collection was obtained.

Body Measurements

Stullken and Kirkpatrick (1955) described some of the physical characteristics of the sea otter and reported on physiological studies of captive otters. My observations are intended to supplement theirs.

Body weights and lengths of sea otters captured or found dead on Amchitka beaches, or shot in waters near Amchitka, and of otters taken in other Alaska areas are discussed in this section. Because no anatomical feature is known to reveal the exact age of a sea otter, juveniles and subadults are omitted and only data from newly born and adult animals are presented. Sea otters were recognized as adults by observations of adult dentition, suture closure and sagittal crest development of the skull, and of the baculum size in males.

Total length was obtained by measuring, with a steel tape, each animal from tip of nose to tip of tail as it lay flat on its back. Only the total length is considered in the following discussion. (The mean tail length was found to be 24.5 percent of the total length. The range in 10 adult males was 22.3 to 29.2 percent and in 10 adult females 22.0 to 26.1 percent.) Some animals killed during the Alaska State harvesting operations could not be measured immediately after death. When an animal in rigor mortis was measured, an attempt was made to stretch it to full length. Some of these, however, were probably measured as being slightly shorter than they would have been when relaxed.

The scales most frequently available were spring scales of 50- and 100-lb. capacity. The data as shown in tables were converted to kilograms. Small young were usually weighed on a 15-kg. capacity balance.

NEWBORN YOUNG

The data on body size of the youngest sea otters obtained are reported in table 1. The umbilical scar was fresh on each individual listed and all showed little or no wear of the fetal claw tips (fig. 13). The two smallest, a male weighing 2.6 lb. (1.2 kg.) and a female weighing 2.25 lb. (1.02 kg.), were both dead when obtained, one from the beach and the other from a mother that was netted on the beach while carrying her dead pup. Among the seven largest fetuses (four males and three females), collected at Amchitka in 1963, the largest, a male, weighed 4.12 lb. (1.869 kg.) and measured 61.0 cm. in length. The mean weight was 3.5 lb. (1.598 kg.) and the mean length 57.3 cm. (22.5 in.). Thus it is probable that the two smallest newborn young were stillborn, being abnormally small at birth. All of the others had received at least some nourishment in the form of milk from their mothers before capture, thus were heavier than when newly born. The living young examined indicate that a healthy newly born sea otter may weigh as little as 3 lb. (1.4 kg.). But the fetal material studied (see Reproduction in the Female) and larger newborn young indicate that larger body size of 4.12 lb. (1.869 kg.) to 5 lb. (2.3 kg.) and 61 cm. (24 in.) in total body length is probably normal.

ADULTS

Analysis of the weights and lengths of 84 adult males and 258 adult females that were shot, are given in tables 2 and 3. Animals

TABLE 1.—*Weight and length of newborn pups taken at Amchitka Island, Alaska*

[The umbilical scar or adhering fragments of the umbilical cord were fresh. All except the two dead pups contained small quantities of milk]

Collection number	Date	Weight	Length
		Kg.	*Cm.*
Males:			
	29 March 1955	1.6	58.0
32–56 [1]	26 May 1956	1.2	47.3
D–6–57	18 November 1957	2.5	62.9
62–178	18 February 1962	1.7	52.8
Mean		1.75	55.25
Females:			
32–56 [2]	25 May 1956	1.02	48.4
D–2–57	11 October 1957	1.45	52.1
D–15–57	16 October 1957	2.4	
([3])	15 Apr. 1959	1.7	
60–17	8 July 1960	2.35	53.5
60–21	10 July 1960	2.83	61.6
Mean		1.96	53.9

[1] Freshly dead pup taken from the mother when she was netted.
[2] Freshly dead pup found on beach.
[3] Mother and pup netted and released. The pup was not tagged because it was obviously newborn (umbilicus still attached and fresh).

FIGURE 13—At birth the claws are white and curved. Soon after birth the young otter attempts to groom its fur, and the soft tips are lost. (KWK 62–16–21)

found dead on beaches (table 4) and those which died in captivity (tables 5 and 6) are compared and the differences are discussed below.

Scheffer (1951) published information on the body size of three adult sea otter specimens which he measured. The present data confirm that the maximum length of the adult male sea otter is about 148 cm. (58.25 in.), that the adult female is 140 cm. (55 in.). The adult male may reach a maximum weight of about 100 lb. (45 kg.) and the adult female may reach a weight of at least 72 lb. (32.6 kg.).

It is indicated in other sections (see Food and Feeding Behavior, Mortality Factors, and Distribution and Numbers) that at Amchitka Island a dense sea otter population has depleted food resources. Additional evidence for this is revealed by comparing the body weights of Amchitka sea otters (table 2) with animals from a sparse population (table 3).

TABLE 2.—*Total length and body weight of adult sea otters killed at Amchitka Island, Alaska*

Item		Male					Female				
		1959 [1]	1962 [2]	1962 [3]	1963 [4]	All	1959 [1]	1962 [2]	1962 [3]	1963 [4]	All
Number		13	24	3	39	79	8	99	16	131	254
Maximum weight	kg.	38.6	36.3	32.6	38.6	38.6	28.1	26.8	26.8	31.7	31.7
Minimum weight	kg.	22.7	22.7	26.3	21.8	21.8	15.4	14.5	15.9	15.4	14.5
Mean weight	kg.	28.7	28.2	28.7	28.1	28.3	20.7	20.4	21.9	21.5	21.1
Standard deviation		7.84	7.45	7.58	6.24	7.93	4.13	5.81	5.15	6.81	6.49
Maximum length	cm.	145	140	145	142	145	135	136	133	140	140
Minimum length	cm.	132	126	132	137	126	124	112	109	107	107
Mean length	cm.	139.7	134.5	137.7	133.6	135.0	129.4	125.3	124.7	124.9	125.2
Standard deviation		4.13	3.53	6.67	3.53	4.30	3.29	4.65	5.77	4.64	4.73

[1] Animals netted on beaches, February-May.
[2] Animals shot, January-March.
[3] Animals shot, October.
[4] Animals shot, March-April. Thirty-four males shown to be subadult by baculum measurements are omitted. Their mean weight was 47.9 lb. (21.7 kg.) and mean length was 123.9 cm. (48.7 in.).

TABLE 3.—*Total length and body weight of adult sea otters killed in areas of sparse population*

[These otters were shot in 1960 in the Shumagin Islands (6), off Unimak Island (2), and Adak Island (1)]

Item	Males	Females
Number	5	4
Maximum weight ....kilograms	44.9	32.7
Minimum weight ....do	34.0	19.9
Mean weight ....do	39.5	25.2
Standard deviation	10.12	13.0
Maximum length ....centimeters	143	139
Minimum length ....do	140	125
Mean length ....do	140.8	129.8
Standard deviation	0.5	6.8

TABLE 4.—*Total length and body weight of adult sea otters found dead on beaches at Amchitka Island, Alaska*

[Weights and measurements could be obtained from relatively few of the total found. All are combined in this table: 1956 (1), 1959 (7), 1962 (20), and 1963 (2)]

Item	Males	Females
Number	13	17
Maximum weight ....kilograms	31.7	18.6
Minimum weight ....do	15.9	12.2
Mean weight ....do	21.4	16.2
Standard deviation	10.20	3.83
Maximum length ....centimeters	145	137
Minimum length ....do	130	122
Mean length ....do	136.5	131.7
Standard deviation	4.39	3.74

TABLE 5.—*Weight loss of 10 adult male sea otters that died in captivity*

[Weight in kilograms]

Collection number	Weight at capture	Weight at death	Weight loss	Percent loss	Days in captivity
II–56	33.6	25.4	8.2	24	15
III–56	32.7	22.5	10.2	31	18
VI–56	33.6	24.0	9.6	28	15
VIII–56	26.3	19.5	6.8	26	8
IX–56	25.8	18.1	7.7	30	47
D–8–57	20.4	17.9	2.5	12	7
D–20–57	30.4	26.3	4.1	13	20
D–21–57	29.5	26.8	2.7	9	13
D–22–57	31.7	20.9	10.8	31	17
D–15–57	28.6	20.9	7.7	27	305
Mean	29.25	22.23	7.03	24	......

TABLE 6.—*Weight loss of seven adult female sea otters that died in captivity*

[Weight in kilograms]

Collection number	Weight at capture	Weight at death	Weight loss	Percent loss	Days in captivity
I–56	21.3	19.3	2.0	9	6
IV–56	23.1	15.0	8.1	35	57
VII–56	24.0	17.0	7.0	29	15
D–7–57	25.4	21.3	4.1	16	6
D–16–57	27.2	23.4	3.8	14	27
D–17–57	22.2	19.7	2.5	11	25
D–23–57	22.5	18.5	2.3	10	10
Mean	23.67	19.17	4.50	19	......

23

Scheffer (1955) concluded that a reduction in body size was correlated with increasing population or crowding in the northern fur seal *(Callorhinus ursinus)*. The data presented below indicate that adult sea otters from a crowded population weigh less than animals from a sparse population. The length of adult otters from sparse populations fell within the length range of otters from the crowded Amchitka population (tables 2 and 3). However, an insufficient number of animals from sparse populations were available to demonstrate a statistically significant difference at the conventional level of 0.05.

Although few adult sea otter specimens (five males and four females) are available from areas where sea otter populations are sparse, the differences in body weight between these animals and the Amchitka collection are noteworthy. Among 79 adult males that were killed at Amchitka, the mean weight was 62.5 lb. (28.3 kg.), and the heaviest weighed 85 lb. (38.6 kg.). Among five that were killed in sparsely populated areas, however, the mean weight was 87.1 lb. (39.5 kg.) and the heaviest weighed 99 lb. (44.9 kg.). The difference between the mean weights of these two samples is 24.6 lb. (11.2 kg.). This indicates that adult males in a sparse population may average about 28 percent heavier than those in crowded populations. The difference is significant at the 0.1 percent level. The mean weight of four females from sparsely populated areas was about 16 percent greater than the mean weight of 254 Amchitka females. When the animals were collected in sparsely populated areas, no effort was made to select large individuals.

The lesser body weights of the Amchitka animals appear to confirm conclusions drawn from food habits and mortality studies that a large population there has created ecological conditions which are below the optimum. Because the sample of adult otters from sparsely populated areas is small, a more thorough statistical evaluation of the apparent differences in mean body weight between crowded and sparse populations must be delayed until more data are gathered.

Most of the sea otters killed at Amchitka were taken during the late winter to early spring period of environmental stress when many of the otters were dying. Thus, it appears appropriate to compare the animals killed at this season with others taken at Amchitka in the fall when body condition would be expected to be optimum. Unfortunately, the only fall (1962) sample of adults is small, consisting of 3 males and 16 females. Comparison of the mean weights of these animals with those taken in the late winter to early spring period indicates no statistically significant difference in body condition (table 2). The sea otter must maintain a high daily intake of food regardless of season. It is reasonable to suppose that those animals capable of maintaining themselves under the feeding conditions imposed by a maximum otter population would show little seasonal differences in body weight.

WEIGHT LOSS PRECEDING DEATH

Death, in the wild and in captivity, is usually preceded by a period of physical deterioration evidenced by gradual or precipitous loss of body weight. The mean weight of 13 adult males found dead on Amchitka beaches was 47.1 lb. (21.4 kg.) (table 4). The mean weight of 79 adult males that were shot near the same places was 62.5 lb. (28.3 kg.) (table 2). The mean weight difference was 15.2 lb. (6.9 kg.), indicating that preceding death the moribund animals lost 24 percent or about one-quarter of their body weight. Similarly, between 254 adult females that were shot and 17 that were found dead on beaches the mean weight difference was 10.8 lb. (4.9 kg.) (21.1 kg. minus 16.2 kg., tables 2 and 4), or an indicated reduction of about 23 percent.

Seventeen adult sea otters (10 males and 7 females) were weighed at capture and again after they died in captivity. These animals were held captive for periods varying from 6 days to 10 months (tables 5 and 6). Among 10 adult males that died in captivity, the mean weight loss at death was 24 percent of the body weight at capture. Three animals in this group lost 30 percent or more of their body weight (table 5). Data for adult females are similar (table 6).

Massive weight loss preceding death appears to result from (1) evacuation of the gastrointestinal tract, (2) consumption of body fat reserves, and (3) dehydration. The usual terminal symptoms, in wild and captive animals, was excretion of black, tarry feces due to enteritis.

After an adult otter enters a period of physical decline, the restoration of normal vigor and weight may be difficult or impossible by any known means. The afflicted animal may become increasingly lethargic and may consume little or no food. Some emaciated juveniles captured on beaches, however, recovered when given adequate food in captivity.

In summary, there is evidence that among adult otters of about the same body length, those from areas of sparse population may weigh about 16 to 28 percent more than apparently healthy animals from a densely populated area and about 50 percent more than emaciated individuals which die on beaches in a densely populated area. Animals in captivity, taken in a densely populated area (Amchitka), lost about 25 percent of their body weight at capture, before death.

MISCELLANEOUS MEASUREMENTS

Skin length and body length

The skin of the sea otter is "loose" and stretches considerably after it is removed from the animal, as shown by the following figures:

Specimen	Sex	Body length [1]		Skin length [2]		Percent increase	Remarks
		Millimeters	Inches	Millimeters	Inches		
KWK 59–61	♀	720	28¾	1,035	40¾	44	Fresh skin.
KWK 59–77	♀	1,320	51¼	1,850	72¾	42	Fresh skin.
BDM 128	♂	1,478	58	1,715	67½	16	Tanned skin.

[1] Tip of nose to tip of tail flesh.
[2] Moderate tension applied.

Thus, a skin freshly removed from the animal may easily be stretched 144 percent and a tanned skin 116 percent of the animal's body length. It is concluded that measurements taken from skins are of little use in establishing body size in the sea otter.

Intestine length

Length of intestine in four adult sea otters is shown in table 7. Shortly after death, the intestinal tract was removed, laid on flat ground, and measured. An effort was made to obtain the relaxed length (not the stretched length). The mean length of the small intestine was 9.0 times body length (table 7).

In general, carnivores have shorter intestines than herbivores but the variation among strictly carnivorous mammals is great.

TABLE 7.—*Intestine length of adult sea otters*

[Length in centimeters]

Collection number	Sex	Body length	Intestine length [1]	Small intestine [2]	Ratio, small intestine to body length
59–60	female	124.	1,214 (39.5 feet)	1,154	9.3:1
61–2	do	127.	1,076 (35.3 feet)	1,016	8.0:1
62–11	do	128.	1,313 (43.1 feet)	1,253	9.8:1
62–10	male	136.	1,290 (42.3 feet)	1,230	9.0:1
Mean		128.7			9.0:1

[1] From stomach to anus.
[2] No caecum is present in the sea otter. The small intestine gradually expands into the large intestine. The approximate length of the large intestine is 60 cm. This amount is subtracted from the total intestine length to obtain the approximate length of the small intestine.

Among pinnipeds, which subsist entirely on flesh, the ratio $\frac{\text{(small intestine length)}}{\text{nose-tail length}}$ ranges from 5.2 in *Monachus* to 42.0 in *Mirounga* (King, 1964). The sea otter, which subsists on marine invertebrates and fish, falls within this general range. Apparently animals which feed primarily on warm-blooded vertebrates have relatively shorter intestines. The above ratio is 5 for the dog and cat (King, 1964).

Organ weights

The relative sizes of body organs may give a clue to the adaptations of an organism to its environment. I have undertaken no physiological studies, but the following comparisons of the relative size of selected body organs of the sea otter with those of other mammals indicate that such studies would be interesting and desirable.

Organs were weighed on a balance having a maximum capacity of 15 kg. Sample organ weights were obtained from six adult male and nine adult female sea otters that were shot while apparently in normal health at Amchitka Island and other areas (table 8). Comparison of the organ weight expressed as percent of body weight indicates that in some respects the sea otter is quite

TABLE 8.—*Weights of body organs in nine adult female and six adult male sea otters*

[Weight in grams. All apparently healthy adults shot at Amchitka Island, except 60–4 to 60–8 which were shot in the Shumagin Islands and off Unimak Island]

Collection number	Body weight	Liver		Heart		Kidney		Spleen	
		Weight	Percent of body weight	Weight	Percent of body weight	Weight	Percent of body weight	Weight	Percent of body weight
Females:									
62–2	21,770	1,219	5.60	182	0.84	409	1.88	65	0.30
62–6	20,410	1,130	5.54	152	.74	340	1.67	59	.29
62–8	19,950	1,135	5.69	130	.65	367	1.84	65	.33
62–11	20,410	1,730	8.48	126	.62	346	1.69	90	.44
62–12	23,130	1,632	7.06	160	.69	425	1.84	90	.39
62–15	21,300	1,226	5.76	135	.63	385	1.81	92	.43
62–19	19,050	955	5.01	134	.70	315	1.65	85	.45
62–20	17,690	1,000	5.65	142	.80	350	1.98	58	.33
60–4	32,500	1,450	4.46	175	.54	470	1.45	150	.46
Mean	21,800	1,275.2	5.85	148.4	.68	378.5	1.74	83.8	.38
Males:									
62–1	29,940	1,479	4.94	185	.62	700	2.34	86	.29
62–10	36,290	2,685	7.39	211	.58	821	2.26	177	.49
60–5	35,500	1,650	4.65	230	.65	870	2.45	100	.28
60–6	45,000	2,390	5.31	270	.60	1,120	2.49	110	.24
60–7	41,300	1,860	4.50	272	.66	997	2.41	113	.27
60–8	41,700	2,086	5.00	227	.54	1,026	2.46	113	.27
Mean	38,280	2,025	5.29	233	.61	922	2.40	116	.31
Mean, all	28,410	1,575	5.67	182.1	.66	596.1	2.01	96.9	.35

similar to other mammals but in other respects it may be unique. Among mammals in general (but with exceptions) total body weight increases at a greater rate than organ weights. It is presumed in the following comparisons that the reader will keep this generalization in mind.

Liver.—To remain healthy the sea otter must consume about one-sixth to one-fourth of its body weight in food daily. Apparently the air blanket in its fur is a less efficient means of insulation in its chilly habitat than the blubber of other marine mammals. The need for a relatively large amount of food indicates an unusually high metabolic rate in the sea otter. Slijper (1962) believes that marine mammals, and particularly cetaceans, have a high metabolic rate. Since the liver is an important organ for the production and storage of energy-producing substances, it is not surprising that the sea otter's liver is relatively very large; the mean is about 5.7 percent of body weight. In this respect it surpasses fur seals of comparable body size (mean 3.1 to 3.5 percent; Scheffer, 1960), porpoises (3.2 percent), and dolphins (2.2 percent; Slijper, 1962), and the river otter (4.85 percent; Jensen, letter, 30 Nov. 1964), although the river otter is a smaller animal.

Heart.—The heart of the sea otter constitutes about 0.66 percent of body weight. The ratio is similar to that of fur seals of comparable size (about 0.6 percent of body weight; Scheffer, 1960), and to dolphins (0.6 percent; Slijper, 1962). As Jensen (1964) points out, sea water gives more support than fresh water and therefore the sea otter may not need as large a heart as the river otter (0.98 percent of body weight).

Kidney.—The marine environment may account for a large difference in relative size between the sea otter kidney, mean 2.01 percent of body weight, and that of the river otter, 0.85 percent of body weight. The sea otter appears to have overcome the physiological problem of the marine environment by developing a lobulate kidney relatively twice as large as that of the river otter. I have observed sea otters in captivity drinking sea water.[2] A study of the physiology involved has not been undertaken. That the sea otter obtains liquids of appreciably less salinity than sea water from food is improbable, since body fluids of invertebrates,

---

[2] The captives were held for 2 months on dry bedding at Amchitka. Frequently when I held a pan of sea water before them they placed their mouths in the water and sucked and lapped it up with their tongues. In their eagerness to drink, they also placed their forepaws in the dish and eventually spilled and splashed so much of the water that I did not measure the quantity that was actually drunk. When given a choice of sea or fresh water they drank either unselectively. Except for one experimental offering of fresh water the captives were given only sea water.

upon which some otters feed almost exclusively, are isotonic, or nearly so, with sea water (Sverdrup, Johnson, and Flemming, 1942, p. 269).

Fisler (1962) demonstrated that even a mouse (*Peromyscus* sp.), that was adapted before capture to a salt marsh environment, survived when given sea water exclusively.

Slijper (1962, p. 314) considers that the kidneys of cetaceans (from 0.44 percent to 1.1 percent of body weight) are, because of great body size, exceptionally large. In general, a large kidney appears to constitute an important aspect of mammalian adaptation to the marine environment.

Spleen.—In the sea otter the spleen is about 0.35 percent of total body weight, which is similar to "0.3 percent in most other mammals" (Slijper, 1962, p. 175). In 62 female fur seals similar in size to the sea otters studied, Scheffer (1960) found that the spleen was from 0.11 to 0.31 percent of body weight. Thus, in the sea otter and river otter (0.46 percent, Jensen, 1964) the spleen is relatively large.

Although the mean percentages of organ size to body weight of all sea otters studied were used in the foregoing general discussion, it appears that in the male, which is larger than the female (see Body Measurements) the kidney is relatively larger than in the female. Also, the spleen of the female is slightly larger than in the male (table 8).

Body temperature

The body temperature of two apparently healthy animals, a juvenile male (59–156) and an adult female (59–157), were obtained when both had lost consciousness after injections of "Lethol" (proprietary name for a compound containing N-amylethyl-barbituate, sodium sec-butylethyl-barbituate, isopropyl alcohol, and sodium carbonate). The deep body temperatures (intracardiac insertion of the thermometer before cardiac activity ceased) and rectal temperatures were the same. The temperature of the juvenile male was 38.0° C. (100° F.) and that of the adult female was 37.5° C. (99° F.).

Body temperature may drop before death under certain conditions. On 1 April 1959, at Amchitka Island, an emaciated adult female (59–98) was lying on a bed of grass above the high tide line, breathing but unconscious. Her intracardiac temperature was 28.0° C. (84° F.). An autopsy revealed extensive enteritis.

During an experimental transplant, observations were made of a juvenile subjected to unusual stress. The otter, a female about

1 year old and weighing 22 pounds, was liberated in cold water (0° C.) on 9 April 1955. The fur had become saturated with filth after 8 days in captivity. Within 1 minute after entering the water the otter uttered loud distress screams and swam toward our dory. After she was retrieved she was placed on dry straw. When we returned to the ship, about 20 minutes later, the otter was unconscious. The rectal temperature was 30.3° C. (86° F.). In a warm room, the fur was vigorously rubbed and dried with a towel and consciousness was restored. At 0700 the following morning the rectal temperature was 38.5° C. (99° F.); the animal appeared weak but ate. She was kept in a warm room (about 22° to 24° C. or 72° to 75° F.) and given almost constant attention until she died on 15 April. During this period her body temperature fluctuated erratically each day from 30° to 36° C. (86° to 96° F.). When her temperature was low, I recorded that she was "almost in a coma." Apparently after chilling, the temperature control mechanism of this otter was upset.

Blood quantity

An approximation of the blood content of sea otters was obtained from five freshly killed animals (table 9). All appeared to be in normal health when killed. The technique used in each case was the same: After capture the animal was given a lethal injection of Lethol. When the animal lost consciousness, it was weighed and measured. The thoracic cavity and heart were opened. The animal was suspended, by means of lines attached to each leg, over a container into which the blood drained. In all cases the heart was still beating when the incisions were made. The blood weight and volume were measured directly.

The percentage of blood weight to body weight of four of the

TABLE 9.—*Blood quantity in sea otters*

[The weight of blood is minimal. The blood was drained from animal directly into a container. No correction was added for the slight amount that was spilled, or for the blood remaining in tissues]

Collection number	Age	Sex	Blood weight	Body weight	Percent, blood weight of body weight
			Grams	*Grams*	
59–62	Adult	male	2,694	31,297	8.6
59–156	Juvenile	do	767	11,566	6.6
59–48	Adult	female	8,106	28,122	[1] 28.8
59–60	do	do	2,100	20,978	10.0
59–157	do	do	1,531	20,865	7.34

[1] Apparently this animal was abnormal. Pathological conditions such as hydrothorax and heart failure occur in other mammals. The large quantities of fluids that accompany these conditions may be difficult to distinguish from blood.

animals (mean 8.1 percent) fall within the expected range (rabbit, 6.2 percent; dog, 7.2 percent; and horse, 9.7 percent (Dukes, 1943); and walrus, 8.4 percent (Fay, 1958)). In the fifth animal, the blood constituted nearly one-third of the body weight. This animal, when captured, was sleeping on the beach and behaved in a normal energetic way. I noted, however, that it appeared "fat" and the abdomen was round and firm. I suspected then that it was pregnant, but found later that it was not.

There was no food in the gastrointestinal tract. In addition to the blood quantity, the only abnormality found were two cysts (congenital? 1.5x1 cm. and 1.5x1.5 cm.) containing clear, yellowish fluid, on one kidney. The gross appearance of blood was normal. Why this animal retained such a large amount of fluid is unknown. There was no mistake about the quantity of fluid (table 9).

Pelage and Skin

Preliminary descriptive studies of the pelage, skin, and molt have been made.

PELAGE

Victor B. Scheffer (Marine Mammal Biological Laboratory, U.S. Fish and Wildlife Service) has made a cursory examination of pelage samples from three sea otters and has kindly offered the following notes (in letter, 13 August 1964). Unless otherwise stated, the notes are based on a sample from the midback of "Pappy," an adult male, specimen D22–57, which died in Seattle Zoo on 16 December and was autopsied on 17 December 1957.

The pelage is an extremely fine wool or fur with the tips of thinly scattered guard hairs protruding from it. It is light smoky gray near the skin, darkening gradually to smoky brown at the surface of the pile. The *larger guard hairs* are dark; their tips make a layer about 34 mm. (1.5 in.) from the skin. The *smaller guard hairs* are more numerous than the larger ones; their tips make a layer about 28 mm. (1.25 in.) from the skin. The *underfur hairs* are by far the most numerous; their tips make a layer about 23 mm. (1 in.) from the skin. The outer surface of the underfur layer is not distinct; the soft, wavy tips of the fur hairs blend with the tips of the smaller guard hairs (fig. 14).

The *pelage unit* consists of: a bundle of many underfur hairs and one guard hair at or near the anterior side of the bundle (fig. 15); a sebaceous gland on right and left sides of the bundle, joined at the anterior side; a coiled sweat gland beneath and partly adjacent to the follicles of the bundle; and other minor structures. There is apparently no hair-erecting muscle.

The guard hairs vary widely in diameter and length, though they fall into

31

FIGURE 14.—Hair from the midback of adult male sea otter D22–57. The outer surface of the underfur layer is not distinct; the soft, wavy tips of the fur hairs blend with the tips of the smaller guard hairs. (VBS 5710)

two overlapping groups which I call "larger" and "smaller," with few intermediates. For example, here are the diameters of 10 roots in one field of view under the microscope: 14, 15, 16, 18, 20, 25, 26, 33, 38, and 64 microns (cf. fig. 16). Cross sections of the guard hair roots are oval to nearly round in outline; they vary in diameter from 13 to 64 microns (average 25).

In five bundles I count 60 to 80 (average 71) underfur roots per bundle. The counts in two other specimens are: (KWK 59–13, old female, 9 February 1959) 79–110 (average 91); (KWK 59–51, young male, 7 March 1959) 40–45 (average 43). Comprehensive studies of pelage samples from different seasons and different age groups of otters will be necessary before the extent of holdover of pelage hairs can be evaluated. Cross sections of the underfur roots are roundish oval, smooth, fairly uniform, and 6.3 to 8.5 microns (average 7.2) in diameter (fig. 16.)

A disc of skin-with-pelage cut by trephine from the formalin-preserved, mid-back specimen measured 0.4 cm². It contained 520 bundles or 1,400 per cm² (fig. 17). [That there is considerable variability is demonstrated by the finding by J. K. Ling (MS) of 2,176 follicle bundles per cm² on a sample of facial skin.] On the basis of 71 underfur hairs and 1 guard hair per bundle, (hairs per cm² = 72 × 1400 = 100,800 or 650,160 per in.²) and an estimated area of 8,000 cm² for the total hair-covered surface of the body, the pelage of an adult male sea otter would contain about 800 million hairs.

Above the surface of the skin, the shaft of each larger guard hair is a typical awn or shield hair, flattened into a blade near the tip. At a level 10

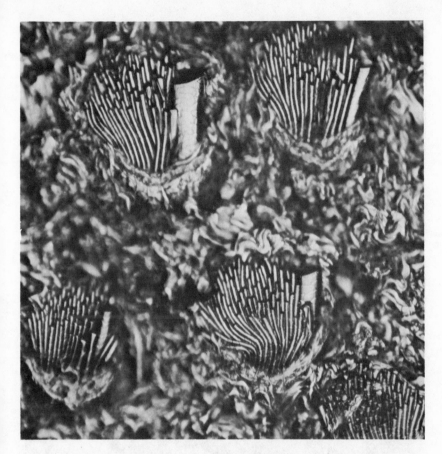

FIGURE 15.—Plastic impression of pelage sheared near skin surface from midback of adult male sea otter D22–57. Anterior at right. Variation in the diameter of guard hairs is demonstrated and their characteristic scale-pattern. Magnification ca. × 75. (VBS 5718)

mm. from the skin, the cross section is oval, slightly wavy in outline, and 55 to 67 microns (average 63) in diameter. The shaft of each smaller guard hair has a small blade. The cross section of the smaller guard hair at the 10 mm. level is 23 to 56 microns (average 42) in diameter. All guard hairs are medullated. Near the surface of the skin, the guard hair root is often displaced from the anterior side of the bundle by pressure of the underfur roots.

The cross section of the underfur hair at the 10 mm. level is irregularly 3- or 4-sided (fig. 18). In this respect it resembles the underfur of the land otter (*Lutra*) (Wildman, 1954, fig. 98b). The underfur shaft is about 7 to 8 microns in cross section diameter, only slightly greater than the root.

In general, the pelage of the sea otter is similar to that of the land otter. The guard hairs seem to be scarcer and more variable in size than those of the land otter, though I have not made a quantitative comparison. The remarkable arrangement of hairs in bundles, outside of which there are no isolated

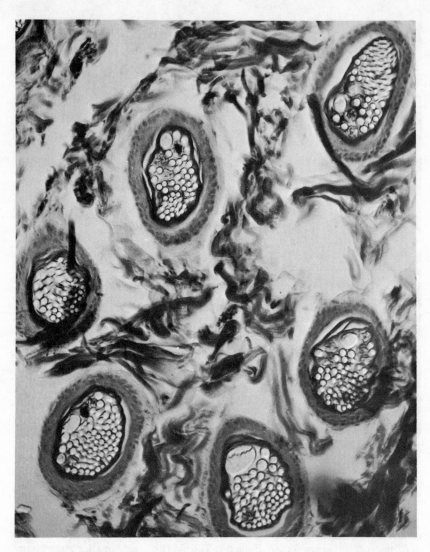

FIGURE 16.—Horizontal section through skin near surface, midback, adult
male sea otter D22–57, anterior at top. The large guard hair in each pelage
unit may measure 64 microns in diameter. The fur hairs average 7.2 microns
in diameter. At this level the hairs are round to slightly oval in cross
section. (VBS 5716)

hairs, resembles the pattern in all pinnipeds, especially in the fur seals
Callorhinus and *Arctocephalus*. Dead underfur hairs probably (?) accumulate
from one year to the next in the bundles of older animals as they do in
Callorhinus. The only evidence is that the count in a young sea otter is 43 as
compared to 71 and 91 in two adults. This "reluctant shedding," if actually
a feature of sea otter pelage, would help to maintain a heat-insulating coat

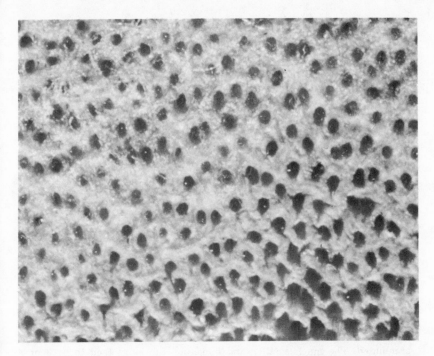

FIGURE 17.—Sheared surface showing skin and distribution of pores from which hair bundles emerge, anterior at top. Sample is from midback, adult male D22–57. Magnification × 24. (VBS 5721)

during molt. The underfur hairs seem to be equal in diameter, though twice as long, as those of *Callorhinus* (Scheffer, 1962, p. 22 and 72). On a disc cut from the fresh skin of an adult female fur seal there are 939 bundles and about 50,000 individual hairs (Scheffer, 1964). On a disc of the same area, though from preserved skin, of the adult male sea otter "Pappy" there are 1,300 bundles and about 100,000 hairs. Because of sampling variables, however, it cannot be said conclusively that the fur of the sea otter is twice as dense as that of the fur seal.

SKIN

John K. Ling (Department of Zoology, Massey University, Palmerston North, New Zealand) contributed the following description, based on examination of a small sample of skin from the facial region of one animal (D22–57).

The formalin-fixed skin was sectioned parallel and at right angles to the skin surface along the hair follicle axes and stained with haematoxylin, eosin, and picric acid. Measurements are uncorrected for *post mortem* changes and are to be regarded as approximate only.

The skin is 3 mm thick from the surface to the panniculus carnosus; the epidermis averages 50 microns in thickness, the papillary layer of the dermis

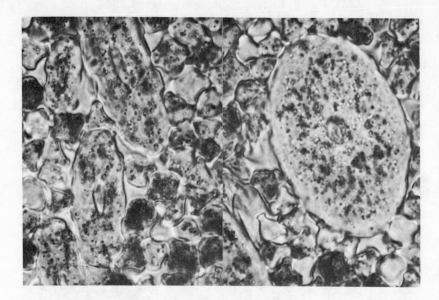

FIGURE 18.—Cross section of pelage (by Hardy device) about 10 mm. from surface of skin, near midback, adult male sea otter D22–57. The large guard hairs are oval in cross section at this level, and their surface is crenulated. The much smaller and numerous fur hairs tend to be 3 or 4 sided. Magnification × 430. (VBS 5712 and 5713)

also 50 microns, and the reticular layer makes up the remainder. The longest underfur hairs measure up to 22 mm in length, of which 19 mm may protrude beyond the surface pore of the hair canals.

Five layers, stratum corneum, stratum granulosum, stratum lucidum, stratum spinosum and stratum germinativum, are recognizable in the epidermis. The granular layer is not uniformly dense throughout and pigment is absent. . . . The epidermis is thrown into a series of folds which are reflected by similar folding of the papillary zone of the dermis. Collagen fibres in the deeper dermis are oriented both randomly and parallel to the skin surface. Arrector pili muscles are absent.

Hair follicles are arranged in bundles and are aligned at an angle of about 70° to the skin surface. Each bundle comprises a guard hair follicle and underfur follicles, which are separated from each other near their base but are held together closely at higher levels. In cross section there is some suggestions of trio grouping with a central guard hair follicle between two other guard hair follicles. The underfur follicles open into the guard hair canal and all hairs emerge at the skin surface through a common pore [fig. 17].

Cutaneous glands associated with each guard hair follicle and opening into the bottom of the guard hair canal comprise a bilobed sebaceous gland and a greatly coiled apocrine sweat gland. The sweat duct opens posterior to, and slightly higher than the common sebaceous duct formed by the union lower down of separate ducts from each gland. Keratohyalin granules abound near the exterior ends of the cutaneous gland ducts. There are no glands opening into the underfur follicles (fig. 19).

Adaptations of the sea otter integument to an aquatic habit include (1) only periodic occurrence of the granular layer which may confer upon the horny layer different properties from those arising from the continuous presence of granules, thereby contributing to its water-resisting function; (2) the flattened guard hairs; and (3) the absence of arrector pili muscles enabling the hairs to lie close to the skin surface when the animal enters the water. These features are exemplified by the fur seals and they may be common to all semi-aquatic mammals. In common with other densely furred species the sea otter has large functioning apocrine sweat glands associated with each guard hair follicle.

Sensory vibrissae

Sensory vibrissae are in three locations: mystacial, superciliary, and nasal. The numbers of vibrissae are for the left side only of an adult male. There were 8 rows including 62 mystacial vibrissae (i.e., total both sides 124 mystacial vibrissae). The largest was 53 mm. long and the shortest 2 mm. There were four superciliary vibrissae, the largest (dorsal) was 33 mm. and the three others were about 12 mm. long. There were three nasal vibrissae (along the dorsal anterior nasal area), each about 14 mm. long.

The mystacial vibrissae are the most important as sensory organs. They are voluntarily controlled and are frequently extended forward. In this position they are used as sensory aids when walking among rocks or when examining a strange object. Presumably they are used when exploring the bottom of the sea for food. In the wild they are often worn off short but in captivity, where a search for food is not necessary, they may reach a length of 100 to 120 mm.

MOLT

Maynard (1898) wrote that "Their fur is considered equally good at all seasons; hence they are hunted throughout the entire year." Similar statements were made by many other authors.

The lack of an observable molting season may perhaps be explained by analogy with molt in the fur seal. Scheffer and Johnson (1963, p. 32) found that "The number of underfur follicles per bundle in the first adult-type pelage . . . remains unchanged throughout life" but that the number of fibers in each bundle increases with age. "The rise in the fiber count means that up to 60 percent of the fibers are not shed in late molt but remain fast in the bundle."

Scheffer demonstrated earlier in the present report that a young

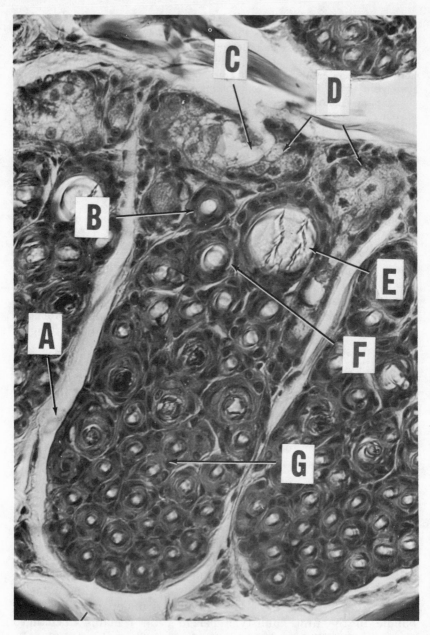

FIGURE 19.—Horizontal section through the sea otter skin showing deeper layer, near hair roots, with one complete pelage unit. *A*—connective tissue, *B*—sweat duct, *C*—sebaceous duct, *D*—sebaceous glands, *E*—large guard hair, *F*—large underfur hair, *G*—smaller underfur hairs. (JKL photo)

sea otter in its first adult pelage had fewer fur fibers (43) per bundle than two adults (adult male 71 and adult female 91). That the fiber population is denser in the sea otter than in the fur seal (adult female 51, adult male 68) is not surprising. Insulation in the fur seal is provided by both blubber and fur but the sea otter, having no blubber, must depend for insulation only on its fur. It seems reasonable to conclude that fur fibers are retained in the sea otter as they are in the fur seal, thus "masking" the period of molt.

John Vania, Leader, Marine Mammal Studies, Alaska Department of Fish and Game, visited the Marine Mammal Biological Laboratory in Seattle from 8 to 19 November 1966 to work with V. B. Scheffer on the examination of skin samples from sea otters. Of 26 sea otters taken in winter and 20 taken in summer, all showed evidence of molt in some of the fiber roots. This evidence is puzzling; the molt deserves further study. A tentative conclusion is that, throughout the year, at various places on the body, individual fibers are in molt while others are at rest.

Observations of captive sea otters also suggested that the period during which fur is shed is prolonged. In all seasons fur fibers were seen on the paws of otters during grooming activity and quantities of fur accumulated at the drain of their pool.

To estimate the periods of maximum and minimum molt, Cecil Brosseau, Director, the Tacoma Aquarium, collected samples of fur for me from a screen over the drain of a pool that held an adult male sea otter (Gus). The uniformly collected samples consisted of the accumulation of fur and guard hair for a 15-hour period at 7-day intervals from October 1967 through October 1968. The samples were dried, cleaned manually (fish scales, fragments of bone, and other debris were removed), and weighed on a beam balance to the nearest 0.01 g. The mean weights of the samples for each month show that shedding is maximal in late spring and summer (mean of 4 August samples = 59 cg.) and minimal in midwinter (mean of 4 January samples = 25 cg.) and that appreciable shedding occurs in all months (fig. 20).

This study suggests that the sea otter exhibits one period of maximal follicular activity (molt) annually in the spring and that it may be similar to the European otter (*Lutra lutra*) which is said to molt almost imperceptibly during a prolonged period (Novikov, 1956), as does the polecat (McCann, 1955).

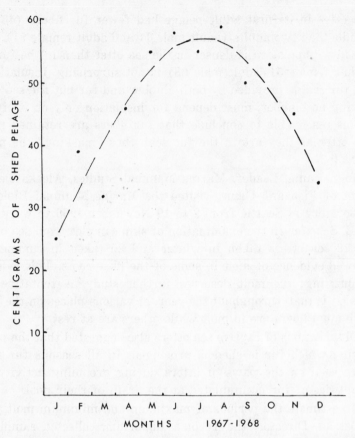

FIGURE 20.—The shed pelage of an adult male sea otter was collected from the drain of his pool at 7-day intervals from October 1967 to October 1968. The mean weights in centigrams of three to five samples (four samples were discarded) collected each month are indicated by dots. The curve shows maximal and minimal periods of shedding during the year and suggests one annual maximal period of molt.

THE PELT IN COMMERCE

Processing

Concerning the processing of sea otter skins, Poland (1892) stated: "The skins are occasionally smoked, and are also dyed or topped." To clarify the meaning of this statement I wrote to Dr. J. L. Stoves of Martin-Rice Ltd., fur processors, London, England, and received the following information (letter, 7 May 1963):

Sea otter fur was dressed in the 19th Century by the conventional method, i.e. fatty tissue was removed by scraping or fleshing after which the skins were smeared with grease or oil (butter rejected for human consumption was also used). The greased skins were then trampled underfoot in large barrels or tubs (so called 'tubbing'). Excess grease was removed by tumbling the skins in sawdust contained in revolving drums ('drumming'). After this the leather was reduced in weight by cutting down or shaving (by hand or by machine). The guard hairs were not removed. . . .

With regard to the quotation from Poland's book, he is referring to the colour of the fur. Poor quality furs were sometimes up-graded (temporarily!) by hanging the skins in smoke from a smouldering, smoking fire whereupon a thin film of soot and tarry matter deposited on the fur turned light yellowish fur into a darker richer brown. The effect was purely temporary but was an unethical way of up-grading fur prior to sale.

The remarks on "dyeing or topping" refer to more lasting improvement of colour (after the raw skins have been auctioned) by deliberate use of dyes. These could be applied by immersing the skins in solutions of the metallic mordants and vegetable dyes then used, or alternatively the materials could be applied to the fur only by brushing, i.e. "topping", a method which left the leather undyed and the article then looked more like a better grade skin which had been dressed only.

Skins taken in recent years were tanned by modern conventional methods. In describing the color, a fur dealer who examined several typical specimen pelts used the following terms: "dark brownish underwool," "brown wool," "very silvery-good top hair," "brownish with a greenish cast."

Value of pelts

Fisher (1941a) summarized information on prices paid for sea otter skins from the time of Bering to 1940: In the mid-1700's skins sold for 20 rubles (about $10) in Kamchatka to 100 rubles (about $50) at the Chinese frontier. During the 1880's prices on the London market ranged from about $105 to $165. By 1903, when sea otters had become scarce, extra rich, large skins sold for as much as $1,125. Fisher was unable to verify or find the source of the statement by Evermann (1923) that during the 1920's (after the sea otter received protection) the prices paid for sea otter pelts ranged from $2,000 to $3,000 each. Among 54 confiscated sea otter skins sold at auction for the account of the U.S. Government from 1924 to 1940, the most valuable brought $465. Only 3 skins were sold for more than $400, 7 for $300 to $350, 7 for $200 to $295, 12 for $105 to $190, and the remaining 25 for less than $100. The average price per skin was $148.54.

On 12 April 1957 at public auction, 117 dressed skins sold for the account of the U.S. Government brought an average price of $22.88 per skin (F. G. Ashbrook, letter 29 April 1957).

On 1 January 1968 the first collection of sea otter skins taken for commercial use since 1911 was offered for sale at the Seattle Fur Exchange, Seattle, Wash. The auction was held for the account of the State of Alaska. Among 1,000 available skins, 905 were considered acceptable for commercial use and were offered for sale.

To prepare them for sale the skins were cased (skinned through a single slit along the hind legs from heel to heel) and dried on frames. The pelts were cleaned and brushed and displayed fur side out. They were divided into 197 lots. The lots ranged in size from one to eight skins matched according to size and color. The bid price for a single skin determined the price for all skins in that lot.

Skins taken in 1962 and 1963 and held since then were less valuable, because of depreciation of quality in storage, than pelts taken in 1967. The earlier collection sold for an average price of about $80 each. The more recently taken skins averaged $280 each. One lot of four skins was sold at the maximum price of $2,300 per skin.

The auction was attended by buyers representing 33 companies from 7 states and 6 foreign countries. All skins offered for sale were sold.

Feeding Mechanisms

Dr. Robert P. Scapino, Department of Oral Anatomy, University of Illinois, has undertaken continuing study of the jaw mechanics and feeding behavior in carnivores. He accomplished a preliminary study of the skull and musculature of the sea otter and kindly contributed an anatomical description, excerpts from which are quoted below (letters, 1963 and 1964). He plans an extensive publication on his studies of carnivore feeding mechanisms.

MASTICATORY MUSCLES

I have completed gross dissection of the masticatory musculature in *Enhydra*. The descriptive terminology used is somewhat different than what you will find in works on *Lutra* (Fisher, 1942; Schumacher, 1961), however, the terms used to designate the various muscles are perfectly acceptable and, in my view, the most useful. My division of the superficial temporal muscle into superior and inferior heads is somewhat unusual and later, when I have examined the muscle in a sufficient number of other mustelids, I may decide to label it differently. But right now the separation seems warranted, at least from an anatomical standpoint.

The masseter muscle of carnivores is usually described as having incompletely distinct superficial and deep parts, but in the sea otter these divisions are even more indistinct than usual.

The anatomy of the jaw muscles in *Enhydra* is essentially the same as in other carnivores. Two features of the temporalis, however, are noteworthy. The superficial temporalis in most other carnivores arises from the entire undersurface of the superficial aponeurosis and is not confined to the anterior part as in *Enhydra*. Of the carnivores I have examined the only two that are like *Enhydra* in this respect are the mink and river otter.

The inferior head of the superficial temporalis is well developed in *Enhydra* and distinct from the superficial head. In other carnivores this muscle seems relatively smaller and blends with the superior head. The functional significance of these differences is not clear.

MANDIBULAR JOINTS

Most carnivores have three jaw joints. The two temporomandibular joints are obvious, but the third, the symphyseal joint has escaped the serious attention of comparative morphologists. My studies indicate that the latter joint has crucial functions in carnivore jaw mechanisms.

The morphology of the temporomandibular joints in carnivores is distinctive. The condyle of the lower jaw takes the form of a transversely oriented cylinder that articulates more or less snugly in a trough-like glenoid fossa. The temporomandibular joint of *Enhydra* does not appear significantly different from that of other carnivores.

The symphyseal joint of carnivores is more varied. This joint consistently shows high mobility (i.e., high mobility for carnivores) in those large carnivores that are powerful crushers. The mobile type of symphysis typically has relatively flat articulating plates that are separated by a well-developed fibrocartilagenous cushion along their anterosuperior borders. The symphysis of *Enhydra* fits this model. Also in *Enhydra*, the articulating plates are bound together by stout cruciate ligaments below and behind the fibrocartilage.

The mobile type of symphysis seems to function to facilitate fitting the teeth to the object that is to be crushed and the fibrocartilage cushion as a shock absorber to reduce the biting force that is transmitted to the skull when the resistance of the object is overcome (Scapino, 1965). The cruciate ligaments allow symphyseal movement, but stabilize the joint by preventing direct lateral separation of the articulating plates.

The teeth and symphysis of *Enhydra* appear to be primarily adapted for crushing hard objects. The sea otter easily cracks the shells of mollusks with its posterior teeth (Kirkpatrick *et al.*, 1955). The combination of a loose symphysis with bunodont teeth in this animal is also observed in other large carnivores that are crushers.

DENTITION

The teeth of the sea otter, particularly the molars, are flattened and rounded. They are not adapted to cut or shear flesh but to crush invertebrates, the preferred food. Even the canines are rounded, having a blunt point and no sharp edge (fig. 21). Because these are used to open the valves of such organisms as the rock oyster (*Pododesmus*) the tips are often worn or broken. Fisher (1941b) described the dentition of the sea otter on the basis of fragmentary material (particularly from younger ani-

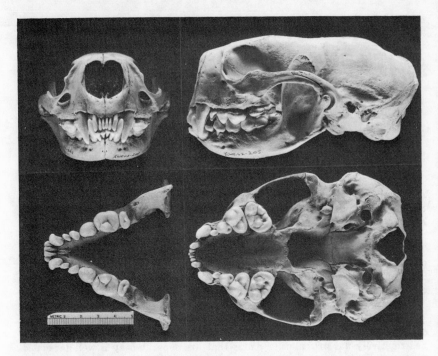

FIGURE 21.—Fresh young adult dentition in the late juvenile or early subadult stage of development. Note the rounded, blunt canines and spade-shaped lower incisors which are used to scoop invertebrate organisms from their shells. Found dead on the beach, 5 March 1962, Amchitka Island, Alaska, weight 24 lb. (10.9 kg.), length 1,005 mm. (KWK 66–9–9)

mals) then available. For this reason, the present description of premature dentition differs somewhat from hers.

In the following discussion, the terminology of Scheffer and Kraus (1964, p. 296–298) is used. The ages at which individual teeth erupt are approximations and are based primarily on body size. A limited number of specimens was studied to determine the progression of tooth eruption from birth to the adult dentition. A detailed study of dental development remains to be undertaken.

In a newborn sea otter (fig. 22), weight about 1.7 kg. (3.7 lb.), the four canine teeth, two upper incisors and two lower first and second pairs of postcanine teeth are erupted from the gums. At birth there are a total of 26 deciduous teeth of which 10 are visible (see formula). The fate of the fetal teeth that are erupted from the bone at birth but are not gingivally erupted is not known, but it appears that they are exfoliated without becoming functional.

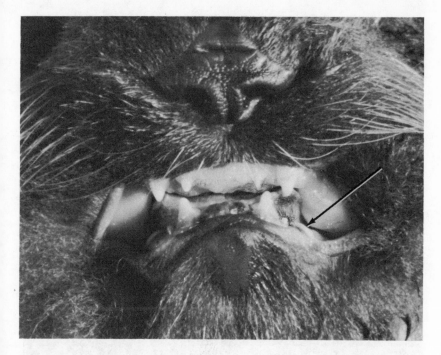

FIGURE 22.—Dentition of newly born male sea otter (62–178), taken at Amchitka Island, 18 February 1962, weight 1.7 kg. (3.7 lb.), length 528 mm. The canines and one pair of upper incisors are clearly shown. The barely erupted first postcanine is visible and the second postcanine is indicated by an arrow. The young sea otter pup probably receives most of its nutrition from mother's milk but soon after birth its mother gives it soft bits of solid food. (KWK 62–14–28)

The complete juvenile dentition (fig. 23), consisting of 44 teeth of which 26 are gingivally erupted, is obtained within about the first 2 to 3 months after birth when the young otter has reached a body weight of about 4 kg. (8–9 lb.). This mixed or transitional dentition is retained for several months.

The complete permanent or adult dentition (fig. 21) consisting of 32 teeth is attained toward the end of the first year of life and before sexual maturity is attained.

The dental formulae given below were determined from skulls that appeared to be typical of the stages of development. These skulls were chosen after examining several dozen specimens.

Dental formulae

Figures represent the number of teeth present on one side; those in parentheses are not yet gingivally erupted. Lower case=deciduous tooth;

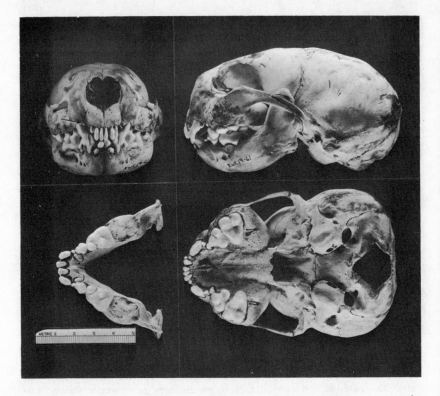

FIGURE 23.—Complete juvenile dentition of a female aged 2 to 3 months, weight 8.75 lb. (3.9 kg.), length 720 mm., captured 12 March 1959. The permanent incisors have all erupted and the permanent first postcanines are erupting and displacing their fetal antecedents. The second and third pairs of deciduous postcanines are well developed. No indication of molar eruption is visible but the tips of the erupting canines are visible (arrow). (KWK 66-11-11)

upper case=permanent tooth, (I=incisor; C=canine; PC=postcanine; M= molar).

Newborn (fig. 24 and fig. 22):

$$\text{i } \frac{1+(2)}{(2)} \qquad \text{c } \frac{1}{1} \qquad \text{pc } \frac{(3)}{2+(1)} \quad = \quad \frac{2+(5)}{4+(2)}$$

Total on one side, 4+(9); total teeth, 26.

Juvenile (mixed or transitional) (fig. 23):

I 3	C (1)	PC 1+(2)	M (1)		4+(4)
i -	c 1	pc 2	-		3
i -	c 1	pc 2	-	=	3
I 2	C (1)	PC 1+(2)	M (2)		3 + (5)

Total on one side, 13+(9); total teeth, 44.

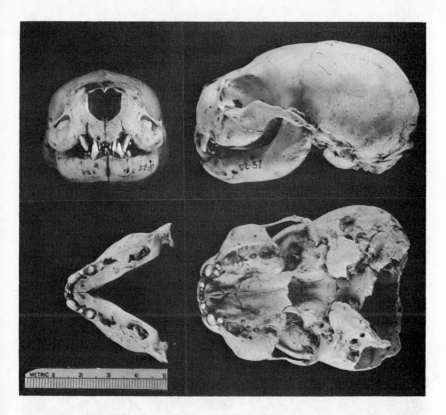

FIGURE 24.—Dentition at birth. The tiny fetal teeth are not erupted from the gums. The canine teeth, a pair of upper incisors, and the first and second pair of lower postcanine teeth are erupted from the gums at birth. Female, captured with mother, Amchitka Island, Alaska, weight 1.5 kg. (3.2 lb.), length 521 mm., umbilical cord attached. (KWK 66–11–2)

Adult (fig. 21):

$$\text{I} \ \frac{3}{2} \quad \text{C} \ \frac{1}{1} \quad \text{PC} \ \frac{3}{3} \quad \text{M} \ \frac{1}{2} \ = \ \frac{8}{8}$$

Total on one side, 16; total teeth, 32.

Incisors

At birth the deciduous caniniform incisors (No. 3 pair) are erupted (fig. 22). These are the first functional teeth to be lost, and are replaced after the two central pairs of permanent upper incisors and the two pairs of permanent lower incisors have erupted gingivally at about 2 or 3 months after birth. The four pairs of central incisors are the first permanent teeth. Their antecedents are small and nonfunctional; they are probably shed when the permanent incisors erupt.

As Hildebrand (1954) has pointed out, the spade-shaped and somewhat protruding permanent lower incisors are used to scoop food organisms from their shells when the sea otter is feeding. In older animals they show wear (fig. 25).

The sea otter is the only member of the order Carnivora with only two pairs of lower incisors. In this respect, it resembles the pinnipeds, most of which also have only two pairs of lower incisors. The walrus has no lower incisors in the adult dentition.

Canines

At birth the deciduous canines are erupted. They are shed and replaced following the loss and replacement of the deciduous caniniform incisors at about 5–6 months of age.

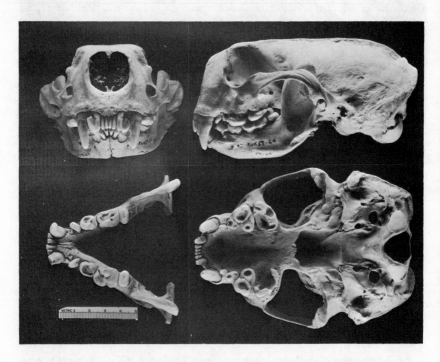

FIGURE 25.—"Old" adult dentition. No method of determining chronological age has been found, but animals with severely worn teeth like this were classified as "old." The worn lower incisors and canines and severely eroded postcanines and molars result when hard-shelled organisms are crushed by the teeth. This male, weight 55 lb. (25 kg.), length 1,420 mm., was captured on a beach at Amchitka Island, 14 March 1959. (KWK 66–12–10)

Postcanines

The deciduous lower 1st and 2d postcanines are erupted at birth. The other four pairs erupt a few weeks later. The postcanines are the last deciduous teeth to be replaced by permanent teeth, at an estimated age of 8 to 12 months. The 2d and 3d permanent postcanines erupt in the last quarter of the first year of life. These are the last of the permanent teeth to erupt. As they push upward the deciduous postcanines are raised above their neighbors but remain anchored to the alveolar bone for a considerable period. This condition results in poor occlusion of all tooth surfaces (fig. 26).

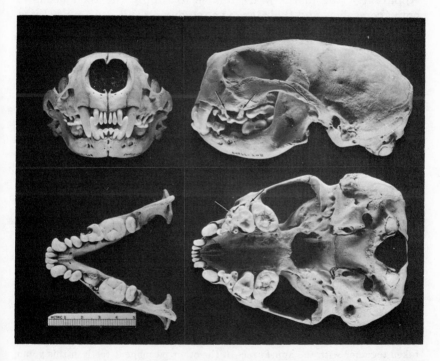

FIGURE 26.—Intermediate juvenile-adult dentition. At this stage the incisors, two pairs of lower postcanines, one pair of upper postcanines, and molars of the adult dentition are almost fully erupted. The remaining postcanines of the juvenile dentition, however, are still held in place by their extended roots (arrows) above the erupting permanent teeth. The upper photographs demonstrate that these teeth prevent occlusion of the molars and incisors. Many young at this stage are found dead of starvation on beaches. Note abrasion-caused attrition of juvenile teeth. (Juvenile female 62–208, weight 22 lb. (10 kg.), length 1,000 mm., found dead on beach, 5 March 1962. (KWK 66–10–15)

Molars

The upper and lower molars have no antecedents. They erupt in the late juvenile period somewhat later than the permanent canines and somewhat earlier than the permanent postcanines.

Many young are born in the late winter-spring period. In the following late winter and early spring period of stress, the food intake of these large juveniles is inhibited by the eruption of the permanent postcanine teeth and the accompanying loss of deciduous teeth. In the crowded Amchitka population where food resources are heavily exploited, such young, still dependent on their mothers for much of their food, are deserted and die at this time. Apparently, the mothers are unable to supply the food needs of both themselves and their large young during this season of stress.

Because poor occlusion, as described above, was observed in many young otters found dead of starvation on beaches, it was assumed that this condition was a factor in their failure to survive (see Mortality Factors).

Dental attrition

The teeth of many sea otters at Amchitka Island show severe tooth wear (fig. 27). In order to learn something of the nature of this damage, sample skulls with worn teeth were sent to Dr. David B. Scott, Chief, Laboratory of Histology and Pathology, National Institute of Dental Research. After he and his associates had examined the teeth they contributed information in a letter of 23 May 1963. Excerpts are quoted:

> None of us feels that the pitted and worn areas have the requisite characteristics of dental caries. The alterations are quite curious. Since we were not familiar with the dentition in the otter, we removed an unerupted permanent tooth and uncovered two others from under the deciduous teeth of a juvenile male (KWK 59–105), and also removed one of the more interesting atypically pitted ones from an adult female (KWK 59–11). One of the former teeth split well enough for us to get an idea of the enamel thickness; taken together with the appearance of the other permanent teeth in this young skull the impression is gained that deep pitting is not a feature at the outset.
>
> The most interesting and confusing configuration in the pitting of the type found in the tooth from KWK 59–11, is the tips of the cusps. As seen in the sectioned tooth, the hole in the underlying dentin is actually broader than the opening through the enamel, resulting in a sort of undermining. [Examination of many teeth indicate to me that these pits are formed when a piece of hard sand is pressed into a newly formed break in the enamel. Movement of the sand grain and pressure on it when food is chewed cause it to rotate and create a cavity in the dentin larger than the hole through which it entered.] This is not expected in attrition, but all of us feel that the classical signs of caries are not present. There is quite a deposit of secondary dentin

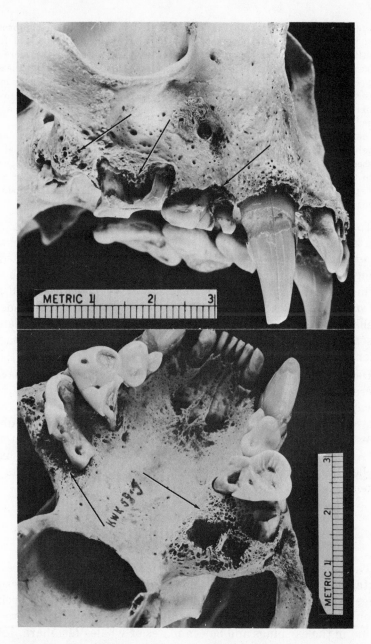

FIGURE 27.—Dental attrition and bone damage in the adult sea otter. Adult otters found dead on beaches at Amchitka Island often have severely worn teeth. Bone resorption (indicated by arrows) and periapical abscesses accompany severe tooth attrition. All teeth showing severe wear were loose. The crushing of hard-shelled organisms, such as mussels and sea urchins, is a suggested cause of severe tooth wear. (KWK 66–14–10 above, 66–13–20 below)

in the pulp chamber beneath the large pit that has resulted in obliteration of the pulpal horn. This phenomenon is ordinarily considered as a defense reaction against trauma or caries. Looking at these pits and the more advanced damage in the other skulls, we are tempted to conclude that some sort of peculiar attritional sequence is represented. The later flattening can be more easily explained in the usual terms of wear and tear. I suspect that a rather large-scale study would be required before the facts could be ascertained as to how the early pitting occurs.

There is a good bit of calculus on the teeth. The bone resorption in an adult female (KWK 59–153) suggests that there may have been periapical abscesses in the lower left molar region, probably as a result of pulp exposure from the attrition. The bone damage in the upper left posterior region could be explained in the same way, or equally well as an outcome of periodontal disease. There are also other areas of bone damage.

Tooth attrition and its relationship to feeding habits and mortality at Amchitka Island are discussed elsewhere. It is apparent that a dense otter population at Amchitka has resulted in a shortage of soft-bodied invertebrate food species. Hard-shelled forms are eaten in large quantities. Sea otters often chew mussels *(Mytilus)* and sea urchins *(Strongylocentrotus)*. The sounds of shells crushed by the teeth are often audible for many meters. Also, sand is ingested with food organisms and sand grains are often found imbedded in teeth.

Dental attrition is less prevalent in sea otters from areas having uncrowded populations than from the crowded Amchitka area. A captive female sea otter that was fed primarily on soft foods showed no dental attrition when she died at the age of about 7 years. It is thus concluded that dental attrition of the kind found at Amchitka is the result of a diet that includes many hard-shelled organisms with which abrasive sand, and even rocks are taken (see Food and Feeding Behavior).

Age Determination

The chronological ages of certain wild animals may be ascertained from anatomical specimens. In pinnipeds the teeth show rings or annuli (Scheffer, 1950a) which are related to cyclical annual phases of fasting and feeding. Similar growth layers are found in the ear plugs and baleen plates of whales (Ichihara, 1966) and in bones (Chapskii, 1952). To a limited degree of accuracy, eye lens weights may indicate age in long-lived mammals, such as the fur seal (Bauer, Johnson, and Scheffer, 1964).

In any study of age determination in mammals it is desirable to have a collection of known-age specimens. The isolation of sea otter populations, problems yet unsolved in keeping a captive colony, and the fact that a regular annual harvest of wild animals has not been taken, have prevented the accumulation of known-age specimens.

Lacking such basic material, but drawing on his experience in the study of teeth for indications of growth layers and age estimation, V. B. Scheffer studied a number of sea otter teeth from young and old animals. Techniques that reveal growth layers in teeth of other mammals revealed nothing that could be related to the annual growth cycle in the sea otter.

Dr. A. F. Forziati and Mrs. M. P. Kumpula, Research Division of the American Dental Association, National Bureau of Standards, Washington, D.C., undertook a study of sea otter teeth. Teeth were sectioned and subjected to techniques such as X-ray photography and exposure to ultraviolet radiation. These and other techniques useful in revealing growth layers in other mammalian teeth showed faint lines (fig. 28) but gave no useful indication of annual growth layers.

In a further effort to "mark" stages of tooth growth, three captive sea otters on Amchitka Island were injected periodically during a 3-month period with alizarin red S dye. It was hoped that visible growth lines would be formed. When the teeth of these animals were studied by Dr. Forziati and Mrs. Kumpula, however, no consistent markings were revealed. Further studies of structures that may indicate age in the sea otter are reserved for the future.

Karl Schneider, Alaska Department of Game (letter, Nov. 1968), tells me that he experimented with a number of different stains and techniques and is now able to differentiate cementum layers which appear to indicate age.

The sea otter is a permanent resident in a relatively uniform environment. It requires a daily food intake of uniform amount (a captive consumed 15 lb. [6.8 kg.] of food per day during all seasons). There is no abrupt molt or distinct period of fasting. In the absence of marked seasonal environmental changes or periodic metabolic changes during the sea otter's life, it is not surprising that the usual indicators of chronological age are not evident.

One captive otter (Susie) was about 1 year old when captured and died of abnormal causes after 6 years in captivity. Her teeth and bone structure at death appeared to be those of a young adult. On this basis it is estimated that in ideal habitat a wild sea otter might be expected to live for from 15 to 20 years. A captive river

FIGURE 28.—Cross section of the right upper canine tooth of an adult female sea otter, weight 47 lb. (21.3 kg.) taken at Amchitka Island, 12 June 1956. Although various zones and lines are revealed by refracted light in this thin section, no series or rhythm of growth layers relating to the annual cycle could be defined. No technique is yet developed to reveal chronological age from a study of the teeth. (National Bureau of Standards photo 45–56)

otter lived to the age of "14 years and 4 or 5 months" (Scheffer, 1958).

The Senses

The various senses are mentioned or discussed in context under different subject headings in other parts of the text. A brief summary of observations of the use of the senses is given below.

SIGHT AND SMELL

The sense of sight appears moderately well developed but, on land at least, is less important than smell as a warning sense. The following observation illustrates this:

I approached a dispersed group of 25 otters sleeping on the rocks. The S. W. breeze of ca. 4–6 knots was such that I could approach cross wind. I moved quietly to within about 10 feet of a group of six sleeping animals and made a noise to awaken them. The animals looked at me but were not alarmed. After taking photos I made some quick movements and they became mildly alarmed and went slowly to the water which was in a channel about 15 feet wide among the rocks. Here they preened—not alarmed. Then they swam slowly to a point directly down wind of me. As they got my scent, all dived in great alarm and swam frantically away under water.

One old male awoke of his own accord and walked leisurely over the rocks on my upwind side. He was only 3 feet away. He looked at me with no recognition—I moved slowly and took a picture, the click startled him but he was not alarmed and ambled around behind me, to a point downwind of me. When he caught my scent he took extreme alarm and scrambled frantically over the rocks, dived into the water, and did not come up until 100 feet away. (Field notes, 12 March 1962, East Cape, Amchitka Island, Alaska.)

When otters feeding or resting in the water are approached by a human observer and the wind is blowing from the observer to the otters, they become restless. Feeding and resting animals rise high in the water and sniff the air. Although there is no rapid movements or indication of alarm, it is generally true that all animals will leave the area within about 10 minutes after the observer's arrival. In the same locations, when the wind blows from the otters toward the observer, the otters remain unconcerned even though the observer moves about on land in clear view.

As mentioned under "Food and Feeding Behavior," sight under water may be useful in finding food. Gentry and Peterson (1967) demonstrated that a sea otter was capable of quite a high degree of accuracy in distinguishing, under water, the size of experimental disks.

HEARING

No observation that I know of demonstrates that the sense of hearing is either particularly acute or poor. The sound of a camera shutter clicking at a distance of 3 to 5 m. usually causes an otter to glance alertly about, but does not cause alarm. Both wild and captive otters soon become accustomed to routine sounds of human activity.

TASTE

Captive otters, when given a variety of foods, often licked each item, then went back to eat first the food which they apparently considered most tasty. Certain foods were obviously preferred, presumably because of their taste.

TOUCH

The forepaws and vibrissae appear to be very sensitive, and they are important in finding food (see Food Gathering and Sensory Vibrissae).

HABITAT REQUIREMENTS

Sea otters inhabit waters of the open coast of the North Pacific Ocean. Although they enter bays on outer sea coasts, there is no evidence that they ever occupied inland waters far from the sea, such as Puget Sound and the extensive inside passages of the Alexander Archipelago of Southeastern Alaska.

They obtain food from the ocean bottom and are seldom seen in waters deeper than 30 fathoms (54 m.), indicating that this may be the approximate limit of their feeding habitat.

Since sea otters are often seen sleeping and diving for food in and near kelp beds (*Alaria, Macrocystis,* and *Nereocystis*), it has often been assumed that kelp beds are a habitat requirement. That this is not true is demonstrated by the fact that a large, permanent sea otter population remains throughout the year in the Bering Sea off Unimak Island and off the western tip of the Alaska Peninsula. There are no kelp beds here and in certain other areas occupied by permanent sea otter populations.

In general, however, sea otters favor waters adjacent to rocky coasts near points of land, or large bays where kelp beds occur. Coasts adjacent to extensive areas of underwater reefs are particularly attractive. In such areas, especially where large rocks or islets are located near shore, some feeding and resting areas are sheltered from wind and storm waves regardless of their direction (fig. 29).

In the Aleutian and Shumagin Islands sea otters regularly haul out on land and they may do so elsewhere. Rocky points are favored but sand beaches, islets, or spits are sometimes used. When a sea otter comes ashore it usually remains within about 1 to 6 m. of the water. Where human disturbance is minimal, as on some Aleutian islands, I have found them sleeping in grass (*Elymus*) as far as 50 to 75 m. from the water. Sea otters tend to concentrate and form colonies in areas which offer an abundant invertebrate bottom fauna and sheltered feeding and resting areas.

FIGURE 29.—Favored sea otter habitat in the Aleutian Islands is characterized by having extensive underwater reefs to a depth of about 20 fathoms, kelp beds, and points of land or offshore rocks that give shelter during storms. This photograph shows an example of favored habitat on Kirilof Bay at Amchitka Island, Alaska. (KWK 55–16–35)

GENERAL BEHAVIOR

Observations of the habits and characteristic behavior of sea otters were obtained in their natural habitat and in captivity. Quantitative studies of behavior and experimental studies were undertaken in only a limited way (Gentry and Peterson, 1967; and in section "In Captivity"). Certain characteristic habits and behavioral traits are discussed in context as they relate to various subjects in other sections of this report.

Daily Cycle of Activity

It was shown in the section "In Captivity" that when an abundant food supply was available a captive animal spent relatively little time feeding as compared to a wild otter. It appears that the abundance of food in the wild also strongly influences the daily cycle of activity of otters in different areas of the Aleutian Islands.

In general, at Amchitka, otters begin to dive for food within the first hour after sunrise. Feeding, interspersed with short periods of grooming and rest, then continues until mid- or late-morning. Sometime between 1100 and 1300 the otters sleep or doze, usually while floating on their backs in a kelp bed. The duration of this rest period usually varies from about one-half to three-quarters of an hour. One mated pair rested from 1225 to 1302 (37 minutes). After this nap, feeding, interspersed with short rest periods for preening and grooming the fur, continues until mid-afternoon when the otters may sleep soundly, usually while floating, but in male areas a number of animals may haul out for the afternoon nap. This nap usually continues for about an hour. The same pair mentioned above rested from 1446 to 1548 (62 minutes).

After this rest period, feeding again occurs and may continue until sunset or after. At dark or shortly before, some animals haul out to sleep, usually within a meter or two of the water but on rare occasions as far as 75 m. up on the beach. Others spend part or all of the night sleeping in a kelp bed while floating on the back.

In areas where populations are less crowded than at Amchitka, and presumably food is more abundant, general observations indicate that rest periods are of longer duration because food needs may be satisfied in a relatively short time.

Mothers accompanied by young, especially large young at Amchitka, often continued to dive for food long after all other otters in the general vicinity had retired for the night. On several occasions I watched mothers feeding until they were obscured by darkness. This is another indication that food species in the Amchitka habitat have been overutilized by that local population. To obtain sufficient food for herself and her young, a mother must search for it after other otters have retired.

The general daily cycle of behavior described above continues throughout the year. When prolonged storms create violent wave action, the daily cycle is disrupted and animals unable to obtain sufficient food die (see Mortality Factors).

Locomotion

SWIMMING

Methods of swimming

Taylor (1914, p. 491) pointed out that the outer or fifth digit of the sea otter's hind foot is the longest (fig. 8). In this respect the sea otter differs from its nearest relative the river otter, from seals, and from most if not all land carnivores. He considered that "extra support" (presumably in walking) is furnished by this unusual feature. Howell (1930, p. 284–287), however, after studying the musculature of the pelvic limbs, surmised that the sea otter swims by means of vertical undulations of the posterior part of the body; that it uses the hind flippers held in the horizontal plane, palms up, in combination with the tail to "present in a satisfactory degree the lunate rear border theoretically desirable." Thus, "the long fifth toes would form the outer borders of the swimming organ." He was unable to confirm this theory by observation. He felt some doubt as to its validity because "It is true that no other mammal is known ever to have employed this method of swimming."

On many occasions, from boats and cliffs, and in captivity, I have watched sea otters swimming in clear water beneath the surface. Howell's deductions were entirely correct.

While the sea otter is swimming beneath the surface or diving, vertical undulatory movements of the body, as described above, furnish propulsion. While near the bottom, maneuvering and searching for food, stroking or paddling movements of the hind flippers are also used.

Unlike other marine mammals, the sea otter habitually swims on the surface when it is moving from one area to another. It usually swims on its back and paddles with alternate strokes of its hind flippers (fig. 30). In this position the long fifth digit dips most deeply into the water and in combination with the other webbed digits produces forward motion.

Thus, the fifth digit is a useful adaptation to two unusual methods of swimming in a mammal: (1) Progression beneath the surface through undulations of the hind flippers and tail in the vertical plane, and (2) progression on the surface by paddling while resting on the back. Whether the fifth digit became elongated as an adaptation to swimming beneath the surface or as the dominant member used in surface propulsion is difficult to surmise.

The sea otter infrequently swims belly down at the surface, with the head and shoulders above the surface (fig. 86). At such

FIGURE 30.—Three adult males in typical swimming attitude. The forepaws are folded across the chest or pressed palmside down against the chest. Forward progress is obtained by alternate strokes of the hind flippers. Maximum sustained surface speed is about 2.5 km per hour (1.5 knots). (KWK 62–27–14)

times the hind feet are used to deliver paddling strokes similar to the stroking movements employed when swimming on the back. Progress on the surface appears to be slower when swimming on the belly than while swimming on the back.

The front feet are not used in swimming either on the surface or beneath it. They are pressed palmside down against the chest or folded across the chest when not in use to manipulate food or to preen the fur or hold young (fig. 30).

The tail is flattened in the horizontal plane and tapers only slightly, so that it presents a broad surface for most of its length. The tail of an adult female measured 317 mm. long, 44 mm. thick, and 64 mm. wide near its base. In addition to its use in conjunction with the hind flippers in underwater swimming, the tail is used as a "sculling oar." Slight alterations of positions are made when the otter is floating on its back. Frequently I observed resting otters floating in this position with front and hind feet folded on the chest and abdomen. Normally the tail floats on the surface while the otter rests, but if it wishes to make slight movements, for example to face away from a light breeze, the tail is projected downwards and by means of circular sideward movements the body is rotated in the desired direction. Also, when captives were eating and they wished to pivot about on the surface to avoid food pilferage by other otters, the tail was used in sculling to assist the stroking hind flippers.

Swimming speed and agility

The sea otter is a slow swimmer but it moves more rapidly beneath the water than on its surface. Two methods were used to measure swimming speed: (1) From the shore, otters traveling from one area to another were timed as they passed beach points. The distances were then measured on nautical charts and the speed computed. (2) Otters were pursued with a motor-driven dory while they swam beneath the surface. In clear water the otters could sometimes be seen as they attempted to escape pursuit. Presumably, at such times they moved at maximum velocity. The speed of the dory was measured by timing its passage over a known distance.

Examples, surface speed: (1) An adult female swam parallel to the coast of Kirilof Point on a nearly windless day. For the most part she swam on her back but occasionally she rolled over and "porpoised" (exposing the back, but not leaving the water) for 10 to 15 yards. During the observation period she made one food dive and when she emerged ate the several urchins she had gathered while she continued on course at the surface. In 44 minutes she covered exactly 1 nautical mile, thus her speed was 2.3 km. per hour (1.4 knots). (2) An adult female, carrying a sleeping pup on her chest, moved hurriedly and steadily on the surface from an area where a rising wind caused rough water. The wind was from her side, so she was neither swimming with or against it. She passed over a measured distance of about 800 m. in 20 minutes, or at the rate of 2.4 km. per hour (1.5 knots). (3) After emerging from a food dive with a fish (weighing about 0.5 kg.), an adult male swam on his back while he consumed the fish and moved with moderate speed to another area. His departure from the feeding area was apparently prompted, to some degree at least, by the presence of three Glaucous-winged Gulls (Larus glaucescens) which swam beside or flew above him while they retrieved discarded fish scraps. The otter was able to outdistance the birds that alighted beside him on the water. In 675 seconds he traversed a measured distance of 300 m. at an average speed of 1.6 km. per hour (0.9 knots).

The top speed of our dory was approximately 11 km. per hour (6 knots). On many occasions we chased sea otters in order to catch them in a dip net. When the water was clear and smooth, we could watch the otters swimming beneath the surface as they attempted to escape. It appeared that their top speed for brief intervals, less than 1 minute, was not more than 9.25 km. per hour (5 knots) and probably somewhat less. When we were unable to see otters beneath the surface, we often overran them. Occasionally during escape attempts, otters would porpoise clear of the water ahead of the boat. When this was done they were most readily captured.

Thus it appears that when an otter moves from one area to another on the surface, its near maximum sustained rate of travel may approach 2.5 km. per hour and the underwater, briefly maintained (up to about 1 minute), maximum escape speed is about 9 km. per hour. This compares with a near maximum, briefly sustained (3 to 5 minutes), escape speed of the northern fur seal, which we pursued in a vessel having a maximum speed of 26 km. per hour (14 knots), of about 18.5 km. per hour (10 knots). A Pacific bottlenose porpoise (Tursiops gilli) sustained a speed of 29 km. per hour (16.1 knots) for 7.5 seconds (Lang and Norris, 1965).

Although a slow swimmer, the sea otter is remarkably agile. On one occasion I plunged the dip net directly in the path of an otter as it swam just ahead of the dory and at a depth of about ½ m. The otter, unable to avoid entering the net, rolled forward, completed a 180° reversal of course, and escaped before I could pull the net from the water.

DIVING

Duration of food dives

In water depths ranging from about 2 to 25 m. food dives were timed with a stop watch from observation points on the cliffs of Amchitka. Several factors render such observations somewhat difficult to obtain and evaluate. Usually several otters were diving for food in an area under observation. Although an otter may make several food dives in a rather limited area, perhaps 15 m. in diameter, the animal may unexpectedly move 100 m. or more beneath the surface to a new feeding location. Also, a nearby otter may move to the vicinity of an animal that is being timed, causing confusion. The positive identification of the sex of a diving otter is sometimes difficult to ascertain at the distances and with the frequent poor visibility caused by weather conditions.

General observations indicate that the duration of food dives by adult males exceeds that of adult females. The following data probably exaggerate this difference because the females' dives were, to a greater extent than the males', in shallow water:

| | Number of animals observed | Duration of food dives (seconds) | | | |
		Timed food dives	Average duration of dives	Maximum duration	Minimum duration
Adult male	4	20	100	160	72
Adult female	6	41	49	82	15

The few observations presented are not strictly comparable, because water depth varied and the animals under observation may have had differing food preferences which caused some of them to search longer for a particular item. Males feed on fish to a greater extent than females. Among 50 stomachs of adult males which contained food, 82 percent contained fish, and 62 percent of 178 stomachs of adult females contained fish. The search for and capture of fish would probably require more time than the gathering of invertebrates.

The best data on the duration of dives of the female were obtained on 20 and 21 August 1955. On these two days a mated pair of otters remained in a small cove at Amchitka and no other otters fed in the area. During the period of mating the two otters dived and emerged from their food gathering dives simultaneously. Because the male followed the female closely, the duration of her dives appeared to determine the duration of his. The mean duration of food dives was 65 seconds and the extremes were 20 and 95 seconds. The majority of the dives (69 percent) lasted between 50 and 80 seconds (fig. 31).

In generalizing on the duration of food dives in the usual foraging depths, between 10 and 25 m., it may be said that the adult female usually stays beneath the surface for about 1 minute and the adult male for about 1½ minutes.

The number of dives in a feeding period varies. In 9 hours and 8 minutes when records were kept the mated pair spent 4 hours and 45 minutes in feeding activity, making 87 dives in water approximately 23 m. deep. Nikolaev and Skalkin (1963) report observations of 63 dives in 1 hour and 18 dives in 12 minutes. Presumably these data were obtained from animals feeding in shallow water.

Duration of escape dives

The sea otter, however, is capable of dives of long duration. This was demonstrated when we pursued a female otter for 50 minutes on 10 July 1960 in the Bering Sea off Unimak Island. During the chase she made 13 dives averaging 120 seconds beneath the sur-

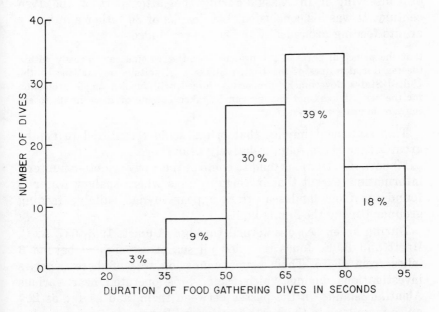

FIGURE 31.—Duration of 87 timed food dives made by a mated pair of otters. The water depth was 23 m. The male followed the female closely, both in submerging and emerging.

face. The longest dive lasted for 250 seconds (4.2 minutes) and the shortest 30 seconds. The last timed dive of 205 seconds indicated that the animal had not become exhausted and we abandoned the chase as futile. Barabash-Nikiforov (1947) says that "the longest time that the sea otter can submerge is not more than 6 minutes." My conclusion is that the maximum duration of a dive is probably less than 6 minutes.

Depth of diving and distance from shore

The maximum depth to which a sea otter may descend to gather benthic food organisms is not definitely known. Consideration of the historical record along with modern observations and data, however, indicate certain tentative conclusions.

The greatest diving depth I find in the historical record is quoted from Chase Littlejohn, a sea otter hunter of the 19th century. He said "There is a [place] . . . about 50 fathoms deep where they go to the depth of the water to feed" (Hall, 1945). Other otter hunters indicate lesser diving depths. Snow (1910, p. 281) stated that the sea otter appears to prefer to get its food at depths of 10–25 fathoms.

Captain C. L. Hooper (1897) studied the sea otter and problems of conserving it in Alaska during the latter part of the 19th century. It was his conclusion that "banks of 30 fathoms of water are its feeding grounds." Further, he concluded—

that the principal parts of the present sea otter grounds are already within the territorial waters of the United States. . . . suitable regulations by the United States Government, properly enforced, will furnish ample protection for the sea otter, as not enough can be taken outside of these limits to encourage hunting to any extent.

This statement implies that otters seldom ventured to depths greater than those found relatively near shore.

Modern observations tend to confirm the early sea otter hunters' information, except that in certain areas where shallow water is found far from land sea otters appear to find suitable feeding grounds beyond the 3-mile limit.

During seven seasons (April through August, 1957–63) A. C. Hartt and B. F. Jones recorded all sea otters sighted beyond 3 miles from shore. Their primary mission was offshore fisheries investigations during which their ships operated near various Aleutian islands, in the passes between them, and as far as 200 miles from land in the North Pacific and Bering Sea.

Their observations of otters over deep water (table 10) are of interest, because in each case the otters were near areas where shallower water was only a few miles distant. Also, the observations were in areas where strong tidal currents are prevalent. These could quickly move an otter sleeping on the surface several miles from a feeding area.

The observation of two otters 32 miles west of Kiska in the 55-mile wide pass between Buldir and Kiska Islands on 27 May 1959 (A. C. Hartt, letter, 1960) is of particular interest. Their presence there may be explained by the fact that they were near an underwater mountain ridge, Buldir Reef, which is about 20 nautical miles long and over a mile wide, and which offers considerable area having depths of from 17 to 30 fathoms.

The only available authentic record of an otter far from shore and away from passes between islands was recorded by G. T. Joynt (letter, 1957). While flying as a naval aviator in the Aleutians in the spring of 1943, Joynt saw an otter—

a little over 50 miles due south of East Cape on Amchitka Island. On this particular day the open ocean was as smooth as a mill pond . . . This animal was observed at very close quarters and identity was certain because of the rarity of anything on the surface making a wake so far from land. I have often conjectured that this particular animal could have been a victim of an unintentional ride in a large free-floating kelp raft. Whenever sea otter were observed more than a half-mile from the nearest kelp patch it was usually a single animal and they were most frequently in the straits between two of the larger islands. On these occasions they were usually headed to one island or the other and not aimlessly swimming about.

Joynt was a trained biologist before becoming a naval aviator and gathered much useful information about sea otters in the Aleutians.

The large amount of time spent by the several observers (table 10) in offshore areas and the dearth of observations of sea otters at an appreciable distance from depths of 20 to 30 fathoms, demonstrate the tendency of otters to remain in shallow water.

On 10 July 1960, an adult female sea otter (KWK 60–19) was shot 9 nautical miles north of the Alaska Peninsula (55°20′ N. lat., 163°11′ W. long.) in water 20 fathoms (120 ft.) deep. The stomach contents (see Food and Feeding Behavior) consisted of benthic organisms. During aerial surveys of the area off the north coast of Unimak Island and south of Amak Island on 8 April 1962, the majority of 811 otters recorded were seen between 3 and 10 miles from shore in water from 10 to 25 fathoms deep. The majority were near or inside the 20-fathom curve. The 20-fathom curve where this large number of otters were seen ranged from 5 to 8 miles from the north shore of Unimak Island. I presumed that

TABLE 10.—*Observation of sea otters beyond 3 miles from shore in waters off Alaska*

Date	Number of otters	Nautical miles from land	Location	Water depth (fathoms)	Observer	Remarks
Spring 1943	1	50+	S. of E. Cape, Amchitka	2,000+	GTJ [1]	Aerial observation.
31 July 1957	Groups	6-7	S.W., Cape Sujaka Tanaga I.	200-300	J [2]	Floating kelp patches present.
15-19 Aug. 1957	do	ca. 8	S., Little Kiska I.	70-90	H [3]	Seen while en route from Kiska I. to fishing grounds.
27 May 1959	2	32	W. by N. of Sirius Point, Kiska I.	ca. 900	J	Floating kelp patches present; otters 25 yards from vessel.
11 May and 23 June 1960	Several	ca. 7	Sitkin Sound	40-60	H	Scattered otters seen en route Adak I. to Great Sitkin I.
10 July 1960	2	5	Bering Sea, S. of Amak I.	20-22	K	Specimen collected had food in stomach.
8 April 1962	811	3-10	Bering Sea, N. of Unimak I.	10-25	S & K [4]	Otters seen singly and in groups; feeding observed.
3 July 1963	2	6	S. by E. of Kagalaska Strait	ca. 100	J	Resting on surface.
9 July 1963	1	17	N. of Unimak I.	31	F [5]	Resting on surface.

[1] G. T. Joynt, Naval Aviator on patrol from Amchitka I.
[2] B. F. Jones, Fisheries Research Institute.
[3] A. C. Hartt, Fisheries Research Institute.
[4] D. L. Spencer and K. W. Kenyon, Bureau of Sport Fisheries and Wildlife.
[5] C. H. Fiscus, Bureau of Commercial Fisheries.

light-colored objects seen on the chest of some of these animals were food items.

Aerial observations of most of the Alaskan areas populated by sea otters indicate that otters prefer to feed in depths of 5 to 15 fathoms and that most of them, except off Unimak Island, are within about one-half mile of the shore. Weather conditions and lack of time prevented aerial examination of all shallow banks far from land where otters might be expected. On 3 May 1965, however, Tahoma Reef (51°51′ N. lat., 175°50′ E. long.), Middle Reef (52° N. lat., 176° E. long.), and Buldir Reef (52°10′ N. lat., 176°30′ E. long.), respectively, 30, 20, and 20 miles from the nearest land (Buldir Island) and having considerable water areas from 3 to 20 fathoms in depth, were examined. Observation conditions were excellent. We saw a number of birds and sea lions, particularly in the kelp beds over Tahoma Reef, but sea otters were absent.

Numerous observations of feeding otters near Amchitka Island, at all seasons, indicate a preference there for depths of 5 to 20 fathoms. Also, during rough winter weather otters are inclined to search for food to a greater degree near shore. When the weather is mild they tend to move offshore to the vicinity of submerged reefs.

Several otters were observed over deep water and far from shore in the vicinity of drifting patches of floating kelp. This suggests that the otters could obtain food organisms that gathered in the shelter of the kelp. It is known that pelagic fishes accumulate under and around floating objects in the sea. That sea otters might rarely adapt to pelagic feeding is intimated by Snow (1910, p. 280):

On one occasion I found the stomach of an otter I killed some 8 or 10 miles offshore filled with the remains of a quantity of small fish with no signs of the remains of any crustaceans.

He does not, however, identify the area or state the depth of water where this otter was taken. Marakov (1965, p. 214) also reports sea otters up to "15 miles from the coast in comparatively deep places." No authentic record, however, indicates that the sea otter is capable of adapting itself to the capture of pelagic organisms where great depth prevents food gathering from the bottom.

In consideration of all the data available, it is my conclusion that sea otters feed in shallow water (1 to 15 fathoms deep) when sufficient food is available there. When food resources are more abundant offshore and particularly in mild weather, they move to feed in depths of 20 or, rarely, 30 fathoms. Food dives to depths as great as 50 fathoms for food may be possible but otters are rarely seen in water as deep as 30 fathoms (180 ft.). No specimen is available to give positive evidence of food gathering at depths greater than 20 fathoms (120 ft.).

Our observations tend to confirm the conclusion of Barabash-Nikiforov (1947) that "the greatest depth to which it can go is 50 meters [164 ft.]"

WALKING AND RUNNING

Progression on land is similar but less agile than in other mustelids. The long, outer 5th digits of the hind flippers, which particularly aid progression when the otter swims on its back, hinder progress on land. Snow (1910, p. 275), however, exaggerated this hindrance when he wrote:

The use, however, of the hind limbs is very limited, the toes appear to lack all muscular power, and the otter cannot place its hind-feet flat upon the ground; when it attempts to walk, the toes are doubled back under the soles.

As figure 32 illustrates, Snow's statement is not true. He probably received his impression from otters that were cornered

FIGURE 32.—Because the fifth digits of the hind flippers are long, the sea otter walks with a somewhat clumsy rolling gait. It moves somewhat more slowly than normal human walking speed. (KWK 62–10–29)

on land and trying frantically to escape the clubs of hunters. His impression that the toes of the hind flipper were doubled back under the foot when walking was so strong a conviction that he figured this unnatural position in the frontispiece of his book.

When the sea otter walks unhurriedly on land, it moves with a rolling gait, raising one foot at a time and with the back arched (fig. 32).

When animals some distance from the water are startled, they arch the back and bound or hop, moving both forefeet then both hind feet forward in rapid succession (fig. 33). Juveniles and young adults are more agile than large, heavy adults. Some large animals seem unable to raise their bodies from the ground and slide, with the help of the feet, across the beach on the belly.

Sleeping

The sea otter may sleep while floating on its back (fig. 34) or when hauled out on shore (fig. 84).

FIGURE 33.—Adult sea otters, startled on a favorite hauling-out beach at Amchitka Island, bound toward the water in a typically mustelid manner. Speed of movement is somewhat less than the running speed of a normally agile man. (KWK 1027)

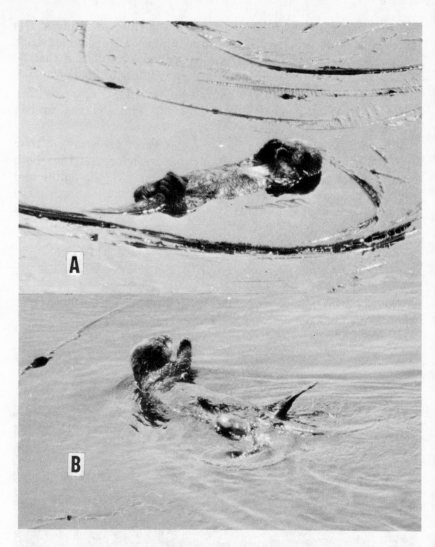

FIGURE 34.—A—Otters usually attempt to find a sheltered kelp bed before
sleeping. After grooming is finished, the hind feet are folded on the abdomen.
The forepaws may be placed over the eyes or against the side of the head
or folded across the chest while sleeping. (KWK 56-4-4) B—This recently
awakened otter is swimming languidly from its resting place while attempting to keep the head and forepaws dry. After awakening, otters appear
reluctant to immerse the feet and head. (KWK 56-4-19)

Where kelp beds are available, the otters sleep in their protection. When surrounded by strands of kelp, the sleeping otter is protected from rough water and from movements by wind and water currents. Often, before going to sleep the otter uses its forepaws to pull one or several strands of kelp over its body; or it may make a shallow dive under the kelp strands, emerging with the strands in place over its body (fig. 35). In certain areas, for example off the north shore of Unimak Island, no kelp beds occur. In that area otters gather in large groups to sleep on the open sea (fig. 81).

Before going to sleep, otters scrub and groom their fur for about 5 to 15 minutes in the water. Then, if they haul out to sleep, the fur is preened and rubbed dry before sleeping.

On land the otter may sleep in many positions, from lying on the back as when sleeping in the water to stretching out flat on the belly or curling up nose-to-tail (fig. 84).

When otters awaken, they appear reluctant to get wet. If floating, they hold the feet, head, and tail aloft while rolling the body from side to side. Often they roll completely over, arching the back to avoid wetting the extremities. The head and forepaws are

FIGURE 35.—A drowsy otter preens its cheeks with its forepaws before going to sleep. The hind flippers and tail protrude beyond strands of kelp (*Macrocystis*) that lie across its chest and belly and prevent movement by wind or current while the otter sleeps. (Photographed near Monterey, Calif., by Wm. F. Bryan)

usually the last to be immersed as the otter swims leisurely from its resting place (fig. 34).

When sleeping on land, an otter usually spends a variable time languidly preening its fur before entering the water. Then it may follow the procedure described above to delay wetting the feet, head, and tail.

Grooming

Pelage care is of primary importance to survival in the sea otter. Grooming is essential to maintain pelage cleanliness and waterproofness, and thus insulation against the chilly marine habitat. A blanket of air remains trapped among the dry underfur fibers which serves as insulation. A captive female sea otter spent 48 percent (about 7.5 hours) of the daylight hours grooming her fur and a wild female, observed for about 7½ hours, spent 11 percent of the time in grooming activity (table 64, Comparison of daily activities of wild and captive female sea otters, see In Captivity).

Grooming takes place either in the water or on land. Energetic grooming is done before rest periods and languid grooming (fig. 36) at intervals during a resting period and at the end of a rest period. Grooming may be divided into two primary phases, (1) washing the fur and (2) drying the fur.

Grooming is accomplished primarily by rubbing the fur with the palms of the forepaws, but the hind flippers may be rubbed together or against the fur of the abdomen and sides. The fur of all parts of the body is rubbed by the forepaws. To accomplish this and reach remote parts of the body, the otter may twist and squirm within its loose-fitting skin, so that areas of the mid-back can be reached. The flexible body may be rolled in a ball so that the forepaws reach beyond the root of the tail to the lower back (fig. 37). Also, loose skin of the sides and belly may be rolled over a foreleg while water is pressed from the pelage and removed with the tongue (fig. 38).

Water may be pressed from the fur by the palms of the forepaws (fig. 39). A fold of skin and fur may be pressed between the forepaws, squeezing water from the fur and the moisture removed with the tongue (fig. 40). The fur may be rubbed in a circular motion or by rapid strokes in many directions. The retractile claws (fig. 2) (see Physical Characteristics) are occasionally extended to aid in grooming but usually they remain retracted. Figure 41, illustrates a typical grooming posture.

FIGURE 36.—While dozing on the surface of her pool, a captive female sea otter languidly grooms the fur of her chest and sides. (KWK 61–10–34)

The fur is washed by rubbing submerged parts of the body with the forepaws and by rolling, head first, over and over at the surface. Rolling may be accomplished just prior to sleep on the water's surface. It smooths the fur and leaves a thin film of water in the outer pelage tips.

In the final stages of a grooming session the otter may rest belly down at the surface, the head bent under the body while blowing air into the fur. Simultaneously the sides and belly are rubbed vigorously with the forepaws (fig. 42). The fur may also be aerated by a rapid churning motion of the forepaws, beating the water to a foaming froth (fig. 43).

If the otter intends to rest on land, it swims to a point near the desired resting place. Here it goes through a 5- to 10-minute grooming routine before leaving the water. After hauling out, the otter energetically rubs and dries its fur (fig. 44).

In general, females tend to be more thorough than males in grooming their pelage. I sometimes saw males, but not females, after hauling out, that failed to thoroughly groom and dry their fur before sleeping.

FIGURE 37.—The sea otter curls its long flexible body into a ball and reaches between the hind flippers to groom the tail and lower back. (KWK 1028)

Casual observers of grooming sea otters often misinterpret grooming for "scratching" and ask if sea otters have lice. They do not.

Voice

BABY CRY

This cry is uttered from birth until the large juvenile stage is passed. The pup cries when in distress or when it wants attention from its mother. The sound: a sharp, high pitched "waah-waah." This may be repeated constantly for long periods if the pup is

FIGURE 38.—Using its left paw, a grooming sea otter pulls the loose skin from its right side over the right foreleg in order to press water from the pelage and lick away the moisture. Moisture in the tips of the fur give the pelage a slick, wet appearance except on the head where dry, light-colored underfur is exposed by parting of the wet tips. (KWK 61–10–19)

separated from its mother and no tranquilizer is given. The sound resembles the cry of a young gull. The mouth is open wide when the cry is uttered.

SCREAM

This is uttered (1) when an adult is in severe distress—as when held in unsatisfactory captive conditions. Often it indicates that the animal is near death. It is not uttered when an animal is captured. (2) When a female has lost her young, as when the pup strays behind a rock, she screams repeatedly. This cry is the adult version of the baby cry. It is earsplitting at close quarters and can be heard at a distance of ¼ to ½ mile in the wild and as far away as 200 meters when an animal is in a closed building. The mouth is open wide when the otter screams.

WHISTLE OR WHINE

This is uttered to denote frustration or mild distress. Captives

FIGURE 39.—While grooming, water is squeezed from the fur of the foreleg under pressure and by rubbing with the palm of the paw. (KWK 61–10–25)

whistle when the feeding schedule is delayed, and when they are carried on a truck or aircraft. The sound is uttered by adults and subadults primarily and to a lesser degree by juveniles. The whistle is loud enough to be heard to a distance of about 200 meters. It is a high pitched vocal sound that resembles a human whistle and is uttered with the mouth slightly open. "Wheeee wheeee" repeated often and of varying duration.

COOING

Females coo during premating and postmating behavior and also when grooming and fondling young. The coo appears to come from the throat and to denote satisfaction and contentment. Females coo while eating if the food is particularly pleasing. The mouth appears to be closed when it is uttered. Cooing can be heard up to a distance of about 15 to 30 m. on a quiet day. The sound "ku-ku-ku" may be continued for considerable periods either steadily or intermittently.

SNARL OR GROWL

This sound appears to originate deep in the throat and is uttered

FIGURE 40.—While drying its pelage, a fold of skin is pressed between the palms of the forepaws. Water expelled from the fur is removed with the tongue. (KWK 61–10–10)

when a newly captured animal is attempting to escape from a net. The snarl or growl is audible only a few meters away.

HISSING (NONVOCAL)

Females hiss during capture, after capture, and before becoming tame. The sound is similar to a cat's hiss (as noted by Steller in his Journal) but more explosive and of short duration. The sound is characteristic primarily of females and juveniles. If a person appears unexpectedly near a caged otter the hiss may be uttered in the first moment of fright.

GRUNTING

When a hungry animal is eating voraciously it utters soft grunting sounds that appear to denote satisfaction. In the male this appears to be equivalent to the cooing of the female.

FIGURE 41.—A mother otter rubs the top of her head with one paw and her elbow with the other. Both paws are in constant motion during grooming. After grooming her own fur, the mother took her pup onto her chest and groomed and dried it before allowing it to nurse from her two abdominal nipples. (KWK 57–29–14)

BARK

A yearling male during pool cleaning, while trapped in the empty pool and resenting thus being "cornered," uttered a staccato bark which trailed off into the whistle, apparently to denote frustration.

COUGHING, SNEEZING, AND YAWNING

Sounds as in other animals.

Handedness

During many hours of watching wild sea otters feeding, I noted that when the animals emerged from a food gathering dive the food items were carried to the surface under the left forelimb. Only if a large quantity of food was brought to the surface, i.e.,

FIGURE 42.—Near the end of a grooming period the sea otter rests belly down at the surface, bends the head to the belly, and vigorously blows air into the fur. At the same time it scrubs the fur on both sides with the forepaws. Note bubbles of exhaled air on water and splash caused by scrubbing paw. (KWK 61–10–26)

too much to be held under the left forelimb, did the otters place food under the right forelimb.

I have watched through calm, clear water while both captive and wild otters gathered food from the bottom. In all cases the right paw appeared to be used dominantly in gathering food and placing it under the left forelimb. Both paws were used to pick the food from the bottom, then with the right paw the food was pushed under the left forelimb.

When food was eaten on the surface, the food item was retrieved from the "chest pouch" under the left forelimb by the right paw, aided by the left paw, then held between both paws while being eaten. The teeth were usually employed to break the shells of small sea urchins. Before a large hard-shelled green sea urchin was eaten, however, the top of the urchin was cradled in the left paw while pressure was exerted by the heel and sometimes the toes of the right paw to crush the test around the oral opening of the urchin. The urchin was rotated against the left palm, so that the

FIGURE 43.—During the grooming period, before hauling out, the sea otter may beat the water to a froth with the front legs, perhaps aerating the fur to some degree. (KWK 55–19–3)

test was broken completely around the oral orifice before the teeth were employed to remove the broken shell.

From these observations I have concluded that the sea otter is right-handed. In hundreds of animals observed I have never seen food items brought to the surface under the right forelimb unless the quantity was too great for the left limb to accommodate.

Handedness in other animals is variable. Warren (1953) demonstrated that in the Rhesus monkey the right and left hands are used with about equal frequency. Lane (1946) indicated that birds of prey tend to be left-footed, and parrots (Friedman and Davis, 1938) are similar. Pigeons, Fisher (1957) concluded, tended to be right-footed.

Further study under experimental conditions may reveal if sea otters invariably exhibit right-handedness.

Tool-using

The use of a rock or hard-shelled mollusk held on the chest as an "anvil" for breaking the shell of a clam held in the forepaws is discussed under Food and Feeding Behavior. Chest pounding with the forepaws commonly occurs as an apparent expression of frus-

FIGURE 44.—After hauling out, the otter usually rests on its back while grooming and drying its fur before sleeping. (KWK 57–32–4)

tration, as when an otter has been robbed of its food by another otter. Perhaps the pounding of a hard-shelled mollusk against another originated because of frustration when the otter could not break, with its teeth, the shell of a food organism. At Amchitka, where the shells of mussels are crushed by the post-canine teeth, food pounding behavior is not observed. Where feeding was observed in Alaska, hard-shelled clams were not eaten and mussels *(Mytilus)* do not grow as large as those in California where they are commonly pounded against a hard object (Hall and Schaller, 1964).

When captive otters from Amchitka were presented with clams that could not be broken with the teeth or crushed between the paws, they broke them against a rock or another clam on the chest (fig. 45) or by pounding them on the cement edge of the pool (fig. 59). A female also pounded smelts (Osmeridae), and herring (Clupeidae) which she did not particularly relish (fig. 46), and she pounded a rock on the edge of her pool. Thus, animals that came from an area where food organisms were not observed to be broken by pounding, used this technique when frustrated by

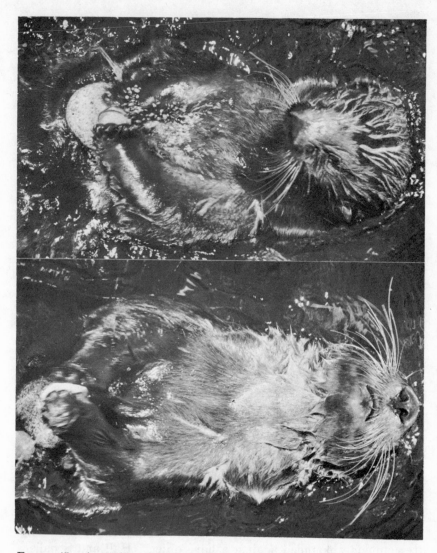

FIGURE 45.—A captive adult male sea otter from Amchitka Island pounds a clam, held between his forepaws, against a rock resting on his chest. Usually the head is held erect (above) but not infrequently it is extended during food pounding behavior (below). (KWK 67–15–7 above, 67–14–30 below)

hard-shelled organisms or by fish they did not care for. Also (Kenyon, 1959), a sea otter pounded a drain cover with a rock when the cover frustrated a desire to explore the drain. I consider the sea otter's tool-using behavior, as derived from chest-pounding,

FIGURE 46.—A captive otter pounded herring (*Clupea*) against the cement edge of her pool. The otter did not particularly relish this species as food, and the pounding behavior appeared to denote frustration when more appetizing food was not available. The irregular surface of the pool edge shown was produced when the otter pounded this area with a rock, cracking away the finishing layer. Rock pounding behavior appeared to express frustration when food was not available in the pool. (KWK 61–10–27)

frustration behavior. Also, I agree with the statement of Hall (1965) that the pounding behavior in the sea otter is—

but a behavioural adaptation that has no special relevance to the evolution of the sort of intelligent, anticipatory skills which are most highly developed in man and which he uses for the manufacture of a standard set of tools to be kept in store and used on different occasions for various purposes.

Thus, tool-using behavior in the sea otter might be likened to the use of gravity by gulls and ravens. These birds commonly break the shells of clams and mussels by carrying them aloft and letting them fall on a rocky beach.

Defense and Escape

ON LAND

When a sea otter on shore finds itself cornered and cut off from escape to the sea it stiffens, faces the approaching intruder, and begins to rear backward (fig. 47). If the intruder continues to approach, the otter flops onto its back (fig. 48). If it is approached more closely, it may hiss and the stiffened forelegs are extended (fig. 49). The animal may attempt to bite any object extended toward it, while using the forepaws to push it away. I have never seen a cornered animal attempt aggressively to attack human intruders. Defense and escape are the only reactions.

IN THE WATER

When a sea otter is surprised at close quarters by an intruder it first rises high in the water. It faces the intruder and extends

FIGURE 47.—A juvenile sea otter, cornered on an Amchitka beach, prepares to rear backwards to assume the defensive posture illustrated in figure 48. (KWK 62–10–10)

FIGURE 48.—In the defensive position a sea otter lies on its back, faces the source of danger, and is alert to repel an attack. If an advance is made to touch an animal in this position, it attempts to bite and to push the adversary with its forepaws. The forepaws may also be used to aid in bringing the teeth into contact with the adversary. (KWK 62–10–26)

its forelegs, stiffly, palms of the forepaws outward toward the intruder. It then submerges vertically, pushing the forelegs above the head. It sinks backward beneath the surface, rather than plunging forward as in a normal dive.

Maternal and Filial Behavior

DURATION OF DEPENDENT PERIOD

The place of birth is discussed under "Reproduction in the Female." In her paper on the "Early life of a sea otter pup," Fisher (1940a) described many aspects of the behavior of mother and pup. Other writers have remarked on the unusual care of the mother for her young.

FIGURE 49.—When closely approached, a cornered sea otter hisses, extends its stiffened forelegs, and rears backwards as far as possible. No aggressive behavior is displayed. (KWK 59–8–6)

The period of dependence is unusually long. This was not ascertained directly from known individuals, but indirectly through various observations at Amchitka. Female reproductive tracts from there indicate that the majority of young are born from early spring to summer (see Reproduction in the Female). In the fall and early winter, large juveniles are numerous. During the late winter and early spring period of high mortality (March to May), most of the juveniles that die weigh 20 to 30 lb. (9 to 14 kg.). At the end of the annual "die-off" few large juveniles can be found alive. Observations during this period of juveniles crying and swimming about, apparently in search of their mothers, plus data compiled under "Mortality Factors" and "Home Range" indicate that most of these young animals are abandoned by mothers in the period of stress caused by storms and depleted food resources.

It is assumed that this group of young, most of which were dead by May, were the young that were born in the previous spring and early summer, in which case they would be 10 to 12 months old at time of death. Young that were born in the fall and winter were small (5 to 10 lb., 2.3 to 4.5 kg.) during the period of stress, and being less a burden to their mothers were cared for during this season. These were the young that survived to augment the population.

During summer, some dependent juveniles were larger than those that were deserted and died during the season of stress, indicating that they were probably more than a year old. Thus, I believe that the period of dependence of the young is normally at least a year and probably somewhat longer. Young somewhat less than 1 year old and in the 15 to 25 lb. (7 to 11 kg.) group do not usually survive in the wild if premanently separated from their mothers, particularly if separation occurs shortly before or during the season of stress.

At birth the pup is helpless and remains so for several weeks. When the mother dives for food the pup is left floating on its back at the surface, where it usually sleeps. If the pup awakens while its mother is diving, it may squirm and move its hind flippers about in an uncoordinated way. A very young pup appears unable to roll over onto its belly, which the pup apparently attempts to do by twisting the forward half of its body (fig. 50).

The ages of pups in the wild are estimated on the assumption that during the first year of life a pup grows at a nearly constant rate from about 5 lb. (2.3 kg.) at birth to about 30 lb. (14 kg.) when mother and young may separate. The sizes of pups are estimated by visually comparing pups in the wild with animals of similar body size that are weighed. On this basis, it is estimated that the pup remains nearly helpless during the first month, although it is able to crawl weakly for a meter or so on land (fig. 51) and swim weakly in an uncoordinated fashion.

SOLICITUDE

Much has been written of the solicitude of the mother sea otter for her young. Snow (1910, p. 142) noted the reluctance of a mother to abandon her pup.

For two hours we chased this otter, pursuing her between the rocks. The pup had been killed during the first hour, but she was holding it as firmly as ever, until a shot, striking one of her paws, made her drop it; and in trying to regain it she was once more wounded. Again and again she made the attempt, all the time giving utterance to the most plaintive and sorrowful cries . . .

After retrieving the pup, which the mother was unable to pick

FIGURE 50.—(Above) After a feeding period and before taking her 3- to 4-week-old pup ashore, the mother sea otter scrubs and grooms her fur with her forepaws. The pup at this stage is unable to swim. By aimless strokes of its hind flippers it may move about in a circle or attempt to roll over (as shown here) to grasp a kelp strand. While she washes and grooms, the mother seldom moves more than a meter from her pup and usually stays close beside it (below). She watches it constantly. (KWK 55–19–7 and 9; 11 September 1955)

FIGURE 51.—A captive mother sea otter leads her 3- to 4-week-old pup from the water. This appeared to be a "walking lesson." At other times the mother carried her almost helpless pup from the water in her mouth. (KWK 57–27–8)

up because of her wounds, the hunters started to return to their ship and later that same night, Snow wrote:

We had traveled some distance, when all at once, right under our stern, we heard the most unearthly crying imaginable; . . . another cry alongside showed us the dark form of the otter we had been chasing. It was now following the boat, lamenting the loss of her offspring.

The possessiveness of the mother sea otter is evident from birth until the young one is one-half to nearly two-thirds the mother's size (fig. 52). Virtually the only time that the mother is apart from her pup is while she is diving for food, while preening, or when swimming beside the pup. On one occasion I watched a mother with a juvenile nearly as large as she. They rested together on a rock until the energetic young one began to explore nearby. When it went to the water as if to depart, the mother rolled forward, grasped the juvenile's hind flipper in her teeth, and did not release it until the young one turned and resumed its position near her.

Many observations of mothers and young at Amchitka indicate that the ties between them may be strong but that the strength of the mother-young bond varies with each individual.

FIGURE 52.—The mother is solicitous of her young for a long period. *A*—A large juvenile, probably weighing about 20 lb. (9 kg.) and about 8 months old, nurses while its mother preens its fur. *B*—Alarmed by the photographer, the mother grasps her young one by the side of the head and, *C*, plunges with it into the water. (KWK 62–19–31, 32, and 37)

On 6 May 1959, a juvenile (about 16 lb., 7 kg., in weight), sleeping beside its mother on rocks near deep water, was captured in a dip net after the mother awoke and escaped. Three times within the next 5 minutes, while a metal tag was being attached to the pup's flipper, the mother partially emerged from the water, grasped the net in her teeth, and attempted to drag it and her pup away.

A captive mother and her very young pup were held in a high-walled enclosure. During the windy night of 28 November 1957, the enclosure door blew open and the mother escaped. When I arrived soon after sunrise, I found her swimming about in the surf near shore and shrieking repeatedly. On entering the enclosure I found her pup still sleeping soundly. When I awoke the pup and carried it outside, it began to cry in answer to its mother's calls. In response, she rushed ashore and was easily recaptured.

The fearlessness of a mother in coming to the aid of her pup is often less strongly expressed than in the above two examples. During tagging operations we frequently netted mothers with large young. Usually when the mother was liberated in advance of her pup, she swam 50 to 100 m. from shore where she uttered repeated shrieks until joined by her pup.

Whenever a mother with a small helpless pup was captured, we attempted to return the pup to its mother as she was liberated. Usually, the mother grasped the side of the pup's head in her teeth and swam rapidly away. Occasionally, however, the frightened mother failed to take her young one. On 5 April 1959 a mother and her pup were captured and tagged on an Amchitka beach. In my field notes I recorded:

The mother of the newborn pup (Tag. No. EL 12938) was released close to her helpless pup so that she brushed over it as she ran to the water, but she failed to pick it up. This was at 1445. I watched from a hiding place until 1720 (2 hrs. and 35 min.). During this time, the mother swam about in a 200 m. radius, screaming frequently. She made 13 approaches to the beach, then swam out among the reefs, and continued to utter loud screams. On the 4th and 8th trips toward the beach, she approached to within 3-4 m. of the pup, then became frightened and swam out. Three other otters hauled up on the beach near the pup but the mother was not reassured and would not come out onto the beach. When I left, because of cold, she was still in the vicinity screaming.

Because of the possible loss of the young during tagging operations, the capture of mothers with helpless pups was discontinued.

A young otter may also demonstrate concern for its mother, as suggested by my field notes (27 February 1962):

A mother and her 15-pound male pup were captured as they slept side-by-side on the beach today at St. Makarius Pt. W. (Amchitka Island). They were caught in separate nets. The pup was tagged first and released. Instead of heading for the water he ran to his struggling mother, put his forepaws on her side and began tearing at the net with his teeth and tried to climb up on her side. He had to be dragged away while a tag was placed on the mother's flipper. As soon as she was released, he rushed to her side and then followed her to the water. After a dive of about 50 meters, the two came up. The pup immediately clasped his mother about the neck and she pulled him toward her with her forepaws. This was a healthy, energetic pup.

Fright during capture may temporarily upset the normal behavior of a pup towards its mother (Field notes, 27 March 1962):

Today we captured in the same net a mother with a large pup as they slept beside each other on the cobble beach at Rifle Range Point (Amchitka Island). After the net was placed over them, they both began to struggle violently and the pup attacked the mother, biting her wherever it could. The mother paid little attention to the pup except that when its head came near hers she attempted to grasp the back of its neck in her teeth—as if to carry it off with her. We removed the pup from the net and tagged it. It was released about 2 feet from the struggling, still netted mother. It rushed to her and bit her on the side in several places. The mother ignored the bites and struggled on with the net. After tagging, the mother was released. As she ran to the water, the pup followed her. The mother swam rapidly for about 100 m., then stopped and the pup surfaced beside her and put its forepaws around her neck while both looked back at us before swimming out together—their fright apparently forgotten.

ATTENTION TO DEAD YOUNG

Mothers were occasionally seen carrying dead pups. I watched a mother carrying a dead, watersoaked pup while she emerged from the water and rested on kelp-covered rocks. For nearly an hour she licked the water from the pup's pelage and groomed its fur with her forepaws. When it was fluffy and dry, she went to sleep with it on her chest. How long a mother will attend a dead pup is not known but one was observed in which patches of skin and hair were slipping from the body, indicating that it had been dead for several days. A dead pup was removed from beside a sleeping captive mother after she had carried the carcass with her for 31 hours. On several occasions we attempted to take dead young from mothers seen resting on tidal rocks. Mother otters, however, are wary and in each instance, the mother escaped, carrying the carcass with her.

Although mother otters carry their pups beneath the surface during escape dives, they normally leave the young one floating on the surface when they dive for food. Dead pups, however, were carried by the mother while food diving. Unanswered questions are: Did the pup die because the mother carried it while diving for food? or did the mother carry it to avoid its loss because the fur became watersoaked causing it to sink after the pup died?

MOVING YOUNG

While swimming on her back, the mother sea otter carries her pup clasped between her forepaws (fig. 53). After a feeding or preening period, when the pup floats near its mother, she may grasp the pup with her forepaws and lift it onto her chest or she may roll on her side, clasp the pup to her chest and then roll again onto her back. If a mother with a pup is frightened or pursued, she holds the pup tightly with her forelegs and grasps the side of its head in her teeth as she turns to dive. Small young may drown during escape dives if the mother must dive repeatedly at short intervals (see Diving).

On land the mother otter grasps the side or back of the pup's head in her teeth and drags it. The pup is limp and relaxed, as if dead, while it is being dragged. Large juveniles usually walk beside the mother when they haul out but if alarmed, the mother grasps the youngster by the head and drags it. Although a juve-

FIGURE 53.—The mother sea otter carries her pup high on her chest, clasped by both front paws. White scar tissue was seen frequently on the noses of adult females but rarely on juveniles or adult males. It is presumed that these scars are inflicted by the male during mating when the nose of the female is grasped by the male's teeth, usually causing it to bleed. (KWK 57–29–27)

nile weighing 15 to 20 lb. (7 to 9 kg.) may be at least as agile on land as its mother, it relaxes completely when grasped by the mother and allows itself to be dragged, even over rough terrain, making no effort to assist in its own progress (fig. 54).

NURSING

The mother sea otter nurses her pup from two abdominal nipples, usually while floating on her back. Nursing may also take place on land (fig. 55). When the pup is small it usually rests on the mother's chest and abdomen while nursing, both on land or while the mother is floating. If the pup becomes hungry and cries while its mother is feeding, she grasps it around the chest with her forepaws and rolls it onto her chest, then turns it around, pushing it headforemost toward her abdominal nipples, allowing it to nurse.

As the pup grows larger it nurses while floating belly down, its body at right angles to that of its mother. Nursing periods are short, lasting 2 to 5 minutes. The pup kneads its mother's abdomen while nursing. It was difficult to time the duration of the nursing period because pups often fell asleep within 5 minutes and the actual duration of the nursing period was in doubt.

FIGURE 54.—This mother sea otter and her large juvenile (estimated weight 20-22 lb., 9-10 kg.) were surprised on land. Although the pup was capable of running at least as fast as the mother, she grasped the side of its head in her teeth and dragged it. On the rough terrain the pup bounced and caught in crevices but it remained relaxed and limp. When the two reached the water the pup was allowed to swim free of its mother's grasp. (KWK 62–17–37)

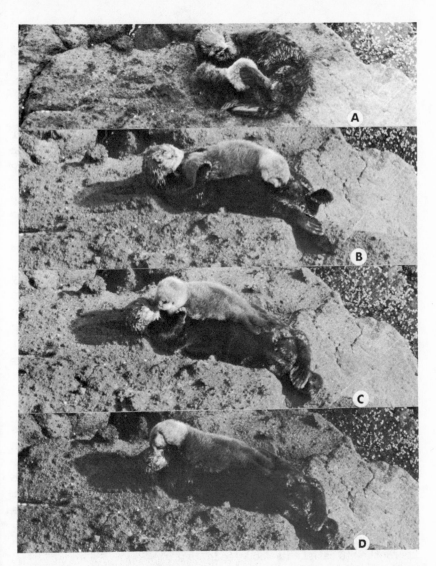

FIGURE 55.—*A*—After dragging her pup onto a rock, a mother sea otter preens and dries her fur while she supports the head of her nursing pup with a hind flipper. *B*—After drying her fur, the mother takes her pup on her chest and while she preens its fur with her forepaws she allows it to nurse from one of her two abdominal nipples. *C*—After the pup has nursed for 3 to 5 minutes the mother turns it around and fondles and plays with it. *D*—Mother and pup sleep, their fur dry and fluffy. This pup is probably a month to 6 weeks old. Its natal coat, particularly the long yellow guard hairs have grown considerably since birth. During the approximately 30-minute period when this sequence was taken, the mother frequently made soft chuckling or cooing sounds. (KWK 55–20–36, 55–934, 936, and 938)

Large juveniles often attempt to nurse. When the mother is reluctant, she rolls over. If the young otter is persistent and clasps her firmly with the forelegs, she may roll on a horizontal axis rapidly through 5 to 10 rotations, which usually dislodges it.

SWIMMING

At an early age, while the pup is still nearly helpless, the mother occasionally lifts it from her chest, places it in the water, then swims slowly away from it. The pup swims belly down paddling clumsily with all four feet. During these early swimming sessions, the pup frequently cries. The mother may remain just beyond the pup's reach for 50 m. or more before she allows it to overtake her when she again rolls or lifts it onto her chest. By the time the pup reaches an estimated age of 2 to 3 months, swimming ability is improved and it appears more at ease, crying less when swimming. When the mother swims near the pup it does not attempt frantically to reach her but swims quietly beside her (fig. 56). At this stage the pup apparently has not learned to swim on its back. Swimming on the back appears to develop slowly. While the mother is resting the pup often plays, swimming and making shallow dives near her. During these periods the pup appears to develop the ability to swim on its back.

DIVING AND FOOD GATHERING

After a pup learns to swim, it attempts to dive. Its first dives barely take it beneath the surface and considerable effort over a period of time is required to overcome the buoyancy of its air-filled fur. When the pup finally learns to reach the bottom in shallow water it brings up starfishes, bits of kelp, and pebbles. Seldom does it obtain edible items. Even after the pup is nearly a year old and about three-quarters as large as its mother, and may obtain much of its own food by diving, it continues to depend on its mother to satisfy its food needs.

From the time of birth the young otter is able to consume solid food which its mother gives to it. In the early weeks of life, however, stomach examinations indicate that milk predominates in its diet. After the pup is a month or two old it frequently pesters its mother for food. When she emerges from a food dive, the pup climbs onto her chest to beg for and receive part of the food she has brought to the surface (fig. 57). Large juveniles, able to dive well but unable to satisfy their food needs, may snatch food forcibly from the tolerant mother while she is floating on the surface and eating.

FIGURE 56.—This pup, probably about 2 months old, swims beside its mother. The mother removed the pup from her chest, placed it in the water, then swam slowly away while the pup followed. Swimming sessions, such as this, were seen often at Amchitka. They usually lasted for from 3 to 5 minutes and terminated when the mother again lifted the young one onto her chest. (KWK 1022)

SLEEP

Resting and sleeping are more frequent on the water than on land but mother otters may bring their young ashore to sleep. Newly born young often sleep while pressed against the mother's neck, under her chin. As the pup grows, it usually sleeps sprawled farther down on her chest or abdomen. When the young has reached a weight of about 10 lb. (4+ kg.), the mother holds the sleeping juvenile's head on her chest or abdomen (fig. 7) while its body floats at right angles to hers. Large juveniles sleep floating close beside and parallel to the mother. When mother and young rest on land, sleeping positions are similar (fig. 55).

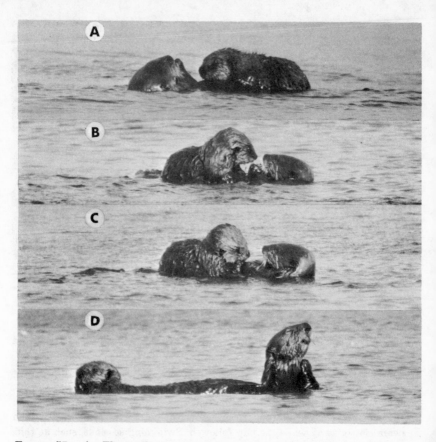

FIGURE 57.—*A*—The mother sea otter has just emerged from a feeding dive. While she eats, her pup (about 2 to 3 months old) crawls onto her belly. *B*—The pup tries to take food from the mother's paw. *C*—The mother reaches forward, placing food (a sea urchin) in the pup's mouth and paws. *D*—After finishing her food the mother rises vertically in the water while inhaling before rolling forward in another food dive. The pup continues to eat the food obtained from its mother. (KWK 65–24–13, 14, 15, and 16; 31 October 1965)

GROOMING

Shortly after birth the sea otter pup makes uncoordinated attempts to rub and groom its fur. Young animals are, however, dependent upon their mothers to keep their fur fluffy and dry. After a feeding period and before resting, the mother otter first grooms and washes her own pelage thoroughly while her pup floats nearby (figs. 41 and 43). When she has finished, she either takes her pup on her chest to preen and dry its pelage or drags it ashore. She licks the pup's fur thoroughly, then fluffs it and rubs it dry with her forepaws. When the pup defecates, the mother cleans it by licking the fur in the anal region—often while doing this she holds the pup's hind flippers above her head with her forepaws. Mothers may continue to groom the fur of large juveniles to some degree even after these animals are capable of caring for their own pelage (fig. 52).

PLAY

Large pups frequently play. If two mothers with large young are feeding in the same area, the two pups may wrestle and chase each other. Frequently the mothers disapprove of such play as one or the other will break up the playing pair, take her young one onto her chest, and swim to another feeding area.

During a feeding period the mother sea otter satisfies her pup's food needs before she satisfies her own. While the mother continues to dive and eat, her pup explores the vicinity. If the pup sees an adult sleeping in floating kelp, it approaches quietly, then rising high in the water descends with both forepaws on the adult's chest or abdomen. Adults are tolerant of such behavior and usually indulge in a period of rolling and chasing play before abandoning the activity to leave the vicinity and continue resting.

ADOPTION

Juvenile otters, lost from their mothers, may join company with a tolerant adult, either male or female. Such pairs may be confused for mothers with pups. Figure 90 shows an adult male and juvenile. The two had been sleeping close to each other. The young animal was first to become alarmed by my presence. Besides retreating behind the adult, it placed its paws on the adult's back and sides. When the adult eventually was aroused and moved into the water, the juvenile followed him closely and remained in company with him as he swam to deep water.

On 16 February 1964, a newly captured adult female (which had been given a mild injection (1 cc.) of Sparine) was placed in an enclosure with an orphaned juvenile female several months of age (wt. 18 lb., 8.2 kg.). Within a few minutes the juvenile approached the adult and was allowed to nurse. Two hours later the adult clasped the juvenile around the neck with her forelegs when I entered the enclosure and alarmed them. Similar nursing and protective behavior was repeated but at increasingly long intervals until 24 February. By this time the adult pushed the juvenile away when it attempted to nurse and when fish were given to each animal at feeding time, robbed it of food. During rest periods,

101

however, the two slept in close proximity and when alarmed by a human visitor or unexpected noise they clasped each other with their forelegs.

An adult female and two juveniles of about the same size were netted together on a beach at Amchitka Island on 2 April 1955. The adult showed maternal attention to one pup and tolerated the other, allowing both to nurse. The adult, however, groomed only one juvenile and my conclusion was that the other was a stray or an orphan that had joined company with the mother and pup. Additional evidence that this may have been the situation was observed on 9 April. The pup presumed to be the mother's offspring died shortly before this group of sea otters was to be liberated at the Pribilof Islands. The surviving juvenile and the adult female were liberated together. In the water, the juvenile attempted to climb onto the adult but she ignored it and swam quickly away. We then retrieved the screaming juvenile.

The above observations indicate to me that under certain conditions a tolerant adult otter might contribute to the survival of an orphaned juvenile. It appears, however, that under conditions of stress and during times of food shortage an adult might give little more than companionship toward the survival of an "adopted" juvenile.

Relation to Other Animals

Within its usual habitat, which includes the beach, offshore rocks, and water out to a depth of about 30 fathoms (60 m.), the sea otter is often near other mammals and birds. Two species, the Bald Eagle and killer whale, are discussed under "Predation."

Harbor seals and sea otters often haul out on the same rocks and rest or sleep near each other. Each species appears to ignore the other; no interspecific strife of any kind was ever seen. In general, harbor seals and sea otters appear to prefer slightly different resting places. At St. Makarius Point on Amchitka several large rocks are located a few meters offshore. Some of these were habitually used by sea otters and others by harbor seals. If a sea otter found a harbor seal on a favorite resting spot, it selected another place. On several occasions a harbor seal was seen to cause a sea otter to move. When the moving seal jostled the sea otter in attempting to pass, the otter got up and moved.

Interspecific competition for food is probably negligible. The harbor seals at Amchitka feed primarily on octopus and Atka mackerel (Kenyon, 1965a). Both of these species may be taken by sea otters but our fishing operations indicated that fish populations at Amchitka are large. Also, sea otters tend to feed on sedentary fish that were not found in seal stomachs.

Steller sea lions seldom chose places that were favored by sea otters for resting on land. When sea lions passed near sea otters that were diving for food, the otters usually raised themselves high in the water to stare at the sea lions. Otherwise the two species ignored each other.

Parasitic worms *(Terranova decipiens*, for example) which commonly infest the harbor seal and sea lion, enter the encysted stage in fishes. Sea otters that eat fish also become infested. *Halarachne miroungae*, a nasal mite commonly found in harbor seals, were rarely found in wild sea otters. These may have been picked up by the sea otters at a location commonly used by the two species. In the wild these pinniped parasites seemed not to seriously affect sea otters.

Glaucous-winged Gulls frequently obtained scraps from otters while they fed on fish. I did not see gulls attempt to take fish away from a feeding otter but they swam close to feeding otters or hovered above them ready to take scraps (fig. 58). When we were searching for sea otters during census studies, we found that gulls were a useful indicator of the location of feeding otters. A group of gulls sitting together on the water usually marked the location where an otter would emerge from a food-gathering dive.

Unlike many other mammals, sea otters at Amchitka did not appear to recognize the calls of birds as possible indicators of approaching danger. On a number of occasions, Black Oystercatchers *(Haematopus bachmani)* and Emperor Geese *(Philacte canagica)* were alarmed by our approach when we were stalking sea otters that were hauled out on the beach. Although the calling birds sometimes flew directly over the otters, they appeared to pay little or no attention to them.

Rats *(Rattus norvegicus)* introduced to Amchitka during World War II often entered the sea otter enclosure to search for food scraps. On one occasion a rat approached a sea otter that was grooming its fur while resting on its back beside the pool. After sniffing at the sea otter's side, the rat suddenly jumped onto the otter's chest. Quickly the otter struck the rat with its forepaw, knocking it a distance of nearly a meter.

In general, it did not appear that the sea otter was in serious competition with other mammal and bird species within its environ-

FIGURE 58.—An immature Glaucous-winged Gull waits expectantly for fish scraps discarded by a feeding sea otter. Groups of two or three gulls sitting together on the surface in the Aleutian area usually indicated the location of a sea otter feeding on fish. While the otter was beneath the surface the gulls waited near the location where they expected it would emerge from a food-gathering dive. (KWK 57–31–2)

ment at Amchitka or that any interspecific strife existed. Perhaps in periods of food scarcity, survival of gulls is enhanced through their utilization of the otters' discarded food scraps.

FOOD AND FEEDING BEHAVIOR

In this section, methods of food gathering and consumption, the kinds and quantities of foods eaten, and the food requirements of sea otters in the wild and in captivity will be discussed. This information was gathered by means of field observation, quantitative and qualitative studies of stomachs and feces, and data gathered from otters held on Amchitka Island, the Woodland Park Zoo, Seattle, and the Tacoma Aquarium.

The amount of food required by the sea otter is greater than that of most animals of comparable size. The sea otter stores body fat but it does not accumulate fat in quantities comparable to the blubber stored by most marine mammals. Because it lacks an insulating blubber layer, the sea otter is dependent for warmth in its chilly habitat upon its fur and upon the rapid metabolic use of energy from food. Passage of food through the gastrointestinal tract is rapid. Food marked with red dye passed through an otter in about 3 hours (Dr. James A. Mattison, personal communication).

Periods of fasting which are characteristic of other marine mammals, such as certain cetaceans and pinnipeds, would prove fatal to the sea otter. Its vitality is maintained by a relatively high and constant consumption of food.

Studies comparable to ours in Alaska were conducted in the Kuril Islands by Soviet biologists Nikolaev and Skalkin (1963) and Nikolaev (1965b).

Feeding location

Sea otters habitually gather their food from the bottom or near it in salt water ranging in depth from a few feet, in the intertidal or littoral zone, to about 20 fathoms (40 m.). This is the greatest depth from which we took an otter having food in its stomach. The majority of otters feed within about one-half mile of shore. In certain areas, particularly off the north shore of Unimak Island in the Bering Sea, where shallow water extends far from shore, they commonly range 3 to 10 miles offshore and one was seen in this area about 17 miles from shore in water about 30 fathoms (56 m.) deep (see table 10).

That certain individual animals would learn to feed on pelagic forms and thus divorce themselves from the necessity of remaining in relatively shallow water is improbable. Observations indicate that the sea otter subsists only on benthic organisms. Wide, deep passes between islands, which prevent bottom feeding, appear to act as a barrier to the spread of sea otter populations. (See Distribution and Numbers.)

Food Gathering

Many observations indicate that the sea otter uses its forepaws primarily to gather food and that the tactile sense is important in locating food organisms. A captive female with good eyesight was offered food in a bucket about half full of turbid water. In one instance the bucket contained about 200 small crabs *(Pachygrapsus)*, 4 blue mussels *(Mytilus edulis)*, and a number of pebbles of various sizes. The otter had eaten both organisms before but showed a preference for mussels. When the bucket was presented to her, she immediately reached to the bottom with both forepaws, her chin on the edge of the bucket, and within a few seconds retrieved the four mussels. She made no attempt to place her head in the bucket or to look into it. Thus, she demonstrated a high reliance on her tactile sense in selecting the mussels from among pebbles and crabs.

Numerous observations of Susie, during the 6 years that she lived at the Woodland Park Zoo, indicated that she relied heavily on her tactile sense while retrieving food placed in her pool. She was blind in her right eye when captured and blind in both eyes for over a year before death. During this period of total blindness she continued to find food and to select the most desired kinds, using her paws to select it. I have observed several healthy wild otters that were blind in one eye but have seen only one that was apparently blind in both eyes. This animal was emaciated and near death. Existence without sight among breakers in the harsh coastal environment would probably be impossible even if food could be found.

Wild otters normally terminate feeding activities before dark and do not begin morning feeding until after sunrise. Mothers which must provide for their young, however, may continue diving for food after dark. I watched a mother diving one evening until darkness prevented further observations. During the period shortly before visibility was lost, the otter continued to bring food items (mostly sea urchins) to the surface in the usual quantities.

I thus inferred that she relied primarily on her tactile ability to find food.

Sight under water, however, is apparently sometimes used in locating food. Captive otters on Amchitka often searched the bottom of their pool by swimming on the surface, head submerged. Food items on the bottom were quickly located visually in this manner and retrieved.

The vibrissae may also aid in the search for food. Captive otters, having an abundance of easily located food, abrade the vibrissae to a minor degree; they may reach a length of 10 to 12 cm. (fig. 59). The vibrissae of wild otters may be worn off short, to a length of about 1.5 to 2.5 cm. Presumably the abrasion occurs during the search for food among rocks.

FIGURE 59.—A captive otter pounds a clam (*Protothaca*) on the cement edge of her pool. This otter came from Amchitka where breaking shells of food organisms by pounding was not observed. The whiskers of captive otters grow long, as illustrated here. In the wild the whiskers are usually abraded and short. Presumably wear occurs during the search for food among rocks. (KWK 57–24–16)

It would appear that under usual circumstances the sea otter does not use its teeth under water. On many occasions I have seen sea otters come to the surface clasping living fish to their chests with their forepaws. After surfacing, each otter grasped the fish's head in its jaws and killed it, suggesting that the teeth are not used to kill fish beneath the surface.

That otters may use their teeth beneath the surface when necessary to obtain food was demonstrated at Amchitka. In Constantine Harbor the otters apparently learned that our net floats marked an abundant supply of fish. We often saw an otter on the surface, eating, near the floats. When we pulled the nets, we found fish that the animals were unable to remove but which they had partly eaten underwater. Usually about half the fish was left, but occasionally only the head and pectoral girdle remained. The fish were not bitten off cleanly; they were chewed, leaving strips of skin and tooth-marked shredded flesh attached to the entangled portion. The frequency with which we saw otters eating fish on the surface near the nets indicated that they were able to remove a considerable number. Rarely did otters become entangled in the nets and drown.

The stomach of one adult male contained a number of large clam siphons. The siphons, with adhering fragments of mantle and muscle tissue, appeared to have been ripped from the clams by the otter's paws or teeth. Visceral material from these clams was lacking in the stomach. Presumably the siphons protruded from the sea's floor and the remainder of the clam was not dug out.

Fisher (1939) postulated that the sea otter used either a rock or its canine teeth to remove abalones from the bottom. Cox (1962) presents convincing evidence that the sea otter uses a rock to break the abalone shell; that the otter then removes the viscera and, after the abalone dies and releases its hold on the rock bottom, brings it to the surface where it eats the muscle from the remainder of the shell. The behavior of a captive otter, which persistently pounded a rock against an underwater drain cover until it was able to damage the fastening and remove it (Kenyon, 1959), lends strong support to the use of a rock rather than the teeth in obtaining abalones. The canine teeth are probably not of sufficient strength to remove any but small abalones from the bottom.

A unique habit related to feeding in the sea otter, that of pounding hard-shelled mollusks against a stone or other mollusk held on the chest, has been given much attention, most recently by Hall and Schaller (1964). Although this habit is frequently observed in California sea otters, it is rarely observed in the parts of Alaska where I have watched sea otters feeding or in Soviet waters (Barabash-Nikiforov, 1947). At Amchitka, I have twice observed subadult otters pounding a chunk of coralline algae held between the forepaws against another resting on the chest. This behavior appeared, however, to be play as the animals did not attempt to find food in the algae after breaking it but discarded the material after a few minutes of intermittent pounding.

That Alaska sea otters are capable of using the pounding technique was demonstrated by a captive taken at Amchitka Island. Soon after Susie had become accustomed to captive conditions at Seattle, several small stones and whole butter clams *(Saxidomus)* were placed in her pool. Although she used a stone as an anvil on which to break the clams, she used it in other ways too. The stone was also held in the paws and used as a hammer. Also, if a large number of clams were given to her she often neglected to obtain the stone but pounded the clams against each other (fig. 60). Clams, sea urchins, fish, and rocks were pounded against the cement-constructed side of the pool (fig. 59).

FIGURE 60.—Clams *(Saxidomus)* were broken open by pounding one against another held on the chest. If a rock was handy, this captive otter pounded clams against it. Clam meats are scooped from the shell with the tongue and lower incisors. (KWK 57-22-32)

What Food is Eaten

The food of the sea otter consists predominantly of benthic invertebrates and fish. At Amchitka Island fish predominate (50 percent by volume), mollusks are second in importance, and echinoderms (mostly sea urchins) third (table 11). In other areas, mollusks and echinoderms are found to predominate.

That the feeding habits of the sea otter vary in different areas, in accordance with the abundance of food organisms, is indicated by the statements of Snow (1910), who claimed to have examined hundreds of stomachs. He stated that he did not find clams among the food species eaten by the sea otter and that—

I have never noticed any traces of the shells of clams, or limpets, or mussels in the stomachs I have examined, but found as a rule, the remains of crabs, sea urchins, sea-squirts, and what looked like fish spawn.

He also said that he very seldom found any remains of "ordinary fish, the bones of which would immediately prove its presence." He adds that the sea otter "finds no difficulty in chewing up good-sized crabs, which judging from the contents of the many stomachs I have opened and examined, appear to be its chief food." Mr. H. P. Hansen, a king crab *(Paralithodes platypus)* fisherman told me (1964) that in the Andreanof Islands he "often sees sea otters eating king crabs, sometimes quite large ones."

Although a large variety of organisms is eaten, individual otters appear to have certain food preferences. "Individual sea otters often prefer a certain food in the assortment of food characteristic to them" (Barabash-Nikiforov, 1947). Some adult males at Amchitka subsist primarily on fish and rarely eat sea urchins. In general, at Amchitka it appears that the otters fall into two groups—those eating mostly fish and those eating mostly invertebrates. The fish eaters, as would be expected, show a higher degree of infestation with certain parasites (principally *T. decipiens*)

TABLE 11.—*Volume and classification of food found in 309 sea otter stomachs from Amchitka Island, Alaska*

[Only stomachs containing food are considered. The samples include 107 stomachs collected in January and February 1962, 20 stomachs collected in October 1962, and 182 stomachs collected in March and April 1963]

Food item	Total volume (milliliters)	Percent of total volume
Annelid worms	929	1
Crabs, shrimp, etc.	467	<1
Mollusks	34,895	37
Echinoderms (mostly sea urchins)	10,020	11
Tunicates	363	<1
Vertebrates (fish)	46,518	50

than those subsisting primarily on invertebrates. Also, the bones of "fish-eaters" are white but the bones of those otters utilizing invertebrates—including many sea urchins—are stained purple by the biochrome polyhydroxynaphthoquinone (Scott, *in* Fox, 1953, footnote p. 195).

Much indigestible material is swallowed incidentally in the consumption of nourishing food. Part of the test of almost every sea urchin eaten is crushed by the postcanines and swallowed. Many stomachs contain scraps of red and brown algae. Seaweeds, as Barabash-Nikiforov (1947) and Fisher (1939) indicate, cannot be considered an otter food. This material appears in the feces unaltered in appearance, except for the wear and abrasion encountered during passage. I have often seen such scraps of kelp eaten when entangled among the spines of sea urchins. Its occurrence in stomachs is accidental.

Small pebbles, gravel, and bits of hard clay occurred in 14 percent of 475 stomachs from Amchitka. One stomach contained 325 small stones. Stones are also commonly found in the stomach of fur seals and sea lions (*Eumetopias* and *Zalophus*) and no sure explanation of their presence is known. Although the "gastroliths" of pinnipeds are usually waterworn or smooth, the stones we found in sea otter stomachs often looked as if they had been freshly broken apart; they were seldom waterworn or smooth. No reason for the swallowing of this indigestible material is known.

After food has been selected from the substrate, it is stored for transportation to the surface in folds of loose skin (fig. 11) which extend from the axilla across the chest (see Kirkpatrick et al., 1955; Barabash-Nikiforov, 1947). If only enough food is gathered to fill the pouch on one side, it is stored under the left foreleg and paw. If a large quantity is gathered, it may be stored and carried in the chest pouches under both forelegs.

When an otter captures a large octopus or fish and satisfies its appetite before it consumes the entire organism, it often sleeps on the water's surface with the remains of such an uneaten meal clasped to its chest. After sleeping for awhile, the otter awakens and continues to eat. Uneaten food, however, is not retained for an extended period. After the animal has nibbled its food intermittently for perhaps 2 hours, and then begins to groom, the food is forgotten and allowed to sink. Captives retrieve discarded food and again eat after grooming and resting.

On occasions when we have pursued otters with an outboard motor-powered dory we have interrupted their feeding. When this occurs, the otters do not relinquish food remaining in the chest pouches. In one instance we interrupted a feeding adult male and pursued him for nearly 2 hours. He invariably evaded us by surfacing at unpredicted places. We finally abandoned as futile our effort to capture him and he immediately continued to eat the sea urchins he had carried under his left foreleg during the entire chase.

When captive otters are given food on land, the items are transferred to the chest pouch under the left foreleg with the assistance of the right paw. The otter then walks on three legs to return to the water with the food. If the quantity of food exceeds the capacity of the pouch under the foreleg, additional food may be grasped and carried in the jaws.

A captive, resting on her side near her pool, was able to place 18 clams *(Protothaca)*, ranging from about 3 to 4 cm. in greatest diameter, under her left foreleg. When a 19th was added, most of the others fell out. Eight clams were easily carried under the left foreleg while the otter walked on three legs about 3 m. to the pool.

Where Food is Eaten

Sea otters normally bring food items to the surface and, using their forepaws, pass the food to the mouth and eat while floating on their backs. Hooper (1897) probably misinterpreted a statement by Steller (1751) when he stated that "the otter haul out upon the land to feed on the sea urchins and the other shellfish exposed at low water." Wild sea otters do not carry food from the water to exposed rocks or beaches and normally do not emerge from the water to obtain food. I know of no record of a wild otter voluntarily consuming food on land.

A wild otter that habitually frequented the inshore water near our fish-cleaning platform quickly learned to take fish scraps from our hands. After several weeks he often left the water to beg for food while following us about. Even though he accepted pieces of fish as far as 25 m. from the water (fig. 61), he always carried the food back to the water before eating it.

Captive otters, if they are denied access to water, will eat while lying on a dry surface, but usually reluctantly. Captives having free access to water and dry areas, voluntarily leave the water to obtain food when they are hungry (fig. 62) but return to the water to eat it.

Periodically (usually at intervals of 20 to 30 seconds) while consuming food at the surface, the sea otter stops eating and rolls

FIGURE 61.—A wild sea otter accepts a fish head from Innokenty Golodoff. This otter frequented the area where we discarded fish scraps. He soon became tame and emerged from the water to follow us as far as 25 meters from the water to beg for food. He never consumed food on shore but carried it in his mouth or under the left foreleg to the water where he ate while floating on his back. (KWK 57–34–31)

over (fig. 63). This action washes food scraps from the chest where they were either purposely discarded or accidentally dropped.

Stomach Analyses

The best information available on food habits of the sea otter was derived from the examination of 475 stomachs from otters most of which were shot at Amchitka Island (table 12). Previously Wilke (1957) studied stomachs from five otters taken there. Also, we examined a number of stomachs of otters found dead or dying on beaches.

Stomachs were removed from sea otters as soon as practicable, usually within 2 to 3 hours after death. They were then injected with a 10 percent formalin solution and immersed in a large container of formalin solution, where they soaked for several days.

FIGURE 62.—A captive adult female sea otter clasps one piece of fish to her chest under her left foreleg while she reaches with her teeth to grasp another. After receiving all the food she could carry under the foreleg and in her teeth, she returned, walking on three legs, to the water before she consumed her food. The long outer or fifth digit of the hind foot is illustrated. (KWK 59–13–10)

TABLE 12.—*Sea otter stomachs examined*

[This listing includes animals presumed to be healthy. Most of them were shot. Animals found dead and dying on beaches are excluded]

Date	Location	Stomachs empty		Stomachs with food		Total examined
		Number	Percent	Number	Percent	
6–10 June 1960	Shumagin Islands	4	67	2	33	6
8–10 July 1960	Bering Sea [1]	2	50	2	50	4
22 Jan.–9 March 1962	Amchitka Island	32	23	107	77	139
26–29 Oct. 1962	do	4	17	20	83	24
14 March–2 April 1963	do	119	39	183	61	302
Total		161	34	314	66	475

[1] Otters were taken at sea off the north coast of Unimak Island.

FIGURE 63.—At frequent intervals, while floating on the surface and consuming food, the sea otter stops eating and rolls about its longitudinal axis through 360°. This action washes food slime and scraps from the chest. It is an important behavioral characteristic that helps to keep the fur clean and waterproof. Food slime destroyed the water-resistant and insulating qualities of the fur of captive otters that were not given access to water. In nature, sea otters eat only in the water—never on shore. (KWK 1021)

After removal from the pickling bath, they were packed in wide-mouthed, 5-gallon cans and shipped to the Seattle laboratory. After removal from the stomach, the weight and volume of the contents were measured, the food species were identified, the percentage composition of each species was evaluated, and all pertinent data for each specimen was entered on a 3-by-5 card. A collection of identified invertebrates and fish, accumulated at the Seattle laboratory for the study of marine mammal food habits, aided identification of food species. Food organisms that could not be identified locally were sent to specialists who examined them and made identifications whenever this was possible.

If a feeding otter swallows the test, shell, or bony parts of a food organism, the identification of food species may not prove difficult. Such hard parts are usually not crushed sufficiently to obliterate all diagnostic characteristics. Often, however, the feeding otter discards most or all of the hard parts, making identification of food species difficult or impossible. As the stomachs were examined, a collection of unknowns was accumulated. Food organisms found in various stages of mutilation in different stomachs eventually furnished material that made possible the recognition of small fragments or badly mutilated food in other stomachs. The food species found in sea otter stomachs taken at Amchitka are shown in table 13 and a general account of these organisms and the sea otter's habits relating to their consumption follows.

Annelid worms were usually torn into pieces several centimeters long and the pieces swallowed with minor damage from mastication. Considerable slimy mucus accompanied annelid remains.

Crabs were torn to pieces and usually the carapace was not among the stomach contents. The larger legs and chelipeds were usually thoroughly crushed.

Among the mollusks that were found, various techniques of ingestion were indicated. Small chitons were slightly crushed and often swallowed nearly intact. Large ones *(Cryptochiton stelleri)* were thoroughly crushed and torn, reducing them to small pieces. The flesh of limpets was scooped from the shell and swallowed nearly intact and the shell discarded. Rarely was a fragment of limpet shell swallowed.

TABLE 13.—*Frequency of occurrence of food species in 309 sea otter stomachs from Amchitka Island, Alaska*

Food organism	Number of stomachs having item—				
	Of 107 stomachs February–April 1962	Of 20 stomachs October 1962	Of 182 stomachs March–April 1963	Total	Percent
Annelida			5	5	
Ribbon worm *Emplectonema* sp.	1	—	—	1	
Sand worm *Nereis* sp.	2	—	—	2	
Lug worm *Arenicola* sp.	5	—	—	5	
Total	8	—	5	13	2
Arthropoda:					
Crustacea:					
Olive green isopod *Idothea (Pentidotea)*	6	—	3	9	
Amphipods (probably incidental)	5	—	6	11	
Shrimp *Sclerocrangon boreas*	1	—	—	1	
Hermit crab *Pagurus* sp.	3	3	9	15	
Crab:					
Cancer sp.	1	5	—	6	
Telmessus cheiragonus	1	1	—	2	
Paralithodes? (larval)	2	—	—	2	
Placetron wosnessenski	5	—	1	6	
Hapalogaster sp.	—	—	5	5	
Unidentified	—	—	4	4	
Shrimp unidentified	—	—	1	1	
Total	24	9	29	62	7

Food organism	Of 107 stomachs February–April 1962	Of 20 stomachs October 1962	Of 182 stomachs March–April 1963	Total	Percent
Mollusca:					
Amphineura:					
Lined chiton *Tonicella* cf. *T. marmorea*	1	—	—	1	
Mossy chiton *Mopalia* sp.	1	—	—	1	
Giant chiton *Cryptochiton stelleri*	4	5	8	17	
Chiton unidentified	—	—	2	2	
Gastropoda:					
Limpet *Acmaea* sp.	5	5	10	20	
Snail:					
Thais sp.	1	—	4	5	
Natica clausa	1	—	—	1	
Buccinum sp.	10	—	7	17	
Argobuccinum oregonensis	6	—	8	14	
Gastropod unidentified	—	—	3	3	
Pelecypoda:					
Cockle *Clinocardium ciliatum*	2	—	1	3	
Clam:					
Liocyma viridis	1	—	—	1	
Serripes	1	—	—	1	
Macona sp.	—	—	3	3	
Unidentified	—	—	2	2	
Mussel:					
Musculus vernicosa	10	12	24	46	
Volsella volsella	22	6	21	49	
Pearly monia *Pododesmus macroschisma*	28	2	20	50	
Cephalopoda: *Octopus* sp.	12	4	14	30	
Mollusk unidentified	—	—	3	3	
Total	105	34	130	269	31
Echinodermata:					
Asteroidea:					
Blood star *Henricia* sp.	15	2	11	28	
Six-rayed star *Leptasterias* sp.	29	—	28	57	
Starfish *Ceramaster* sp.	6	—	6	12	
Brittle star Ophiuroidea	1	—	13	14	
Echinoidea: Green sea urchin *Strongylocentrotus drobachiensis*	71	17	92	180	
Holothuroidea: Sea cucumber *Cucumaria* sp.	17	4	5	26	
Total	139	23	155	317	37
Chordata:					
Tunicata: Tunicate (2 species)	4	1	6	11	1
Vertebrata:					
Osteichthyes:					
Sablefish *Anoplopoma fimbria*	1	—	—	1	
Rock greenling *Hexagrammos superciliosus*	5	1	9	15	
Atka mackerel *Pleurogrammus monopterygius*	4	2	3	9	
Red Irish lord *Hemilepidotus hemilepidotus*	18	4	14	36	
Globefish *Cyclopterichthys glaber*	22	—	87	109	
Cottidae unidentified	1	—	—	1	
Fish and fish eggs unidentified	5	—	—	5	
Total	56	7	113	176	22
Grand total				848	100

Snails were recognizable in stomachs because the tough muscular foot was usually little affected by chewing and often the chitinous operculum remained intact and attached to the foot. The shells of small snails (*Buccinum* sp.) were often swallowed but those of large ones (*Argobuccinum oregonensis*), except the operculum, were not.

Clam shells, except those from small individuals, were seldom present in the stomach. One stomach contained about 2 liters of clam meats, the foot and viscera of many almost intact, but not one scrap of shell. The shell of thin-shelled clams (*Serripes groenlandicus*) were fragmented and swallowed in considerable quantity.

The small mussel *Musculus vernicosa*, which was consumed in large numbers, was usually swallowed whole. Individual mussels may appear in the feces with the valves still intact. Many fragmented shells of larger mussels, such as *Volsella volsella*, sometimes appeared in feces. Often, however, stomachs having a number of mussels contained little or no shell. The viscera were recognizable by their orange color and attached byssus.

The pearly monia (*Pododesmus macroschisma*) appeared in 50 stomachs, often in considerable quantity but only a few tiny fragments of shell were found. Observations of feeding otters revealed that, after slightly loosening the valves with one canine tooth, the two valves were twisted horizontally past each other between the paws so that the viscera could be quickly scooped with the lower incisors and tongue from the half shell to which it adhered. Seldom are the shells broken during this procedure. Since few hard parts of this species are ingested, it is not revealed as an important food species in fecal examinations.

Octopuses are eaten with particular enthusiasm by captive otters and wild otters also appear to relish them. Because of its size (commonly 2 to 4 lb.), the octopus constitutes an excellent food source at Amchitka. Apparently otters are not disturbed by the writhing tentacles of this mollusk. Pieces of arms are bitten off and eaten when one moves within range of the paws and mouth. Other tentacles wrap themselves about the otter's head, legs, and body while the otter continues to tear off and swallow chunks of flesh (fig. 64). Occasionally a sucker attaches itself to the otter's palate but it is quickly torn loose by the extended claws of the forepaws. A large octopus may furnish sufficient food for more than one feeding period. The chitinous beak of the octopus may or may not be swallowed. Even if it is, fecal examinations do not reveal the importance of this food species.

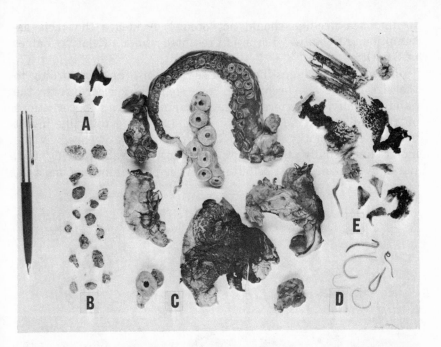

FIGURE 64.—Food taken from a sea otter stomach: *A*—fragment of octopus jaws; *B*—small pebbles; *C*—octopus tentacles and mantle; *D*—ascarid worms (probably *Terranova decipiens*); *E*—fins, skin, and opercular spines of the red Irish lord (*Hemilepidotus hemilepidotus*). The sea otter's teeth are not adapted to cutting; the tough octopus flesh is swallowed in chunks that show little effect of chewing. (The pencil is 12 cm. long.) (KWK 1013)

A captive otter was fed 5 lb. (2.3 kg.) of squid *(Loligo)* daily. Before beginning to eat each squid he removed the pen by grasping its tip between his incisors and drawing it from the mantle. He then discarded it over his left shoulder by turning his head quickly to the side.

Starfish of several species are of minor value as a sea otter food. Although a number of stomachs (111) contained starfish remains, the volume was small. I have seldom observed a feeding otter that ate an entire starfish. The otter usually tears off and eats one or two arms of a starfish, then loses interest and discards the remainder.

Fecal and stomach examinations indicate that the green sea urchin *(Strongylocentrotus drobachiensis)* is frequently eaten and this food has been considered the most important, if not essential, item in the diet of the sea otter. With captive sea otters, Shidlovskaya (1947) stated that "Longer interruptions than 5 days in feeding sea urchins should not occur." Evidence that this assumption is not always true is presented under "Relative Values of Sea Otter Foods."

The method of ingesting green sea urchins varies according to the size of the sea urchin and also somewhat according to the habits of individual otters. Stomach examinations and observations of feeding otters indicate that some animals habitually ingest more of the test than others. Small urchins are crushed by the molars and usually at least part of the test is swallowed (fig. 65). Large urchins may first be bitten with the postcanines on one side,

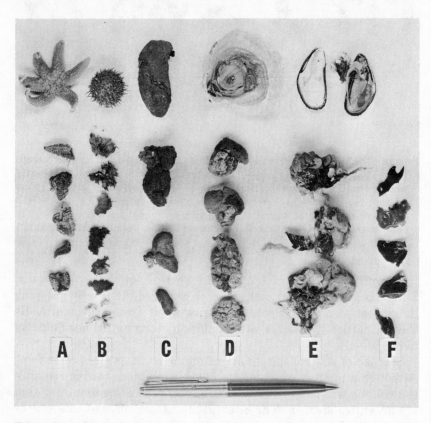

FIGURE 65.—Intact sea otter food organisms are shown at the top of columns *A* to *E*, and partially digested fragments of the same species removed from stomachs are shown below. *A*—six-rayed star (*Leptasterias* sp.); *B*—green sea urchin (*Strongylocentrotus drobachiensis*); *C*—sea cucumber (*Cucumaria* sp.); *D*—pearly monia (*Pododesmus macroschisma*); *E*—mussel (*Mytilus edulis*); *F*—fragments of marine algae. Algae, which is voided undigested in the feces, is not a food species but is eaten accidentally. (KWK 1011)

fracturing the test. Then, with the aid of paws and teeth, the otter is able to open the test and with the lower incisors and tongue to scoop out the exposed viscera and gonads (Hildebrand, 1954). Large urchins may also be opened primarily with the paws. The top of the urchin is cradled against the palm of one paw while the digits and palm of the other exert pressure on the test surrounding the urchin's oral opening, crushing it inward. The urchin may be rotated to facilitate application of pressure. When the test is sufficiently weakened the teeth are used to remove the broken test so that the contents may be scooped out. The empty test may be tossed aside with the paws or dropped on the chest or belly while another item is eaten.

Sea cucumbers appear to be of minor importance in the diet of the sea otter, they appeared in only 26 stomachs. They are tough and showed relatively little multilation from chewing (fig. 65). We did not give them to captive otters but Shidlovskaya (1947) says that they were eaten reluctantly by her captives.

Tunicates, having a tough leathery covering, do not appear to be an important food. A few individuals were in 11 stomachs.

Fish, particularly the globefish *(Cyclopterichthys glaber)*, contributed the greatest food volume (50 percent of all food volumes combined) among stomachs taken at Amchitka. It is evident that this food source, along with mollusks, is of major importance.

The identification of fish species eaten is sometimes difficult because sea otters often discard diagnostic bony plates from the heads of fish. Also, the bones that are swallowed may be severely crushed during mastication. The variety of fish eaten is not large and a series of specimens was accumulated during stomach examinations that enabled us to identify most fish remains.

The fish taken are usually bottom-inhabiting forms and are somewhat sedentary or sluggish. The red Irish lord (fig. 64) and globefish, both sluggish species, occurred in 75 percent of the stomachs containing fish. Information obtained from hundreds of trammel net hauls at Amchitka, as well as data from the stomachs of harbor seals taken there, indicate, however, that the rock greenling and Atka mackerel may be more abundant than the red Irish lord or globefish. However, they are more active than these two species and possibly for this reason are less frequently captured by the otters.

The sea otter does not appear to be well adapted to the capture or consumption of fish. The dentition is very unlike that of seals and porpoises. All marine mammals that eat fish, except the sea otter, capture them with their teeth and swallow them without mastication (seals and sea lions may, however, tear chunks from a fish that is too large to swallow intact). The sea otter apparently captures fish with its paws and all fish flesh found in stomachs had been torn into chunks that were crushed before swallowing. No fish were swallowed whole.

Thus, the sea otters' manner of capturing and eating fish is unique among marine mammals. After the fish was brought to the surface and killed by a crushing bite at or near its head, it was held in the paws and chunks were torn from it, masticated to a moderate degree and swallowed. Some chunks of fish found in stomachs measured about 3 x 4 x 5 cm. Eating usually began at the fish's tail and often all or most of the head (particularly of the cottids) and viscera were discarded. Strong adult males clasped the fish body firmly with the forepaws and extended claws, then, starting at the anterior end ripped the skin with the canines and incisors from first one side, then the other. The flesh and bones were then rapidly eaten like a candy bar. Globefish, being scaleless and having soft bones, were consumed almost in their entirety.

In the Shumagin Islands four adult male and one adult female sea otters were taken on 6 and 7 June 1960 at Simeonof Island and one female on 11 June at Little Koniuji Island. Four stomachs were empty. The stomach contents of two males are shown in table 14.

Of interest is the fact that among the contents of the two stomachs which had a combined volume of 3.48 liters (3.7 qt.), mostly clam meats, there were no scraps of clam shell. For this reason, the species eaten could not be positively identified. Dr. G. D. Hanna did, however, tentatively identify the large siphons as belonging to the Washington clam (*Schizothaerus nuttallii*). Perhaps this large clam was not removed from the sand bottom or the shell could not be broken or opened by the otter. About 1 inch of the siphons appeared to have been bitten or ripped from the clam bodies. A captive otter demonstrated that clams, even large horse clams (*Schizothaerus*), are cracked either against a

TABLE 14.—*Stomach contents of two male sea otters from Simeonof Island, Shumagin Islands, Alaska*

Specimen and food item	Volume (milliliters)	Individuals
KWK 60–6: Clam feet	2,425	155+
KWK 60–8:		
Large clam syphons	844	59
Small clam feet	206	17
Horse mussel	5	1
Whelk operculum	trace	1
Total	3,480	233

rock or against another clam resting on the otter's chest (fig. 60). It is thus inferred that clams which are buried are not dug from the bottom.

In the Bering Sea on 8 and 10 July 1960, one adult male and two adult female otters and two pups were taken 3½ miles off the north shore of Unimak Island in a depth of 15 fathoms and 9 miles north of the Alaska Peninsula in 20 fathoms. The food habits of these individuals are of particular interest because no other stomach specimens of otters which habitually remain offshore are available. The foods found in three of the stomachs are shown in table 15. All food items (clams, crabs, and a hexagrammid fish) are benthic forms. This indicates that here, as in other areas, the sea otter is predominantly a bottom feeder (see Diving). The lack of feces on the beaches of nearby Amak Island in July 1961 and 1963 indicates that otters in this area seldom come ashore.

Fecal Analyses

Studies of sea otter food habits prior to 1962 were based primarily on analyses of fecal remains (Williams, 1938; Murie, 1940; 1959; Jones, 1951). All of these studies indicated that the sea urchin was the dominant food species.

About 95 percent of 422 fecal samples I examined at Amchitka contained sea urchin remains (table 16). Stomach examinations, however, as well as other studies discussed elsewhere (see Relative Values of Sea Otter Foods), indicate strongly that mollusks and fish are essential foods and that in some areas sea urchins may be of relatively minor importance and then primarily during their season of reproduction.

The examination of feces may contribute certain qualitative

TABLE 15.—*Stomach contents of three sea otters taken in 15–20 fathoms of water in the Bering Sea*

Specimen and food item	Volume (milliliters)	Individual
Adult female (KWK 60–16):		
Clinocardium ciliatum	75	ca. 4
Musculus sp.?	trace	?
Surf clam (*Spisula alaskana?*)	50	1
Fish (*Hexagrammos* sp.?)	125	1
Pup (KWK 60–18):		
Clam, unidentified	20	ca. 4
Milk curd	10	----------
Adult female (KWK 60–19): [1]		
Clam (*Serripes groenlandicus*)	427	ca. 20
Tanner crab (*Chionecetes bairdi*)	48	1
Hermit crab (*Pagurus* sp.?)	150	several
Crab, unidentified	trace	----------
Musculus niger	trace	----------

[1] Both stomach and intestinal contents included.

[The samples were examined on seven habitually used hauling-out beaches]

Food organism [1]	Number of occurrences (frequency) [2]	Percent of fecal samples having item
Arthropoda:		
Crabs (Crustacea)	67	16
Mollusca:		
Chitons (Amphineura)	26	6
Snails (Gastropoda)	11	3
Limpets *Acmea*	10	3
Horse mussel *Volsella volsella*	89	21
Mussel *Mytilus edulus*	1	<1
Varnished horse mussel *Musculus vernicosa*	48	11
Pearly monia *Pododesmus macrochisma*	1	<1
Clam (Pelecypoda)	5	1
Pecten (Pelecypoda)	1	<1
Octopus (Cephalopoda)	3	1
Subtotal	195	46
Echinodermata: [3]		
Sea urchin *Strongylocentrotus drobachiensis*	401	95
Chordata:		
Fish	63	15
Total	726	

[1] Nonfood material, clay, gravel, etc., was found in seven fecal samples.
[2] Frequency refers to the number of samples having the item, not the number of individuals present.
[3] Starfish were probably broken into fine pieces and thus not detected.

information concerning the food habits of sea otters but, because hard parts of some food species are not ingested, information derived from fecal examination contributes distorted information on both the qualitative and quantitative aspects of food habits.

Otters must defecate on land if fecal samples are to be studied. In many areas otters defecate on land infrequently or not at all. Weather conditions, geographical features (such as sheltered beaches above the tide line), and the presence of a human population appear to influence the frequency with which sea otters haul out on land. Like all other marine mammals, and unlike many terrestrial ones, the sea otter is not selective in choosing a defecation site. When sleeping or resting on land, the otter usually rises to its feet and expels the feces at the edge of its resting place. As it changes position for comfort during several hours on shore, feces may be deposited in several locations around the resting spot and the animal may, in changing position, lie in its own feces. Defecation in the water is also a random function and may occur while the animal is eating, swimming, or resting on its back on the surface. Although, as noted above, defecation on land is frequent, I have often noted that captive otters, after a rest period beside their pool, may defecate immediately upon entering the water.

Where otters habitually use certain hauling-out areas, as they do at Amchitka Island, a large number of fecal deposits may accumulate. Because these are composed primarily of the hard parts of marine organisms (fig. 66), they may remain in recognizable form for a number of weeks or, in well-protected locations, for months.

The analysis of fecal deposits from the Shumagin Islands and from Amchitka are presented in tables 16 and 17. The fact that sea urchins appeared in 95 percent of the droppings found on Amchitka and only in 4 percent of those from the Shumagins is significant. Sea urchins are available in the Shumagin Islands. It thus appears that the sea otter may feed selectively. No evidence,

FIGURE 66.—Contents of a large (286 g. dry weight) sea otter fecal deposit: *A*—more than 100 varnished horse mussels (*Musculus*) (10 g.); these are usually swallowed whole, the viscera are digested, and the valves pass intact through the gastrointestinal tract. *B*—fragments of the tests, spines, and Aristotle's lanterns of an unknown number of green sea urchins (*Strongylocentrotus*) (159 g.). *C*—broken shells and *D*—byssus threads, of more than 40 horse mussels (*Volsella*) (117 g.). Sea urchins and large mussels are crushed by the teeth, and parts of the test or shell are swallowed. Specimen was collected on an Amchitka beach, 21 July 1956. The rule is 5 cm. (KWK 68–13–4)

TABLE 17.—*Analysis of 75 fecal samples from the Shumagin Islands*

[15 samples were taken at Simeonof Island, 5–9 June 1960 and 60 at Eagle Harbor, Nagai Island on 16 June 1960]

Food organism	Number of occurrences (frequency)	Percent of fecal samples having item
Arthropoda:		
Crabs (Crustacea)	12	16
Mollusca:		
Snails (Gastropoda)	4	5
Horse mussel *Volsella volsella*	3	4
Mussel *Mytilus edulus*	58	77
Clam (Pelecypoda)	6	8
Subtotal	71	94
Echinodermata:		
Sea urchin *Strongylocentrotus drobachiensis*	3	4
Chordata:		
Fish	8	10
Total	94	

such as high winter mortality, indicates that the sea otter population has approached its maximum size in the Shumagin Islands as it has at Amchitka. It might therefore be concluded, in the light of all available evidence (see Relative Values of Sea Otter Foods), that the sea otters of Amchitka consume a large number of sea urchins because other food resources have been depleted. In areas where otter populations have not yet approached maximum size, food species more nourishing than sea urchins are still abundant and the sea urchin may be eaten to a minor degree.

The fecal analyses presented here give useful qualitative information on food habits. They show that the food habits of otters in a crowded population differ from those in areas where crowding is not a factor. It is, however, evident that stomach analyses are necessary to reveal the food habits in their proper perspective. A discussion of the method of ingestion of each group of food organisms indicates in more detail why fecal examinations are of only limited use in food habits studies of the sea otter.

Food Quantities Required

The food requirement of the sea otter is great. Captive juveniles held on Amchitka Island during the 1957-59 study periods required from 25 to 30 percent of their body weight of food per day.

The quantity of food consumed by captive adult otters did not vary according to season. The required amount for an adult male and female was similar, about 20 to 23 percent of the body weight per day. The data are discussed in the section on the sea otter "In Captivity."

Relative Values of Sea Otter Foods

Miss Neva L. Karrick, Assistant Laboratory Director, Food Science Pioneer Research Laboratory of the Bureau of Commercial Fisheries at Seattle, has furnished proximate analyses of certain representative sea otter foods (table 18). From these data and the known quantities of food consumed by captive otters and data obtained from stomach examinations, it is evident that the sea urchin is seldom as important a food item as previously supposed and that the sea otter is primarily dependent for survival on other foods with more calories and higher protein content.

A captive sea otter weighing about 40 pounds required an average of about 8.4 lb. of food, primarily rockfish, per day (24-hour period). This diet supplied about 3,400 calories (about 89 calories per 100 grams of fish). Sea urchins with gravid gonads can supply roughly 58 calories per 100 grams of gonads and 16 calories per 100 grams of viscera. If large gravid sea urchins were available, about 200 would be required to supply 3,000+ calories to a sea otter in a 24-hour period.

Most of the sea urchins now available at Amchitka are small. The reason appears to be that a large sea otter population is over-utilizing this food resource (see Depletion of Food Resources). Mature gravid green sea urchins, weighing about 115 g. each, were obtained for analysis from an area at Cold Bay, Alaska, where there are no sea otters. At Amchitka, the size available in greatest quantity weigh about 6 to 10 g. These are consumed in large numbers, particularly by juvenile otters. The gonads in these immature sea urchins are almost microscopic. The amount of visceral material available in them is small and is a poor

TABLE 18.—*Proximate analysis of important sea otter food species*

[Averages. These data were furnished by Bureau of Commercial Fisheries Technological Laboratory, Seattle, Wash.]

Species	Moisture (percent)	Oil (percent)	Protein 6.25 × %N. (percent)	Ash (percent)	Calories per 100 grams [1]
Dungeness crab meat *Cancer magister*	77.2	0.90	20.8	1.61	91
Butter clam *Saxidomus nuttalli*	83.0	1.30	13.3	1.9	63
Octopus [2]	85.7	0.86	12.1	1.3	56
Sea urchin *Strongylocentrotus drobachiensis:*					
Gonads	85.9	2.70	8.4	2.51	58
Viscera	92.2	0.72	2.3	3.72	16
Rockfish *Sebastodes* sp.	79.0	1.50	19.0	1.18	89

[1] Calories per 100 grams = average percent oil × 9 plus average percent protein × 4.
[2] Sea otters usually discard most or all of the viscera of octopus; therefore only the flesh was analyzed.

nutritional source. Because of the general depletion of invertebrates and the apparent inability of juvenile otters to obtain an
adequate number of fish and mollusks, these young animals are
compelled to eat the abundant and easily obtained immature sea
urchins. An otter would have to consume nearly 6,500 of these immature urchins daily to supply the 3,000+ calories which appear
to be required.

Depletion of Food Resources

The requirement for large amounts of food by sea otters has
been discussed. Feeding grounds are limited by depth to relatively
shallow waters and tag returns indicate that individual sea otters
do not range widely along the coast (see Home Range). Because
of these circumstances which concentrate feeding activities in
rather limited areas, it appears probable that a large population
of sea otters could seriously deplete food resources within their
home range. Evidence is available that this does in fact occur.

SEA URCHIN DEPLETION

McLean (1962) presents convincing evidence that the sea urchin
Strongylocentrotus franciscanus has been nearly exterminated in
a particular area on the California coast which is occupied by a
considerable number of sea otters. Of the area he studied he says
(p. 101) "the large sea urchin was totally absent, although spines
and test fragments were present in gravel samples."

Indirect evidence from Amchitka Island, where a large sea otter
population exists, indicates that sea otter predation has drastically
reduced certain food species there. Small green sea urchins are
abundant. It is not possible, however, to find large individuals in
the intertidal zone and I seldom saw an otter eating an urchin
that approached in size the large individuals which are abundant
in other Aleutian areas where the sea otter is scarce or absent.
Bottom samples obtained by R. D. Jones, while diving with
SCUBA equipment, both at Amchitka and in comparable areas
at Adak (where at the time few sea otters occurred), showed that
sea urchins at Amchitka are relatively scarce and small.

In a recent letter (16 December 1966), Jones reported on a
subsequent visit to the Adak area he had explored prior to the
time that it was occupied by a large number of sea otters:

In 1957 the green sea urchin was numerous and obvious in this area, and this
time I saw none. I have no quantitative data because I had neither the equip-

ment nor time to gather it. This same thing is reported to have happened in the Sandman Reefs and Sanak Reefs when the sea otters reappeared in numbers.

John Nevzoroff, a native of the Aleutian Islands who worked with me on Amchitka in 1962, told me that in the early 1930's, when he trapped foxes on Amchitka with his father, sea otters were considerably less numerous, particularly along the Bering Sea coast, than they are today. He also said that he found large sea urchins ("sea eggs") abundant along the shores of Constantine Harbor where we were unable to find them in the 1955–63 study period.

Tons of fragments of large sea urchin tests are contained in kitchen middens at Amchitka Island. These indicate that in prehistoric times large sea urchins were abundant there. Presumably the aboriginal human population was able to obtain these large sea urchins because the sea otter population had been utilized and reduced. Thus, the sea urchin resource was not overexploited by the otters as it is today, and the urchins were allowed to grow to maximum size.

It is evident that at Amchitka, where mature sea urchins are scarce, the diet of the sea otter must be supplemented by other foods, such as fish and mollusks, to prevent starvation. That starvation does, in fact, occur in winter and early spring, particularly among young otters, is discussed in the section on Limiting Factors.

THE ABALONE–SEA OTTER PROBLEM IN CALIFORNIA

J. H. McLean writes (letter, December 1964):

20 miles of coastline below San Simeon which formerly produced abalone year after year under continuous commercial exploitation has been completely ruined for abalone as a result of the southern migration of the California herds. It has nothing to do with the number of divers now working because the otters take the entire population, not just those of legal size. The fact is that otters, urchins and abalones do not coexist and the entire commercial abalone fishery is very seriously threatened by possible southern expansion of range.

Cox (1962), who has conducted comprehensive studies of the abalone (*Haliotis*) along the California coast, says (p. 57) "all evidence indicates they [sea otters] pose a threat to human exploitation [of the abalone] when the two are competing in the same area." Data gathered in Carmel Cove and Stillwater Cove before and after the areas were occupied by sea otters demonstrated that the local abalone beds were seriously decimated but not entirely eliminated by sea otter predation.

In a public statement, additional information was given by Cox (California Senate, 1963):

In 1956 we went into Shelter Cove right off Monterey and over a period of several days tagged 513 abalone. One year later we came back in the area and we spent approximately three days searching and we found five abalone . . . one of which had a tag. The area where we were able to collect five hundred abalone in an hour we couldn't find any. On one dive I brought up over two dozen broken shells . . . characteristic of broken ones of the sea otters. We were told . . . by the caretaker, that a herd of sea otters had spent the winter in this cove . . . I had been called to task for not reporting this. . . . However, I felt this was not an adequate experiment.

In a recent study of sea otter feeding habits on the California coast, Ebert (1968) concluded that "sea otters exert a profound influence upon benthic communities."

During 1963, abalone fishermen in San Luis Obispo County, California, complained that sea otters were destroying the abalone resource of that area. Claims of spectacular damage to abalone beds appeared in many newspapers. In response to these complaints a hearing was held at the City Hall, San Luis Obispo, on 19 November 1963. At this hearing Mr. Harry Anderson, Deputy Director of the California Department of Fish and Game, presented testimony to the California Senate Fact Finding Committee on Natural Resources. He compared commercial landings of abalones in certain areas before and after sea otters were present in these areas. In 1961 when sea otters were present "the catch was over 1,550,000 pounds, by far the largest catch of any year in the 10-year period." He indicated further that competition among abalone fishermen has increased greatly. In 1928 there were 11 licensed commercial abalone fishermen in California. The number has increased to 505 in 1963. Since the abalone resource is limited, it becomes apparent that the individual fishermen can expect to obtain fewer abalones than when competition among them was less. It was concluded that "all the evidence we have indicates that the sea otter has not seriously harmed or threatened the abalone resource."

The data indicate that the depletion of food resources at Amchitka has resulted in an abnormally high winter die-off of sea otters as well as a population of undersized animals (see Mortality Factors and Body Measurements). Evidence from California reveals that when sea otters feed for an extended period in a limited area they may seriously deplete local populations of their prey species.

Unusual Food Items

BIRDS

On 27 March 1962, at Amchitka Island, I watched an adult female sea otter through a 50-power telescope while she consumed what appeared to be a shearwater *(Puffinus)* or Fulmar *(Fulmarus)*. When first seen she was carrying the carcass on her chest. She stopped in the shelter of an islet to groom, leaving the bird floating beside her. After about 5 minutes of grooming she picked up the bird and tore flesh from the breast. She alternately groomed and ate for about 30 minutes. While she ate, the bird's intestines streamed out across her chest and feathers littered the water around her. After apparently satisfying her appetite she swam away carrying the carcass, bloody sternum erect, on her chest.

On 13 November 1957, I found sea otter feces at East Cape, Amchitka Island, which consisted of feathers, skin, fat, and flesh (breast muscle) of what appeared to be a cormorant *(Phalacrocorax pelagicus)*. The chunks which were torn from the bird showed little indication of having been affected by passage through the digestive tract.

Hungry captive otters consumed Emperor Goose *(Philacte canagica)* flesh (Kirkpatrick et al., 1955) but Jones told me that the meat passed undigested through the alimentary tract.

It appears that the flesh of birds is eaten only under the stress of hunger, particularly in winter. Also, the sea otter, adjusted to a diet of fish and invertebrates, seems unable to derive nourishment from the flesh of birds.

MISCELLANEOUS

On several occasions sea otters were seen to eat unusual food items that zoo visitors threw into their pool. These included a slice of white bread, a marshmallow, and peanuts. The animals appeared to suffer no ill effects from ingesting these items but the keeper reported that the peanuts passed through the animal undigested.

Conclusions

It is evident that fecal examinations give less adequate information about sea otter food habits than similar studies for other species. Certain food species (clams and certain fishes) may not appear in recognizable form at all in droppings because shells are not swallowed and the bones of some fish *(Cyclopterichthys)* are soft and are digested. On the other hand, when sea urchins are eaten some part or all of the test may be swallowed. The important quantities of high protein food contained in mollusks and fish cannot be evaluated by the examination of feces.

It has been wrongly assumed that sea urchins held first-rank importance as a sea otter food. Barabash-Nikiforov (1947) believed that sea urchins were essential to survival. There can be no question but that where and when mature gravid sea urchins are available they are an important food source. That they are not essential to sea otter existence is demonstrated by: (1) A captive sea otter was given no sea urchins for a period of 4 years and remained in good health; (2) numerous captives held on Amchitka refused to eat urchins after being introduced to a diet of fish; (3) each winter many juvenile sea otters (apparently incapable of obtaining fishes) died of enteritis (probably induced by shock or stress accompanying starvation) and were found to have the remains of considerable numbers of sea urchins in the intestines; (4) feces and stomachs of sea otters taken, for example, in the Shumagin Islands, contained few, if any, sea urchin remains (although sea urchins occur there).

My conclusion is that sea urchins may, during their season of reproduction in areas of abundance, rank high in importance as a sea otter food source. Where an abundance of mollusks and fish may be obtained, however, the sea urchin is at no time an essential food species. The food value of the sea urchin may vary from poor to good, depending on maturity and the season of reproduction. Mollusks and fish, however, when available and to those animals able to obtain them, furnish an adequate and consistently nourishing diet. Mollusks (37 percent) and fish (50 percent), relatively high in calories, account for 87 percent by volume of the sea otters' food at Amchitka.

DISTRIBUTION AND NUMBERS

Original

The sea otter originally ranged at least as far south as Morro Hermoso (27°32′ N. lat.) on the Pacific Coast of Lower California (Ogden, 1941, p. 7). Scammon (1870) noted that it occurred at Cedros Island, about 30 miles north of Morro Hermoso, and at Guadalupe. From these locations its distribution continued northward along the coast of North America to Prince William Sound and westward through the Aleutian, Pribilof, and Commander Islands to the coast of Kamchatka and south through the Kuril Islands at least to northern Hokkaido and southern Sakhalin (Barabash-Nikiforov, 1947) (see map, fig. 67).

ICE AND THE NORTHERN LIMIT OF RANGE

The northernmost permanent sea otter population in the Western Hemisphere is in Prince William Sound (60°30′ N. lat.) where the sea does not freeze. In the Bering Sea the aboriginal population on the Pribilof Islands (57° N. lat.) and that along the northwest extremity of the Alaska Peninsula (55° N. lat.) overlap the southern limit of winter drift ice. That the sea otter is able to survive limited winter ice conditions is also indicated by the fact that the aboriginal Pribilof population was apparently a large and permanent one, and that on occasion the sea freezes there for brief periods. Winter drift ice reaches the southeastern Kamchatka coast and Kuril Islands where early sea otter populations were apparently prosperous and are today increasing. Nikolaev (1965b) found in the Kuril Islands that when sea otters were unable to move to ice-free locations in winter they died of starvation. When closed in by ice they crossed its surface or even went overland in search of open water.

Bee and Hall (1956) record two unsubstantiated sight records of sea otters far north of their usual range in the Arctic Ocean. One was reported in 1951 at Cape Halkett, 70°49′ N. lat., 142°16′ W. long. and another at Atigaru Point, 70°35′ N. lat., 151°50′ W. long. C. H. Fiscus, who obtained these reports from other observers, told me in 1964 that he is now doubtful of their authenticity.

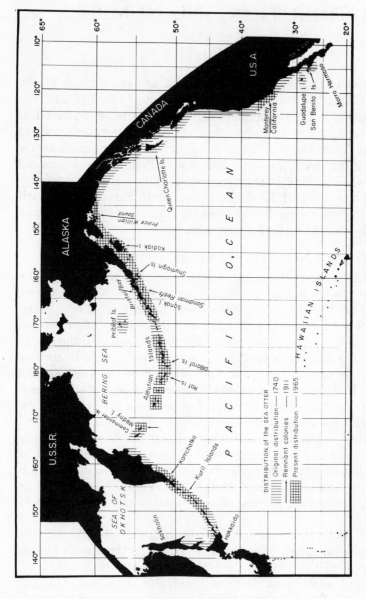

FIGURE 67.—Distribution of the sea otter in 1741 and 1965, also showing the locations where remnant colonies survived in 1911 when protection was given. Two of these known remnant colonies, in the Queen Charlotte and San Benito Islands, were exterminated by 1920.

Barabash-Nikiforov (1947) and Nikolaev (1960) indicate that on the east coast of Siberia the sea otter may have ranged to 64° N. The records, however, are vague. Gulin (1952) photographed the skin of a sea otter said to have been taken by local hunters at Lavrentiya (65°08′ N. lat., 171° E. long.) near Bering Strait on the Chukotsk Peninsula. No date or other specific data are given. Such a casual report in a popular magazine of a sea otter so far north of the usual range must be regarded with skepticism.

Specific records as far north as 64° do not appear to be available. Gribkov (1963) says that the known boundary of the sea otter's range is 57° N. on the east coast of Kamchatka but mentions that in 1960 sea otters "were bagged" north of this point.

The occurrence of a permanent sea otter population in the northern Bering Sea or Arctic Ocean where the sea freezes is quite unlikely. That a stray otter might have traveled north with pack ice in spring from the lower limit of winter drift ice in southern Bristol Bay and the southeastern shore of Kamchatka, is a possibility. Retreating winter ice might account for the presence of three sea otters at the Pribilofs in 1889, 1892, and 1896 (Preble and McAtee, 1923) long after they were extirpated there. A sighting in Norton Sound (64° N.) in June 1941, was reported by Frank Glaser (*in* Lensink, 1958).

In general it is true today, as it was in early times, that the prosperous sea otter colonies are south of areas where sea ice forms regularly and remains for long periods in winter months.

The environmental factors that control the southern limit of distribution, other than predation by man and environmental pollution caused by him today, are unknown. Additional sources of information on aboriginal distribution are cited by Barabash-Nikiforov (1947).

POPULATION REDUCTION THROUGH EXPLOITATION

Intensive exploitation of the sea otter by Europeans began with the voyage of Vitus Bering in 1741 and continued unregulated for 170 years. Exploitation was halted and protection was given to the sea otter by international treaty in 1911.[3]

---

[3] Convention between the United States, Great Britain, Russia, and Japan for the preservation and protection of fur seals. Proclaimed 14 December 1911 and approved 24 August 1912. Article V of this Convention extended protection to the sea otter. Further protection was extended by the "Presidential Proclamation for the preservation and protection of fur seals and sea otter," signed by Woodrow Wilson on 31 May 1913, and an "Executive order regarding the protection of fur seals and sea otters," signed by Calvin Coolidge on 14 January 1929 (U.S. Bureau of Fisheries, 1929).

The sea otter was then commercially extinct and nearly extinct as a species. The number of sea otters that were taken during the period of unregulated exploitation is not known because proper records were not kept. Most records are vague concerning where skins came from, except that they came from the New World. Fisher (1940b) states that her summary is not complete but lists records of 359,375 skins taken between 1740 and 1916. Between 1745 and 1867, "260,790 sea otter skins were reported as having been shipped from Alaska" and from 1868 to 1905 the take was 107,121 skins (U.S. Bureau of Fisheries, 1906). From 1906 to 1910, 240 skins are recorded taken by U.S. and Canadian hunters (U.S. Bureau of Fisheries, 1907 through 1911). Thus the total recorded number of skins taken in waters off Alaska, prior to 1911, was 368,151. Skins taken by hunters of other nationalities are not recorded. Lensink (1960) presents figures and broad estimates which place the take of sea otters from Alaska at over 906,500 animals.

POSTULATED SIZE OF ABORIGINAL POPULATION

From data gathered during recent studies, some idea of the possible take may be postulated. Today it appears that about 30,000 sea otters occupy approximately one-fifth of the original lineal coastal range of the sea otter. Some of the presently occupied habitat is of superior quality. Islands contribute more usable habitat than do unbroken continental coastlines. Thus, it is probable that the population of sea otters in 1740 may have been no more than five times the present number, probably between 100,000 and 150,000 animals. If the annual increment that could be cropped on a sustained yield basis was about 2.5 percent per year (the approximate annual yield of the Pribilof fur seal (*Callorhinus ursinus*) herd is 5 percent per year and fur seals normally bear one pup each year; 2 years elapse between sea otter pups), then the take in 170 years could have been between 425,000 and 637,500 if cropping had been rational. The killing of sea otters, however, was unregulated and for periods of many years the take was at the expense of the population "capital." Probably certain populations were wiped out during an early part of the exploitation period. Thus the yield over the entire period was less than it would have been if only the annual increment had been taken. Reasoning on this basis, it appears that the probable take of sea otters between 1740 and 1911 was less than a million and more likely about a half million animals.

In the following section, sea otter population studies in Alaska are reviewed and a summary of information on the past and present world populations is presented. Field counts of living sea otters (omitting pups carried by mothers) furnish the information on which this study of population and distribution is based. To obtain a knowledge of population dynamics, studies of mortality, reproduction, food habits, and movements of sea otters were also undertaken.

Modern

ALASKA POPULATIONS

The greatest population of sea otters in the world today is in the central to outer Aleutian Islands (table 36). This is also the area where repopulation of available habitat, from which the sea otter was extirpated before 1911, is apparently occurring the most rapidly. It is also the location where most of our studies were concentrated.

Data were made available by individuals who visited or worked in Alaska during the 1930's and 1940's. Additional data were obtained, particularly after 1955, by observers who made extensive aerial and surface surveys. During these studies, areas occupied by sea otters as well as areas to which otters have not yet returned were surveyed.

The Aleutian Islands chain consists of five named groups of islands from west to east (subgroups are in parentheses): the Near (Semichi Islands), Rat, Andreanof Islands (Delarof Islands), the Islands of Four Mountains, and Fox Islands (Krenitzin Islands) (see map, fig. 68). Important island groups which furnish suitable sea otter habitat are separated from each other by passes up to 55 miles wide, hundreds of fathoms deep, and swept by swift tidal currents. These wide passes appear to hinder seriously the movements of otters from a heavily populated area to a neighboring island group having vacant habitat.

Today (1968), a sea otter "population explosion" is occurring in the Andreanof Islands. The early expansion of this population was sketchily documented during the late 1930's and early 1940's. More thorough observations were made in the 1950's and until 1965. A similar "population explosion" in the Rat Islands apparently reached a climax in the mid-1940's. The historical data on these two populations are reviewed below and compared with modern findings.

The locations in which sea otters survived the 1741–1911 period

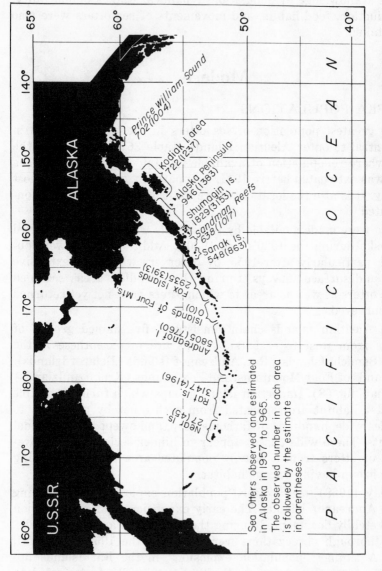

FIGURE 68.—Beginning in 1957, aerial surveys of sea otter habitat were undertaken (see appendix 1). From the recorded counts of otters, calculated estimates of the various populations were derived. Because the figures on this map were taken from tables in the text, they are not rounded.

of unregulated hunting are indicated by (1) areas where large populations are found today, and (2) areas where sea otters were taken shortly before and after 1911. Fragmentary data on otters that were taken between 1906 and 1936 are reviewed briefly below.

Records of the U.S. Bureau of Fisheries (1907–37) indicate that at least 302 otters were taken in Alaska from 1906 through 1936. Of these, 240 were taken between 1906 and 1911 and 62 from 1912 to 1936. For 213 skins (186 before 1911 and 27 after 1911) no location of origin is given, but many apparently came from the Aleutian, Sanak, and Kodiak Islands areas. The specific locations of origin of the remaining skins were often not stated clearly. It appears, however, that the remaining 89 skins may be allocated to the following areas: Aleutians, 7 (4 in 1910 and 3 in 1929); Southern Bristol Bay and Bering Sea north of Unimak Island, 15 (all before 1911); Alaska Peninsula, south coast (about 56° N.), 6 (1918, 2; 1929, 2; 1931, 2); Sanak Island area, 3 (1926, 2; 1934, 1); Shumagin Islands, 1 (1910); Kodiak area, 52 (31 before 1911 and 21 after 1911); Prince William Sound and Kayak Island area, 5 (1910, 3; 1924, 2). Within these areas otters probably survived along exposed coasts that offered few if any anchorages and where offshore reefs made hunting hazardous. Such areas also offered otters feeding habitat well offshore.

The map (fig. 68) and table 19 summarize modern field counts and estimates of sea otter populations in Alaska and indicate that most of the population is concentrated in an area about 500 miles long which includes the Rat and part of the Andreanof Islands (9,605 observed, 1965, table 19). From the present spearhead of population expansion in the central Andreanofs eastward to the next small colony at Atka (228 observed, 1965, table 25) is about 75 miles. The next colony (159 observed, 1965, table 25) is 50 miles farther east, near the east end of Amlia. Moving eastward 30 miles, the next colony (28 observed, 1965, table 25) is at Seguam. From here to the small Samalga-Umnak colony (9 observed, 1965, table 30) is 140 miles. The next small colony (32 observed, 1965, table 30) is at Tigalda Island 175 miles to the east. From here to the Unimak–Amak–Port Moller colony (2,892 observed, 1965, table 30) is 75 miles. Along the south side of the Alaska Peninsula and northeastward to the Kayak Island area, a distance of about 800 miles, the colonies (5,748 observed, table 36) are not separated by any known geographic barriers.

After the publication of population and distribution studies by Lensink (1960) considerable field work was undertaken. The data

TABLE 19.—*Summary of sea otters observed and estimated in Alaska*

[See tables in sections for counts by islands. Most areas have now been surveyed several times. The highest counts which were made under optimum conditions were selected for this summary. Three observers, D. L. Spencer, C. J. Lensink, and K. W. Kenyon gathered most of these data]

Area	Aerial surveys		Estimated total otters [1]	Estimated total 1965 [2]
	Year	Otters observed		
Near Islands	1965	27	45	45
Rat Islands	1965	[3] 3,147	4,196	4,196
Delarof Island	1965	[3] 653	871	871
Andreanof Island	1965	[3] 5,805	7,760	7,760
Islands of the Four Mountains	1965	0	0	0
Fox Islands	1965	2,935	3,913	3,913
Bogoslof Island	1962	0	0	0
Sandman Reefs	1962	638	879	1,017
Sanak Island area	1962	548	746	863
Shumagin Islands	1957	1,829	2,724	3,153
Pavlov Islands	1962	4	8	12
Alaska Peninsula	1962	949	1,317	1,383
Semidi Islands	1957	5	10	12
Kodiak area	1957–59	722	973	1,237
Prince William Sound and Kayak Island	1959	702	1,004	1,004
Total		17,964	24,446	25,466

[1] See Aerial Surveys for method of estimating.
[2] Projected in the regions where growth was observed on the assumption that the increase is at the rate of 5 percent per year.
[3] Total 9,605.

now available indicate that in significant areas sea otter populations have declined and are less than the estimates which Lensink computed on the basis of figures then available to him. Lensink (1960) considered that sea otter feeding habitat included waters to a depth of 50 fathoms, but no evidence is available that they descend to this depth (see Diving). Because of this assumption a greater area of available habitat and greater population potential was postulated by Lensink than is indicated by information now available. Also, Lensink's (1960) estimates for a large sea otter population at Amchitka do not agree with the modern or historical data for this area. The rate of population growth which he postulated is greater than indicated by the data now available. In addition, as shown later, the Amchitka population "crashed" in the 1940's and now fluctuates annually near a population about one-half its maximum size.

Aerial surveys

The most extensive aerial surveys consumed about 200 hours of flight time in a DC–3 aircraft (table 20). Air speed was maintained at 120 knots and flight altitude varied from 200 to 400 feet, depending on winds and nearby terrain. Two observers counted otters from the aircraft's cockpit. Some groups were so large that

TABLE 20.—*Summary of aerial surveys of sea otters, 1957–65*

[Before these surveys, organized surveys were not undertaken]

Date	Method	Hours of flight time	Observers	Areas surveyed (inclusive)
1957: 6 May–28 Sept.	A variety of air and surface craft used	(?)	C. J. Lensink, D. L. Spencer, R. D. Jones, W. A. Troyer, F. Wilke.	Various areas, Cook Inlet to Kanaga Island (Aleutians).
1958: August.	Aircraft.	(?)	W. A. Troyer.	Shuyak area.
1959:				
21–27 May	DC–3 aircraft.	56.8	D. L. Spencer, K. W. Kenyon.	Attu Island (Near Island group) to Herbert Island (Island of Four Mountains).
13 July	UF–2 aircraft (U.S. Coast Guard).	3	K. W. Kenyon.	Outer coast, Olympic Peninsula, Washington.
July	Aircraft.	(?)	C. J. Lensink	Kodiak area.
August.	Cessna 180 aircraft.	(?)	C. J. Lensink, R. Pirtle.	Prince William Sound, Kayak-Wingham Island.
1960: 3–5 March	DC–3 aircraft.	28	D. L. Spencer, K. W. Kenyon, D. W. Rice.	Herbert Island to Amak Island.
1961:				
27 March	DC–3 aircraft.	4	D. L. Spencer, K. W. Kenyon.	Amak area (failed because of fog).
27 October	UF–2 aircraft (U.S. Navy)	1.8	L. W. Croxton, K. W. Kenyon	Adak area. (all data lost in crash of survey aircraft).
1962: 29 March–10 April	DC–3 aircraft.	53.6	D. L. Spencer, K. W. Kenyon, J. J. Burns	Rat Islands to Amak I.; Sanak, Sandman Reefs, Shumagin Is., Alaska Peninsula.
1965: 19 April–9 May.	DC–3 aircraft.	49.2	D. L. Spencer, K. W. Kenyon, E. G. Klinkhart.	Aleutian Is., Alaska Peninsula (part), Cook Inlet (part).
Total		196.4+		

141

all individuals could not be counted in the time available. In such groups we counted a sample of 10 to 50 animals. We then visually divided the remainder of the group into sectors equivalent to the counted sector to obtain an estimate of the total number of animals. Aerial photographs were taken of unusually large groups to ascertain the accuracy of the field estimates (see Aerial Photography). The flight path was divided at the center line of the aircraft. One observer stood behind the pilot and the other behind the copilot. Otters were seen to a distance of at least 1 mile on each side of the aircraft during excellent survey conditions and to at least ½ mile under good conditions.

The width of the survey track was ascertained by flying at survey height over an air strip of known length. In this way each observer obtained a reference point on the wing of the aircraft, which from his position in the aircraft during surveys delimited a known distance on the surface.

Observation conditions were evaluated during the surveys and were classified as follows:

> Excellent—no wind, high overcast (water glassy and no glare).
> Good—light wind (to 6 or 8 knots) and overcast; or no wind (glassy water) but sun glare present.
> Fair—light wind to 10 knots and surface glare or wind 8 to 15 knots and sky overcast.
> Poor—winds over 10 knots and glare on water, or wind over 15 knots regardless of sky cover.

When possible, survey operations were suspended during fair or poor conditions, because too few otters could be seen and the errors in the census could not be properly evaluated.

Observations were recorded by one of the biologists, or by a third person assisting him. Each observation was immediately plotted on a U.S. Coast and Geodetic Survey chart.

Several aerial surveys which supplemented the comprehensive surveys were conducted from single engine aircraft and from a Grumman Widgeon. Also, the U.S. Navy cooperated by sending Fish and Wildlife observers on survey flights in a UF–2 Grumman Albatross aircraft.

Data were gathered in 1959 to provide a factor for computing estimated total sea otter populations from aerial counts.

In an effort to ascertain as nearly as possible the number of sea otters occupying a particular coastal area at Amchitka Island, inshore and offshore surface surveys were repeatedly conducted by dory. A total of 17 survey counts were made along a 13-mile section of coast from (and including) Crown Reefer Point

(51°28′ N. lat., 179°11′ E. long,) to (but not including) East Cape (51°22′32″ N. lat., 179°27′45″ E. long.) The surveys were conducted in February, March, and April of 1959 (see Kenyon and Spencer, 1960).

These surface surveys differ from the others because an intensive effort was made in a limited area to observe, by repeated trips, the available sea otter habitat at close range in locations familiar to the observer. The mean number of otters observed was 254. On an aerial survey of the same section of coast in May 1959, 192 otters were counted. Thus, approximately 76 percent of the number seen from the surface was observed from the air.

If only the highest surface counts for the section of the coast are considered, the total count for the area is 295 otters. This figure would indicate that on the aerial survey about 65 percent of the otters in the survey area were seen $(\frac{192 \times 100}{295})$.

Based on the premise that the maximum number of otters seen on surface surveys failed by 15 percent to include all those present, an aerial survey would reveal 50 percent of the otters present. This correction factor was used previously (Kenyon and Spencer, 1960).

The correction factor indicating that about 75 percent of the otters were seen is a conservative one and is used to estimate total populations in the following discussion for these reasons: (1) Tag recoveries at Amchitka revealed that the home range of a sea otter may include about 10 miles of coastline. It therefore appeared reasonable to use the mean of counts for each part of the area studied. In this way some compensation is made for the movements of individual otters in and out of the study areas during intervals between surveys. (2) Many observations during aerial surveys, when the same locations were flown over repeatedly, indicated to us that, in general, under excellent conditions we saw at least 75 percent of the otters present. In some places, having a minimum number of rocks and kelp breaking the surface, where the shoreline was even and the band of water furnishing available feeding habitat was narrow, we felt reasonably certain that, in calm weather, we saw more than 75 percent of the otters present. (3) We found that water depths as shown on USCGS charts constituted a dependable guide to locations inhabited by sea otters. A large majority occur within the 20-fathom curve (waters less than 120 feet in depth). Rarely do sea otters occur in water as deep as 30 fathoms. Therefore we consider that no significant number of sea otters was missed during the aerial surveys.

Future studies may show that we were unable to estimate the

error in our counts accurately. Nevertheless, the results of the surveys are comparable and they establish the order of magnitude of populations in the locations that were surveyed. For the purpose of this report, comparability of field observations in different areas is more important than an estimate of absolute population magnitude.

On calm days, when the sea was glassy and a floating otter could be seen at a distance of more than a mile on each side of the aircraft, we carefully examined many extensive offshore areas between islands. Where the water is shallow and otters occur in numbers well offshore (as off the north shore of Unimak Island) we systematically flew sectors through the area covering most of the sea's surface where otters occurred.

In areas of dense population, the otters tend to gather in groups or "pods" of variable size numbering from 10 to 30 animals. Groups of 100 or more animals were infrequent (fig. 69) and rarely were more than 200 otters together (the maximum observed was 440, fig. 70). In sparse populations, relatively fewer groups

FIGURE 69.—A group of 157 sea otters resting in a kelp bed in Kagalaska Strait (between Adak and Kagalaska Islands), Aleutian Islands, Alaska. Flight altitude about 150 feet, air speed 120 knots; 6 April 1962. (KWK 62–35–19)

144

FIGURE 70.—Part of a group of 440 sea otters in Kujulik Bay on the south shore of the Alaska Peninsula. This was the largest group observed on the aerial surveys. Flight altitude 200 feet, air speed 120 knots; 10 April 1962. (KWK 62–39–13)

of animals were seen; most animals were scattered. Because it is easier to see a large group of animals than scattered individuals, we realized that, in our aerial surveys, we saw a greater proportion of the animals where populations were dense than where they were sparse. For this reason, a sliding scale based on numerous field observations was chosen to compute an estimate of total populations in various areas.

Otters counted	Estimation factor to obtain total
1-15	Estimate 50 percent were seen
16-100	Estimate 60 percent were seen
Over 100	Estimate 75 percent were seen

Aerial photography

Aerial photography is a useful censusing tool when views of animal concentrations may be obtained. A large majority of sea otters are scattered as individuals or gathered in small groups of 5 to 20 animals, which may be counted directly. Therefore we have used aerial photographs primarily to assist us in improving our technique of estimating occasional large concentrations of otters. The mean of 1962 and 1965 data listed below shows that the field estimates of large concentrations were 12 percent below the number counted on photographs. The 1965 field estimates, made after studying earlier results, however, averaged only about 2 percent below the counts from photographs. Relatively few groups as large as 100 animals were seen, therefore no general correction factor is applied to the field count, as this would not materially affect the overall estimate.

Date	Location	Field estimate	Photo count	Percent error in field estimate
6 Apr. 1962	Kagalaska Str.	150	157	−5. ⎱ −36.
10 Apr. 1962	Kujulik Bay	250	387	−35. ⎰
25 Apr. 1965	L. Tanaga I.	300	334	−11.0 ⎫
25 Apr. 1965	Umak I.	275	274	+0.4 ⎬ −2.
25 Apr. 1965	Box I.	450	440	+2.0 ⎭
Total		1,425	1,592	[1] 12.

[1] Average.

Surface surveys

Surface surveys were made in limited areas from an outboard motor-driven dory and by observers using binoculars and telescope from shore (Lensink, 1958; Kenyon and Spencer, 1960).

A review of observations of sea otters from 1933 through 1962 in many Alaska areas indicates that observations of numbers of animals made from the surface are generally less useful than aerial observations. When a local otter population is small, surface observers may miss the animals altogether. For example, on aerial surveys in 1959, 1962, and 1965 Spencer and I were able to count 8 to 10 otters in the vicinity of Samalga Island and Cape Sagak, Umnak Island. Reports from Aleut hunters at nearby Nikolski Village during the past 10 years indicate that this population, though small, is permanent. In 1961, R. Thomas and in 1963, G. Baines, fur seal research biologists, Bureau of Commercial Fisheries, visited Samalga. They each spent a 24-hour period on or near Samalga and looked specifically for sea otters. Neither saw otters or any indication on beaches that they were present.

Lensink (1958) counted otters in the Shuyak and Barren Islands in the summer of 1957, first from the surface and then from the air. The surface count was 211 otters. On an aerial survey of the same area he recorded 515 otters, indicating that at least 59 percent of the otters in an area may be missed on a surface survey. On the basis of these surveys, a correction factor of 60 percent is applied to certain surface counts that are discussed.

Area of habitat

Sea otter feeding habitat was ascertained to consist of waters

30 fathoms or less in depth (see Diving). Where population and distribution surveys were made, the area of available habitat was measured on U.S. Coast and Geodetic Survey charts. A modified acreage grid, 64 dots per square inch, was used to obtain measurements which were converted to square miles of available habitat. Estimates of populations (exclusive of pups carried by mothers) were applied to the square miles of habitat to obtain the population densities that are presented in the following discussion and tables.

The entire Aleutian Chain, waters adjacent to the Alaska Peninsula, the Sanak Islands and Sanak Reef area, the Sandman Reefs, and the Shumagin Islands were surveyed one or more times under good to excellent observation conditions during our comprehensive 1959, 1960, 1962, and 1965 surveys. During these surveys and those by other individuals in different Alaska areas, 17,964 (table 19) otters were observed. The highest count obtained in each area surveyed was used to obtain this total.

As the aerial surveys and surface studies proceeded, it became evident that the population of sea otters in the various geographically separated areas exhibited different stages of population development. For example, in the Rat and Delarof Islands a crowded population heavily exploited available food resources (see Food and Feeding Behavior), and in certain of the Andreanof Islands dense local populations were expanding into adjacent areas of vacant habitat. These observations are discussed in the perspective of available data from earlier observers under the geographical headings that follow.

The Near Islands

This Aleutian group (fig. 71), the western extremity of U.S. territory, is separated from Buldir, the westernmost of the Rat Islands by 55 miles of open water. Attu and Agattu are the largest islands but Shemya is today more important because of its airfield and military base. A small military base has been maintained on Attu since World War II. Early in the war, the native Aleut population was removed from Attu by the Japanese and was never reestablished there (Golodoff, 1966).

In the early years of sea otter exploitation, the Near Islands yielded many furs. The Alaska survey expedition of the U.S. Navy Department in 1932 searched for sea otters at Attu but found none. Information was received, however, that "the Chief of the Attu natives assured the commander of the expedition that there were a few [sea otters] at Agattu which would soon be gone because the Japanese come frequently to take them" (Hutchinson, 1935).

147

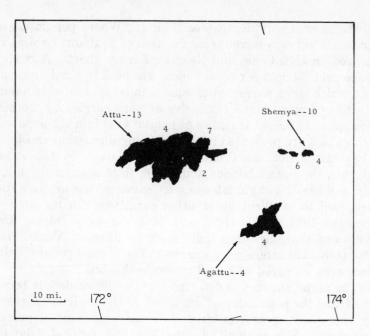

FIGURE 71.—The sea otter was exterminated from the Near Islands during the late 1800's or early 1900's. Probably because wide passes separate these islands from the heavily populated Rat Islands, it was not until July 1964 that the first authentic observations of otters were obtained in the Near Islands. Our aerial survey of 2 May 1965 revealed that at least 27 otters are now established there.

Whether the remnant population was exterminated before 1911, or by poaching in later years, is not known. Beals (1943) visited the Near Islands but was unable to find any clue that the sea otter existed there. That the aboriginal sea otter population of the Near Islands was in fact extirpated is beyond doubt.

In 1956, Refuge Manager R. D. Jones moved five otters to Attu from Amchitka on a U.S. Navy ship and liberated them. It is not known whether any of these survived. Before our 1959 aerial survey, no surface observer had reported seeing otters.

Our aerial survey of 19 May 1959 included all of the Near Islands and was conducted under excellent conditions. We made repeated sweeps to inspect areas appearing to offer ideal sea otter habitat but we saw no sea otters.

B. F. Jones, while a biologist with the Fisheries Research Institute, told me that on 12 June 1959 he sighted one otter one-fourth of a mile off Chirikof Point at the eastern extremity of Attu. An additional report from R. D. Jones (letter, 25 March 1964) states that a warrant officer stationed at Shemya "is convinced he has seen a sea otter several times" there. In July 1964, R. D. Jones (1965) saw eight otters in the Near Islands and obtained skeletal remains of another at Agattu. On an aerial survey, 2 May 1965, we saw 13 otters at Attu, 4 at Agattu, and 10 at Shemya. These observations indicate that the Near Islands population is now established. The Near Islands were probably repopulated by otters from the heavily populated Rat Islands. The statement by Nikolaev (1960) that "movements occur ... from the Commander to the Aleutian Islands" is not documented, and the present study indicates that such movement across 185 miles of open sea is improbable.

The Rat Islands

The Rat Islands (fig. 72) extend 160 miles from Buldir eastward to Semisopochnoi. During World War II large military installations existed on Kiska and Amchitka, with small outposts on several other islands. Since about 1948 none of these was occupied, except for brief and intermittent military occupation of Amchitka, par-

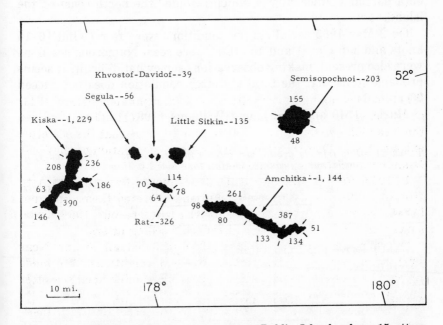

FIGURE 72.—The Rat Islands group, except Buldir Island, where 15 otters were recorded. The aerial survey was conducted on 2 and 3 May 1965 under good to excellent survey conditions. The numbers near the islands indicate the approximate distribution of the 3,147 otters that were observed.

ticularly in 1964 and 1965, and present day Defense Department–Atomic Energy Commission weapons testing activity.

The Rat Islands are noteworthy because it was at Amchitka Island that the first indication of substantial recovery of a sea otter population was noted in 1935. An aerial survey covering all of the Rat Islands was conducted in 1959. Attempts to repeat the survey in 1962 failed because of prolonged harsh weather, but a successful survey was made 2 May 1965. The survey data are recorded in table 21.

Individual islands from which data of particular interest are available are discussed below.

Buldir Island.—This island is 55 miles west of Kiska and is the most isolated of the Rat Islands group. Apparently, for this reason it was the last to be repopulated. No otters were seen during an aerial survey 19 May 1959, but this survey was unsatisfactory because of poor weather conditions (wind and fog). The first modern report of sea otters at Buldir was made by R. D. Jones (1963). He saw an adult male and three females with young there during a visit, 25–28 June 1962. In 1963, between 7 and 19 July, our party recorded five mothers with young and four lone adults on a partial surface survey which included the north coast of the island.

On 2 May 1965 aerial survey conditions were fair (wind 10–15 knots and sun glare) and 15 otters were seen. Numerous sea lions were also present, making observations somewhat difficult. It seems probable to us that the total sea otter population does not exceed 30 animals.

Murie (1940 and 1959), and Williams (1937) did not find sea

TABLE 21.—*Rat Islands group, sea otter population density, estimated from aerial survey counts, 19 May 1959 and 2–3 May 1965*

Island	Otters counted		Estimated total		Square miles of habitat [1]	Otters estimated per square mile	
	1959	1965	1959	1965		1959	1965
Buldir [2]	—	15	—	30	13	—	2
Kiska, L. Kiska, Tanadak I. and Pass	1,127	1,229	1,503	1,652	78	19	21
Segula	47	56	63	75	7	9	11
Pyramid, Davidof, Khvostov	33	39	44	52	8	5	7
Little Sitkin	50	135	66	180	15	4	12
Rat	270	326	360	435	30	12	15
Amchitka	1,560	1,144	2,078	1,525	110	19	14
Semisopochnoi	393	203	524	271	32	16	8
Total	3,480	3,147	4,638	4,220	293	12	11

[1] Square nautical miles of water 30 fathoms or less in depth.
[2] At Buldir Island in July of 1963, 9 otters were counted from the surface along 4 miles of the 10-mile shoreline. The estimated total in that year was 25 otters.

otters at Buldir. The present breeding population probably became established there in recent years. This fact is important because the sea otters must have crossed 55 miles of open water to reach Buldir from Kiska. Buldir reef, a 20-mile strip of relatively shallow water, extends 20 miles west of Kiska to 15 miles east of Buldir. It offers depths of less than 30 fathoms where food might be found en route, and otters were seen in this area on 27 May 1959 (A. C. Hartt, letter, 1960).

The observed absence of sea otters at Buldir after intensive exploitation ended in 1911, and their reappearance there in 1962, furnishes another example that, given time, sea otters will find their way from one island group to another across broad expanses of deep open water.

Rat Island.—The available observations of numbers of sea otters at Rat Island are listed in table 22. These data indicate that population changes at Rat Island followed a pattern similar to the changes observed at Amchitka during the same period and in more recent years in the Andreanof Islands. No observations are available from Rat Island to indicate that population reduction there was caused by mortality. Presumably, though, as was observed at Amchitka, mortality at Rat Island caused population reduction from a high of 31 otters per square mile of habitat to 12 to 15 per square mile in recent years.

Amchitka Island.—A number of surface and aerial counts and estimates of the Amchitka sea otter population have been made since 1935. Estimates of the total population, because of the variety of methods used in obtaining the basic field data, are approximations and are given to represent an order of magnitude. That these approximations are within reasonable limits is indicated by the fact that they reveal a history of population growth, decline, and stabilization (with annual fluctuations) that is typical of animals when a "seed population" is given complete protection in ideal vacant habitat.

The first observation of significant recovery of a sea otter popu-

TABLE 22.—*Rat Island sea otter population density in 30 square miles of feeding habitat*

Year	Count	Estimate of total	Otters per square mile	Authority and survey method [1]
1943	705	[2] 940	31	F. Beals and G. T. Joynt, aerial count-estimate.
1949	234	312	10	R. D. Jones, aerial survey.
1959	270	360	12	Spencer-Kenyon, aerial survey.
1965	326	435	15	Spencer-Kenyon, aerial survey.

[1] All unpublished reports in U.S. Fish and Wildlife Service files.
[2] Estimate based on the assumption that 75 percent of the otters were recorded.

lation was reported at Amchitka Island by Lt. H. B. Hutchinson, U.S.N., Commander, Aleutian Islands Survey Expedition, in a memorandum of 21 June 1935. The investigation by Naval personnel at Amchitka was in response to a request by the U.S. Department of the Interior. Hutchinson (1935) stated "there are more than one thousand (1,000) adult animals and half that number of pups on the waters surrounding the island." Possible poaching of sea otters by the Japanese was suspected when a vessel believed to be the *Hakyuo Maru* was observed attempting to enter Constantine Harbor, Amchitka Island, on 24 June 1935 (Hutchinson, 1935).

Also, unidentified men were seen on the island in August 1936 (Swicegood, 1936). Accordingly, buildings were erected on Amchitka by the U.S. Bureau of Fisheries in July 1937 (U.S. Bureau of Fisheries, 1938). Sea otter wardens were stationed there intermittently during parts of each year from 1937 through 1940.

During World War II, specific observations of sea otters were recorded by G. T. Joynt (1957) and Beals (1943). Beginning in 1949, many observations were obtained from Amchitka. Selected population counts and estimates that were made are shown in table 23. Other estimates not based on field counts are omitted.

The tendency of a sea otter population to expand to new areas primarily at the periphery of a dense population is illustrated by observations from Amchitka.

Lt. Cdr. S. P. Swicegood (1936), commanding officer of the *Chelan*, conducted field counts of otters at Amchitka on 14–16 August 1936. Although 804 otters were counted along 24 miles of the Pacific coast of the island, only 10 were seen on the Bering Sea coast. A similar condition was observed in the summer of 1937 when C. L. Loy and O. A. Friden (1937) counted 1,241 otters along the Pacific coast of Amchitka and only 80 along the Bering Sea coast. The aerial count by Beals (1943) when he recorded 2,198 otters along the Pacific coast and 1,219 along the Bering Sea coast indicates that between 1937 and 1943 a movement of otters from the Pacific to the Bering Sea coast of the island occurred, probably because the large Pacific coast population caused food depletion along that side of the island.

A review of the field counts at Amchitka between 1936 and 1965, summarized in table 23, demonstrate that a dense population existed on the south side of the island in 1936 (42 otters per square mile) while a sparse one (3 otters per square mile) occupied the north side. Emigration was not rapid but it was appreciable by the year 1939 (south side 40 otters per square mile, north side 14

TABLE 23.—*Amchitka Island sea otter population density in 110 square miles of feeding habitat*

[Only the counts that included all or substantial areas of Amchitka are included. Area measurements from USGCS charts show 72 square miles of feeding habitat on the Pacific (south side) and 38 square miles on the Bering Sea (north side) of Amchitka. Habitat is considered to be water 30 fathoms or less in depth]

Year	Counts			Estimates			Otters per square mile			Authority and survey method
	North side	South side	Total	North side	South side	Total	North side	South side	Total	
1936	10	804	814	[1]100	3,000	3,100	3	42	28	Swicegood (1936)[2]
1937	80	1,241	1,321	[3]200	3,102	3,302	5	43	30	Loy and Friden (1937)[2]
1939	217	1,138	1,355	[3]542	2,845	3,387	14	42	31	Loy (1940)[2]
1943	1,219	2,198	3,417	[4]1,625	2,931	4,556	43	41	41	Beals (1943)[5]
1949	528	559	1,087	704	745	1,449	19	10	13	Jones (1949)[5]
1959	537	1,023	1,560	716	1,364	2,080	19	19	19	Kenyon and Spencer (1959)[5]
1965	720	424	1,144	960	560	1,520	25	8	14	Kenyon and Spencer (1965)[5]

[1] Estimates made by Swicegood on the basis of counts made along 24 miles of coast and other observations at Amchitka.

[2] Surface surveys.

[3] The estimate given by Loy and Friden in 1937 was 1,760, and by Loy in 1939 was 1,700. Both estimates are given above on the assumption that about 60 percent of the otters are not seen on a surface survey (Lensink, 1958).

[4] Beals did not give a calculated estimate of the totals. This estimate, like other aerial surveys is based on the assumption that about 75 percent of the otters present were recorded.

[5] Aerial survey.

otters per square mile). By 1943 the population density was high on both north and south sides of the island but nearly equal (43 and 41 otters, respectively, per square mile). The difference observed in 1949 (10 otters per square mile of habitat on the south side of the island and 19 on the north side) probably resulted from mortality and emigration caused by depletion of food species that must have occurred in earlier years when the population on the south exposure was very dense (42 otters per square mile). By 1959 the population reached a condition of relative equilibrium with the population evenly distributed (19 otters per square mile) on both north and south shores of the island (fig. 73). By 1965 considerable divergence again occurred, the density on the north side increasing to 25 otters per square mile and on the south side decreasing to 8. Additional detailed studies over a period of years will be necessary to understand the observed population fluctuations. It is possible that significant numbers of otters might move across Oglala Pass to Rat Island.

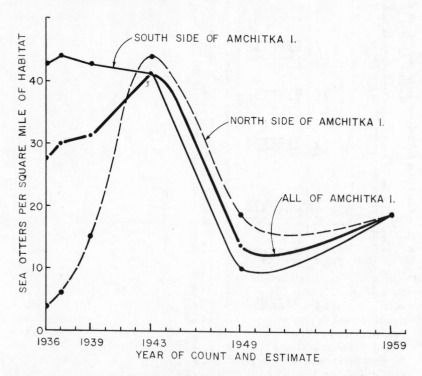

FIGURE 73.—Changes in population density on the north and south coasts of Amchitka Island, 1936–59. Estimates of the population density are based on field counts (see table 23).

Available information indicates that in the 1909–11 period the Amchitka sea otter population may have numbered about 100 animals (fig. 74), and that this population reached maximum size of about 4,500 otters in the early 1940's and then "crashed" to about 1,500 animals by 1949. A gradual increase to about 2,000 otters apparently occurred between 1949 and 1959, but mortality in the winter-spring period of environmental stress caused the population to stabilize or possibly to decrease in the early 1960's.

A curve based on field counts and population estimates is shown in figures 73 and 74. An estimated rate of increase of 10 percent

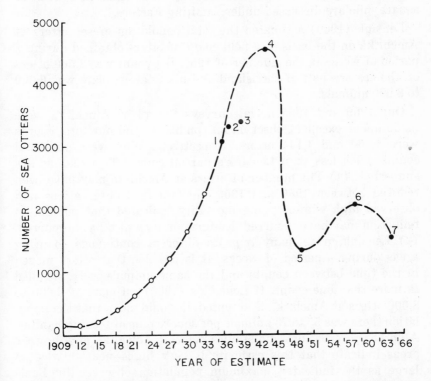

FIGURE 74.—Estimated curve of the Amchitka sea otter population, 1909–65. No data are available before 1936. The curve from 1909 to 1936 is a projection back from the estimated 1936 population, assuming that the population increased in this period at an exponential rate of 10 percent per year (see section on Seguam Island). Point 1: Population estimate by Swicegood (1936) based on extensive surface counts and observations. Points 2 and 3: Population estimates based on the surface counts of Loy and Friden (1937) and Loy (1940). Point 4: Estimate based on aerial count by Beals (1943). Point 5: Estimate based on aerial count by Jones (1949). Points 6 and 7: Estimate based on aerial counts by Kenyon and Spencer (1960) and Kenyon (1965).

per year in early stages of growth (fig. 74) is based on the observed growth rate in a part of the Andreanof Islands (Seguam Island) where conditions seemed similar to the Amchitka area. The field counts of otters by Loy and Friden (1937) and Loy (1940) are projected to estimated totals on the basis of Lensink's (1958) data indicating that about 60 percent of the otters present may not be seen on a surface survey. These estimated totals assume logical positions (Points 2 and 3) on the curve between the estimated totals of Swicegood (1936), Point 1, and Beals (1943), Point 4. The observations of mortality which occurred after the Amchitka population reached a density of at least 42 otters per square mile are discussed under Limiting Factors.

Lensink (1960) estimated the total population of sea otters at Amchitka on the basis of a field count of otters obtained during a period of weeks in the summer of 1956. His count was 2,568 otters on the eastern half of the island and his total estimate was 6,000 to 8,000 animals.

Our 1959 and 1965 aerial surveys for all of Amchitka were made under excellent observation conditions and our total counts were 1,560 and 1,144 otters, respectively. Why were our total counts much less than Lensink's partial count? Two reasons are suggested: (1) The number of otters at Amchitka may have been reduced between 1956 and 1959. General field observations and observed high winter-spring mortality indicated that population reduction may have occurred. Emigration may also have occurred. (2) Lensink made many trips to different contiguous counting areas during a period of weeks. It is possible that otters moved in the time between counts and the same animals were included in more than one count. If Lensink's (1960) estimate of 6,000 to 8,000 otters at Amchitka is accepted, it would mean that the population there was 55 to 73 animals per square mile of feeding habitat. All other observations and studies made at Amchitka and in other areas indicate that this estimate is very high—nearly twice as large as the indicated maximum population observed by Beals (1943).

In summary, our studies conducted since 1955 and intermittent surveys made since 1935 have indicated that the sea otter population on Amchitka Island grew to a large size, causing overutilization of food resources during the mid-1940's. Population reduction through starvation was then observed and a fluctuating population in balance with the habitat resulted.

It was not surprising, therefore, that our 1965 observation of 1,144 otters at Amchitka was less than our 1959 tally of 1,560, a reduction of 416 animals, or 27 percent. It is interesting to note that during the interval between surveys 637 otters were taken, either by the Alaska Department of Game for their pelts (502 in number) or by the Fish and Wildlife Service for research. Apparently reproduction during the 1959–65 period compensated only partially for the natural and artificial mortality that occurred. It may be concluded that either the habitat limited the otter population below the 1959 level, or the slow rate of reproduction prevented compensatory population growth.

A summary of the probable history of the rise and fall of the Amchitka sea otter population, as deduced from field studies at Amchitka and by analogy with observed rates of growth in other populations, is given below:

1. The 1911 population of otters, at Amchitka, was about 100 animals.

2. At a rate of growth of about 10 percent per year, this population increased to about 3,000 animals in 1935.

3. In the 1935–43 period, the south side of the island was overpopulated and otters moved to the north side. The rate of increase decreased because of mortality caused by overuse of food resources.

4. By 1943 both the north and south shores were crowded by a total population of over 4,000 otters (more than 40 otters per square mile of habitat) and mortality increased.

5. By 1949 field observations indicated that the population had crashed to less than one-third of its 1940–43 maximum. Mortality rather than emigration apparently accounted for much of the decline.

6. Since about 1949 high mortality annually among juveniles and old adults in the late-winter, early-spring season of stress has caused the population to fluctuate within the range of about 1,500 and 2,500 animals (exclusive of dependent young).

Semisopochnoi.—Available information indicates that the sea otter was exterminated at Semisopochnoi during the pre-1911 period of unregulated exploitation. They were vulnerable to hunters because the island is relatively small, the band of feeding habitat along the shore is narrow, and there are no offshore reefs.

No mention is made that sea otters were seen there during the 1936–38 expeditions by Murie (1959) and his assistants. V. B. Scheffer told me in 1964 that sea otters were not seen when he landed on Semisopochnoi on 4 July 1937.

Beals (1943), speaking of military pilots who developed much interest in the distribution and abundance of sea otters while stationed on Amchitka, says "These same pilots have made many scouting flights around Semisopochnoi Island and report that they have never seen sea otters in that vicinity."

On the aerial survey of 19 May 1959, when observation conditions were excellent, we saw 393 otters (16 per square mile of habitat) at Semisopochnoi Island. It thus appears that the animals moved from Amchitka across nearly 30 miles of open water to this island after 1943, when the Amchitka population approached maximum size and population pressure stimulated emigration. By 1965, the population at Semisopochnoi had decreased to an estimated 8 otters per square mile of habitat (table 21).

Delarof Islands

This small group (fig. 75) is technically part of the Andreanof group (U.S. Board on Geographic Names, 1963), but is treated as a separate unit here. The group includes a distance of about 33 miles from east to west and is separated from Tanaga Island

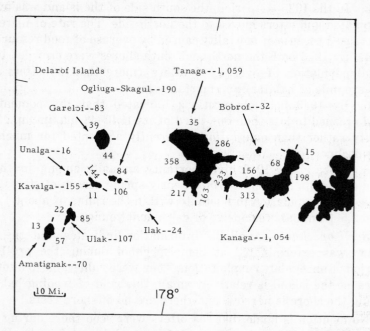

FIGURE 75.—The Delarof Islands of the western Andreanof Islands were apparently among the few Aleutian areas where the sea otter remained in 1911 when it was given protection. A large population developed here and at Kanaga and Tanaga Islands by the late 1940's, but population pressure did not cause repopulation of nearby Adak until the mid-1950's. The number of otters observed on aerial surveys of 2 and 3 May 1965, as shown on this map, was 2,790.

on the east by 14-mile-wide Tanaga Pass and from the Rat Islands on the west by 50-mile-wide Amchitka Pass. The Delarofs have no human inhabitants.

Murie (1940) found a thriving sea otter population at Ogliuga in 1936. Joynt (1957) says of his 1943 aerial observations that—

The most densely grouped of any pod of sea otter observed was on one end of the sand bars exposed at half tide that lies between Kavalga Island and Ogliuga Island in the Delarof Islands group.

Data from the 1930's, as cited above, indicate that the Delarof and Rat Islands populations approached maximum size at about the same time. Because of the width of Amchitka Pass (50 miles), it appears probable, as pointed out by Lensink (1960), that remnant populations remained in 1911 in both the Rat and Delarof Island groups. The habitat at Amchitka and in the Ogliuga-Kavalga Islands areas, is similar in having extensive shallows dotted by submerged or partially submerged reefs. Although these offered feeding habitat and a place of refuge to the sea otter, they presented considerable hazard to early sea otter hunters and were probably instrumental in preserving the species.

On 26 May 1959, our aerial observations (table 24) revealed that the number of otters per square mile of habitat in the Delarofs was the highest of any island group that we surveyed. This condition is of particular interest because the Delarofs were among the first Aleutian islands to be repopulated. By May 1965, our observations indicated that the Delarof population had dropped by approximately 50 percent (table 24).

It may be postulated that after the population peak, which probably occurred in the 1930–40 period, emigration to Tanaga

TABLE 24.—*Delarof Islands sea otter population density estimated from aerial survey counts of 26 May 1959 and 2–3 May 1965*

Island	Otters counted		Estimated total		Square miles of habitat [1]	Otters estimated per square mile	
	1959	1965	1959	1965		1959	1965
Gareloi	41	83	68	111	9	8	12
Unalga	51	16	85	27	8	10	3
Kavalga	275	155	367 ⎫	207 ⎫			
Ogliuga	112	144	149 ⎪	192 ⎪			
Skugul-Tag-Ugidak	281	46	375 ⎬ [2]1,152	77 ⎬ 529	52	22	10
Gramp Rock	134 ⎫ 32		179 ⎪	53 ⎫			
Ilak	49 ⎭		82 ⎭				
Ulak	352	107	469 ⎫ [2]605	143 ⎫ 260	20	30	13
Amatignak	102	70	136 ⎭	117 ⎭			
Total	1,397	653	1,910	927	89	Av. 21	10

[1] Includes water of 30 fathoms or less in depth as measured from U.S. Coast and Geodetic Survey charts.
[2] Closely associated islets and islands.

took place. After the Tanaga population exceeded the carrying capacity of the available habitat, otters moved westward to the Delarofs again as well as eastward to Kanaga and Adak. Thus, we observed a second population peak in the Delarofs in 1959. This resulted in food depletion and a subsequent "population crash" bringing the population density from 21 down to about 10 otters per square mile by May 1965 (table 24). Whether oil from the San Patrick, which was wrecked on the south shore of Ulak Island during the winter of 1964–65, was a factor in population reduction is not known.

Andreanof Islands

The Andreanof Islands (figs. 76 and 77) (excluding the Delarof group) extend for a latitudinal distance of about 230 miles from Tanaga on the west to Seguam on the east. Human populations in this group are at the U.S. Naval Station on Adak, and Atka

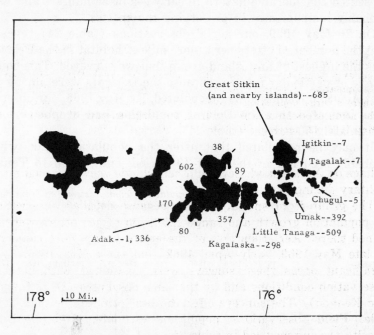

FIGURE 76.—The Adak–Great Sitkin Island areas in the central Andreanofs were repopulated during the 1950's and early 1960's by otters from the Delarof and Kanaga and Tanaga Islands. No otters were found on a survey of Adak in 1952, but on an aerial survey in 1954 a count of 48 was obtained, and by 1965 the count increased to 1,336. On aerial surveys of 25 and 26 April 1965, 3,239 otters were observed in the area shown.

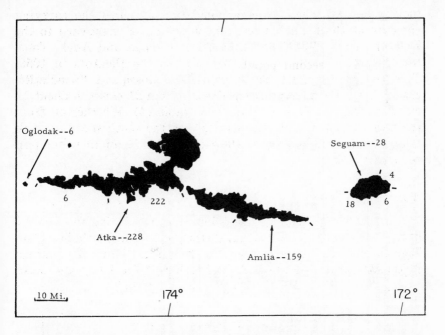

FIGURE 77.—The colonies on the southern exposures of Atka and Amlia Islands, in the eastern Andreanof Islands, appear to be augmented from the large population in the central Andreanofs (Adak–Great Sitkin area). Repopulation is proceeding at Atka and Amlia as it did at Amchitka, where a large population developed on the south side of the island before the north exposure was repopulated. On aerial surveys of 21 April and 6 May 1965, 421 otters were observed in the area shown.

Village on Atka Island. Several other islands were occupied by the military during World War II.

The group is of special interest because detailed observations on population growth and range extension of sea otters were obtained there. Aerial surveys of the entire group were conducted in late May 1959, early April 1962, and early May 1965. In all significant areas these surveys were conducted with excellent observation conditions and by the same observers (D. L. Spencer and Kenyon). The surveys offer the best comparable data available. Field observations, population estimates, and population density are summarized in table 25.

Analyses of observed population growth and of population fluctuations are presented for individual islands on the following pages and a discussion of the group as a unit is presented below.

The sea otter populations at islands from Tanaga on the west to Seguam on the east (exclusive of Bobrof Island, which is small

161

TABLE 25.—*Andreanof Islands counts and estimates of sea otters obtained on three aerial surveys to show movements of otters*

[Surveys were made on 25–27 May 1959, 5–6 April 1962, and 19 April to 8 May 1965. The islands are listed in geographical sequence, top to bottom from west to east. Counts made at small islets closely associated with large ones are combined with the count for the large island].

Island	Otters counted			Otters estimated			Square miles of habitat	Otters per square mile of habitat		
	1959	1962	1965	1959	1962	1965		1959	1962	1965
Tanaga	902	898	1,059	1,203	1,197	1,412	83	14	14	17
Bobrof [1]	57	—	32	76	—	53	2	38	—	26
Kanaga	1,822	846	1,054	2,429	1,128	1,405	95	26	12	15
Adak	1,718	2,260	1,336	2,291	3,013	1,781	75	31	40	24
Kagalaska	1	251	298	1	335	397	15	<1	22	26
Little Tanaga	0	214	509	0	285	679	22	0	13	31
Umak	0	94	392	0	157	523	9	0	17	58
Anagaksik	0	14	0	0	28	0	1	0	28	0
Great Sitkin [2]	33	325	710	44	433	947	80	<1	5	12
Atka	0	50	228	0	83	304	200	<1	<1	1.5
Kasatochi	0	0	[3]NS	0	0	—	5	0	0	—
Koniuji	0	0	NS	0	0	—	1	0	0	—
Amlia	83	91	159	111	152	212	150	<1	1	1.4
Seguam	14	23	28	28	38	47	28	1	1	2
Total	[4]4,630	5,066	5,805	[4]6,183	6,849	[4]7,760	766			

[1] Bobrof is a small island and was not surveyed in 1962. It is omitted frorm certain calculations based on this table.

[2] In addition to Great Sitkin the counts made at 12 small islands from north of Umak to Atka are included.

[3] NS = no survey was conducted.

[4] When Bobrof Island is excluded the total becomes 6,107 in 1959 and 7,707 in 1965.

and was not surveyed in 1962) increased from 6,107 otters in 1959 to 6,849 in 1962 (table 25), a gain of 742 otters or 12.1 percent in 3 years. In the next 3-year period (1962–65) the same area gained 858 otters (7,707 minus 6,849, table 25) or 12.5 percent.

Within the Andreanofs, emigration occurred when islands became densely populated. For example, the Kanaga population lost 1,301 otters (2,429 minus 1,128, table 25) between 1959 and 1962, while nearby islands (Adak, Kagalaska, Little Tanaga, Umak, Anagaksik, Great Sitkin, and adjacent islets) increased from 2,292 to 4,269 (table 25), a gain of 1,977 otters or 86 percent. Because immigrating otters may have moved into the available vacant habitat surrounding the above named islands from Tanaga as well as Kanaga, it is not possible to separate the increase representing reproduction from that caused by immigration in these areas. The conclusion is indicated that in the Andreanofs the total sea otter population may grow at a rate of about 4 to 5 percent per year and that in the 1975 to 1980 period the population there may number over 12,000 otters or about 14 animals per square mile of habitat.

Tanaga Island.—The repopulation of Tanaga Island appears to have been well underway by the mid-1930's. Williams (1937) mentions it along with Amchitka and Ogliuga as being one of the "most productive" islands. D. Hooper (*in* Jones, 1953) indicated that the otter population there was large in 1953. Until our aerial surveys, no comprehensive quantitative assessment of the otter population at Tanaga was made. Available population data are summarized in table 26.

The few observations available indicate that population overflow from the Delarof Islands repopulated Tanaga during the 1930's, and that during the late 1940's or early 1950's the local population reached maximum size. During the mid- or late-1950's, the population density probably became reduced through emigration to Kanaga Island and remained stabilized from 1959 to 1962 at about 14 otters per square mile of habitat. The increase to about 17

TABLE 26.—*Tanaga Island sea otter population density in 83 square miles of feeding habitat*

Year	Count	Estimate of total	Otters per square mile	Authority and survey method
1937	(?)	150+	2	O. J. Murie and V. B. Scheffer, surface survey.
1953	1,000 (ca.)	1,000+	12+	D. Hooper, surface survey (*in* Lensink, 1960).
1959	902	1,203	14	Spencer and Kenyon, aerial survey.
1962	898	1,197	14	Spencer and Kenyon, aerial survey.
1965	1,059	1,412	17	Spencer and Kenyon, aerial survey.

otters per square mile in 1965 may have resulted from emigration from densely populated Kanaga.

Kanaga Island.—The Murie expedition visited Kanaga in 1936 and Williams (1937) states that no sea otters were seen. Natives reported to him, however, that otters did "occur occasionally or sparingly" there. By 1943, Kanaga was apparently only sparsely repopulated. Joynt (1957) says that in 1943:

A few stray animals were observed along the south shore of Kanaga but I do not recall ever observing more than 6 or 8 animals on the three or four flights over this area.

By 1953 the population had increased greatly. In June of that year D. Hooper (*in* Jones, 1953) spent 21 days on Kanaga. He walked 40 miles of beach and counted 575 otters. After examining a number of inshore areas at Tanaga he estimated that the otter populations of Kanaga and Tanaga Islands were large, "probably numbering several thousand" animals.

Data obtained on the 1959 and 1962 aerial surveys indicate that the Kanaga population was near maximum size in 1959. The precipitous population drop from an observed total of 1,822 otters in 1959 to 846 in 1962 indicates that the estimated 1959 population of 26 otters per square mile of available feeding habitat may have depleted food resources and precipitated substantial emigration (and mortality?) during the elapsed 3-year period. By 1965 a slight increase, probably resulting from crowding at nearby Adak, had occurred (table 27).

On a dory survey in 1957 along a 19-mile sample of coast, Lensink (1960) recorded 566 otters. Along the same coastal sample on our 1959 aerial survey we recorded 549 otters and in 1962 the aerial count there was 404. The similarity of the 1957 surface

TABLE 27.—*Kanaga Island sea otter population density in 95 square miles of feeding habitat*

Year	Count	Estimate of total	Otters per square mile	Authority and survey method
1943	6–8	few	(?)	G. T. Joynt (1957) flew repeatedly over area.
1953	575	many	(?)	D. Hooper (*in* Jones, 1953) walked 40 miles of beach and counted otters.
1957	566	[1] 3,000–5,000	32–53	C. J. Lensink (1960), dory survey along 19 miles of coast.
1959	1,822	2,429	26	Spencer and Kenyon, aerial survey, entire island.
1962	846	1,128	12	Spencer and Kenyon, aerial survey, entire island.
1965	1,054	1,405	15	Spencer and Kenyon, aerial survey, entire island.

[1] Because this estimate was made from data gathered along the south shore, where more habitat is available than along the north shore, the estimated upper limit may be somewhat high.

and 1959 aerial observations indicate that the total populations in these two years were at least similar, or perhaps larger in 1957, since aerial counts usually include a higher percentage of animals present. The number of otters seen along different parts of the coast on aerial surveys when correlated with the distribution of available feeding habitat around the island, indicate that the distribution of otters along the shores of the entire island varies according to the amount of habitat available.

The coastal zone of sea otter habitat is narrow along much of the north shore of Kanaga. In 1959, along 30 miles of the north shore, we observed 415 otters (14 otters per mile of coast), while along 45 miles of the mostly southern and eastern coast, where the habitat zone is wider, we recorded 1,407 otters (31 per mile of coast).

These data suggest that Lensink's (1960) "somewhat conservative" estimate of 3,000 to 5,000 otters at Kanaga (32 to 53 otters per square mile of feeding habitat) based on his sample count along the south shore may have been quite realistic (table 27).

Adak Island.—The U.S. Naval Station, Adak, was established in the early 1940's. It remains today the most important center of human population in the Aleutian Islands and furnished facilities for sea otter studies in the outer Aleutian area.

The Murie expeditions did not find sea otters at Adak and obtained no information from natives that they were observed there in recent years (Williams, 1937).

Although 14 otters were seen in 7-mile-wide Adak Strait between Kanaga and Adak in 1943 (Lensink, 1960), few if any crossed the strait and became established at Adak during the 1940's.

When I visited Adak on 31 October to 5 November 1947, I saw no sea otters and could find no report of an observation there. Neither did R. D. Jones see any otters (table 28) on a complete circuit of Adak by dory in 1952. The first indication that sea otters had become established at Adak was an observation of 48 animals during an aerial survey in 1954 by Lensink (1960).

The influx of otters that began from Kanaga to Adak in the early 1950's proceeded rapidly and was documented during the 1959 and 1962 aerial surveys. It appears that emigration from Kanaga (26 otters per square mile in 1959) to Adak (31 otters per square mile in 1959) continued during this period and that a large population at Kanaga during a period of years had depleted food resources there. Adak, on the other hand, was repopulated only recently (in 1959) and serious food depletion did not occur until the

TABLE 28.—*Adak Island sea otter population density in 75 square miles of feeding habitat*

Year	Count	Estimate of total	Otters per square mile	Authority and survey method
1947	0	0	0	Kenyon field notes. No otters seen or reported seen.
1951	0	0	0	R. D. Jones, surface survey, west side only.
1952	0	0	0	R. D. Jones, surface survey entire island.
1954	48	80	1	C. J. Lensink (1960), air survey. All otters seen on west side of island.
1954	1	—	—	R. D. Jones. First recorded sighting at Adak Naval Station, on east side of island.
1957	399	997	13	C. J. Lensink (1960) and R. D. Jones, surface survey. Most otters on west side of island.
1959	1,718	2,291	31	Spencer and Kenyon, aerial survey.
1962	2,260	3,013	40	Spencer and Kenyon, aerial survey.
1965	1,336	1,781	24	Spencer and Kenyon, aerial survey.

1962–65 period. All available observations are listed in tables 27 and 28.

Kagalaska Island.—Kagalaska is uninhabited by man. Most of the island is precipitous. Although its coastline is about 35 miles long, the band of shallow water surrounding it and offering sea otter feeding habitats is relatively narrow. As at nearby Adak, sea otters were apparently exterminated at Kagalaska before 1911.

On the 1959 aerial survey we recorded one otter there. Between then and the 1962 survey the influx from nearby Adak was rapid and had apparently passed its peak in 1965 (table 29 and fig. 78).

Atka Island.—The village of Atka is the farthest west location of a small Aleut population today. The village is on Nazan Bay near the eastern end of the 55-mile long island.

Both R. D. Jones and I were told repeatedly by Aleuts living at Atka that during the 1940's sea otters were occasionally seen at Vasilief Bay near the east end of Atka. The 1959, 1962, and 1965 aerial surveys confirmed that a small and growing sea otter colony is resident in this area (table 25).

Vasilief Bay offers ideal sea otter habitat. The main body of the bay is dotted with rocks and islets. Numerous channels among them and irregular shores offer many areas that are sheltered

TABLE 29.—*Kagalaska Island sea otter population density in 15 square miles of feeding habitat*

Year	Count	Estimate of total	Otters per square mile	Authority and survey method
1954	0	0	0	Lensink, aerial survey.
1959	1	2+	<1	Spencer and Kenyon, aerial survey.
1962	251	335	22	Spencer and Kenyon, aerial survey.
1965	298	397	26	Spencer and Kenyon, aerial survey.

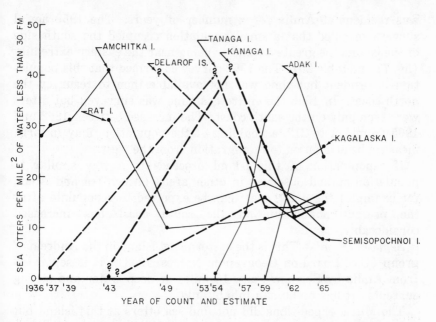

FIGURE 78.—Populations of sea otters at several Aleutian Islands have increased to maximum size and then crashed between 1936 and 1965. Estimates of otters per square mile of habitat (waters within the 30-fathom curve), which are based on extensive field counts, are shown as dots which are connected by solid lines. Observations of "few," or "many," or "thousands" are shown by question marks and connected by broken lines. (For data, see tables 21–29.) Population peaks apparently occurred between aerial surveys at Adak and Kagalaska Islands.

from wind and rough water in storms. This habitat apparently attracted the occasional otter that wandered eastward from the large population in the western Andreanofs, causing the colony to form and to be augmented by further immigration. In the 1959 to 1962 period, the colony increased by 86 percent and between 1962 and 1965 by 375 percent. Repopulation of the north side of Atka had not begun in 1965.

Amlia Island.—It is 40 miles long, has no human inhabitants and except near the west end is seldom visited by the Aleutian natives of nearby Atka Village. The U.S. Coast and Geodetic Survey has not as yet (1965) issued a chart showing soundings of Amlia's inshore waters. The area of sea otter feeding habitat (table 25) was estimated on the basis of measurements taken at Atka because the two islands appear similar.

Vague reports that I received from the hunters of Atka during the 1940's and 1950's indicated that a small number of sea otters was resident at Amlia for a number of years. The 1959 aerial surveys revealed that a small population occupied the south side of the island, the greatest number being near the eastern extremity (fig. 77 and table 25). The 1962 survey confirmed that this population is resident but time was not available then to resurvey the north coast. In 1965 the entire coastline was surveyed but otters were seen only on the south coast. The increase between 1962 and 1965 from 111 to 212, a doubling of the population, may in large measure be attributed to immigration from the west.

If repopulation of this island proceeds in a way similar to population spread observed in other areas (Amchitka and Adak, for example) the north coast can be expected to repopulate after the present population on the south coast has increased considerably.

Seguam Island.—This is the easternmost island in the Andreanof group (U.S. Board on Geographic Names, 1963). It is separated from Amlia by Seguam Pass, 16 miles of deep water and strong currents. It has no human inhabitants.

The Murie expeditions did not find sea otters at this island but information from Aleutian natives indicated that otters had been seen there (Williams, 1937). The first specific evidence that sea otters occupied Seguam was found on our 1959 aerial survey. The 1962 and 1965 surveys confirmed that the small population is resident and is growing slowly. An increase of approximately 10 percent per year (from 28 to 47 otters in 6 years) may represent the rate of increase due to reproduction in an isolated, uncrowded population.

Because the population today is so small (table 25), it seems unlikely that otters survived the period of unregulated exploitation in this location. It appears more probable that wanderers from the larger populations in the west reached Seguam in recent years and remained there either because the habitat is desirable or because the width of Amukta Pass discouraged emigration to the Islands of Four Mountains. The relatively slow rate of increase, however, indicates that immigration is, as yet, not appreciable at this rather isolated location.

Islands of the Four Mountains

From Amukta Island northeastward to Kagamil Island on Samalga Pass is about 70 miles. There is no human population in this island group, therefore few surface observations are available. The survey of 3 March 1960 covered all coastlines and was made under excellent conditions. On 7 April 1962, survey conditions were fair and only about 50 percent of the coastline of each of the main islands was surveyed. On neither survey were otters seen. It is probable that no sea otters occupy this group at present.

The available sea otter habitat around the seven steep-sided islands in this group is 88 square miles. When compared with Gareloi, a similar island having a sea otter population of 8 otters per square mile of habitat, the estimated future population in the Islands of Four Mountains may be about 700 otters.

Fox Islands

This group (figs. 79 and 80) includes the islands in the 240-mile sector of the Aleutians between Samalga Pass and Isanotski Pass at the western extremity of the Alaska Peninsula. Amak Island, off the north coast of the Alaska Peninsula, although not one of the Fox Islands, is included in this discussion because of its proximity to Unimak Island.

Among the Fox Islands at present there are two small, widely

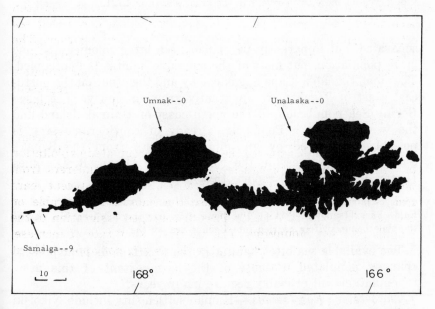

FIGURES 79.—The colony at Samalga Island and in the vicinity of Cape Sagak, Umnak Island, at the western extremity of the Fox Islands, is a small but permanent one. Otters were observed there during aerial surveys in 1960 (6), 1962 (10) and, as shown on the map, in 1965. This is the most isolated Aleutian colony. Complete surveys of Umnak and Unalaska Islands were made in March 1960 and April 1962. Only the south exposures were surveyed on 8 May 1965.

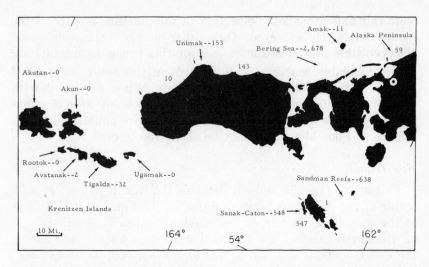

FIGURE 80.—The Sanak–Caton Islands and Sandman Reefs areas were last surveyed on 8 April 1962. All other surveys of the eastern Fox Islands shown on this map were made on 8 May 1965. The total number of otters observed on these two surveys in the areas shown is 4,121.

separated, but apparently permanent, sea otter colonies and one large population, but most of the available habitat is unoccupied. The small Samalga–Cape Sagak colony and the other on the northeast coast of Tigalda are apparently growing slowly. The large Bering Sea population off the north coast of Unimak Island and the western Alaska Peninsula, already of considerable size, is possibly augmented by an influx of otters from the Sanak–Sandman Reefs areas in the North Pacific Ocean. R. D. Jones (letter, 10 April 1964) reports that he—

observed an adult otter right smack in the narrows of the north end of False Pass [Isanotski Strait]. I've never seen one there before. He was at the time being swiftly carried into Bering Sea by the tide.

The available sea otter habitat in the Fox Islands is at present sparsely populated. Because of the large extent of this area, repopulation will probably require many years.

The western Fox Islands.—Human settlements include Nikolski Village, a sheep ranch, and a DEWline site near the south end of Umnak Island, and a sheep ranch and Reeve Aleutian Airways' installation near Cape Tanak on the north end of 65-mile long Umnak. On Unalaska Island the village of Unalaska is the largest of the extant native Aleutian settlements. There is also a DEWline site at Driftwood Bay on Unalaska Island. Counts of otters from several sources and estimates of all otters in this area are summarized in table 30.

Several Aleutian natives who hunt and fish in the waters off the south end of Umnak and near the east end of Unalaska have given me verbal reports over a period of several years (1950–62). Fred and Antone Bezezekoff of Nikolski Village, Umnak Island, have told me of repeatedly seeing a small number of otters in the vicinity of Samalga Island and Cape Sagak at the southwest end of Umnak Island. Their highest count was 14 otters (F. Bezezekoff, letter 13 March 1961). The three aerial surveys of the Fox Islands indicate that the small colony at the western extremity of Umnak Island is permanent but no increase is indicated. Apparently few wanderers enter this extensive western Fox Islands area which is isolated from other populations.

No one at Unalaska reported a sea otter sighting in the 1950–62 period. That sea otters are now repopulating Unalaska is indicated by a recent report. On 19 and 20 July 1968, C. H. Fiscus, A. M. Johnson, and H. Kajimura (personal communication) saw an otter in Kismaliuk Bay, on the north coast of the island, and another off Tiderip Point at the island's southwestern extremity.

The available sea otter habitat adjacent to the islands from Samalga Island to Akutan Pass is about 570 square miles. If this habitat can support about 12 otters per square mile, the estimated future population of this area may eventually be about 6,800 otters.

Krenitzin Islands.—The Krenitzin Islands occupy a 45-mile sector of the Fox Islands from Akutan Pass on the west to Unimak Pass. The village of Akutan, on Akutan Island, is the only human settlement in the Krenitzins. Occasional otter sightings near Akutan are reported by native Aleut fishermen (Lensink, 1958).

TABLE 30.—*Numbers of sea otters observed and estimated population in the Fox Islands group*

[The many islands, islets, and rocks where no sea otters were observed are omitted]

Island and year	Otters counted	Estimated total
Samalga-Umnak:		
1962	10	20
1965	9	20+
Egg and Old Man Rocks: 1957 [1]	1	2
Tigalda:		
1960 [2]	11	22
1965	32	53
Unimak-Amak:		
1962	811	1,081
1965	2,892	3,856
Total (highest counts)	2,935	3,931

[1] Lensink (1958) aerial survey.
[2] Surface survey of June 1960.

On 23 August 1962, R. Thomas (fur seal research biologist) sighted one otter in Akutan Bay (personal communication).

On 3 and 4 March 1960, D. L. Spencer and I surveyed this island group in detail under good weather conditions. On 7 and 8 April 1962 and again on 8 May 1965, wind permitted us to make only an inadequate survey of a small area off Tigalda Island, the only place where sea otters were previously seen. Only three otters were sighted in 1959 and 1962. In addition to the aerial survey data, I obtained information during surface surveys by dory on 26–29 June 1960 when I counted 11 adult otters and 6 young with mothers at Tigalda Island. During the 1965 survey, in spite of wind and rain, we sighted 32 otters there (table 30).

During May and June of 1960 and 1962, C. H. Fiscus (fur seal research biologist) spent considerable time in the Krenitzins while conducting pelagic sealing investigations in Unimak Pass and Bering Sea. The sealing vessel anchored on numerous occasions in different bays and bights and Fiscus went along the shore by dory in several areas. These included Avatanak Strait, Akun, Seredka, and Trident Bays at Akun Island; Rootok Strait, Durbin Strait, Durbin Bay at Tigalda Island; Ugamak Strait, Ugamak Island; and the south shore of Akutan. Although a careful search was always made for sea otters, Fiscus told me that none was observed. It therefore appears probable that the small colony along the northeast shore of Tigalda Island is the only one in the Krenitzin Islands and that otters reported occasionally from Akun Strait are wanderers.

The area of sea otter habitat adjacent to the Krenitzin Islands is about 200 square miles. If it may support about 12 otters per square mile, the future otter population may be about 2,400.

Unimak and Amak Islands.—Unimak Pass separates Unimak Island from the Krenitzin Islands. The distance from Unimak Pass to Amak Island is about 100 miles. A Coast Guard Station at Cape Sarichef is the only human settlement in the study area.

The greatest number of sea otters in this area inhabit the shallow waters of the Bering Sea off Izembek Bay in the vicinity of Amak Island and off the north central portion of Unimak. Depths of 20 fathoms or less extend to about 8 miles from shore and the 30-fathom curve extends to about 15 miles from shore. The majority of the 811 otters observed on the 8 April 1962 aerial survey were seen near the 20-fathom curve. Observation conditions were good to excellent during this survey and sectors were systematically covered between 1 and 15 miles from the shore of Unimak Island and the tip of the Alaska Peninsula. In addition, I conducted surface investigations in these waters with C. H. Fiscus and his crew of biologists from 7 to 10 July 1960 while on board the M/V *Windward*. Otters were found over waters as deep as 23 fathoms. An investigation of about 2 miles of beach on Amak Island in 1960 revealed no remains of sea otters or droppings. While walking the same beach in 1963, Fiscus found the remains of two adult sea otters but saw no living animals on shore. It appears that this population leads a predominantly offshore existence. Some observers (Lensink, 1958) speculate that this group of otters migrate seasonally. No evidence to support this supposition is available.

During aerial surveys of walruses on 27 March 1961, the Amak Island area was visited. Fog, however, prevented a satisfactory survey. A few otters were seen through gaps in the fog northeast of Amak Island, north of Izembek Bay, indicating that a number were present. It seems reasonable to conclude that, as in other areas, otters are resident there throughout the year. Where they bear their pups is unknown.

In 1963, R. D. Jones and C. P. McRoy (Jones, letters Dec. 1963 and March 1964) found five dead sea otters in April, June, August, and November on the Kudiakof Islands which separate Izembek Bay (55°20' N. lat., 162°30' W. long.) from the Bering Sea. They also saw several living otters in Izembek Bay, 17–19 December 1963. These observations and the lack of similar ones in past years indicated a population increase in the southwestern Bristol Bay area which was confirmed during the 1965 aerial survey.

One of the significant observations we obtained during the 1965 aerial survey was of the very large number of otters occupying shallow water north of the Alaska Peninsula and Unimak Island (table 30). Many of these animals were gathered into large rafts well outside the surf line, apparently sleeping on their backs at midday when we made our survey (fig. 81). Scattered individuals were feeding. Although the 1965 survey showed that the majority of the otters in this area were within the 3-mile limit, the 1962 survey demonstrated that numbers of them may feed in waters near the 20-fathom curve, which in this area is from 5 to 8 miles from shore. A possible reason that more otters were near shore during the 1965 survey was that a north wind of approximately 30 knots had blown steadily for several days before our survey. At the time of the survey, the wind had dropped to 10–15 knots but was still from the north.

The indicated great increase in the otter population from Fox Islands to Port Moller may probably be attributed primarily to

FIGURE 81.—This group of 128 otters slept on the open sea about 2 miles off the north coast of Unimak Island, Alaska. No kelp beds are found in this offshore location. Available evidence indicates that animals in this area rarely come ashore. (KWK 65-17-8)

three factors: (1) An influx of otters from the Sanak Island–Sandman Reefs area. (2) A north wind of several days' duration before and during our 1965 survey may have concentrated large numbers of otters near shore from their extensive offshore feeding grounds. During the 1962 survey of this same area, we found otters more scattered than in 1965. In 1962 they were spread over many square miles of open water. Possibly we failed to see many of them in 1962. (3) A large number of mothers carrying young were observed during both surveys—obviously reproduction accounted for some but certainly not all of the observed population increase in this area.

If the habitat (more than 1,000 square miles) may be populated as densely as some of those of the Aleutian Islands, the population might reach from 10,000 to 15,000 otters. No quantitative study of the marine invertebrate fauna of southwestern Bristol Bay has been made. A qualitative study by McLaughlin (1963), however, revealed a variety of crustaceans and molluscs in this area and suggests that it is rich. The large numbers and variety of aquatic birds and marine mammals there indicate that food species are abundant.

We extended the 1965 survey along the north shore of the Alaska Peninsula about 10 miles northeast of Port Moller but found no sea otters beyond the mouth of that bay. Our observations suggest that Port Moller (56° N. lat., 160°50′ W. long.) is near the northeast extremity of the sea otter's range in Bristol Bay. A sea otter taken ". . . near the Naknek River . . ." at about 58°40′ N. lat., in northeastern Bristol Bay ". . . where they are rarely to be found" (U.S. Bureau of Fisheries, 1911, p. 56) was probably a wanderer from southwestern Bristol Bay.

Sanak Island and Sandman Reefs

Sanak Island (fig. 80), which supports a small village, is approximately 20 miles southeast of the eastern extremity of Unimak Island. Between Sanak Island and the Alaska Peninsula the Sandman Reefs consist of extensive shallows having a number of exposed rocks and islets.

Sea otters were reported in the Sanak Island-Sandman Reefs area as early as 1922 (McCracken, 1957), but must have been very scarce at that time (Lensink, 1962). The Murie expedition received reports of otters in this area in 1936 but found none (Williams, 1937). Aerial surveys in 1957 and 1962 indicate that a substantial population now in this area is increasing (fig. 80 and table 31).

Aerial surveys in 1957 by Lensink (1958) and my observations obtained on dory surveys of 20–23 June 1960 indicated that few sea otters occupied waters surrounding Caton Island and that the animals were more numerous among the reefs off the southeast coast of Sanak. Aerial surveys of 10 April 1962, during excellent weather conditions, confirmed these observations. The majority of the otters observed on both aerial surveys were concentrated among reefs and islets off the southwest coast of Sanak Island

TABLE 31.—*Numbers of sea otters observed and estimated population in the Sanak Islands and Sandman Reefs areas*

Area	Aerial surveys		Estimated total in 1962
	1957 [1]	1962 [2]	
Sanak area:			
Sanak Island and associated reefs	236	525	700
Caton Island and associated reefs	15	23	46
Total	251	548	746
Sandman Reefs:			
Cherni Island	271	259	345
Clubbing Rocks	33	2	4
Little Goose Island	76	82	137
Deer Island and all reefs not named above	123	295	393
Total	503	638	879
Total both areas	754	1,186	1,625

[1] Aerial survey by Lensink (1958) on 19 July 1957.
[2] Aerial survey by D. L. Spencer and Kenyon on 10 April 1962.

within the 20 fathom curve. Lensink (1958) saw no otters in the relatively deep waters off the northeast shore of Sanak and only one was seen there during the 1962 survey.

Flights over the Sandman Reefs on 10 April 1962 were undertaken when conditions were excellent. We viewed the exposed rocks and islets and examined most of the open water. Otters could be seen on the glassy surface within a track about 2½ miles wide.

Because of the irregular bottom topography of this area, it is difficult to measure from charts the amount of available sea otter habitat. The approximate measurements obtained, however, indicate that the Sanak Island-Sandman Reefs area may furnish nearly 900 square miles of feeding habitat. With about two otters per square mile of habitat this area appears underpopulated.

Since the surveys of 1957 and 1962 were undertaken under excellent observation conditions, they may be comparable. If the total count in the Sandman Reefs area is projected forward at an increase of 5 percent per year (see Andreanof Islands) the estimated 1962 count would be 637. The aerial count of 1962 was 638 otters. The 1957 survey may have missed a number of otters in the Sanak Island area, since Lensink's (1958) figures when projected to 1962 at 5 percent per year fall short of the count obtained in 1962.

Shumagin Islands

This group lies 100 miles east of the tip of the Alaska Peninsula and reaches its southern extremity at Chernabura Island about 100 miles south of the Peninsula's south shore.

Sea otters apparently survived the 1741-1911 period of exploitation in the Shumagin area where offshore feeding areas offered them refuge. Japanese poachers worked the area until at least 1910. An estimate of 4,000 otters in the southern Shumagins was made in 1920, but this population was certainly reduced when a tanker and a freighter were wrecked and spilled oil in this area during World War II (Kenyon, 1964).

A small human population lives at Unga Village on Unga Island and another at Sand Point on Popof Island. Reports from surface observers at these locations indicate that occasional otters wander to the vicinity of these two islands but that no sizable population exists there. About half of Unga Island was surveyed in 1962 and only four otters were seen, confirming reports of surface observers. The sea otter population of the outer Shumagins is, however, large (table 32). Many shallow areas with underwater reefs, particularly

TABLE 32.—*Numbers of sea otters observed and estimated population in the Shumagin Islands*

Island	Aerial survey		1962 estimate of total
	1957 [1]	1962 [2]	
Unga	2	4	8
Nagai	149	338	676
Near	3	14	28
Bird	160	38	76
Chernabura	132	79	158
Simeonof	455	294	588
Little Koniuji	430	255	510
Big Koniuji	220	222	444
Peninsula	0	3	6
Spectacle, Bendel, and Turner	268	105	210
Popof (plus rocks)	2	—	4
Andronica	1	—	2
Twins	7	—	14
Total	1,829	1,352	2,724

[1] Complete aerial survey, 20 to 24 July 1957 (Lensink, 1958).

[2] Aerial survey, 10 April 1962, by D. L. Spencer and Kenyon. The survey of shallow areas offshore was incomplete. Therefore all 1962 field enumerations are increased by a factor of 50 percent to obtain the estimated total. If Lensink's 1957 count is used, the estimated total in that year is 2,440 (assuming 75 percent were seen). If population growth is considered to be 5 percent per year the 1962 population was 3,045 otters based on Lensink's field count.

between Chernabura and Simeonof Island, furnish sea otter habitat well offshore.

Surface observations at Simeonof Island between 4 and 10 June 1960 did not give an adequate indication of the number of sea otters inhabiting this area. On 8 June a dory survey around Simeonof Island yielded a count of only 75 adult otters.

When the aerial observations of 1957 and 1962 are compared (table 32) it appears that many of the 1962 counts are substantially less than those obtained in 1957 (Lensink, 1958). I believe that, because of the very calm weather conditions prevailing before and during the 1962 survey, many otters had moved to shallow offshore feeding areas, as they were observed to do in June 1960, and were thus not seen. Lack of time prevented a comprehensive survey in 1962 of rather large offshore shallow areas.

U.S. Coast and Geodetic survey charts indicate that water depth is not known in much of the Shumagin Islands area. A careful measurement of available sea otter habitat could therefore not be made. The available soundings suggest that large shallow areas exist. I have estimated that about 700 square miles of habitat are available around the islands and that in 1962 the population density was about four otters per square mile of habitat.

Alaska Peninsula

The south shore of the Alaska Peninsula, which offers considerable sea otter habitat, extends for over 400 miles from False

Pass to Cape Douglas at the mouth of Cook Inlet. The north shore of the peninsula is discussed under "Unimak and Amak Islands."

D. L. Spencer has flown over the coastal waters of the peninsula many times. Because of his previous knowledge of sea otter distribution and because of a shortage of time, our 1962 survey included primarily those areas where a significant number of sea otters was known to exist.

Otters were counted in the Cape Kumliun–Sutwick Island area in 1951 and 1957 (table 33). This area appears to be the center of the population along this coast. The 1962 survey was made from Cape Kumliun northeastward. The greatest concentration of sea otters was in Kujulik Bay and around Sutwik Island. One large group which was photographed (fig. 70) contained 440 otters, by a count from the photograph, the largest assemblage that was seen on the aerial surveys up to that time. From this area northeastward the number of otters seen decreased as shown in table 33. In 1957 Lensink (1958) found none east of Chiginagak Bay. Our observation of five otters east of this point in 1962 indicates a slow population spread eastward.

The difference in distribution of otters in the area between Cape Kumliun and Cape Kunmik, including Sutwik Island, between the 1957 and 1962 surveys, probably indicates that this rather large local population shifts about in this area in response to weather or food supply.

It is not possible from available charts to measure the square miles of sea otter habitat along the southeast coast of the Alaska Peninsula. We believe, however, that the increasing population may fill much vacant habitat in future years before maximum population is reached.

TABLE 33.—*Numbers of sea otters observed and estimated population along the Alaska Peninsula*

Area	Surveys			Estimate of total [4]
	1951 [1]	1957 [2]	1962 [3]	
Univikshak Island area	13	180	86	143
Kujulik Bay (C. Kumlik)	12	103	684	912
Sutwick Island area	355	581	109	145
Aniakchak Bay and Amber Bay (C. Kunmik)	8	6	47	78
Cape Kunmik to Cape Igvak (55 miles)		19	22	37
Cape Igvak to Cape Kuliak (70 miles)		0	1	2
Total	388	889	949	1,317

[1] Aerial surveys during the May to August period by R. D. Jones (*in* Stiles, 1953).
[2] Aerial survey, 25 July 1957 (Lensink, 1958).
[3] Aerial survey, 10 April 1962, by Kenyon and Spencer.
[4] Estimated population as of April 1962.

Kodiak Island to Cook Inlet Area

From the Trinity Islands, off the south shore of Kodiak, to the Barren Islands, in the mouth of Cook Inlet, is about 180 miles.

Records of confiscated sea otter skins in reports of the U.S. Bureau of Fisheries (1912 to 1936) and the observation of four otters near Afognak Island in 1922 (Eyerdam, 1933) indicated that sea otters survived after 1911 in the Kodiak area.

Lensink (1958; 1960; 1962) conducted both aerial and surface surveys in this area and reviewed the numerous reports available from various individuals who lived in or visited the area during a period of many years. The historical record of 18th and 19th century otter hunters, as well as midden excavations reported by Laughlin (1963), reveal that the sea otter was once numerous in the Kodiak area. Today repopulation is proceeding slowly. The majority of observations of otters come from waters off the north coast of Afognak Island and nearby Shuyak Island or from the Barren Islands. Lensink (1958) says of the few Kodiak Island reports that "The observations of otters on Kodiak are believed to be stray animals from the Shuyak area."

During the 1957 surveys Lensink did not find otters in the Trinity Islands but reports that R. Lopp observed 14 in 1957 (Lensink, 1958). The results of surveys by Lensink and W. Troyer are shown in table 34. D. L. Spencer has flown over and visited on the ground much of the coastal Kodiak area in recent years. He told me in 1962 of reports from many local inhabitants. These all indicate that the Kodiak area has not been repopulated to a significant degree.

On the west side of Cook Inlet, in Kamishak Bay, Spencer (letter, 1957) observed 40 otters at Augustine Island and one at Shaw Island.

Kenai Peninsula, Prince William Sound, and Kayak Island areas

The distance from the tip of the Kenai Peninsula to Kayak

TABLE 34.—*Numbers of sea otters observed and estimated population in the Kodiak Islands*

[Data for 1957 and 1959 are from Lensink (1962), except the estimates based on field observations; 1965 data is from aerial survey by Spencer and Kenyon]

Island	Survey date	Otters observed	Estimate of total
Augustine and Shaw Islands and Cape Douglas area	April 1965	120	200
Barren	July 1959	272	363
Shuyak	July 1959	395	527
Trinity	July 1957	14	28
Total		801	1,118

Island off the coast is about 250 miles. Sea otters are scarce along the coast of the Kenai Peninsula. The center of the sea otter population in this area is in Prince William Sound.

Many reports of otters, particularly from Prince William Sound, were made during past years by personnel of the U.S. Fish and Wildlife Service, the Alaska Department of Fish and Game, and the U.S. Coast Guard (Lensink, 1962). That the population is a long-established one is indicated by the seizure by the Government of two illegally taken skins at Seward in 1924 (U.S. Bureau of Fisheries, 1925).

Aerial surveys made in 1959 by Lensink (1962) furnish the best modern information on sea otter populations in this region (table 35). We did not conduct an aerial survey of the Kenai Peninsula but a number of biologists have visited this coast. The lack of sea otter observations by them and by residents indicates that no significant population of otters occupy this area.

The long-established Prince William Sound sea otter population may have reached maximum size some years ago followed by a decrease in recent years, or, possibly the surveys are not comparable (table 35). The reason for the indicated decline is a matter of speculation. It may be that ecological conditions are marginal. Much of the coastal area is precipitous, furnishing only a narrow zone of shallow water where sea otters may obtain food. The Prince William Sound population, being the most northerly in Alaska, may suffer during severe winter weather. Available food species may be heavily infested with parasites to which the sea otter is poorly adapted. F. H. Fay found an individual more massively infested than any animals taken from other areas (see Parasites and Miscellaneous Diseases). Lastly, it is possible that the relatively

TABLE 35.—*Number of sea otters observed and estimated population in the Kenai Peninsula, Prince William Sound, and Kayak Island areas*

Area	Aerial survey observations		Estimated populations	
	1959 [1]	1964 [2]	1959 [3]	1964
Kayak-Wingham Islands	138	24	184	40
Hinchinbrook Island	58	167	93	223
Montague Island	349	42	465	70
Green and Little Green Islands	42	116	70	155
Latouche and Erlington Islands	87	1	145	2
Other, including unsurveyed areas	28	42	47	70
Total	702	392	1,004	560

[1] Data from aerial surveys made in April and August 1959 using a Cessna 180 aircraft.
[2] John Vania, letter of 30 October 1964. Aerial surveys made 1 and 2 October 1964.
[3] Estimates, although similar to Lensink's estimate of 1,000 to 1,500 (1962), are not taken from his report. For the sake of uniformity in this report they were computed on the same basis as other estimates.

large human population of the Kenai Peninsula and Prince William Sound area may in some way inhibit sea otter population growth.

The Prince William Sound area was greatly affected by the earthquake of 27 March 1964. An expedition to discover the effects of the earthquake was undertaken by the U.S. Geological Survey in May and June 1964. An indication of the damage to some of the sea otter habitat is told in letters of 4 June and 20 July 1964 from Dr. G. Dallas Hanna who was a member of the expedition.

The destruction of animal and plant life in the former intertidal zone where we have been is catastrophic. Not a living thing is left on the upraised section. I think it will be many years before a new zone is formed.

Sea otters have been the most common of the marine mammals thus far. Usually we are in small boats close in shore or on land in daylight hours and opportunity for observation has not been the best. . . . Where the rise was greatest (7 to 33 feet) the kelp beds were destroyed so the animals seem to range out in the channels.

Dr. Hanna recorded 70 otters observed by himself and other members of the expedition in the vicinity of Hinchinbrook, Latouche and Montague Islands.

Further studies will be required to determine if the reduced number of sea otters observed in 1964 (table 35) was related to the March 1964 earthquake.

Earthquake caused disturbances have drastically affected sea otter populations. Voronov (1967) observed starvation and changes in distribution of sea otters in 1963 and 1964 following massive destruction of bottom fauna by tsunami in the Kuril Islands.

Pribilof Islands

The sea otter was numerous at the Pribilofs at the time of their discovery in 1786. Elliott (1875) says—

when the Prybilov Islands were first discovered, two sailors, Lukannon and Kaiekov, killed at Saint Paul's Island, in the first year of occupation, *five thousand;* the next year they got less than a *thousand,* and in six years after not a single sea otter appeared, and none have appeared since.

Lutke (1835), however, indicates that in the first 2 years [ca. 1786–88] the take was "plus de 200 loutres" and by 1828 "il n'y eut bientot plus une seule loutre." The number taken during Pribilov's short visit to the Pribilof Islands is given by Nozikov (194?) as 2,325.

I. Veniaminov (*in* Elliott, 1875) indicates that the species was not exterminated at the Pribilofs until about 1840. Records of the sighting of two sea otters and of "one which had been crushed by the ice" in 1889 and 1896 are recorded by Preble and McAtee

(1923). As previously suggested (Lensink, 1960) these may have reached the Pribilofs on drifting ice from the Unimak–Amak Islands area. Preble and McAtee (1923) mention the finding of skulls in subsequent years. I presume that these, like the ones several other biologists and I have found since 1947, had remained buried under sand dunes since the 1700's or even earlier.

The area of available feeding habitat—water 30 fathoms or less in depth—around St. Paul Island is about 395 square miles. If the population there was as dense in 1786 as that now found at certain of the Rat and Delarof Islands (about 16 to 19 otters per square mile), the total population at the Pribilofs could have been about 6,300 to 7,500 in 1786. This estimate indicates that Elliott's (1875) statement is plausible.

In April 1954 we attempted to transplant sea otters by ship from Amchitka Island to the Pribilofs. All 19 animals apparently died soon after liberation on 9 April. None was subsequently seen. Another transplant of seven otters by aircraft on 20 May 1959 was successful in that at least some of them survived. Residents of the Pribilof Islands, believed to be reliable observers, reported the occasional sighting of one or two otters until the spring of 1961. Although the sightings could not be verified, they do indicate the possibility that at least some otters survived for 2 years (see Transplant Attempts).

Isolated as this island group is by 240 miles of open sea from the nearest population, near Unimak and Amak Islands and the tip of the Alaska Peninsula, there is probably little chance that natural repopulation will occur in the near future. The possibility exists that eventually otters associated with floating ice may reach the Pribilofs from the Unimak-Amak-Alaska Peninsula area.

Other western Alaska areas

The Pavlov Islands (55° N. lat., 161°30′ W. long.) are south of the Alaska Peninsula and northeast of the Sandman Reefs. In 1957 (Lensink, 1958) and again in 1962 the group was partially covered during aerial surveys. On each survey four otters were seen near outer Iliasik Island. As the Sandman Reefs population grows, otters will probably move from that area into the Pavlov Islands.

The Semidi Islands (56°10′ N. lat., 156°45′ W. long.) lie about 20 miles south of Sutwik Island. In the summer of 1957 Lensink (1958) recorded five otters there. This isolated group was not subsequently surveyed.

Chirikof Island (55°50′ N. lat., 155°35′ W. long.) is about 40 miles southwest of the Trinity Islands and was not included on sea otter surveys. D. L. Spencer told me in 1962 that he flew around Chirikof and saw no sea otters there.

Southeastern Alaska

Observers occasionally report sea otters from the vast complex of islands, passes, and straits of Southeastern Alaska. Enforcement Agent J. A. Klingbeil, Jr., (letter, 14 October 1950) reported four animals seen at Nakwasina Bay on 2 September 1950, which he believed to be sea otters. He also reported a single otter seen at Silver Bay, Baranof Island (*in* Lensink, 1958). The possible observation of sea otters near Ketchikan was reported by J. Ditcher in 1945 (*in* Lensink, 1958) and by L. W. Croxton in 1961 (letter, 1962). No observation, however, has been confirmed by other observers. It appears that until 53 were transplanted to the area by the Alaska Department of Game in 1965 and 1966 few, if any, sea otters existed in Southeastern Alaska.

Dall (1870) indicates that exploitation of the sea otter in the Alexander Archipelago was intensive. Apparently this population was wiped out before 1900.

Maynard (1898) indicates that otters were most abundant "along the coast as far as Sitka. South of that point they were less numerous and were taken mostly from Queen Charlotte Islands."

There is no record that sea otters occured in the inland passages of Southeastern Alaska and apparently they also shunned parts of the outer coast.

BRITISH COLUMBIA

The sea otter apparently became extinct on the British Columbia coast during the 1920's.

In a conversation, in 1962, A. W. F. Banfield told me of a sea otter skull, deposited in the National Museum of Canada, that was found by Patch in the Queen Charlotte Islands in 1919. Later he wrote (letter, 1963):

I discussed the specimen with [C. A.] Patch some years ago and was under the impression it was a fairly fresh skull, when he picked it up. . . . The National Museum of Canada sponsored an expedition to the north end of Graham Island during the summer of 1919. . . . Concerning the sea otter he [Patch, 1922] writes (p. 103): "I found a sea otter skull in a deserted cabin near Rose Spit. Chief Harry Wiah said that about a year before our visit an Indian shot at a sea otter which was resting on kelp near North Island. He also said that about thirty years ago his father, his wife's father and other Indians—a total of nineteen boats—got twenty-one sea otters in a forenoon and six in the afternoon.

The most recent record is of a sea otter taken at Grassie Island, Kyuquot, in 1929 (Cowan and Guiguet, 1956). Concerning this specimen Guiguet wrote in a letter (1958) that—

We have one specimen record (skin) of an adult sea otter taken at Kyuquot Sound (Grassie Island) in the autumn of 1929 and donated to the Provincial Museum by the B. C. Game Commission. There are few details, the animal was not sexed, measured or the skull preserved. Since that time we have no authentic report, but many "sight" records, and of those investigated all proved to be river otter. . . . As far as we know, the sea otter has yet to re-establish on the British Columbia coast.

WASHINGTON

The last authentic record of sea otters on the Washington coast is of "several" being killed at Willapa Harbor in 1910 (Scheffer, 1940).

The river otter is frequently seen in salt water along the outer coast and among the islands and inland waterways of Washington State. Observers often report these to us as sea otters. To date, all sightings that could be investigated proved to be of river otters. C. Vandersluys of Friday Harbor, Wash., who is familiar with the inland waters, wrote (letter, 1963):

We did see a group of otter last summer, off the San Juan Islands. In fact, this animal seems to be increasing in number in this area each year. Locally we call them land otter, and to my knowledge, I have never seen a sea otter around here.

I have searched the outer coast of Washington many times during the past 10 years but have never confirmed any report of sea otters there (Kenyon and Scheffer, 1962).

Although originally numerous on the outer coast of Washington, it is doubtful whether the sea otter ever occurred on inland waters at any distance from the open-sea coast. Scheffer (1940) says, "There are no authentic records of the sea otter in Puget Sound or the San Juan Islands." Dr. E. Gunther (letter, 1963) told me:

Peter Puget's Journal of the exploration of Puget Sound, May 7 to June 11, 1792 [from] Pacific Northwest Quarterly, vol. 30, no. 2, April 1939 . . . commented on the absence of sea otters in Puget Sound (p. 200). . . . [From] Menzie's Journal of Vancouver's Voyage: "We saw but few sea otter skins amongst them [the natives] which shows that these animals do not much frequent the interior channels."

Dr. R. E. Greengo, Professor of Anthropology at the University of Washington, told me in 1963 that he and his students have carefully examined about 30 midden sites in the Puget Sound area. Among the many bones found, only two, from Sucia Island in the

San Juan group, were from the sea otter. Comparison with specimens in the U.S. Fish and Wildlife Service collection showed them to be phalanges, one from a front and one from a hind paw (University of Washington collection no. 455J105). Dr. Greengo estimates that the remains were deposited at the site 1,500 years ago. Sea otter bones occur quite frequently in midden sites on the outer coast of Washington. It appears that during the time of human occupation, the sea otter was extremely scarce or absent within the enclosed waters of Puget Sound. Certainly the "great numbers of sea otters" in the Columbia River as far up as Celilo Falls recorded by Lewis and Clark (see Burroughs, 1961) were not sea otters but, as Bailey (1936) and Scheffer (1964) point out, harbor seals *(Phoca vitulina)*.

OREGON

Bones found in middens along the Oregon coast indicate that the sea otter was once abundant there, but Bailey (1936) records that after 1876 the species was not again reported from Oregon. Mrs. V. F. Martin (letter, 12 August 1965) told me of an unconfirmed report that may represent the last of the original sea otter population in Oregon:

In answer to my query to Otter Rock, Oregon, a correspondent (signed C. Jones) wrote me on July 29, 1965: "Frank Priest of Newport, Oregon (now deceased) told me several years ago that the last otter taken here was by he and Joe Biggs (deceased) of Agate Beach, Oregon. That was in the year of 1906, and they sold it for $900,00. (Rich Chinese in San Francisco were the otter buyers for local people.)"

A recent sighting about 30 miles north of Tillamook Bay, near Neahkahnie, at about 45°44′ N. lat. (Pedersen and Stout, 1963) has not been confirmed by other observers.

It is a matter of speculation that occasional otters may wander down the coast from Prince William Sound, as far as the outer coast of British Columbia, Washington, and Oregon, or that stray animals move northward from the well-established California population. A linear distance along the Pacific Coast of approximately 2,000 miles separates the sea otter colony at Kayak Island, Alaska, from the central California population.

CALIFORNIA POPULATION

Although reports of fish and game wardens recorded the continual presence of a small herd of sea otters during early years of the present century, it was not until 19 March 1938 that their presence near the mouth of Bixby Creek, Monterey County, became generally known (California Senate, 1965, and Bolin, 1938).

The permanent population of sea otters on the California coast is between Point Conception (34°27' N. lat.) and Monterey Bay (36°33' N. lat.). Here, during an aerial survey on 27 August 1957, Boolootian (1961) observed 638 otters. Because of predation by the sea otter on abalones *(Haliotis* sp.) the opinion was expressed that sea otters were shot or killed with spears by fishermen (H. Shelby, *in* California Senate, 1963). To ascertain the number of otters presently on the California coast, aerial surveys were conducted by the California Department of Fish and Game. The surveys included the areas surveyed by Boolootian (1961). During the first, 26 to 29 January 1964, 236 otters were observed (Commercial Fisheries Review, 1964a). During the second, 13 February 1964, the counts by two observers were 339 and 351 (Commercial Fisheries Review, 1964b). The most recent survey was on 8 June 1966 when 618 otters were counted (J. G. Carlisle, Jr., letter, July 1966). [For recent information see page 200 and footnote 5, table 36.]

These surveys indicate that the California sea otter population has not increased in recent years. Other observations, however, suggest that the population in the area surveyed did not increase because otters wandered to other areas.

R. G. Prasil searched National Park Service files on the Channel Islands and found the following reports (J. C. von Bloeker and R. M. Bond, letter 28 May 1940):

Kenneth E. Stager saw a sea otter asleep in the rocks on the northwest side of Santa Barbara on March 17th [1940]. He approached to within 30 feet of it before it awakened and took to the water. He is familiar with these animals off the Monterey County coast (as I am also) and I see no reason to doubt his record.

Another report was obtained by L. Sumner and R. M. Bond (letter) during a survey at Anacapa Island in 1950. They interviewed a long-time island resident named Raymond (Frenchy) Ladreau and wrote:

Ladreau told us that in 1943 two sea otters came to the kelp beds of the West Island and to the landing area nearby where he has his shack. He said they were quite tame and unafraid and remained there for 2 or 3 days before disappearing. This is the second recent record of sea otters in the Channel Islands area and indicates that if undisturbed they may be expected to increase in that general region. Perhaps some day, if protected from poachers, they will remain permanently around Anacapa and neighboring islands.

Allanson (1955) reported seeing two otters at San Miguel Island in the Channel Islands (34° N.) in 1954.

On 17 and 18 March 1958, I visited Santa Rosa and San Miguel Islands aboard the M/V *Trinity* and observed the inshore waters of both islands from a dory. Much ideal sea otter habitat was examined but no otters were seen. This survey and reports from other visitors to the Channel Islands indicate that, as yet, no substantial sea otter population has developed there.

Orr and Poulter (1964) recorded several observations at Año Nuevo Island (37°7′ N. lat.) in the summer of 1963; and Bentley (1959) noted two near Trinidad Head (41° N.) in December 1956, indicating that individual otters are moving northward.

LOWER CALIFORNIA, MEXICO

The aboriginal population of sea otters reached its southern limit at least as far south as Morro Hermoso (27°32′ N. lat.) (Ogden, 1941) and Natividad and Cedros Islands (27°50′ N. lat.) (Anthony, 1925; Scammon, 1870). Anthony indicates that the last remaining colonies "in the region of certain kelp beds south of Ensenada" were wiped out when about 50 were killed in 1897 and an additional 28, "eight or nine years later at the same point." The last record he gives is of one being "killed by fishermen in 1919, at San Benito Island."

In April and May 1946 and in January and February 1965 I visited many of the islands and inshore water areas along the coast of Lower California from Natividad Island to the U.S. border. I found no information that sea otters might still exist along the coast and saw nothing to indicate their presence. The species was probably extirpated on the Mexican coast in 1919.

SOVIET UNION POPULATIONS

Barabash-Nikiforov (1947) summarizes information on the distribution of sea otters in the Soviet Union. Information on modern sea otter populations in areas under Soviet control became available only recently. The drowning of Scientist S. D. Pereleshin at Paramushir Island in the Kuril Islands in 1959 probably retarded sea otter studies. Pereleshin's successor, Scientist A. N. Belkin, accidentally shot himself in 1965 (pers. comm., V. A. Arseniev) but some of his work was published posthumously.

Commander Islands

Data obtained on a visit to the Commander Islands in July 1961 and the available published information is summarized.

Geologically the Commander Islands (Komandorskie Ostrova)

are part of the Aleutian Chain. They are separated from Attu, westernmost of the Near Islands, by about 185 miles of open sea. Permanent human settlements are Preobrazhenskoe (population about 300) on Copper Island (Ostrov Medny) and Nikolskoe (population about 500) on Bering Island (Ostrov Bering).

Exploitation of the sea otter began at the Commander Islands in 1741 when Vitus Bering's second expedition discovered them. Barabash-Nikiforov (1947) stated that in 1902 the sea otter population there was "at least 2,000 head" but because of excessive killing "the herd numbered 700 head in 1904." The number at Medny "in the winter 1911–1912 . . . was 63 head." After 1924 he says that "Importation of animals was begun and still continues" and the number rose to "over 200 head in 1930." He also says that "An increase in the number of sea otters around Bering Island was observed after the autumn of 1931."

Information now available contradicts some of the data given by Barabash-Nikiforov (1947). The current information is presented.

Marakov (1963) says of the Commander Islands that the sea otter became rare early in the 19th century and then "disappeared entirely, first on Bering Island and then also on Medny Island." They reappeared on Medny toward the end of the century but have never reappeared on Bering Island. "Hunting continued on Medny Island until 1924. When it was completely banned, no more than 350 individuals were left." The herd showed little or no increase during the following 30 years. Marakov believes that various human activities, including the spilling of petroleum products in the sea, prevented population growth. Marakov (1965) states that "the herd of otters on Medny Island numbers more than 1000 adult individuals."

I obtained additional information during a visit to the Commander Islands from 9 to 23 July 1961.

We saw six sea otters (five adults, one pup) during our visit. We found these near the southeast end of Medny Island along about 3.5 miles of coast. Reefs projecting from the shore, outlying rocks, and extensive kelp beds provide excellent habitat in this area. The green sea urchin is abundant at the locations we visited on Medny and Bering Islands. Two sea otter droppings found among the rocks at Medny consisted entirely of sea urchin tests.

Certain of our hosts, the late Dr. S. V. Dorofeev, G. A. Nesterov (biologist), and E. P. Skripnikov (supervisor of sealing activities at Medny and a resident of the Commander Islands for about 25 years—15 years on Bering Island and 10 years on Medny Island) gave us the following information: Hunting of sea otters at the Commander Islands continued until the 1917–22 period. By that time, when protection was enforced, otters had been extirpated at Bering Island. They have never become reestablished there.

Sea otter studies were carried on at the Commander Islands by Barabash-Nikiforov during the late 1920's. The animals were captured in nets set in the water and were held captive for study purposes. During the 1950's, Biologist Fedorof and Scientific Worker Danielov held a male and female captive on Bering Island. The animals were captured at Medny.

Kuril Islands and the Kamchatka Peninsula

In 1943 Nikolaev (1961) estimated that the sea otters in the Kamchatka Peninsula area numbered about 300, and Klumov (1957) estimated from field observations made in 1951, 1955, and 1956 that the Kuril Islands population numbered "at least 1,500 head." Belkin (1966) reviews various studies of sea otters in the Kuril Islands and presents the results of his own work from 1962 to 1964. His count of otters at 22 islands yielded a total of 4,300 animals (3,300 adults and about 1,000 young).

WORLD POPULATION

The preceding sections present the data on the world population of sea otters that were gathered during a period of many years. The most recent estimates derived from field observations, when projected at the observed growth rate (for those populations still growing) of one population (about 4 to 5 percent per year), give a computed estimates of about 33,000 sea otters (table 36) extant in the world in 1965.

On the basis of the historical record and field observations presented in foregoing pages, it appears that sea otters survived at the close of the 1741–1911 period of unregulated exploitation in the following 11 geographical areas: (1) Kuril Islands, (2) Kamchatka Peninsula, (3) Commander Islands, (4) Rat Islands, (5) Andreanof Islands, (6) The Unimak and Sanak Islands-Sandman Reefs area, (7) Shumagin Islands, (8) the Kodiak to Prince William Sound area, (9) near Monterey, Calif., (10) the Queen Charlotte Islands, British Columbia, and (11) the San Benito Islands, Baja California. From the last two locations, however, they were soon extirpated.

TABLE 36.—Estimated world population of sea otters

Area	Date of observation	Sea otters observed	Estimated total [1]	Estimated total in 1965 [2]	Authority
Soviet Union:					
Kuril Islands	} 1962–64	(?)	4,300	4,700	Belkin (1966).
Kamchatka					
Medny Island	(?)	(?)	1,000+	1,200	Marakov (1965).
Alaska:					
Near Islands	1965	[3] 27	45	45	FWS aerial surveys.
Rat Islands	1965	[3] 3,147	4,196	4,196	Do.
Delarof Islands	1965	[3] 653	871	871	Do.
Andreanof Islands	1965	[3] 5,805	7,760	7,740	Do.
Fox Islands	1965	[3] 2,935	3,913	3,913	Do.
Sanak-Sandman Reefs	1962	[4] 1,186	1,625	1,880	Do.
Shumagin Islands	1957	[4] 1,829	2,724	3,972	Do.
Pavlov Islands	1962	4	8	10	Do.
Semidi Islands	1957	4 5	10	16	Lensink (1958).
Alaska Peninsula	1962	[4] 949	1,317	1,525	FWS aerial surveys.
Prince William Sound	1959	[4] 702	1,004	1,004	Lensink (1962).
Kodiak Island area	1957–59	[4] 722	973	1,237	Do.
California [5]	1966	618	600	600	J. G. Carlisle, Jr., letter, 1966.
Total		18,582	30,346	32,909	

[1] At time of observation.
[2] Projected from the year of the original estimate on the basis that in underpopulated areas growth will be at the rate of 5 percent per year. Where field observations indicate that little or no growth is occurring, no projection of growth is shown.
[3] Aleutian Islands total is 12,567. This also includes S.W. Bristol Bay.
[4] Total 5,397. The total for all of Alaska is 17,964 (5,397 + 12,567).
[5] In a series of aerial and surface censuses begun in August 1968, the highest count of sea otters was 1,014 (Peterson and Odemar, 1969).

DISCUSSION

In the foregoing section, observations of sea otter populations obtained between 1935 and 1965 in several geographic areas were reviewed. The data included aerial and surface counts, total population estimates based on them, measurements of available habitat, and population densities in different areas. The field observations and the conclusions derived from them are discussed below.

Rate of population increase

Two methods may be used to ascertain the approximate rate of increase in a sea otter population: (1) The annual rate of reproduction and mortality in a population may be studied; or (2) otters in an isolated population may be counted at intervals and the increment found directly. The first method is treated elsewhere. The results obtained by the second method are discussed below.

Because movements of large numbers of otters from one island to another were recorded, it was evident that the area included in population surveys must be sufficiently large to include locations where both emigration and immigration occurred. The population surveys in the Andreanof Islands furnish the best available information on which to base a study of population growth. On the east, this otter population is isolated from the small population of the Umnak-Samalga Islands by 120 miles, which includes Amukta Pass and the unpopulated Islands of Four Mountains. On the west, the study area is separated from the Delarof Islands by 14-mile-wide Tanaga Pass.

This sample area, about 210 miles in length, includes densely populated islands adjacent to others having unoccupied habitat. Aerial surveys of the Andreanofs in 1959, 1962, and 1965 were conducted under comparable conditions by the same observers. The small, semi-isolated populations at Atka and Amlia at the eastern end of the sample area showed a larger rate of increase than did the total Andreanof population. Probably these colonies were augmented by wandering individuals that formed the vanguard of the massive eastward moving population of the Kanaga-Adak-Kagalaska Islands segment of the sample area.

The rate of the Andreanof population increase of about 12+ percent in each of two 3-year periods or over 4 percent per year, is less than the rate of increase postulated by Soviet biologists. The rate of increase was at first presumed to be 10 to 12 percent per year by Barabash-Nikiforov (1947) but he finally concluded that this rate was not in accord with his field observations and placed the annual rate of increase of a population at 7 percent. In the Commander Islands, however, even this rate appeared somewhat high when compared with his "on the spot observations." Lensink (1962), on the basis of his surveys, concluded that the rate of increase of the Andreanof Islands population was 10 to 15 percent per year. The more comprehensive data gathered in the same areas after his studies were completed, however, indicate that the total population within the Andreanof group is now increasing at a lower rate, probably because of density-caused mortality in the heavily populated areas.

In a local area of sparse population, the 1959–65 data indicate the population may have increased during that period at an annual rate of at least 10 percent. For example, the estimated population at Seguam, the easternmost island of the sample area, increased from 28 to 47 otters (table 25) in the 6-year period 1959–65 or at a mean annual rate of a little more than 11 percent. This conclusion is based on the assumption that Seguam Pass is a fairly effective barrier to immigration.

After a large population is produced, as it was, for example, at Adak (in the Andreanof Islands) in the 1954–62 period (table 28), the overall annual increase of the Andreanof population was at the rate of about 4 percent.

The observed 4 percent annual rate of increase is a generalized figure. At islands where the population exceeded the carrying capacity of the habitat, i. e., more than 10 to 15 otters per square mile of habitat (see table 25), population regression was observed. Stress mortality (starvation), as well as emigration, probably accounted for the local population decreases. Evidence to support this view was found on 28 April 1965 during a brief examination of one otter hauling ground at Shagak Bay, Adak. There I found a large juvenile otter dead on the beach. It exhibited all the characteristics of starvation that I observed at Amchitka. Probably the rate of mortality during the winter-spring season of stress at Tanaga, Kanaga, and Adak in the 1962–65 period was considerably greater than at the relatively sparsely populated islands east of Kagalaska during this same period.

Thus, the rate of population increase varies according to population density and its relation to ecological conditions and may be quite different from the rate of reproduction. Elsewhere it is shown that about 16 young may be born annually per 100 independent animals of both sexes and all ages.

In general, it is concluded that an isolated population having ample unused habitat may grow through local reproduction (no immigration) at a rate of about 10 to 12 percent per year. In a region that includes both densely populated areas (where winter-spring mortality occurs) and adjacent unpopulated habitat, the rate of growth may be about 4 to 5 percent per year.

Optimum population density

No study has yet been undertaken to indicate the productivity of the sea otter habitat or to show what critical differences in food productivity exist in different habitats. Because such studies are not available it is not possible to compute, on the basis of food resources available, the number of sea otters that any particular habitat may support.

On the basis, however, of the observed behavior of several island populations of sea otters it is possible to reach tentative conclusions as to the approximate optimum population density and which areas are overpopulated or underpopulated.

At five locations (Rat, Amchitka, Tanaga, and Kanaga Islands, and the Delarof group) we observed large otter populations which subsequently became greatly reduced (table 37 and fig. 78). The figures available do not necessarily represent absolute maximum and minimum populations because of the infrequency of observations. From these data it appears, however, that a growing sea otter population in an unexploited habitat may reach a temporary maximum density of 40 or more animals per square mile of habitat. After such a high density is attained, a period of population reduction occurs, either through emigration, a high rate of mortality, or both concurrently during seasons of stress. That a depleted feeding habitat may support about 10 to 15 otters per square mile is indicated by the observation that the five densely populated areas dropped to that level.

TABLE 37.—*Changes in sea otter population density in six areas*

Island	High population		Low population		Interval years	Means of reduction [2]
	Date	Number [1]	Date	Number [1]		
Rat	1943	31	1949	10	6	Mortality (?).
Amchitka	1943	41	1949	13	6	Mortality.
Delarof	1959	21	1965	10	6	Mortality (?).
Tanaga	1953	([3])	1959	14	6	Emigration.
Kanaga	1959	26	1962	12	3	Emigration.
Adak	1962	40	1965	24	3	Emigration and mortality.
Mean		30		12		

[1] Otters per square mile of feeding habitat (waters 30 fathoms or less in depth).
[2] It is known that emigration took place because rapid population increase in nearby areas was observed. Mortality was observed and documented only at Amchitka. At Rat Island and in the Delarofs a condition similar to that at Amchitka would be expected.
[3] Unknown but presumed to be high on the basis of reports that otters there numbered in the thousands (Hooper, *in* Jones, 1953; Lensink, 1960).

The Kanaga data indicate that this level may be maintained for at least a 3-year period. The Amchitka data indicate that after the initial population "crash" a period of slow increase, or adjustment, occurred (table 23). During the recovery period the population approached a density of about 20 otters per square mile of feeding habitat. That this is not an optimum population density is indicated by the continued annual occurrence of heavy mortality among juveniles and old adults (see Age Specific Mortality), by comparatively small body size (see Body Measurements), by excessive dental attrition, and by the fact that by 1965 the population had fallen to a density of 14 otters per square mile of habitat.

Optimum population density in the Aleutian area, after a depleted habitat has recovered from the damage caused by overutilization of food resources, may be postulated at about 10 to 15 otters per square mile of habitat. Table 38 shows predicted populations in certain Alaska areas based on data now available. More data are needed, however, to properly estimate optimum population density.

Geographic barriers

Passes between areas of feeding habitat around islands, may act to a varying degree as barriers to the spread of sea otter populations. For example, Buldir, Semisopochnoi, and the Near Islands were not repopulated for a number of years after the islands nearest to them supported high populations. The 55 miles of open water between Buldir and Kiska was an effective but not a permanent barrier. A few otters reached Buldir from Kiska betwen 1936 and 1961. Kiska was densely populated by 1959 and perhaps before that, but not until the 1959–65 period were small colonies established in the Near Islands, 65 miles west of Buldir.

TABLE 38.—*Present and projected sea otter populations in certain Alaska areas*

[Only the areas that have been most intensively studied are included. The projections of future populations are based on the assumption that a population of about 10 to 15 otters per square mile of feeding habitat may be supported]

Area	Square miles of habitat	Projected total number of sea otters	Present population estimate
Near Islands	326	3,300– 5,000	27
Rat Islands	293	3,000– 4,400	4,200
Andreanof Islands	766	7,700–11,500	7,800
Delarof Islands	89	900– 1,300	930
Islands of the Four Mountains	88	900– 1,300	0
Fox Islands	570	5,700– 8,500	25
Krenitzen	200	2,000– 3,000	55
Unimak-Amak Islands	1,000	10,000–15,000	4,000
Sanak Island and Sandman Reefs	900	9,000–13,500	1,600
Shumagin Islands	700	7,000–10,500	2,700
Total	4,932	49,500–74,000	21,337

The 30 miles of deep open water between Amchitka and Semi-sopochnoi Islands was apparently a less effective barrier. No otters had reached Semisopochnoi in 1943 (when the Amchitka population was near maximum size) but by 1959 the population at Semi-sopochnoi was relatively dense (16 otters per square mile). Movement to Semisopochnoi of a substantial number of otters, rather than the slow increase of a small breeding nucleus, during this period is indicated.

The behavioral barrier

Considerable data show that the reoccupation of vacant habitat is dependent to an important degree on the inherent behavioral characteristics of the sea otter.

The sea otter does not undertake seasonal migrations. Recovery of marked sea otters at Amchitka revealed that the home range of an individual otter includes only a few miles of coast. Marakov (1965, p. 212) also found that otters in the Komandorski Islands become attached to a particular area.

Elsewhere (see Amchitka Island) it is shown that otters move into areas of nearby but unoccupied habitat only in response to "population pressure" after a large local population has developed (table 23). The Amchitka data indicate that the remanent colony which repopulated the island was probably on the Pacific coast and that significant numbers of sea otters did not move to the Bering Sea coast until 1940 or soon thereafter (fig. 73).

Substantial population movement from densely populated Kanaga to nearby unpopulated Adak and later from Adak to nearby islands east of it did not occur until dense local populations built up. In 1959 the Adak population had reached a density of 31 otters per square mile of habitat (table 28) but only one otter was observed at nearby Kagalaska (table 29). It thus appears that otters tend to maintain an established home range until the effects of a dense population force movement.

Wandering individuals

Many observations of individual otters at great distances from large local populations are available. That such wanderers eventually settle permanently in a locality that offers ideal habitat conditions is indicated by the existence of small colonies at great distances from large population centers. The small colonies found in the Near Islands, Buldir, Atka, Amlia, Seguam, and in the Umnak-Samalga and Tigalda Islands areas in the 1950–65 period, are examples.

It thus appears that vacant sea otter habitat is repopulated by two means: (1) Movement of large numbers of otters from a densely populated area to adjacent unpopulated habitat, and (2) wandering individuals that accumulate to form colonies where habitat conditions are ideal many miles distant from dense populations.

Because of the indicated 4 percent per year rate of growth of the Andreanof sea otter population, the repopulation of vacant habitat at the periphery of a densely populated area, is, today, the most important means by which the sea otter is reoccupying the places from which it was exterminated during the 18th and 19th centuries.

Dispersal of sea otters and population density

Most animals included in tagging studies at Amchitka were adults when marked and the recoveries indicated that they remained permanently along a limited area of coast (see Home Range). By analogy with other species it would seem probable that wanderers, contributing to range extension, might be composed mostly of subadult animals. That this may be true also of sea otters is indicated by our failure to observe as many mothers accompanied by small young in newly populated areas as in other areas. In 1959, we saw no otters in Kagalaska Strait, but in 1962 we observed 348 there. Aerial photographs of a group of 157 animals and another of 59 revealed not one small pup among them. In mid-November of 1965, when this area was well behind the vanguard of population expansion, I spent 2 days in Kagalaska Strait and saw a number of mothers accompanied by young.

Two possible conclusions concerning the otters which first appeared in Kagalaska Strait are indicated: (1) All were males, and (2) they were mostly subadults of both sexes and had not born young.

Estimates of population density, or the number of sea otters per square mile of available habitat, were obtained in several Aleutian areas. Among these were locations where substantial populations have existed for many years, and also recently repopulated areas.

On the basis of geographical barriers and population density, sea otter populations in Alaska may be classified according to four general categories (two densities of isolated populations and two densities of populations adjacent to available habitat).

1. Dense isolated populations

This category includes populations of sea otters that have

reached a size which heavily utilizes food resources in the available habitat. Significant population dispersal to new habitat is hindered by broad expanses of deep water which prevent feeding.

The Rat Islands (except Buldir Island) population is an example. Significant emigration of sea otters from this island group appears to be slowed by passes hundreds of fathoms deep and about 50 miles wide on the eastern and western extremities of the group. The average population density was about 14 otters per square mile of available habitat (table 21). When such populations increase and exceed the carrying capacity of the habitat, heavy mortality occurs because substantial emigration does not occur.

2. Sparse isolated populations

The recently established Buldir Island colony and the Samalga and Tigalda Islands populations are examples. Many years may elapse before these populations approach maximum size. The Samalga-Umnak population is separated from the nearest Andreanof population at Seguam by Amukta Pass, 35 miles wide, and by the Islands of Four Mountains, a total distance of 120 miles, where no otters are found. The Tigalda Island colony is about 140 miles east of Samalga. Such small colonies grow slowly because they are rarely augmented by immigrants.

3. Dense local populations adjacent to areas of vacant habitat

The Andreanof, Sanak, Unimak, and Shumagin Islands, and the Alaska Peninsula areas furnish examples of populations which today are large but may expand into adjacent vacant habitat. During aerial surveys, comparable observations of expanding distribution and increasing abundance of sea otters were obtained in these areas. Such populations expand rapidly because movement of part of the population increment to new areas is possible and minimum mortality probably occurs except at densely populated islands after they are left far behind the spearhead of population growth.

4. Sparse local populations adjacent to areas of vacant habitat

In the Aleutian Islands three local populations of sea otters—at Atka, Amlia, and Seguam Islands—are placed in this category. These populations occupy a tiny part of the habitat available to them. They are separated from other populations by many miles but not by geographical barriers. They may be augmented by an influx of otters from the western Andreanofs. Narrow passes between islands of this group are easily crossed.

The rate of increase of these three colonies is related inversely to their distances from the large western Andreanof population:

| Colony | Distance from large population (miles) | Annual rate of increase | |
		1959–62 (percent)	1962–65 (percent)
Seguam	130	10	10
Amlia	100	12	13
Atka	60	30	85

Possibly the annual rate of increase of the Seguam colony represents the rate of increase that may be attributed to local reproduction in an uncrowded population.

Summary

1. In 1741 when unregulated exploitation of the sea otter began, the species ranged from central Lower California, Mexico, north along the coast of the North Pacific Ocean, through the Aleutian and Kuril Islands to the northern islands of Japan.

2. The northern limit of the sea otters' range overlaps but slightly the usual southern limit of winter drift or pack ice in the Bering Sea. The farthest north colony in Alaska is in Prince William Sound (60°30′ N. lat.) where the sea does not freeze.

3. The total population of sea otters in 1740 was probably between 100,000 and 150,000 animals.

4. The number of sea otters taken during 170 years of unregulated exploitation is not recorded but probably did not much exceed one-half million animals.

5. The total world population in 1911, when exploitation of the sea otter was halted, probably numbered between 1,000 and 2,000 animals.

6. Small sea otter populations apparently remained in 1911 at the following 11 areas: Kuril Islands, Kamchatka Peninsula, Commander Islands, Rat Islands, Andreanof Islands, the Unimak, Sanak Islands-Sandman Reefs area, Shumagin Islands, Kodiak Island and Prince William Sound area, in the Queen Charlotte Islands, British Columbia, on the coast of California near Monterey, and in the San Benito Islands, Baja California.

7. The first modern data on the recovery of sea otter populations were obtained in the Aleutian Islands in the mid-1930's and considerable miscellaneous data were subsequently gathered during the 1940's. Detailed field studies of population and distribution were begun by the Fish and Wildlife Service in 1954 and continued through 1965.

8. The sea otter is limited to a relatively narrow band of water around islands and along mainland shores where water depths do not exceed 30 fathoms. Under the prevailing weather conditions when aerial surveys were made, sea otters were easily observed. We concluded that in most areas about 75 percent of the sea otters present were recorded. Comparative surface and aerial surveys indicated that about 60 percent of the otters seen on an aerial survey may be missed on a surface survey.

9. Data obtained on aerial surveys in the Andreanof Islands in 1959, 1962, and 1965 indicated that in this area, having much available and unpopulated habitat, the population is growing at an exponential rate of between 4 and 5 percent per year.

10. Aerial surveys and other studies conducted between 1954 and 1965 in Alaska reveal that large areas of sea otter habitat are not yet repopulated. In certain areas repopulation of vacant habitat is proceeding rapidly (the Andreanof Islands). In isolated areas the habitat may be heavily utilized by a dense population (the Rat Islands).

11. In all observed areas where estimated sea otter populations reached 20 to 40 otters per square mile of habitat, the populations decreased to about 8 to 15 otters per square mile of habitat. The decrease occurred through mortality (e. g., Amchitka Island) or emigration (e. g., Kanaga and Adak). In years following a population "crash" the populations at islands may fluctuate between about 10 and 20 otters per square mile of habitat.

12. Reoccupation of available sea otter habitat is hindered by wide, deep passes between islands. Sea otters readily cross passes about 10 miles wide. Significant numbers may cross 30 miles of open water (e. g., Amchitka to Semisopochnoi). Passes 50 miles or more in width may be crossed by a few individual otters that wander great distances from densely populated areas (e. g., from Kiska to Buldir and from there to the Near Islands). These individuals may eventually concentrate in locations having unusually desirable habitat.

13. The most significant factor that limits the spread of sea otter populations is the tendency of individual otters to occupy a limited home range. Feeding habitat on one side of an island, or at an island near another having vacant habitat, may become densely populated (to about 40 otters per square mile of habitat) before a significant number of otters move into adjacent vacant habitat even at the home island. Where repopulation was observed, the south sides of islands were repopulated prior to the north exposures (e. g., Amchitka, Atka, and Amlia).

14. In addition to the many areas in western Alaska offering sea otter habitat which today is unpopulated, approximately 2,000 miles of coastline, including much sea otter habitat, separates the colony at Kayak Island, Alaska, from the small central California colony.

15. Several aerial surveys were made in 1958 and 1964 to 1966 along the California coast. The highest counts in 1958 and 1966 yielded 638 and 618 sea otters, respectively. Further surface and aerial surveys, begun in August 1968, yielded a high count of 1,014 otters (Peterson and Odemar, 1969), indicating a population increase since 1958 of about 5 percent per year.

16. The number of otters recorded during aerial and limited surface surveys in Alaska was 17,964 and the total population in Alaska waters in 1965 is estimated to be about 25,000.

17. The most recently published Soviet total estimate of sea otters in Soviet waters is 5,300.

18. On the basis of all data available, the world population of sea otters in 1965 was computed to be 32,909. A general estimate of the world population, presuming that some populated areas have not been observed, is about 32,000 to 35,000 animals.

19. Measurements of available sea otter habitat, much of which was not occupied in 1965, and the observed population density of relatively stable populations (10 to 15 otters per square mile of habitat) indicate that the Aleutian Islands and closely related areas of the Alaska Peninsula may eventually support a population of about 50,000 to 74,000 sea otters.

Home Range

The purpose of permanently marking sea otters is to obtain from field observations and recovery of tags, over a period of time, the following information on the life history of individual animals: (1) Maturation, (2) aging, (3) longevity, (4) reproduction, and (5) movements and home range.

Sea otters were captured on shore with a sport fisherman's landing net (fig. 82). While the netted otter struggled to free itself, using forepaws and teeth on the net, one rear flipper was grasped and a cattle or sheep ear tag of monel metal (table 39) was clamped to the web of the hind flipper with a special pliers. Two men were required, one to hold the net and the other to affix the tag. Colored plastic strips were attached experimentally to some tags, so that individual animals might be recognized in the wild.

FIGURE 82.—John Nevzoroff holds an adult female sea otter which he captured while it slept on an Amchitka beach. After capture, at least two men are required either to tag an otter or to place it in a carrying cage. (KWK 62–15–20)

All animals that could be captured were tagged, but when a choice was possible juveniles were captured in preference to adults. When studies were begun, an effort was made to capture mothers having with them very young pups. This practice, however, was soon discontinued.

Tags were recovered (1) when marked animals were recaptured, (2) from animals found dead on beaches, and (3) during harvesting operations.

Tags were placed on the hind flippers of 224 sea otters (table 39), 107 adults and 117 juveniles or pups. Among them were 88 males, 135 females, and 1 of unknown sex.

In 1956, 1959, 1961, 1962, and 1963, a total of 28 recoveries were recorded (table 40). The intervals between tagging and recovery ranged from 10 minutes to 35 months. Thirteen tagged animals were recovered dead on beaches, eight were captured and released, five were shot, a colored plastic marking device from

TABLE 39.—*Sea otters tagged at Amchitka Island, Alaska*

Year	Tag numbers	Juvenile			Adult		Total
		♂	♀	?	♂	♀	
1956	EL 401–409 [1]	1	1	—	4	3	9
1957	EL 12908 and 12910 [2]	1	—	—	1	—	2
1959	12901–12903; 12926–13000; [3] EL 426, 427, 429–431, 433, 440–442, and 444.	25	21	—	9	31	86
1962	EL 446–565	27	34	—	16	43	120
1963	EL 566–572	4	2	1	—	—	7
Total		58	58	1	30	77	224

[1] This series sheep-ear size.
[2] This series cattle-ear size. The high numbers (12,000 to 13,000) are the result of using tag remainders from Pribilof fur seal series. The prefix EL was hand stamped on only a few. The tags were obtained from the National Band and Tag Company, Newport, Ky.
[3] Except two ruined.

one animal was recovered at a hauling-out place, and one color-marked individual was observed repeatedly.

Two hundred and eight of the animals were captured and tagged at nine traditional hauling-out areas; the remaining 16 were marked at scattered locations on Amchitka Island. Three hauling-out areas are on the Bering Sea coast, five are on the Pacific coast, and one is at East Cape where the Bering Sea and Pacific coasts meet. The minimum distance between the hauling grounds used as tagging locations is 1 mile and the maximum distance is 9 miles. Eight animals tagged at one hauling-out place were subsequently recaptured at the next nearest one.

Three females, tagged as adults and recovered nearly 3 years later, were found 2.5, 2.5, and 5 miles, respectively, from the locations of tagging. One female recovered 2 years after tagging was ½ mile from the location of tagging. Two females recovered about 1 year after tagging were 2.5 and 2 miles from the location of tagging and two others were recovered at the location of tagging.

One young adult male, whose tag bore a colored plastic flag, was observed repeatedly. This animal visited the location where we discarded fish remains in Constantine Harbor, near Kirilof Dock. He was present daily for a period of about a month and a half. He became tame and was captured by hand when he came ashore to accept food. Because of the artificial food source, the sedentary behavior of this animal may not represent the normal behavior of the adult male. One juvenile male, tagged at East Cape, was found dead 24 days later in Constantine Harbor, 9 miles from the location of marking. Among five juvenile males, recovered within a month of tagging, however, only one was as far as 3 miles from the tagging location.

TABLE 40.—Recoveries of tagged sea otters at Amchitka Island

Tag number	Date[1] Tagged	Date[1] Recovered	Period free[2]	Location[3] Tagged	Location[3] Recovered	Distance moved[4]	Sex	Age[5] Tagged	Age[5] Recovered	How observed[6]
EL 401	21-5-56	23-5-56	3 da	CH	CH	¼ mi	♀	J	J	BD
EL 402	26-5-56	31-5-56	6 da	SMP	RRP	3 mi	♀	A	A	PS
EL12910	28-11-57	11-12-57	1 mo+	CH	CH	O	♂	A	A	BD[7]
EL12951	2-3-59	26-3-59	24 da	EC	CH	9 mi	♂	J	J	BD
EL12903	1-4-59	2-4-59	24 hr	RRP	RRP	100 me	♀	A	A	O
EL12902	2-4-59	4-4-59	19 da	SMB	SMB	¼ mi	♂	J	J	CR
EL12972	2-4-59	4-4-59	2 da	SMB	SMB	½ mi	♂	J	J	BD
EL12975	2-4-59	14-4-59	12 da	RRP	RRP	O	♀	J	A	CR
EL12941	5-4-59	13-2-62	34 mo	CP	KB	5 mi	♂	A	J	S
EL12945	7-4-59	15-4-59	8 da	RRP	RRP	¼ mi	♀	J	J	BD
EL12948	8-4-59	18-3-62	35 mo	SMP	AB	2.5 mi	♂	A	A	BD
EL12993	15-4-59	10-2-62	34 mo	RRP	SMB	2.5 mi	♀	A	A	S
EL12995	15-4-59	8-5-61	25 mo	RRP	RRP	0.5 mi	♀	A	A	BD
EL13000	18-4-59	8-5-59	20 da	SMP	SMB	O	♂	J	J	C
EL 456	15-2-62	18-2-62	3 da	RRP	SMB	3 mi	♂	A	P	CR
EL 455	15-2-62	19-3-62	1 mo	RRP	B	5 mi	♂	A	A	BD
EL 457	15-2-62	16-2-62	1 da	RRP	RRP	1 mi	♀	J	J	CR
EL 457	15-2-62	26-2-62	11 da	RRP	RRP	O	♀	J	J	BD
EL 464	16-2-62	27-3-62	39 da	RRP	RRP	1 mi	♂	J	J	BD
EL 490	26-2-62	19-3-62	21 da	RRP	AB	0.4 mi	♂	J	J	BD
EL 497	27-2-62	31-3-63	13 mo	SMP	SMB	2 mi	♀	A	A	S
EL 499	1-3-62	5-3-62	6 da	RRP	AB	2.5 mi	♂	J	J	BD
EL 502	3-3-62	20-3-63	13 mo	AB	AB	O	♀	A	A	BD
EL 513	3-3-62	27-3-63	13 mo	AB	AB	100 me	♂	A	A	S
EL 525	7-3-62	7-3-62	1 da	SMP	SMP	O	♀	A	J	CR
EL 529	7-3-62	8-3-62	1 da	SMP	SMP	O	♀	A	A	BD
EL 526	7-3-62	8-3-62	1 da	SMP	SMP	O	♂	A	A	CR
EL 556	22-3-62	18-3-63	12 mo	RRP	SMP	2.5 mi	♀	J	SA	S
EL 570	25-3-63	29-3-63	4 da	CRP	CRP	O	♀	J	J	BD

[1] Day, month, and year.

[2] Period free, mi = minutes, hr = hours, da = days, mo = months.

[3] Location abbreviations: AB = Aleut Beach (not to be confused with Aleut Point), B = beach, not named, CH = Constantine Harbor, CP = Constantine Point, CRP = Crown Reefer Point, EC = East Cape, RRP = Rifle Range Point, SMB = St. Makarius Bay, SMP = St. Makarius Point.

[4] Distance moved: O = same location, me = meters, mi = miles.

[5] Age at tagging and at recovery, P = pup, J = juvenile, SA = subadult, A = adult.

[6] How observed: BD = beach dead, O = observed, CR = captured and released, S = shot, PS = plastic strip found on hauling ground.

[7] From about mid-October this animal remained near Kirilof Dock. It was given fish heads and became tame. It was easily captured when it came ashore for fish heads on 28 November and was tagged. It was last seen when we left on 11 December.

The tagging of newborn or very young pups was discontinued because the frightened mother, upon release, usually made several long dives. It seemed probable that at least some of these young pups may have died as a result of unusually long periods of immersion. Also, several mothers refused to accept their helpless pups when they were released and later failed to return for them.

DISCUSSION

To date the information from tagging is meager. Many of the animals which were captured on land were there because they were ill or in weakened condition. For this reason, the rate of survival of tagged animals is probably lower than for the population as a whole. There is as yet no reason to believe, however, that the act of tagging increased the mortality within the tagged segment of the population as compared to the untagged segment (except when mothers with small pups were captured). Disturbance of the animals during tagging was brief and care was taken not to injure them. The tag placed in the web of the hind flipper had no noticeable effect on swimming. Marked animals, in the wild and in captivity, ignored their tags, except that certain individuals chewed the colored plastic flags attached to the metal tag.

The data and general field observations lead to the following tentative conclusions: (1) The home range of the female sea otter during at least a 3-year period may include about 5 to 10 miles of coastline. Soviet biologists found that the range from the "basic station is 15 to 17 km. [9.3 to 10.5 miles]" (Nikolaev and Skalkin, 1963). (2) Animals tagged on one side of Amchitka did not move around to the other side of the island (see Distribution and Numbers). (3) Males may have a larger home range than females. (4) Individual otters may use more than one of the traditional hauling-out places.

Additional information from tagged animals is found in sections on "Age at Sexual Maturity," "Age Specific Mortality," and "Juvenile Sex Ratio."

Territoriality

It is difficult to say whether territorialism exists in the sea otter in the same sense that it does in other mammals. Many sea otters, both male and female, share much of the same home range within which the two sexes mingle to some degree. Also they may segregate to haul out in traditionally established locations (see Segregation of Sexes).

I repeatedly saw lone adult male otters in the same locations near the shore of Kirilof Point, a female area. During a period of 3 weeks, one of these slept daily on the same rock. Another habitually rested in a kelp bed or on rocks on the shore of a sheltered cove. Although I saw transient males in the same general vicinity, I did not observe any behavior that might be interpreted as territorial defense.

When a female, searching for food or moving along the coast, passed the area occupied by a sedentary male he swam to her and attempted courtship. If the female was not receptive and passed on, the male returned to a favorite feeding or resting place. If the female was receptive, she chose a rock in the vicinity where the pair slept and groomed during the mated period (see Breeding Behavior) of up to several days.

Thus, males seeking an estrous female may be sedentary and wait for one in some favorite "territory," from which other males are not driven, or may actively search for estrous females. The maximum time that a male may remain in a limited location or remain away from one of the male haul-out areas was not ascertained. It is my conclusion that territoriality is but weakly expressed in the sea otter.

REPRODUCTION

Sex Ratio

Because sea otters segregate themselves according to sex, the raw data from samples killed, captured, or found dead on beaches at Amchitka Island must be carefully evaluated before drawing any conclusions concerning the sex ratio among different age classes.

PRENATAL SEX RATIO

Three samples of fetal sea otters are available from females killed in 1962 and 1963. The data are summarized in table 41. The smallest fetus in which sex was positively determined weighed 8.80 g. Among the 58 fetuses in which sex was determined, the ratio was 45 percent males: 55 percent females. The fact that the two 1963 samples show a nearly 50:50 ratio indicates that until a larger sample is available the prenatal sex ratio may, for practical purposes, be considered to be about 1:1.

JUVENILE SEX RATIO

Data on the sex ratio of juvenile otters were gathered during tagging studies when sea otters were netted, tagged, and released. This work was done mostly before the period in which high mortality occurred. The young otters were in the areas frequented primarily by females with young. Many of the young that were captured for marking were still in company of their mothers or recently separated from them. Mortality among young in company with their mothers is not known but apparently is low or moderate.

TABLE 41.—*Prenatal sex ratio at Amchitka Island*

Date taken	Number			Ratio (percent)	
	Males	Females	Total	Males	Females
22 Jan.–9 Mar. 1962	4	9	13	31	69
17–31 Mar. 1963	18	19	37	49	51
31 July–3 Aug. 1963	4	4	8	50	50
Total	26	32	58	45	55

Little geographical segregation of deserted juveniles had apparently occurred at the time tagging was done. Therefore, this class of animals contributes the best indication of sex ratio among sea otters up to approximately 1 year of age. Among 117 juveniles that were captured and marked, 58 males, 58 females, and 1 of unknown sex were recorded (table 39, section on Home Range). This evidence suggests that the sex ratio is approximately 1:1 during the juvenile period.

ADULT SEX RATIO

The areas in which females predominated were the most accessible to hunters. Also, these areas are more extensive than the locations frequented by males (see Segergation of Sexes). Primarily for these reasons the sex ratio of animals taken during cropping operations in 1962 and 1963 were biased in favor of females. The take consisted of 67 percent females and 33 percent males (table 42). In the section on mortality it was shown that the sex ratio among juveniles found dead on beaches during the late-winter to early-spring period of stress was 58 percent males: 42 percent females. These data suggest that among surviving adults, females outnumber males. The percent by which females predominate among adults, however, cannot be derived from the available data. The difference between the number of males and females taken during killing operations is a result of sexual segregation and is too great to be explained by the apparent difference in male and female mortality among juveniles.

Until further studies are conducted, it may be concluded that a nearly equal number of males and females are conceived and that the sex ratio remains approximately 1:1 until juveniles are deserted by their mothers. At this time, more males than females die of natural causes. Thus, among adults, females probably predominate over males. Harvesting operations tend to confirm this but more data are needed.

TABLE 42.—*Sex ratio of sea otters killed at Amchitka Island during experimental harvests*

[Ratio, males to females, 1:2]

Date	Males		Females		Total number
	Number	Percent	Number	Percent	
Jan.–Mar. 1962	43	28	111	72	154
Oct. 1962	6	25	18	75	24
Mar.–Apr. 1963	109	36	194	64	303
Total	158	33	323	67	481

Segregation of Sexes

Male and female sea otters at Amchitka habitually segregate themselves and, almost always occupy distinct geographical areas at all seasons. This condition first became apparent during observations when otters in various areas were counted and the numbers of each sex recorded. Additional information was obtained when otters were captured on beaches and when those dying of natural causes were recovered. During harvesting operations in 1962 and 1963, more quantitative data on the degree of segregation became available (tables 43 and 44). The terms "male area" and "female area" refer to the geographical locations used predominantly (but not exclusively) by each sex. Marakov (1965, p. 213) noted sexual segregation among otters at Medny Island, Commander Islands, U.S.S.R.

FEMALE AREAS

These are more numerous and less discrete than male areas (fig. 83, map). Seven female areas are listed in table 43. At these places the adult females usually haul out in favored sheltered places near the extremities of points. In general, they appear less bound to a limited hauling out location than the males. Certain locations, however, such as St. Makarius Point W., Rifle Range Point, and Constantine Point, are more favored than others. Tag recoveries reveal that females may use more than one of the favorite hauling grounds (see Home Range). The kill of adult females reveals that they are generally distributed along the coast when feeding. Many were taken a kilometer or more from favored haul-out locations. Observations as well as data from the kill indicate that females not only avoid the male haul-out locations but also avoid the feeding habitat adjacent to them. Among 242 adult otters killed in female areas, 93 percent were females. When 20 animals, not accompanied by a pup but in female areas, were killed selectively (31 July to 3 August 1963) in an effort to take males, only one male was obtained. This sample may indicate that males constitute only 5 percent of the animals in female areas.

MALE AREAS

Three locations on the eastern half of Amchitka (fig. 83, map) are used almost exclusively by males; the southeast tip of St. Makarius Point (SMPE) about 800 m. of beach, the north beach and tip of East Cape (ECN) about 500 m. of beach, and Crown Reefer Point (CRP) about 600 m. of beach. Along each of these

TABLE 43.—*Sex and age of sea otters taken in seven areas frequented mostly by females at Amchitka Island*

[All otters were shot during harvesting operations in 1962 and 1963. The only selection of animals shot was that adults were taken in preference to juveniles when both were present]

Location [1]	Adults					Juveniles					Adults and juveniles				
	Males		Females		Total number	Males		Females		Total number	Males		Females		Total number
	Number	Percent	Number	Percent		Number	Percent	Number	Percent		Number	Percent	Number	Percent	
RRP	0	0	20	100	20	4	50	4	50	8	4	14	24	86	28
SMB	1	9	10	91	11	2	18	9	82	11	3	4	19	96	22
SMPW	7	12	51	88	58	8	62	5	38	13	15	21	56	79	71
CP–IP	1	1	70	99	71	5	31	11	69	16	6	7	81	93	87
CH–KB	7	12	49	88	56	12	34	23	66	35	19	21	72	79	91
AMB	1	9	10	91	11	0	0	1	100	1	1	8	11	92	12
ECS	1	7	14	93	15	0	0	0	0	0	1	7	14	93	15
Total	18	7	224	93	242	31	37	53	63	84	49	15	277	85	326 [2]

[1] RRP = Rifle Range Pt.; SMB = St. Makarius Bay; SMPW = St. Makarius Pt. West; CP–IP = Constantine Pt. to Ivakin Pt.; CH–KB = Constantine Harbor to Kirilof Bay; AMB = Aleut Midden Beach; ECS = East Cape South.
[2] Of the 326 animals taken, 84 (25.8 percent) were juveniles.

209

TABLE 44.—*Sex and age of sea otters taken in three areas frequented mostly by males at Amchitka Island*

[With the exception of the otters taken at CRP, otters were shot in 1962 and 1963 during harvesting operations. There was no selection of animals shot except that adults were taken in preference to juveniles. Because of its remoteness, otters were not harvested at CRP. The animals listed from there were found dead on beaches in 1956, 1959, 1962, and 1963. Remains showing no positive evidence of sex are omitted]

Location [1]	Adults					Juveniles					Adults and juveniles				
	Males		Females		Total number	Males		Females		Total number	Males		Females		Total number
	Number	Percent	Number	Percent		Number	Percent	Number	Percent		Number	Percent	Number	Percent	
SMPE	37	97	1	3	38	14	78	4	22	18	51	91	5	9	56
ECN	46	98	1	2	47	7	78	2	22	9	53	95	3	5	56
CRP	17	100	0	0	17	7	88	1	12	8	24	96	1	4	25
Total	100	98	2	2	102	28	80	7	20	35	128	93	9	7	[2] 137

[1] SMPE = St. Makarius Pt. East; ECN = East Cape North; CRP = Crown Reefer Pt.
[2] Of the 137 animals taken, 35 (25.5 percent) were juveniles.

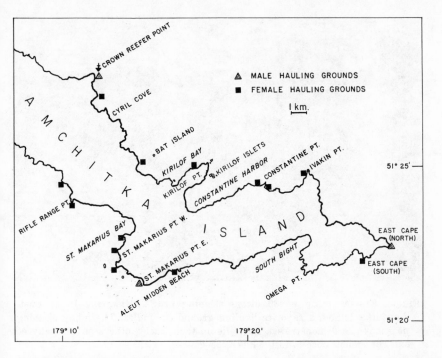

FIGURE 83.—The southeastern end of Amchitka Island showing the most favored male and female hauling grounds. Individual animals may haul out at almost any location along the shore. At the locations indicated on the map, however, aggregations of sea otters are habitually formed when numbers of animals come ashore to rest at all seasons.

beaches the majority of animals habitually haul out on 40 to 50 m. of beach. A few individuals may haul out indiscriminately at various distances from the most favored location. When a number of otters are hauled out, they usually congregate in groups, often sleeping in contact with one another (fig. 84). Among 102 adult otters killed in these areas, only 2 were females (table 44).

It appears that the males, except those actively seeking to mate, limit feeding activities to a radius of several hundred meters from the haul-out location. If they did not do this, more than 7 percent males (table 43) would have been shot in the female areas during killing operations. When mating activity was observed (see Breeding Behavior), males actively sought estrus females and mating was observed only in female areas. Thus, it is reasonable that a higher proportion of males was found in the female areas than females in male areas.

FIGURE 84.—A group of 39 otters sleeping at St. Makarius Point East, Amchitka Island, a favorite hauling ground for males. The many sleeping positions are demonstrated. Some lie on their backs, others on the belly or side, or curled nose-to-tail. (KWK 65–27–34)

JUVENILES

The foregoing paragraphs dealt primarily with adults. Segregation of sexes is more pronounced among adults and subadults than among independent or newly weaned juveniles. Among 35 juveniles taken in male areas, 80 percent were males (table 44). In female areas, among 84 juveniles examined 63 percent were females (table 43).

Since juveniles are or were recently associated with their mothers, it might be expected that a larger number would be found in the female areas than in the male areas. The percent of juveniles taken in both male and female areas was, however, the same, about 26 percent (see footnotes, tables 43 and 44). This may indicate that independent juveniles wander to all areas and mingle with any group of adults. It also appeared, however, that juveniles were more attracted to areas occupied predominantly by adults of their own sex (20 percent female juveniles on the male areas and 37 percent male juveniles on female areas). Perhaps because of the recent mother-young relationship the proportion of young males on the female area was greater than the proportion of young females in the male areas.

Discussion

The largest aggregations (animals hauled out in close proximity on the same rocks) were seen on male hauling grounds at Amchitka. I saw from 70 to over 100 on several occasions at East Cape. I seldom saw more than 10 to 15 females in close proximity on the same rock at any hauling ground (fig. 85). During aerial surveys, certain large aggregations contained few, if any, mothers with small young as far as we could ascertain.

Large aggregations were photographed at sea off Unimak Island (fig. 81) and mothers carrying small pups were not detected on the photograph. In the same general area but away from the aggregations, however, I saw many mothers carrying young on their chests. These mothers with young were usually alone but occasionally two were near each other. It thus appears that males and females habitually segregate themselves, both when on the hauling grounds and in offshore locations.

More observations of this aspect of social behavior are needed

FIGURE 85.—Rifle Range Point, a female hauling ground. Three of the females have entered the water; eleven adults and large juveniles remain on the rocks. (KWK 62–17–31)

in other island populations. Knowledge of the degree of segregation of sexes and the locations of areas where males concentrate may prove useful in management operations.

As mentioned elsewhere (Breeding Behavior), males often patrolled female feeding areas and attempted courtship with all females present. In the course of 3 or 4 hours, two to four males might pass separately through such an area.

Breeding Behavior

Observations at Amchitka are often hindered by dense fog. This fact and the tendency of mated pairs of otters to occupy offshore rocks, have prevented me from following any one pair of otters through all phases of the breeding cycle. I have, however, recorded observations of 41 mated pairs in the wild. Among these, copulation was initiated by 13 males which were not successful in completing it. Copulation was completed, apparently successfully, in eight cases. The remaining 20 observations were of paired animals in close company which, as explained later, exhibited the behavior typical of mated pairs. Excluded from the records are observations of unsuccessful attempts at courtship by males toward unreceptive females. The data on various aspects of the breeding cycle were obtained from many pairs observed briefly and from the observation of one pair which remained for about 3½ days in a sheltered cove (table 45). These observations indicate that the cycle of breeding behavior is rather uniform. A description of behavior during the different phases of the breeding cycle follows:

COURTSHIP OR PRECOPULATORY PERIOD

As mentioned elsewhere, adult males and adult females segregate themselves to a considerable degree. When a male seeks a

TABLE 45.—*Activities of a mated pair of sea otters during observations on 19, 20, and 21 August 1955*

19 August, 1634-1810. The male and female remained in close company at all times.

| Activity | Number of periods | Elapsed time (minutes) | | Total minutes | Percent of time |
		On land	In water		
Copulation	2	—	35	35	37
Grooming	2	39	2	41	43
Sleeping	1	19	—	19	20
Total	5	58	37	95	100

TABLE 45.—*Activities of a mated pair of sea otters during observations on 19, 20, and 21 August 1955—Continued*

20 August, 1542-1910. The male left the female resting on the rock when he continued food diving, but he remained close to her while she was in the water.

Activity	Number of periods	Elapsed time (minutes)		Total minutes	Percent of time
		On land	In water		
Male:					
Feeding	4	—	79	79	38
Groom and wash	4	1	23	24	12
Sleep and rest	2	52	40	92	44
Sexual behavior (play)	5	4	8	12	6
Investigate strange female	1	—	1	1	>1
Total	16	57	151	208	100
Female:					
Feeding	2	—	58	58	28
Groom and wash	1	21	—	21	10
Sleep and rest	3	108	9	117	56
Sexual behavior (play)	2	4	8	12	6
Total	8	133	75	208	100

21 August, 1052–1820. The male left the female resting on the rock when he continued food diving, but he remained close to her while she was in the water.

Activity	Number of periods	Elapsed time (minutes)		Total minutes	Percent of time
		On land	In water		
Male:					
Feeding	10	—	310	310	70
Groom and wash	5	—	40	40	9
Sleep and rest	2	—	72	72	16
Sexual behavior (play)	5	5	20	25	5
Sniff rock	1	1	—	1	>1
Total	23	6	442	448	100
Female:					
Feeding	7	—	247	247	55
Groom and wash	6	9	41	50	11
Sleep and rest	8	61	65	126	28
Sexual behavior (play)	5	5	20	25	6
Total	26	75	373	448	100

On 22 August a dense fog prevented detailed observations.

Summary of activities of mated pair of otters on 19, 20, and 21 August 1955, during three observation periods totaling 749 minutes (12 hours, 29 minutes).

Activity	Total elapsed time			
	Male		Female	
	Minutes	Percent	Minutes	Percent
Feeding	389	52	305	41
Groom and wash	103	14	110	14
Sleep and rest	183	24	262	35
Sexual play	72	10	72	10
Sniff rock	1	>1	—	—
Investigate strange female	1	>1	—	—

female in estrus, he usually swims belly down and rapidly on the surface (fig. 86) and seldom dives for food. He closely skirts favorite hauling-out rocks, and he may rise high in the water to look onto the rocks, or leave the water to walk quickly about, sniffing the rocks. If he sees a feeding female floating on her back he swims directly to her. He may come up beneath her and attempt to put his forelegs around her chest from behind, his forepaws resting in or near her axillae. Or he may rise up beside her. He may rub and pat her chest, belly, and genital area with his forepaws, or he may nuzzle and appear to sniff them with his nose. If the female is unreceptive, she rolls away from him and pushes him away with her flippers and paws, or snaps at him. Before departing he may snatch whatever food items she has on her chest.

If she is receptive, the two may roll and frolic together. During

FIGURE 86.—Adult males actively searching for estrous females in areas habitually frequented by feeding females often swim belly down rather than in the more usual inverted position. (KWK 1026)

this period, the male may grasp the female about the chest from behind with his forepaws and attempt to grasp the side or back of her head or her nose in his jaws. At this rather rough stage of courtship, the female may disengage herself, snap at the male, and push him away with her flippers and paws. The two may now separate, but if the female is not determined in her resistance the male may follow her; or, occasionally, the female may follow the departing male and rough courtship behavior will continue. If the female is in estrus, she becomes increasingly submissive as courtship continues.

After the male has found an estrous female, the two continue actively to roll and splash about on the surface together. They nuzzle each other and fondle each other with the forepaws. Similar behavior was noted in the polecat by McCann (1955). Such behavior apparently lasts for a variable period, perhaps up to an hour. In the course of their activities the animals usually make their way, with the female leading, toward a suitable hauling-out rock which the female selects. This spot becomes the center of their activities during the mating period.

COPULATORY PERIOD

Copulation takes place in the water near the hauling-out rock. When the female is ready for coitus, her body becomes rigid and she lies belly up on the surface, her back somewhat bowed (i.e., concave) and her forelegs rigid and protruding vertically in front of her. The male grasps the female's upper jaw usually, including her nose, in his jaws, or he may grasp the side of her head. If the mated pair are on land during precoital play, the male leads the female into the water after grasping the side of her head in his jaws. He clasps her tightly from the back ("more canum"), his paws resting against her chest in or near her axillae. At the same time the already extruded penis is inserted as the male rests against the female's back, slightly on one side of the mid-dorsal area. The rear feet of the male are in motion, so that the two animals move about in a wide circle and roll from side to side. Periodically they lift their noses above the surface. For the most part, the male is beneath the surface and the belly and chest of the female are above it. The female frequently emits loud shrieks and gurgling gasps which indicate that she experiences difficulty in breathing.

In one case (19 August 1955), after copulation had continued for 14 minutes, the female struggled and wrenched her body, disengaging the male's penis. The male, however, retained his grip

217

on the female's head with his jaws, and the two animals, linked together by their heads, spun rapidly over and over in the longitudinal axis on the surface. The spinning continued for only a few seconds. Then the female became limp, the male again aligned his body with her back and grasped her with his forelegs, and copulation continued for an additional 9.5 minutes. When the male released his grip after an elapsed time of 23.5 minutes, the female's nose was gashed and bleeding. The two animals immediately began to groom and scrub their fur. Then, the female leading, the pair swam to and hauled out on the rock where they had previously engaged in courtship. Here they continued to groom and dry their fur for 10 minutes. The female was particularly vigorous in this activity. During this period and subsequent periods of association with the male on the chosen rock, the female almost constantly uttered a soft chuckling sound. After drying their fur, the pair went to sleep curled up close beside each other. The time was late afternoon and presumably, as was observed on other occasions, they slept in this location until after sunrise the next day.

While most observations indicated that the male initiated mating activities, estrous females were observed to tease or stimulate a reluctant male. In one instance (7 May 1956 at 1715 local time) I saw a male and female sleeping close beside each other in a kelp patch. They appeared to be a mated pair, and I presumed that copulation had occurred. While I watched, the female awoke and began to nuzzle the male about the head and abdomen. The male was slowly aroused from sleep and at first appeared indifferent to the attention of the female. Within about 30 seconds, however, he clasped her with his forepaws, then grasped the side of her head in his jaws. The female then became rigid (as described elsewhere) and copulation was accomplished. Unfortunately, after copulation had continued for 11 minutes, their motions carried them behind rocks, and it was not possible to obtain further observations of the pair.

In one case, a second copulation occurred about one-half hour after the first. Various observations of behavior indicate that more than one copulation may be usual.

Copulation usually occurs in the afternoon. I have 21 observations of copulation and attempted copulation during the afternoon, but only 1 recorded for morning (1030).

Barabash-Nikiforov (1947) says that during coitus the pair "cling to each other, intertwining belly to belly, and revolve around the longitudinal axis." Murie (1940) also said "position

218

apparently being with the ventral surfaces opposed, although of this I could not be positive." In all nine cases of completed copulation that I observed, the male clasped the female from behind and remained dorsal to her but slightly to one side of her median dorsal line during copulation. Because of the position of the female, lying rigidly on her back with forepaws extended, immediately before coitus, it would seem unusual that the position of the male would be other than dorsal to her body during copulation.

POSTCOPULATORY PERIOD

In one case this period was observed to last for 3 days (19 through 22 August 1955, table 45). The pair fed, groomed, and rested in close company (fig. 87). Occasionally they engaged in short periods of play, and the male sometimes attempted copulation. The female, however, appeared to be unreceptive during this period. The pair rested periodically on the chosen hauling-out site and slept beside each other during the night.

FIGURE 87.—A pair of sea otters (female on left) rest and groom beside each other shortly after mating. The light colored head is more typical of males than females. As shown here, females tend to be more alert and watchful than males. Males tend to be phlegmatic and take alarm less easily than females. The nose of the female was grasped in the teeth of the male during mating and is swollen. The broader and heavier head and neck of the male is evident. (KWK 975)

The male followed the female closely, often being in contact with her while the two consumed food, side-by-side on the surface. When the female dived for food the male quickly followed, often discarding a food item that he had not finished eating. When the female surfaced, the male emerged a fraction of a second behind her.

During this period the male left the female's side only after the two had emerged and groomed following a feeding period. While the female remained on the chosen rock to groom and sleep, the male dived for food nearby. While eating he swam back near the chosen hauling-out rock to eat, and often glanced at the female before diving.

On the third day of the mating period the male exhibited less interest than previously toward his mate, and several times stole food from her. Also, he followed her in food dives less promptly. The pair had left the cove by shortly after daylight on the morning of 23 August.

THE SEPARATION PERIOD

The breaking of the pair bond was observed on several occasions. The female, in each case, deserted the male. Probably because the male is larger than the female he requires more food, and as a general rule he returns to the water to continue feeding while the female rests on land. In one instance, the food dives of the male gradually carried him about 50 m. from the female's resting place. She watched him intently and, suddenly, while the male was beneath the surface gathering food, she slipped quietly into the water and swam rapidly away beneath the surface. Apparently the visual acuity of the male was inadequate to detect immediately from his feeding station the absence of the female. When the male returned for one of his periodic visits to his mate on the chosen rock and found her gone, he left the water and walked rapidly about, sniffed the spot where the female had rested, and looked quickly at possible hiding places nearby. Apparently satisfied that the female was gone, he entered the water and swam hurriedly to several nearby hauling-out places, rising high in the water to look onto them. He also rose high in the water to look across the surface in different directions. Although I observed several such episodes, I never saw a male relocate the female after her departure.

In general, it would appear that during the postcopulatory period the female exhibits less interest in retaining the pair-bond than does the male. The female may, however, exhibit sexual interest, or even protective behavior, toward the male. What might be interpreted as protective behavior was exhibited by an adult female of an apparently mated pair that slept close beside each other on tidal rocks at 1630 on 2 March 1962. The more alert female started to leave the rock when she saw me approaching. When the sleeping male failed to awaken and follow her, she returned to him and, after pressing her paws against his face, neck, and chest and crawling on top of him, she finally aroused him. She then pressed her body against him from behind, inducing him to enter the water and follow her out of the area (figs. 88 and 89).

BREEDING BEHAVIOR VS. SOCIAL BEHAVIOR

Barabash-Nikiforov (1947) stated that "A grown cub often remains with the mother even after a new one is born, so that the mother is seen together with the newborn and yearling." This statement implies that a mother accompanied by a pup may participate in breeding activity. Murie (1940) describes a situation he observed in the Aleutians in which it appeared that the mother of a young pup engaged in coitus while the "little one . . . was crying at the far edge of the kelp."

I have observed a mother with a pup engage in rough play with a courting male during which the male attempted coitus. I have not, however, seen a female accompanied by a pup complete coitus or participate with the male in the breeding behavior cycle. In all instances that I have observed, the mother, after a period of play with the male, eventually retrieved her pup and attempted to disengaged herself from the aggressive male. If the pup was large, the mother appeared to be considerably mauled as the crying, clinging pup clasped her about the head and neck from the front and the male clung to her from the rear, or tried to intrude between the mother and pup. My observations lead me to believe that it would be difficult for a mother with a pup to engage in the mating cycle of several days duration.

That a mother accompanied by a pup might become impregnated is a possibility. Further data on the physiology of reproduction in the female must be obtained before a conclusion could be indicated with some certainty. Available observations indicate to me that it is usual for females to enter estrus only when they are not accompanied by a pup.

Certain habits of the sea otter could lead to confusion during field observations. First, rough play might be mistaken for copulation. It appears that Fisher (1939) may have made this mistake. Second, sea otters, especially juveniles which are separated from

221

FIGURE 88.—*A*—An adult male and female slept beside each other on a tidal rock (male right, female left). The more alert female was aroused by the click of the camera and started to leave the rock. The male continued to sleep soundly. (KWK 62–19–6) *B*—The female returned and prodded the male with her forepaws and then climbed on top of him, pressing his head and chest with her paws. The male raised his paws to push her away. (KWK 62–19–5) *C*—The male, finally aroused, looked about sleepily while the female stared in alarm at the camera. The female nudged the male toward the water. (KWK 62–19–3)

their mothers, may attach themselves temporarily to an adult, either male or female, or to another juvenile. The two animals may play together, and when frightened may cling loosely together with their forepaws.

Figure 90 shows a juvenile which took refuge behind an adult male, beside which it slept. After being disturbed by my presence,

FIGURE 89.—*A*—Finally aroused, the male moved ahead of the female while she prodded him toward the water from behind. (KWK 62–19–1) *B*—As the pair slid into the water the female grasped the still drowsy male and gazed over him at the camera. (KWK 62–19–43) *C*—Finally completely aroused, the male stared in mild alarm while the female clasped his back in her forepaws. Shortly after the last photograph was taken the pair dived and made their way through a narrow channel to open water beyond the tidal rocks. (KWK 62–19–40)

the two swam off together. Since an impregnated female separates from the male shortly after copulation, and family groups include only the mother and her young, it appears improbable that such an association as illustrated would involve family ties.

As a general rule, lone females and females with young are observed apart from adult males. But a courting male, after a period of attempted courtship with a female and her young, may

FIGURE 90.—This adult male was tolerant of a deserted juvenile which slept beside him and sought shelter behind him when frightened. When the adult finally became alarmed, entered the water, and swam off, the juvenile remained in close company with him. (KWK 62–25–24)

sleep near them in a kelp bed, or the three may haul out on a rock to groom, rest, and sleep in close association. It would appear that such an association is an expression of gregariousness. On one occasion I watched an adult male and female play roughly together for about 15 minutes. The female was accompanied by a large pup, which during the play period attempted to participate, or swam about nearby and occasionally cried. Although the male tentatively attempted copulation, the female was not receptive. After the three had hauled out and the male had groomed and rested beside the mother and pup for about 20 minutes, he entered the water and left the vicinity. In this case it was apparent that, although the male was sexually motivated, the association of the male and female was casual, and they were not a mated pair. The association described above might lead an observer to form erroneous opinions concerning breeding habits.

Reproduction in the Female

In this section, data from female reproductive tracts, the conceptuses they contained, and field counts of dependent young and independent animals are combined to present an analysis of reproduction in the female sea otter. The fundamental histological study on which much of the present analysis of reproductive tracts is based was done by Dr. A. A. Sinha under the direction of Dr. C. H. Conaway (Sinha, Conaway, and Kenyon, 1966). In that study, 136 mature tracts taken from 1954 through 1962 were used. Some material from that collection, which was not published in Sinha et al (1966), is included in the present study. It was kindly given to me by Dr. Sinha. A study of the histology of the sea otter ovary was recently completed (Sinha and Conaway, 1968).

The 1963 collections (table 46) added data from different seasons which revealed what the earlier material did not: that there is apparently a peak in frequency of births in summer.

Samples representing certain seasons are small. More specimens from summer, fall, and winter are needed before all phases of the reproductive cycle may be based on an adequately large sample. A long-continued field study of marked animals and a captive breeding colony would contribute valuable information on some phases of the reproductive cycle.

My discussion of various aspects of the reproductive material available is followed by a statistical analysis of this material by Dr. Douglas G. Chapman.

REPRODUCTIVE TRACTS

From 1954 to 1963, reproductive tracts were obtained from animals found dead on beaches, from animals captured (netted) on beaches, and from animals shot during experimental cropping studies. The adult female tracts that were collected are listed in table 46. The four larger collections from 1962 and 1963 (table 46) contribute the most useful material. The smaller collections and individual specimens taken in other years are included where useful in the following analyses. In tables 47 through 51, different

TABLE 46.—*Adult female sea otter reproductive tracts from Amchitka Island*

[Except those taken in 1960. These were taken in other areas of Alaska]

Period	Number	Remarks
1954–57	14	Taken at various seasons. Some from animals found dead. Studied by C. H. Conaway and A. A. Sinha.
Feb.–Apr. 1959	14	Most were netted on beaches, several found dead. Studied by Conaway and Sinha.
Jan.–July 1960	4	Shot (FWS). Studied by Conaway and Sinha.
Jan.–Feb. 1962	88	Shot (ADFG). Studied by Conaway and Sinha.
Oct. 1962	14	Shot (ADFG). Studied by Conaway and Sinha.
Mar.–Apr. 1963	125	Shot (ADFG). Studied by Kenyon.
July–Aug, 1963	19	Shot (ADFG). Studied by Kenyon.
Total	278	

TABLE 47.—*Phases of reproduction in the female sea otter as shown by status of ovaries and size of conceptus*

[Information from genital tracts collected from 1954 through 1963 is combined]

	Jan.–Feb.		Mar.–Apr.		May–Aug.[1]		Sept.–Dec.		Total number
	Number	Percent	Number	Percent	Number	Percent	Number	Percent	
Unimplanted blastocyst	35	57	49	50	4	31	6	100	94
Conceptuses:									
Class 1	8	13	9	9	0	0	0	0	17
Class 2	4	7	6	6	0	0	0	0	10
Class 3	4	7	11	11	2	15	0	0	17
Class 4	10	16	17	17	3	23	0	0	30
Class 5	0	0	6	6	4	31	0	0	10
Total conceptuses	26	43	49	50	9	69	0	0	84
Total pregnant	61	70	98	70	13	52	6	27	178
Not pregnant [2]	27	30	42	30	12	48	16	73	97
Total tracts	88	—	140	—	25	—	22	—	275

[1] The 19 adult female sea otters taken between 31 July and 3 August 1963 were killed selectively, mothers accompanied by pups were spared. Thus, the percentage of postpartum nonpregnant specimens in this sample is less than it would have been if the kill had been nonselective.

[2] See table 51 for more details.

TABLE 48.—*Frequency of primiparous and multiparous sea otters*

Period sampled	Total examined	Primiparous		Multiparous	
		Number	Percent	Number	Percent
1963					
15 Mar.–2 Apr.	125	21	17	104	83
31 July–3 Aug.	12	2	17	10	83
Total	137	23		114	

TABLE 49.—*Uterine horn of pregnancy*

Period sampled	Specimens examined	Uterine horn pregnant			
		Right		Left	
		Number	Percent	Number	Percent
Mar.–Apr.	90	46	51	44	49
May–Aug.	7	3	43	4	57
Total	97	49	51	48	49

TABLE 50.—*Weight distribution of embryonic and fetal sea otters*

| Weight class | Collected in period [1] | | | | | | | | | | | | | | |
| | 22 Jan. to 13 Feb. 1962 [2] | | | | | 15 Mar. to 2 Apr. 1963 | | | | | 31 July to 3 Aug. 1963 | | | | |
	Num-ber	Per-cent	Maxi-mum	Mini-mum	Mean	Num-ber	Per-cent	Maxi-mum	Mini-mum	Mean	Num-ber	Per-cent	Maxi-mum	Mini-mum	Mean
No. 1, <1 gram	8	31	0.9	0.5	0.6	8 [3]	16	0.9	0.2	0.2	0	0	—	—	—
No. 2, 1–10 grams	4	15	9.0	7.0	8.0	6	12	8.8	1.1	4.1	0	0	—	—	—
No. 3, 10–100 grams	4	15	80.0	15.0	46.0	11	23	93.0	10.9	39.9	2	25	61.9	36.1	49.0
No. 4, 100–1000 grams	10	39	720.0	140.0	350.0	18	37	882.0	100.5	344.1	2	25	478.0	356.0	417.0
No. 5, 1,000–2,000 grams	0	—	—	—	—	6	12	1,869.0	1,067.0	1,511.2	4	50	1,810.0	1,118.0	1,497.0
Total	26	100				49	100				8	100			

[1] No implanted pregnancies were found in the 1962 fall sample.
[2] Weights from A. A. Sinha (personal communication).
[3] Three of the visibly implanted embryos included here were very small and were not weighed. These are included in the total above but only five that were weighed are represented in the maximum, minimum, and mean weights.

TABLE 51.—*Reproductive status of adult nonpregnant sea otters*

[Nine animals, adult in body size but being nulliparous and showing no follicular activity, are excluded]

Nonpregnant tracts	Samples collected in—						Total
	Spring 1963, Mar.–Apr.		Summer 1963,[1] July–Aug.		Fall, 1957 and 1962, Oct.–Nov.		
	Number	Percent	Number	Percent	Number	Percent	
Postpartum, inactive ovaries:							
Pup present	13	35			8	61	21
Pup absent	16	43	3	60	1	8	20
Inactive ovaries [2]	4	11	2	40	3	23	9
Active ovaries [3]	4	11			1	8	5
Total	37	100	5	100	13	100	55
Total tracts examined and percent not pregnant	125	30	14	36	17	76	156

[1] Animals were killed selectively to exclude all mothers accompanied by young. The objective was to take as many male skins as possible in a female area. Among 19 independent animals, only 1 male was taken.

[2] Multiparous but not showing positive evidence of being recently postpartum.

[3] Estrus and proestrus.

total numbers of specimens are shown because not all specimens could be used for every aspect of this study. I did not examine all collections and samples. Those that I did examine presented adequate information for certain aspects of this study.

The reproductive tracts were removed from the animals from a few minutes to several hours after death, depending on field conditions. They were then fixed entire for 24 hours in AFA solution (95 percent alcohol, 30 percent; commercial formalin, 10 percent; glacial acetic acid, 10 percent; water, 50 percent). After fixing, the tracts were stored for later study in 70 percent isopropyl alcohol.

Sinha et al. (1966) explain how certain aspects of reproductive tract studies were conducted. I examined ovaries with a 10X Loupe after slicing them into sections about 1 mm. in width.

FIELD COUNTS OF SEA OTTERS

Field counts of sea otters were recorded whenever possible. The primary objectives were to obtain information on (1) the season of birth, and (2) the annual rate of reproduction.

Observations were limited by: (1) Environmental conditions such as wind, precipitation, and rough water; (2) a variable degree of sexual segregation among independent animals, including mothers with young; (3) the often indistinguishability of sexes and age classes; and (4) the constant movement of animals to and from local areas. In spite of these factors, useful field observations were obtained.

Counts of otters were made primarily at Amchitka Island, from beaches and cliff tops and during dory trips through inshore waters. Binoculars (7X50) and a telescope (50 power) were used for observation.

DEFINITION OF TERMS

Implanted pregnancy observations are based on visible swellings of the uterine horn, presence of a corpus luteum, and recovery of the conceptus. *Unimplanted pregnancy* observations are based on the presence of a corpus luteum not accompanied by swelling of the uterine horn. Sinha et al. (1966) demonstrated that when a corpus luteum is present and no uterine swelling is visible a blastocyst may be recovered from the uterine horn. *Multiparous* animals were separated from *nulliparous* and *primiparous* animals by the thickened appearance of the uterine horns which, after having held a conceptus, do not regain the smooth, firm texture of the nulliparous uterine horn.

Tracts were classified as *nonpregnant* when no corpus luteum was present. A female was considered to be *post partum* if one or more of the following conditions was observed: (1) lactation, (2) presence of a pup, (3) presence of a corpus albicans, (4) presence of a placental (uterine) scar. Because it appears that the young sea otter remains with its mother for about a year, certain evidence of a post partum condition may be obscure by the time the pup and mother part. The placental scar may virtually disappear and the corpus albicans may be reduced in a female accompanied by a large pup. One lactating female, whose pup was either recently lost or was not seen by the hunters, showed no placental scar and the corpus albicans was very small.

Classification of ovaries as *estrous*, *proestrous*, and *anestrous*, based on macroscopic examination of sectioned ovaries, are considered briefly in the following discussion. The objective of this study is to present a review of the natural history of reproduction.

AGE AT SEXUAL MATURITY

Sufficient data are not available to fix with certainty the age at sexual maturity. Some information was obtained from a juvenile female (approximately 1 year old), weighing about 24 lb. (10. 9 kg.), that was tagged (EL 556, table 39) on 22 March 1962. On 18 March 1963, when this animal was shot 2.5 miles from the place of marking it weighed 33 lb. The dentition was that of a young adult, but the reproductive tract was decidedly immature.

It can thus be said that the female sea otter does not mature sexually until after 2 years of age.

The mean weight of 39 pregnant females was 50 lb. (22.7 kg.) (extremes 36 and 70 lb.). Among 21 primiparous females, the mean weight was 43 lb. (19.5 kg.) (extremes 35 and 52 lb.). If the marked 33-lb., 2-year-old had continued to grow during her third year at the rate she did in her second, her weight would have approximated the mean weight of the primiparous females. This suggests that the female may become sexually mature at 3 years of age.

Among northern fur seals on the Pribilof Islands, the pregnancy rate in 4-year-olds is about 3 percent and in 5-year-olds about 40 percent (Fiscus and Kajimura, 1967). If we assume a somewhat similar condition in the sea otter, it is indicated that a small percentage of females may become pregnant after attaining 3 years of age, i.e., in the fourth year, and that animals 5 or more years of age constitute the important reproducing segment of the population (see also "Implication of Other Observations," p. 245-246).

PREGNANT FEMALES

Table 47 and figure 91 summarize data from 178 females showing evidence of pregnancy. Among pregnant animals, unimplanted pregnancy reached maximum frequency (100 percent) in the fall sample. Implanted pregnancy increased in spring and reached maximum frequency (69 percent) in summer. The high frequency of large (weight class 5) fetuses in summer (50 percent, table 50) and concurrent low frequency of unimplanted pregnancies (31 percent, table 47) indicate, as do the field counts of dependent young, that parturition reaches a peak in summer. Although the fall sample of tracts is small, it demonstrates that parturition in the fall and winter accounts for a minority of births.

Among 137 pregnant females from two samples for which data are available (table 48), it is indicated that annually 17 percent of the pregnant animals became pregnant for the first time and that 83 percent are multiparous.

Location of pregnancy

A record of the uterine horn of pregnancy is available for 97 animals. Although the sample is small, it was gathered unselectively and demonstrates that pregnancy occurs with equal frequency in the right and left uterine horns (table 49). The location of implantation of the conceptus is usually within the center one-third of the uterine horn.

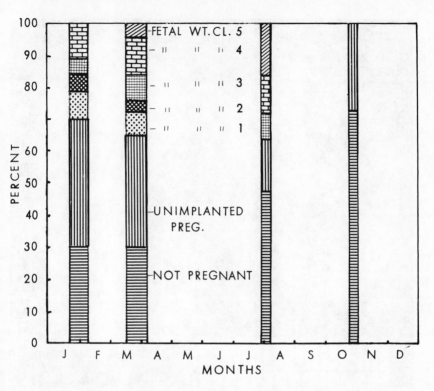

FIGURE 91.—Phases in the reproductive cycle of the female sea otter as revealed by ovary and fetal examinations of four samples of reproductive tracts. Although some of the samples are small, they illustrate that large fetuses and implanted pregnancies predominate in summer and that pregnancy is at a maximum in late winter and spring.

Conceptus size and development

To compare the conceptuses that were recovered from reproductive tract samples, the embryos and fetuses were classified according to five arbitrarily chosen weight classes following a logarithmic scale (table 50). The conceptuses ranged in weight from a fraction of a gram to 1,869 g. (4 lb.). When the weights of fetuses taken in different seasons are compared, it is shown that in winter conceptuses of small size predominate and in summer large fetuses predominate. The series of photographs (figs. 92 and 93) illustrate stages of development. The comparative sizes of the conceptuses in the samples from different seasons were useful in indicating the timing of certain phases of the reproductive cycle (see Chapman's analysis that follows).

The morphology of the female reproductive tract was studied

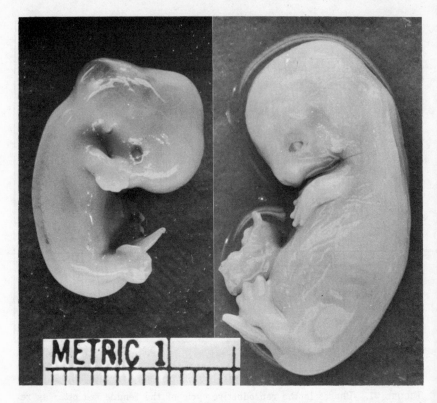

FIGURE 92.—Early fetal stages of the sea otter. Sex could not be determined
in either specimen by gross examination, and the age of the fetuses is not
known. Differentiation of the front and hind limb buds has barely begun
in the larger fetus. Specimens from Amchitka Island, 18 and 19 March
1963: Left—Specimen JEB 63-52, weight 0.692 g., crown-rump length 17
mm. (KWK 65-18-15) Right—Specimen JEB 63-67, weight 1.12 g.,
crown-rump length 24 mm. (KWK 65-18-9).

and described in detail by Sinha (1965). The development of the
fetal membranes, their structures, and evolutionary relationships
were studied and described by Sinha and Mossman (1966). The
general appearance of the gravid reproductive tract is shown in
figure 93.

NONPREGNANT ADULT FEMALES

Spring sample

Although two spring samples (1962 and 1963, table 46) of
female sea otters from Amchitka were taken, I studied only the
1963 specimens.

Between 15 March and 2 April 1963, 125 adult female sea otters

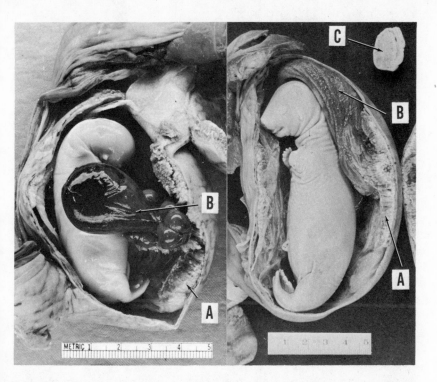

FIGURE 93.—Intermediate fetal development. One side of the uterine wall was removed to show the chorioallantoic placenta (*A*) and the large antimesometrial, pedunculated saclike hematome (*B*). The specimen on the left shows also smaller hematomic pouches surrounding the hemotomic peduncle. The relative size of the ovary is shown. It was sectioned to reveal the large corpus luteum (*C*). Specimens from Amchitka Island: Left—specimen JEB 63–40, weight 11.82 g., crown-rump length 53 mm., sex ♀; taken 17 March 1963. (KWK 65–18–33) Right—specimen ADFG 520, weight 61.95 g., crown-rump length 105 mm., sex ♀; taken 2 August 1963. (KWK 65–13–11) Sinha and Mossman (1966) give a detailed description of placentation in the sea otter.

were taken and their reproductive tracts were examined (table 51). Thirty-seven (30 percent) showed no evidence of pregnancy (no corpus luteum or visible conceptus). Of these, 29 exhibited evidence of being post partum from a few days to perhaps a year. Among these 29 females that were judged to be post partum, 13 (45 percent) were accompanied by a pup. The remaining 16 (55 percent) were not, or the pup was not seen, but the female showed anatomical evidence of having borne a pup. Although it might be inferred that the loss of young is as high as 55 percent, this is not necessarily true. Large young, although still dependent on their mothers, may be some distance (±50 m.) from them and thus not associated with the mother by the hunter's observations. Also, large young may have recently become independent.

Among the eight remaining nonpregnant females, four showed no follicular activity or positive evidence of being post partum. One of these was diseased. It possessed a large ovarian cyst (31×15 mm.) The remaining four were multiparous (enlarged uterine horns) but did not show evidence of being post partum and appeared to be approaching estrus (follicles enlarged) or to have recently ovulated.

Summer sample

Among 14 sexually mature sea otters taken between 31 July and 3 August 1963 at Amchitka, 5 (36 percent) were not pregnant. Three of these were post partum. None was accompanied by a pup. (As explained elsewhere, this collection was selectively taken to exclude mothers accompanied by pups.) Two were multiparous inactive but their reproductive tracts revealed no evidence of being recently post partum (table 51).

Fall sample

Among 17 sexually mature females taken between 12 October and 3 November, 13 (76 percent) were not pregnant. Among these, eight (61 percent) were accompanied by young and one was lactating, indicating that a pup had recently been lost. Of the five remaining, three showed no follicular activity or indication of having recently lost a pup. One showed follicular activity indicating a proestrus condition (table 51).

FIELD COUNTS

An effort was made to record newly born young separately from older dependent young. Because of variable field conditions, the results were inconsistent and not useful to this study. Therefore, all young with mothers were grouped as dependent animals.

Counts were made in many areas but only in a consistent way during all field seasons in the Constantine Harbor, Kirilof Point to Kirilof Bay areas. After all of the data from several other areas were studied, it became apparent that because of different conditions in each area the results of counts in one area were not comparable with those made in another. Also, counts made from a cliff top cannot be compared with counts made from a dory. Females with young among coastal rocks may be missed during an offshore dory count. Also, the number of males, i.e., the degree of sexual segregation, varies in different areas (see table 43, Segregation of Sexes).

I made the field counts from Kirilof Point and vicinity from the same observation stations at all seasons (table 52). Because they were made in different years, they cannot be considered strictly comparable but they do constitute the best material available and general conclusions are based on them.

In the summer of 1955, Kirilof Point (on the Bering Sea shore of Amchitka), bounded on the east by Constantine Harbor and on the west by Kirilof Bay and having a shoreline of about 5.5 km. (3 nautical miles), was chosen as a study area. I soon found that it was frequented primarily by females, and especially mothers with young (see Segregation of Sexes). Counts in this area were thus not representative of the ratio of dependent young to independent animals in the Amchitka population, but were biased in favor of a high ratio of dependent young to independent (includes both sexes and all ages other than dependent young) animals.

PHASES OF REPRODUCTION

Breeding season

Mating behavior (mated pairs, attempted copulation, or copulation) was observed in all months except October and December. Harsh winter weather reduces visibility and I have spent less time in the field in the fall and winter seasons. Barabash-Nikiforov

TABLE 52.—*Sea otters counted along 5.5 km. of shoreline Kirilof area, at Amchitka Island, Alaska*

[This area included parts of Constantine Harbor, all of Kirilof Point, and part of Kirilof Bay. This locality is frequented primarily by females and young. Complete counts of Kirilof Point, as well as counts from parts of the area, are included in this table]

Month and year	Number of counts	Independent animals	Dependent young	Total	Percent dependent young	Season mean percent young
January 1959	6	37	7	44	16	} 15
February 1959	7	104	17	121	14	
March, 1959 and 1962	2	34	5	39	13	} 15
April 1959	5	197	39	236	17	
May 1956	4	164	42	206	20	
May 1959	1	62	11	73	15	} 17
June 1956	3	126	23	149	15	
July 1956	6	258	85	343	25	} 22
August 1955	9	278	59	337	18	
September 1955	12	407	83	490	17	
October 1957	3	132	49	181	27	} 24
November 1957	11	315	117	432	27	
Total	69	2,114	537	2,651		

(1947) did not observe copulation during October and December.

Data from field observations of breeding behavior and from reproductive tracts give conflicting indications of the period of maximum mating activity. Field observations appear to indicate that most breeding activity occurs in June. By months, observations of breeding behavior were as follows:

January	1	May	9	September	2
February	2	June	17	October	0
March	3	July	1	November	1
April	1	August	4	December	0

Field observations of behavior are hampered in fall and winter by stormy weather conditions. Because comparative field observation time was not available in all seasons, I consider that field observations of mating activity are not quantitatively useful. They are qualitatively useful, however, in demonstrating that breeding activity does occur in all seasons.

Because the frequency of pregnancy in our samples increased from 27 percent in early fall (October) to 70 percent in the January-February sample (table 47), the available data indicate that maximum breeding activity occurs in the late fall to winter period. Further studies, particularly of reproductive tracts taken in fall and winter months, are needed to reveal with certainty the period of maximum breeding activity.

Gestation period

Sinha et al. (1966) demonstrated that after fertilization in the sea otter the blastocyst enters a period of rest, i.e., undergoes "delayed implantation." Thus, presence of a corpus luteum indicates pregnancy whether or not a conceptus is visible on gross examination of the tract. When the "resting stage" is completed, the blastocyst becomes implanted in the mucosa of the uterine horn and proceeds through embryonic and fetal stages of growth.

To gain some knowledge of the length of the gestation period and the duration of its unimplanted and implanted stages, data were obtained from the ovaries and conceptuses of 275 reproductive tracts (table 47 and fig. 91).

One method of estimating the gestation period of the sea otter is to assume that during the period of implanted pregnancy the rate of fetal growth may be comparable to that of the European river otter *(Lutra lutra)* and American river otter *(L. canadensis)*. (A more sophisticated method, given below, is employed by Chapman.) The European animal differs from the American river otter and sea otter in that the blastocyst does not undergo a delay in implantation and the gestation period has been determined to be about 63 days (Cocks, 1881).

The data of Hamilton and Eadie (1964) show conclusively that the gestation period of the American river otter includes a period of delayed implantation. The data of Liers (1951) appear to indicate that this period may be variable. He recorded extremes of 9 months 18 days to 12 months 15 days in the total gestation period of captive otters.

Huggett and Widdas (1951) showed that during certain phases of prenatal growth the cube roots of fetal weights fall along a straight line. They indicate that an adjustment can be made for the period before the cube root of fetal weights begins to follow a straight line. This adjustment, however, is minor and, in estimating the period of implanted gestation in the sea otter, is ignored on the graph (fig. 94).

The weights of two young European otters that were presumably

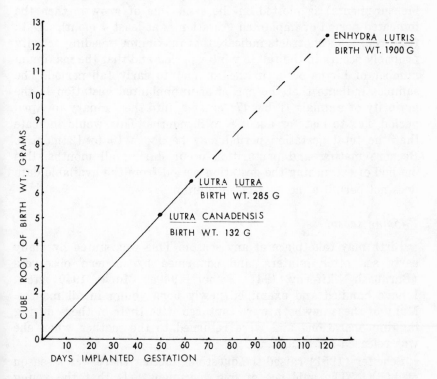

FIGURE 94.—Estimated period of implanted pregnancy. The periods are estimated for the American river otter and sea otter on the assumption that their fetal growth velocities are similar to that of the closely related European river otter (see Huggett and Widdas, 1951).

less than a week old were 285 and 290 g. (Jensen, 1964). If the smaller of the two is presumed to approximate the birth weight and its cube root is plotted according to the method of Huggett and Widdas (1951) for a gestation period of about 62 days, a fetal growth rate line is established (fig. 94). If the full-term fetus weighing 132 g., that was recovered by Hamilton and Eadie (1964), is plotted on the same growth scale as the European otter, it is indicated that the period of implanted pregnancy in the American river otter may be less than 2 months. Liers (1951) states that "The eyes open when the young are about thirty-five days old." This indicates that at birth the river otter is in an early stage of development compared to the sea otter which is born with the eyes open.

To obtain an approximation of the period of implanted pregnancy in the sea otter, it appears reasonable to compare its fetal growth rate with that of its closest relatives. If the cube root of the sea otter weight at birth (generally at least 1,900 g., see Body Measurements) is plotted on the same line of growth, then the indicated period of implanted gestation is at least 4 months. Data from reproductive tracts indicate that maximum breeding activity probably occurs in the fall to winter period and that the maximum number of births occur in the summer to early fall period. The samples indicate that the period of unimplanted gestation in the majority of animals (table 47) extends into the January to April period, i.e., to last for about 6 to 8 months. This would indicate that the total gestation period may be about 10 to 12 months. Because mating and parturition occur during all months, this method of estimating the gestation period from the available data does not permit a more precise definition.

Pupping season

Birth may take place at any season. This was stated by many early sea otter hunters, and confirmed by modern observers (Barabash-Nikiforov, 1947; Fisher, 1940a; Murie, 1940; etc.). I have handled and examined newly born young in all months. Many of these newborn were captured with their mothers during tagging operations and were returned to the mother when she was released after tagging.

Scheffer (1951) raised the question whether there was a season of birth: "The evidence of five specimens...is that the young are born in April and May, rather than the year around." Data from our samples indicate that there is a season of maximum birth frequency. The data in table 52 demonstrate that the percentage of dependent young in the population is relatively low in the winter and spring. After the late-winter to early-spring season of storms, which is accompanied by much mortality among juvenile otters (see Limiting Factors), an increasing number of births is demonstrated in the field counts. A summer peak in the frequency of births is confirmed by high frequency of large fetuses recovered in that season from reproductive tracts (table 47).

The frequency of nearly full-term fetuses in the samples increased from none in the January-February sample to 6 percent in the March-April sample and to 31 percent in the May-August sample (table 47). The number of dependent young with mothers also increased throughout the spring and summer (see table 52, Field Counts).

In the small midsummer sample (August) the fetuses were large, in weight classes 3, 4, and 5, none were in weight classes 1 and 2 (table 50).

These data strongly suggest that birth frequency increases in early spring and reaches a peak in summer. Our samples from the September through February period were too small to confirm the field observations of newly born young in every month.

Although the Steller's sea cow (Hydrodamalis gigas) is a very different animal from the sea otter, it was also a resident inshore marine mammal. It is interesting that Steller noted (in Stejneger, 1936, p. 355) that the sea-cow "brings forth their young at all seasons, generally however in autumn, judging from the many new-born seen at that time." The fact of bearing young at all seasons, while having a season of maximum birth frequency, may be a case of convergent evolution related to the habitat in which these animals were sympatric.

Place of birth and fetal orientation

There is no record that the birth of a sea otter has ever been observed. Fisher (1940a, p. 132) presumed that "The births of the young otters take place on the kelp beds." This infers that the young are born in water. Barabash-Nikiforov (1947, p. 97, English translation), however, saw a mother with a newly born young on shore and recovered the still warm afterbirth.

The place of birth in marine mammals may be related to fetal orientation at birth. For example, in cetaceans birth always occurs in water. Slijper (1956) summarized data on the position of the cetacean fetus at birth. In 22 observed births, all young were born tail foremost. Presumably caudal presentation is a survival factor in an air breathing mammal born under water (Essapian, 1953). Slijper (1956), however, does not subscribe to this theory.

If caudal presentation is a survival factor in aquatic birth and it were the rule in the sea otter, it might be supposed that birth would occur in the water. Among 43 fetuses for which fetal orientation were recorded, delivery would have been cephalic in 22 (51 percent) and caudal in 21 (49 percent). These data indicate that selective evolution for caudal presentation at birth, and by inference for birth in water, has not taken place in the sea otter. By comparison, the fur seal is more specialized for life in the marine environment than is the sea otter but emerges from the water before parturition. Peterson (1965, p. 136) recorded that in 61 percent of 112 observed births the young emerged head foremost. It is thus indicated that birth in the sea otter, as in the fur seal normally occurs on land.

Period between births

Figure 91 and table 47 demonstrate that during the winter and spring when the maximum number of sea otters are pregnant, one-third of the tracts in our sample were nonpregnant. I strongly suspect that all reproductive tract samples are biased toward a low frequency of nonpregnant animals. This assumption is based on three observations: (1) that no female known definitely to be accompanied by a pup was found to be pregnant, (2) that females with young are more wary and secretive than females without young and are thus less available to hunters, and (3) that during hunting operations I noted a degree of reluctance in hunters to shoot a female accompanied by a pup if animals without pups were present. Thus, an unknown degree of bias in favor of single animals, i.e., a high percentage of pregnant animals, is included in all samples. The July to August 1963 sample is particularly biased, since single animals only were selectively killed. At this season the number of mothers accompanied by pups is approaching the annual maximum (see table 52). Thus, the percentage of nonpregnant animals in the adult female population would also approach maximum numbers at this season. This is shown by the sample (fig. 91), but it would be much more apparent had the sample been unselective.

Because the summer sample of reproductive tracts was taken selectively to exclude mothers accompanied by pups it is, in some respects, not comparable with the spring and fall samples. Nevertheless, the following conclusions concerning nonpregnant female sea otters in our samples are indicated. (1) Females accompanied by young do not enter estrus. (2) Even if the pup is lost, estrus may be delayed until after evidence of parturition (lactation, placental scar, or corpora albicantia) has disappeared or nearly disappeared. (3) In fall there is a maximum number of nonpregnant animals in the population, since many females are accompanied by young born in spring and summer. (4) Because the percentage of proestrous and estrous animals in the nonpregnant population is small, it is indicated that impregnation takes place soon after the onset of follicular activity.

With the probability of a sampling bias toward a high frequency of pregnant animals in mind, it may be considered that more than one-third and probably at least half of the sexually mature female population is always nonpregnant (fig. 91). This coincides with general observations that the mother sea otter cares for her pup for about a year. When she separates from her young, she may become pregnant and give birth again about 2 years after the prior parturition (see analysis by Chapman that follows).

The period between normal separation of the mother from the young and the onset of estrus is unknown. If this period is long, the period between births may be longer than 2 years. That the period between separation from the young and the onset of estrus may be extended is indicated by the observation that ovaries were inactive in females which were multiparous but not lactating or accompanied by a pup and showed questionable evidence (indistinct recent corpus albicantia tissue and slight uterine discoloration) of having been post partum for a long time.

Rate of reproduction

The counts recorded in table 52 were made in an area favored by females (see Segregation of Sexes). Data obtained from animals killed in the Constantine Harbor to the Kirilof Bay areas reveal that among 91 animals 19 (21 percent) were males (Segregation of Sexes, table 43).

It was shown that for general purposes the sea otter sex ratio may be considered 50:50 (see Sex Ratio). If 21 percent of the animals in the field counts were males (from table 52: 2,114 $\times$ 0.21 = 444 males, 2,114 − 444 = 1,670 females; males and females in total population = 1,670 $\times$ 2 = 3,340 independent male and female;

3,340 + 537 young = 3,877; $\dfrac{537 \times 100}{3,877}$ = 14 percent, i.e., young to independent animals 14 percent dependent young) then the mean annual percent of young in the entire population is 14 percent. Since the young sea otter remains with its mother for about a year, the annual rate of reproduction is 14 percent, or about 16 young born per 100 independent animals per year.

From Chapman's analysis (see later section) it is shown that each 100 adult females in the breeding population produce 50 young per year. Thus, in the adult population (male and female) there are theoretically 25 dependent young per 100 adults of both sexes. It was calculated that 31 percent of the independent animals observed during field counts are juveniles. Thus, 69 percent of those observed are adults. It follows that, with a group of 69 adults there are 17 (i.e., 25 percent) dependent young, or—

	Number	Percent
Dependent young	17	14.5
Independent animals:		
Juveniles	31	26.5
Adults	69	59.0
Total	117	100

Information from reproductive tracts, from field counts of dependent and independent animals, and the ratio of males to females in the kill are used in two ways to demonstrate that the annual rate of reproduction of the Amchitka population is about 14 to 15 percent.

Twinning

Barabash-Nikiforov (1947, p. 98) and Snow (1910) report observations of mothers with two young, and reproductive tracts containing two fetuses. Our observations indicate that twinning is unusual. In 278 reproductive tracts taken in 1954–63, 178 of which showed an indication of pregnancy, no twin fetuses were found. One specimen (No. JEB 63–166) taken at Amchitka on 25 March 1963, had well-defined corpora albicantia in both ovaries and darkened scar tissue (placental scars) in both uterine horns. This female was not, however, accompanied by young.

That activity in both ovaries is not necessarily an indication of twinning was shown by one specimen (ADFG 515). Both ovaries contained well-defined corpora lutea but only the left uterine horn contained a conceptus.

In early April 1955, a female and two large young (each about 18–20 lb.) with her were captured on shore at Amchitka. They were held in captivity and liberated at the Pribilof Islands. During the days that the three animals remained in captivity, the adult allowed both young to nurse. She appeared equally permissive to both. She groomed only one of the pups, however, and when the three were liberated together, she ignored one and took on her chest the one she habitually groomed. It was our conclusion that the deserted pup was an orphan toward which this mother exhibited tolerance.

Large young, still dependent on their mothers, will frequently play together for long periods while their mothers are diving for food. If one mother should desert her young at such a time, it is possible that an association such as we observed could occur. Although it is possible that a mother may bear twins, I believe it is doubtful that a mother could feed and groom and successfully bring two young to the stage of independence.

In the northern fur seal *(Callorhinus ursinus)* which, like the sea otter, normally bears one young at parturition and is highly specialized to marine existence, twinning is rare. Peterson and Reeder (1966) summarize data derived from Fiscus, Baines, and Wilke (1964) demonstrating the incidence of twin implantation in the fur seal at 0.14 percent among 4,223 pregnant females examined. In spite of the observation that the young fur seal appears less burdensome to its mother than the young sea otter, no evidence exists to date that a fur seal can successfully raise twins to weaning age (Peterson and Reeder, 1966).

Length of Stages of the Reproductive Cycle

Dr. D. G. Chapman, Chairman, Biomathematics Group, Laboratory of Statistical Research, Department of Mathematics, University of Washington, studied the data obtained from female reproductive tracts and prepared the following analysis:

Analysis of fetal weight data; The procedure of Huggett and Widdas (1951) is used to estimate the fetal growth velocity and hence the length of the growth period. Table 53 shows the data of table 50: fetuses classified by weight classes according to time of collection reduced to a percentage basis.

The last row in the table is obtained by (1) calculating an unweighted mean of the mean weights in the three periods; (2) finding the cube root of this mean.

The use of percentages in the table and the unweighted means in the

TABLE 53.—*Percent of fetuses in each weight class*

[This table is derived from data in table 50]

Time of collection after Jan.	Class 1	Class 2	Class 3	Class 4	Class 5
1 month	31	15	15	38	0
3 months	18	12	22	35	12
7 months	0	0	22	33	44
Mean time in months after Jan.	1.7	1.9	4.0	3.5	6.1
Cube root of mean weight	0.74	2.21	3.27	7.18	11.45

calculation are necessary to give equal representation to all times of the year. A regression line fitted to the cube root of the weights against the mean time in months give a regression coefficient of

a=2.292 per month

or on a daily basis

a=0.076

This is an estimate of the specific growth velocity of Huggett and Widdas (1951). In view of the very small samples obtained over all parts of the year except the January to April period, it is subject to considerable sampling error and it seems reasonable to round the estimate to 0.08. While this growth velocity is somewhat below the value calculated for the European river otter, it is quite close to values calculated for the northern fur seal (0.085 has been calculated by Chapman, unpublished manuscript).

If 1850 g. is used as an average fetal size at birth, the estimated period of fetal development after establishment of the fetus is,

$$\frac{\sqrt[3]{1850}}{.08} = \frac{12.3}{.08} = 154 \text{ days}$$

or approximately 5 months.

It is also necessary to estimate the length of the gestation period during which the blastocyst is unimplanted. From table 54 we have the numbers and percentage of pregnant animals with an unimplanted blastocyst and a conceptus during the four seasons.

It might be argued that lesser weight should be given to the two shorter periods, January to February and March to April. If the results of these two periods are averaged, and this average is incorporated into an overall unweighted average, the result is essentially the same. (The average so computed would be 61 percent versus the 60 shown in table 54.)

It thus appears that the period during which the blastocyst is unimplanted is half as long again as the implanted period, or about 7½ months. The full gestation period will also include the period required for establishment of the embryo, i.e., the period before linear growth is established. Huggett and Widdas (1951) indicate a rough procedure to estimate this but it is not known whether their values apply to animals that exhibit delayed implantation. If about ½ month is allowed for this period, it follows that the estimated total length of the period of gestation is about 13 months.

The period during which the female sea otter is not pregnant (lactating and resting period) can be estimated similarly from the data from table 47. This table shows that the percent nonpregnant in the four periods noted is 30, 30, 48, and 73, respectively. In this case the weight to be given to the two first periods does make a difference. The average of the four percentages is

TABLE 54.—*Frequency of unimplanted and implanted pregnancy, by season*

[Data from table 47]

Sample period	Number animals with unimplanted blastocyst	Number animals with conceptus	Percent unimplanted
January, February	35	26	58
March, April	49	49	50
May–August	4	9	31
September–December	6	0	100
Unweighted average			60

45, while the average of the three seasons, if January, February, March, and April are pooled into one value, is 50.

If the length of the gestation period is about 13 months, the first average above, i.e., 45 percent, would imply an 11-month period for lactation and resting and a 2-year total cycle. The other average, 50 percent, would imply a 13-month lactation and resting period or a total 26-month cycle. This seems less probable, though it could be the average of a breeding group in which some proportion of the animals miss being impregnated at the first opportunity after the end of lactation and thus lengthen the average cycle. It is also possible that the estimates of the length of the gestation period are high due to sampling errors and that both gestation and lactation plus resting periods are 12 months in length.

It thus seems that the best estimates available at present are as follows:

Lactation plus resting _____11–12 months.
Unimplanted period _____7–8 months.
Implanted fetus _____4½ to 5½ months.
Gestation period _____12–13 months.
Total length of reproductive cycle _____2 years.
Average birth rate mature female _____0.50.

IMPLICATION OF OTHER OBSERVATIONS

Recruitment and mortality rate: The observations on the proportion of primiparous animals among pregnant animals (17 percent, table 48) taken together with the 2-year cycle indicates that the recruitment rate among mature females is 0.085 per year. If the mature female herd is nearly stable in size, this will also be the mortality rate of this component of the population. This is relatively low but only slightly lower than the corresponding rate among fur seals.

Proportion of juveniles and length of juvenile stage: If 50 percent of the mature females give birth each year and nurse the young animal for nearly a year (say 10 months), this implies the ratio of dependent young to mature females is $\frac{1}{2} \times \frac{10}{12}$ or 0.42. Extensive field observations (table 52, cf. also discussion) show the ratio of dependent young to independent females is $\frac{537}{1670} = 0.32$.

The independent females include both mature and juvenile animals. If it is assumed that the survival rates of both of these groups is 1–0.085 (=.915) *after the initial transition from dependence to independence*, then a comparison of the two ratios given above shed light on both the proportion of juveniles in the herd and the length of the juvenile stage.

For denote by
Y=dependent young (of both sexes)
J=juveniles (females)
A=adults (females)

then the above two ratios are:

$$\frac{Y}{A} = 0.42$$

$$\frac{Y}{A+J} = 0.32$$

so that

$$\frac{A+J}{A} = \frac{0.42}{0.32} = 1.31 \quad \text{whence} \quad 1+\frac{J}{A} = 1.31$$

or

$$\frac{J}{A} = 0.31 \tag{1}$$

Now let J_o=number of juveniles in their first year after dependency let n=
number of years in juvenile stage

$$J = J_o + J_o(.915) + \ldots J_o(.915)^{n-1}$$

$$= \frac{J_o}{1-.915}(1-(.915)^n)$$

Also $A = J_o(.915)^n + J_o(.915)^{n+1} + \ldots$

$$= \frac{J_o(.915)^n}{1-.915} \tag{2}$$

so that

$$\frac{J}{A} = \frac{1-(.915)^n}{(.915)^n} \qquad \text{or from (2)}$$

$$0.31 = \frac{1}{(.915)^n} - 1$$

$$1.31 = \frac{1}{(.915)^n}$$

or

$$(.915)^n = \frac{1}{1.31} = .763$$

Whence $n = 3$ years approximately. This is the estimated length of the period
between the end of dependence and maturity for females.

SUMMARY AND CONCLUSIONS

1. It is indicated that breeding activity reaches a peak in fall,
but breeding activity was observed in all seasons.

2. Unimplanted gestation is estimated to last for 7 to 8 months.

3. Implanted gestation is estimated to last for 4½ to 5½
months.

4. The total gestation period is estimated to last 12 to 13
months.

5. The period between births, i.e., total length of the reproductive cycle, is about 2 years.

6. The average annual birth rate among mature females is
50 percent.

7. Parturition occurs in all months, but a minority of births
occur in fall and winter months. Parturition reaches a peak in
summer, and large fetuses occur with greatest frequency in
summer.

8. Dependent young occur with greatest frequency in fall and
with least frequency in late winter and early spring. In fall, unimplanted pregnancy reaches greatest frequency.

9. Birth normally occurs on land.

10. Caudal and cephalic presentation of the fetus occurs with about equal frequency.

11. Twinning is possible but rare, and if twins are born there is no evidence to show that both survive.

12. Females accompanied by young or showing positive evidence of parturition do not normally enter estrus.

13. Low frequency of estrous and proestrous females among nonpregnant females at all seasons indicate that impregnation occurs soon after the onset of follicular activity.

14. Annually 17 percent of the pregnant animals are pregnant for the first time and 83 percent are multiparous.

15. Pregnancy occurs with equal frequency in each uterine horn.

16. The annual rate of reproduction in the total population is estimated to be about 14 to 15 percent (i.e., about 16 young born per 100 independent animals of both sexes and all ages).

17. It is estimated that the female sea otter reaches sexual maturity at age 4 years (3 years after becoming independent).

Reproduction in the Male

Observations of courtship behavior in all seasons and the occurrence of newborn young in all months indicate that male sea otters may be sexually active at any season.

A preliminary histological study of testes was made of 40 sea otters taken in the January to April period in 1958, 1959, and 1962. These specimens indicate that spermatozoa are produced when the testes attain a weight of about 13 to 14 g. Spermatozoa are probably not produced by animals having a body weight of less than 50 lb., but most of those weighing 55 lb. and all of those weighing 60 lb. or over may produce spermatozoa.

Dr. Edward C. Roosen-Runge, Department of Biological Structure, University of Washington Medical School, Seattle, kindly examined the histological specimens of sea otter testes and contributed the following information concerning the adult:

No quantitative evaluation was attempted. Spermatogenesis was evaluated by the stages of germ cells present. The last stage of spermatogenesis is that in which the late spermatids (with dense and elongate heads) are lining the lumen of the tubule. If an appreciable number of tubular sections were found containing this stage or stages immediately preceding it, it was assumed that many spermatozoa were liberated at this time from this testis. If many stages of spermatogenesis were found, but few of the very late ones, it was assumed that there was a slowing down or a standstill somewhere in the development of germ cells or that some periodicity occurred in the liberation of sperm.

The material examined appeared to indicate quite strongly that there was such a periodicity. All adult animals showed a germinal epithelium in a state of active production of germ cells, but not all showed an appreciable number of late stages of spermatogenesis. No animal indicated as "old," [animals having well-worn teeth were arbitrarily classified in the field as old] showed any signs of diminished sperm output; in fact, all of these animals (3) showed *many* late stages of spermatogenesis.

Two cases (62–92 and 62–228) were probably hypotrophic. Both were poorly preserved (hypotrophic testicles are commonly more difficult to preserve well). It appeared to me that these two cases are possibly significant. They may indicate either a fairly high percentage of males with degenerative testicles and consequently low fertility, or they may indicate a periodicity in the spermatogenic activity which would appear more pronounced when specimens taken throughout the year are investigated. Both hypotrophic testicles showed hypotrophic Leydig cells.

The Leydig cells of the normal, adult sea otter testis appear to be aggregated in huge masses around the rete channels and almost form an "endocrine organ" in this location. From there, long strands of these cells penetrate into the septa, usually in very close apposition to thin-walled veins. The rete itself is fortified very strongly with a coarse network of collagenous fibers. The general structure of the seminiferous tubules is entirely typical for mammals.

One conclusion that appears justified on the basis of the testes examined is that the production of spermatozoa in the sea otter exhibits a mild or modified periodicity. There is no indication that a distinct seasonal periodicity in sperm production exists, as in many distinctly seasonal breeders, or that there is continuous production of sperm as in the rat. A comprehensive study of reproduction in the male sea otter remains to be done.

LIMITING FACTORS

The sea otter is highly specialized to occupy a limited aquatic environment. The feeding habitat lies between the beach and the 30-fathom curve. Its specialized characteristics which confine it to this inshore area offer both advantages and disadvantages to its survival. The advantages are that it may usually find shelter from violent storms and that its prey species, unlike the wandering populations of the pelagic prey organisms of other marine mammals, are localized. A disadvantage, though, is that population growth and expansion of range may be hindered and a local population, isolated by broad expanses of deep water, may overutilize food resources. In times of stress, a large isolated population may suffer heavy mortality caused primarily by starvation.

The sea otter's natural enemies are few. Depredation by man and natural attrition resulting from overutilization of food resources are the mortality factors that limit population size.

Mortality among sea otters was studied during the winter-spring period of environmental stress only at Amchitka Island. In other seasons, different areas were visited and an effort was made to find beach remains that would give an indication of the magnitude of winter-spring mortality.

Amchitka differs from most areas inhabited today by sea otters. It and the other densely populated Rat Islands are isolated from other areas of sea otter habitat by broad, deep passes and the whole island group is densely populated. Emigration of otters from Amchitka appears to be insignificant. Emigration from a crowded population at Kanaga Island was observed (see Distribution and Numbers). Unfortunately, this island is difficult for biologists to reach and no observations of mortality there are available.

The Shumagin and Sanak Islands groups, which I visited, have relatively small otter populations in proportion to available feeding habitat when compared to Amchitka. The observations obtained from these three areas are presented.

Natural Mortality

Data are not available to indicate exactly when the regular annual occurrence of considerable late-winter, early-spring mortality among sea otters on Amchitka Island began. Natives who trapped foxes there in 1938–39 reported that "many" dead sea otters were found on beaches in that winter. Between 10 July 1939 and 15 January 1940, however, a careful search revealed only six skeletons on beaches (Loy, 1940). Sea otter wardens J. B. Mangan and G. Ritter, who were on Amchitka from 1 February to 5 September 1940, reported salvaging only "two sea otter skins and skeletons" (Amchitka Island Report, September 5, 1940, U.S. Fish and Wildlife Service files, unpublished).

During the years that Amchitka was occupied by military forces, 1941–47, no reports of unusual sea otter mortality were made. V. B. Scheffer and I visited Amchitka on 12 November 1947 and recorded (field notes) that in walking about 4 miles of beach we found the remains of six sea otters. At the time we attributed these deaths to military personnel occupying the island, two of whom we saw target practicing along the beach. Only a fraction of the beaches where dead sea otters were found in subsequent years was examined.

In the light of later experience on Amchitka, I am inclined to believe, on the basis of what I saw on that one day in 1947, that considerable natural mortality occurred in the winter-spring period of 1946–47. In the late-winter, early-spring period of 1948, Elmer Hanson, a civilian employed by the Army on Amchitka, estimated that more than 100 otters died on Amchitka beaches. Jones and Hanson recorded 124 dead otters on the beaches in the late-winter, early-spring period of 1949 (Jones, R. D., narrative reports of 1 January to 30 April and 1 July to 30 August 1949, unpublished). Both Jones and Hanson spent much time on Amchitka during or after World War II. Neither remembers observing a significant number of dead otters on beaches before 1948. Thus, it appears that an annual late-winter, early-spring "die-off" began in the late 1940's. All available counts and estimates are shown in figure 95. An analysis of observed mortality from 1955 to 1963 at Amchitka is presented in the following pages.

Studies conducted 1955–63

During the 1955–63 study period, I repeatedly surveyed the same beaches that were searched for dead otters by previous observers. The majority of moribund otters haul out above the high

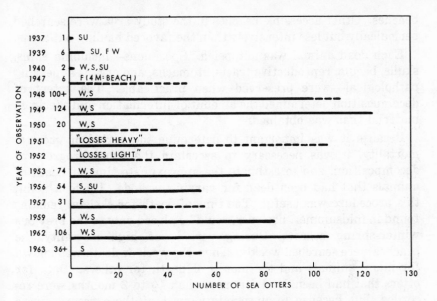

FIGURE 95.—The counts (solid line) and estimates (broken line) of dead sea otters on Amchitka beaches indicate the order of magnitude of annual mortality. Except for the counts of 1949, 1959, and 1962, the figures are only roughly comparable. The information was obtained from unpublished reports in Fish and Wildlife Service files: 1937, C. L. Loy and O. A. Friden; 1939, C. L. Loy; 1940, J. B. Mangan and G. Ritter; 1947, V. B. Scheffer and K. W. Kenyon; 1948, E. C. Hanson; 1949, 1950, 1953, R. D. Jones; 1956, 1957, 1959, 1962, K. W. Kenyon; 1963, J. E. Burdick; and from Rausch (1953). The season of observation is indicated as follows: W= winter; S=spring; SU=summer; and F=fall. In no case were all beaches searched regularly. Counts were obtained mainly on the southeastern half of the island. This data is useful only in illustrating the relative magnitude of mortality in different years.

tideline and die on shore. Dead sea otters float and if they die in the water they usually wash ashore. Thus a high percentage of those that die in study areas may be found if beaches are searched systematically and frequently.

To study annual mortality as a factor in population dynamics, and to ascertain its magnitude and understand its causes, I made an effort to gather comparable mortality data during five trips to Amchitka.

Methods of study

Certain beaches on the eastern half of Amchitka were searched systematically. Observations are available for each month of the year. Most dead otters were on or near favorite hauling-out beaches. Other accessible beaches in the study area were searched periodically but less intensively than the favored hauling-out areas.

Each dead animal was autopsied. Specimens—including skins, skulls, bacula, reproductive tracts, stomachs, and organs appearing pathological—were preserved when practicable. The extent of decomposition determined the amount of information and specimen material that was obtained.

Because it was important to determine the period of greatest mortality, it was necessary to ascertain the usual progress of decomposition, and to estimate the approximate time of death of animals that had been dead for varying periods. Up to a point, this procedure was useful. The time of death for skeletal remains found in midsummer, however, could be placed only to the previous winter-spring season. During periods of high mortality the beaches were searched weekly. Thus, the week of death was known for many animals and the month of death for others. Data for otters that had been dead for more than ½ to 2 months were recorded, but because of uncertainty most of these records were excluded from those aspects of the study which required more exact data. Each carcass was removed from the beach after needed data were recorded and specimens taken from it.

Average daily air temperatures in winter infrequently exceed 36° F., and spring and fall average daily air temperatures above 49° F. are unusual. For this reason, otter carcasses decompose slowly on Amchitka beaches. The study was complicated when scavengers (Bald Eagles and rats *(Rattus norvegicus)*) mutilated carcasses, sometimes preventing the gathering of certain data.

Results

Between July 1955 and April 1963, approximately 15 months were spent on Amchitka. During six study periods, a total of 331 dead otters found on the beaches were examined. Because data from certain individuals were incomplete, these are eliminated, where appropriate, from the following discussions of different aspects of mortality.

THE TIME OF MORTALITY

It would be ideal, in a study of sea otter mortality, if data could be gathered during some period of consecutive months for several years. This could not be done, so the data from various seasons in different years were used to present a composite picture of the annual cycle of mortality. The mortality study included parts of different seasons during the six field study periods. Two seasons, 1959 and 1962, included the entire period of greatest mortality.

Data gathered in midsummer presented fragmentary evidence of the magnitude of mortality that occurred in the preceding winter-spring period. Natural decomposition of dead otters, storm waves that sweep high onto beaches, and scavengers scatter, bury, and break up skeletal remains. By midsummer of 1955, little skeletal material remained on beaches to indicate the extent of mortality that I observed briefly in late March and early April of that year.

Available data indicate that maximum mortality among sea otters at Amchitka occurs annually during the winter and early spring (fig. 96). At this time of year the Aleutians are subject to frequent and often violent atmospheric storms, and also prolonged periods of high seas. In 1962, moderate weather conditions prevailed from mid-January to mid-February and mortality up to that time was insignificant. From this time on, weather conditions were stormy. Mortality increased rapidly after 20 February and remained high until 25 March. A search of all study areas during the last week of March revealed only three freshly dead otters (fig. 97).

In 1959, late winter and early spring were less stormy than in 1962. Appreciable mortality did not occur until early March, but it continued at a high rate until mid-May. During the intensely stormy 1962 season, 106 dead otters were found in only 2 months on the same beaches where 84 dead otters were found during the comparatively mild 1959 season (fig. 96). Thus, it appeared that the magnitude and the time of greatest mortality varied in accordance with the stresses exerted on the animals by the environment.

AGE-SPECIFIC MORTALITY

No technique is known by which the chronological age of a sea otter may be determined. On the basis of body size, suture closure, and dentition, however, certain age classifications are roughly indicated. In this discussion I will distinguish only between immature and adult animals. Table 55 summarizes available data, and indicates that immature otters (fig. 98) constitute about 70 percent of the average annual mortality. Among adults, most of those found dead or dying show signs of aging (fig. 99), such as grizzled pelage and severe dental attrition.

The juveniles weigh from about 10 to 30 lb. and are still in the company of their mothers when the winter period of storms begins. Large juveniles, although capable of obtaining food by

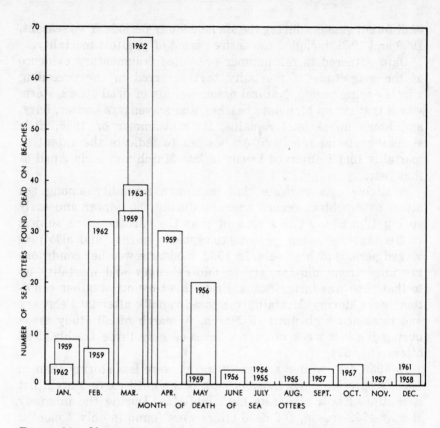

FIGURE 96.—Observed mortality of sea otters at Amchitka Island, 1955–63. Each bar represents the number of otters that were found dead and were estimated to have died in the indicated month and year. Otters dead so long that the month of death could not reasonably be estimated are excluded. Data from 259 dead otters were used in this graph. No freshly dead otters were found in June, July, or August of 1955, in July of 1956, or in November of 1957.

diving, habitually beg for and receive food from the mother. The result of this behavior is that mothers are unable to obtain sufficient food for themselves and their large offspring during periods when heavy seas render food gathering difficult. For this reason, many mothers desert their large young at this season of stress. Deserted juveniles were seen searching and screaming for their mothers in the late-winter, early-spring period.

For example, a mother and a pup, weighing about 12 lb. (5.4 kg.), were captured together and tagged on 15 February 1962. When released they swam off together. Both appeared thin but in normal health. On 18 February, the juvenile was found wander-

TABLE 55.—*Mortality of sea otters, by age and sex, at Amchitka Island, Alaska, 1956–63*

[Certain specimen records are eliminated from this table because inadequate data or specimen material were available]

| Observation period | Juvenile | | | | | | | | Adult | | | | | | | | Grand total |
| | Males | | Females | | Sex? | | Total | | Males | | Females | | Sex? | | Total | | |
	Number	Per-cent	Number	Per-cent	Number	Per-cent	Number	Per-cent	Number	Per-cent	Number	Per-cent	Number	Per-cent	Number	Per-cent	
5 May–26 July 1956	21	39	7	18	10	18	38	70	7	13	3	6	6	11	16	30	54
10 October–11 December 1957	3	10	2	6	10	30	15	48	9	29	—	—	7	23	16	52	31
21 January–20 May 1959	26	31	16	19	10	12	52	62	21	25	9	11	2	2	32	38	84
19 January–4 April 1962	51	48	23	22	7	7	81	76	10	9	15	14	—	—	25	24	106
10 March–12 April 1963	13	36	12	33	9	17	34	94	1	3	1	3	—	—	2	6	36
Total	114	36	60	19	46	15	220	70	48	16	28	9	15	5	91	30	311

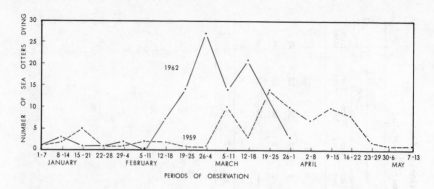

FIGURE 97.—Mortality of sea otters at Amchitka Island during weekly intervals through periods of high mortality in 1959 and 1962.

ing about alone, crying, very weak, and near death from starvation. The mother was found dead on 19 March. It might be concluded that even after deserting her pup, she was unable to regain the strength she sacrificed during storms while attempting to meet the food demands of both herself and her pup. Another pup (weighing about 17 lb., 7.7 kg.) was captured, tagged, and released together with its mother on 27 February 1962. The pup was found dead and emaciated on 5 March.

FIGURE 98.—A moribund juvenile sea otter. During the late winter and early spring season of stormy weather starving juveniles haul out on shore and die. Enteritis is usually a terminal symptom. This animal illustrates the final comatose stage that occurs shortly before death. Amchitka Island, 26 February 1962. (KWK 62–17–22)

FIGURE 99.—This aged male sea otter sought escape from a high wind in a sheltered cove. It was in a final stage of starvation, appeared to be blind or nearly blind, and showed severe dental attrition. Most adults found dead exhibited similar symptoms of aging. Amchitka Island, 26 February 1962. (KWK 62–17–3)

Small helpless pups are present in the Amchitka population at all seasons. They were, however, seldom found dead on beaches. Two were found in 1959 and two in 1962. Three reasons are suggested to explain why few are found dead. (1) Mothers habitually give more care and attention to small pups than to large juveniles. (2) Small pups require comparatively little food and mothers are able to supply their food needs without undue strain on themselves. (3) If a small pup dies it is retained by the mother until it becomes saturated with water. When she finally deserts the body it may sink and not be found on the beach.

Among captive otters we observed that when a mother otter is given a reduced ration of food she steals food from her pup. This behavior suggests that when stormy weather and reduced prey populations make it difficult to obtain sufficient food for herself and her pup, she deserts her large juvenile at an earlier age than she would during moderate summer weather when food gathering is less difficult.

Among animals found dead, the percentage of juveniles in the different study periods varied from 48 to 94 percent. Mortality data obtained in summer, fall, and early winter are not directly comparable with data obtained in late winter and early spring. Between 1 October and 11 December 1957, 48 percent of the remains found were juveniles. The remains of most dead animals were judged to have lain on beaches since the previous winter-spring period. Only seven were judged to have died in September or later. There is a greater probability of finding remains of adults because they are more durable than remains of immature animals. The skeletons of juveniles, unless in sheltered locations well above tide line, suffer environmental attrition more rapidly than the harder bones of adults. Six months or more after the mortality period, remains of many juveniles had disintegrated and were not among the bones still on beaches. This probably explains why juveniles did not predominate.

In 1963, when juveniles composed 94 percent of the dead animals, the study period was 10 March to 12 April. The data from 1962 indicate that mortality among adults may increase as the period of high mortality advances (fig. 100). In January and February 1962, before the height of the mortality period, adults constituted 16 percent of the animals that died. During and after the period when the mortality reached its peak in March, 39 percent of animals that died were adults. This might indicate that adults are better able to withstand environmental stresses than immature animals recently separated from mothers. In 1963 the period of greatest adult mortality may not have been included in the study period, and a disproportionately high mortality of juveniles was indicated by the available data. The 1959 data show, however, that the mortality among adults may, in some years, be high throughout the period of increased mortality (fig. 101).

The 1959 and 1962 study periods are the only two which spanned entire periods of greatest annual mortality (fig. 97). Therefore, the proportion of juveniles (60 and 75 percent, respectively) to adults is probably more representative of the usual mortality pattern.

SEX-SPECIFIC MORTALITY

More males than females were found dead on beaches. Among juveniles, the disparity was greater than among adults. Rausch (1953) noted in his 1951 and 1952 investigations that "the heaviest mortality occurred . . . in subadult males." The raw data from the remains I examined, however, tend to exaggerate this difference. The accurate determination of sex by the examination of juvenile skulls or other bones is perhaps impossible. If a carcass was

258

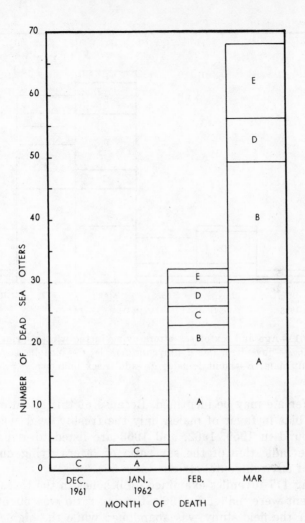

FIGURE 100.—Age and sex of sea otters dying in the winter-spring period of 1961–62. *A*—juvenile male; *B*—juvenile female; *C*—juvenile, sex unknown; *D*—adult male; *E*—adult female.

mutilated by scavengers and the reproductive organs removed, the sex of the animal was in question. On partially mutilated carcasses, the likelihood that a male might be identified was greater. Eagles, for example, usually remove the viscera first. The genitalia of the females are easily taken, but the baculum of the male is attached to the ischium by a strong ligament composed of the ischio- and bulbo-cavernosus muscles. These parts may remain attached to the skeleton, identifying it as a male for weeks longer

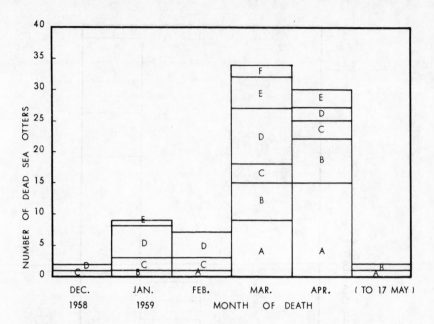

FIGURE 101.—Age and sex of sea otters dying in the winter-spring period of 1958–59. A—juvenile male; B—juvenile female; C—juvenile, sex unknown; D—adult male; E—adult female; F—adult, sex unknown.

than a female may be identified. Because of this situation and to avoid a bias in favor of males, only the freshly dead beach specimens found in 1959, 1962, and 1963 are listed to give the best available indication of the sex ratio of otters dying during the period of environmental stress (table 56).

Among 117 juveniles examined on beaches in the three seasons, 58 percent were males. In 1963, the sex ratio was 50:50, but in this year the field study was abandoned while the high mortality period was probably still in progress and the results may not be representative.

That males are not as hardy as females was repeatedly demon-

TABLE 56.—*Age and sex of otters found freshly dead on Amchitka beaches*

	Juvenile					Adult					
	Males		Females			Males		Females			
Year	Num-ber	Per-cent	Num-ber	Per-cent	Total num-ber	Num-ber	Per-cent	Num-ber	Per-cent	Total num-ber	Grand total
1959	21	57	16	43	37	13	68	6	32	19	56
1962	36	62	22	38	58	8	38	13	62	21	79
1963	11	50	11	50	22	1	50	1	50	2	24
Total	68	58	49	42	117	22	52	20	48	42	159

strated when both sexes were held captive under the same conditions. A similar situation was suggested in the northern fur seal. Chapman (*in* Abegglen, Roppel, and Wilke, 1960) estimated that in the first 3 years of life females outsurvived males by a ratio of 2 to 1. Studies since then indicate that the ratio may be only 1.25 to 1 in favor of females (Chapman, unpublished manuscript).

MORTALITY FACTORS

Physical characteristics and food supply

The terminal conditions observed in a high percentage of otters found dead on Amchitka beaches are emaciation and hemorrhagic enteritis. Enteritis may, however, occur in the final hours before death after other conditions have doomed the animal.

Sea otters found dead on beaches during the late-winter and early-spring period of high mortality may be divided into two primary groups: (1) Those whose death was apparently caused by an injury in rough seas, or disease, and (2) those which showed evidence of starvation and finally exhibited symptoms of enteritis. Many dead animals cannot be placed positively into one group or the other. An emaciated and weakened animal is more subject to injury by large breakers than a strong one. An animal obviously killed by an injury might have died soon of starvation.

The actual cause of death of many animals cannot be determined because of decomposition. Table 57 lists observed conditions which may have caused death of otters that might be considered to be in group (1) above. The section "Parasites and Miscellaneous Diseases" gives additional data on mortality recorded by Dr. Robert L. Rausch in 1952 and more detailed information on several specimens that were examined in the laboratory.

The dead animals which fall into the second group are of the greatest interest from the point of view of population studies. Most of these may be separated into two age groups: (1) Juveniles, many of which approach subadulthood and, (2) old animals having worn teeth and often showing other indications of advanced age, such as gray pelage about the head, chest, and abdomen, and impaired vision caused by injuries or senile cataracts. In the 1959 study period a particular effort was made to record pertinent data from 83 individual otters found dead on beaches. The information is summarized in table 58.

Juveniles and old adults had two characteristics in common at death. Both lacked body fat and both showed a high incidence of defective teeth. In the case of the young animals, 50 percent ex-

TABLE 57.—*Abnormal conditions found in sea otters that died on beaches of Amchitka Island, Alaska*

Collection number	Age	Sex	Date	Condition
59–68	juv.	♂	15 Mar. 1959	Fractured skull.
59–92	ad.	?	29 Mar. 1959	Bruised head.
36–56	juv.	♂	31 May 1956	Bruises, blood clots around head and neck.
B20–57	juv. (pup)	♂	30 Oct. 1957	Broken neck.
59–3	juv.	♀	26 Jan. 1959	Nondraining abscess dorsally in neck and head.
47–56	juv.	♀	17 June 1956	2 broken ribs.
59–73	juv.	♀	14 Mar. 1959	Extensive body bruises and swellings.
59–49	ad.	♂	5 Mar. 1959	Body bruises perforated intestine.
59–100	ad.	♂	31 Mar. 1959	Internal hemorrhage—quantity of blood in abdominal cavity.
59–155	juv.	♀	6 May 1959	Perforated intestine and intus-susception of small intestine.
44–56	ad.	♂	11 June 1956	Bruises in genital area.
59–34	ad.	♂	20 Feb. 1959	Bruised penis.
62–241	ad.	♂	12 Mar. 1962	Penis swollen and extruded.
59–130	ad.	♀	17 Apr. 1959	Uterine cyst 180 × 50 mm.
D7–57	ad.	♀	6 Dec. 1957	Abscess in jaw, liver discolored and with abnormal adhesions.[1]
59–85	ad.	♀	25 Mar. 1959	Liver with abnormal adhesions and discoloration.[1]
59–79	juv.	♀	21 Mar. 1959	Hemorrhagic nasal passages.
59–90	ad.	♂	29 Mar. 1959	Cutaneous emphysema.
59–82	juv. (pup)	♀	25 Mar. 1959	Lungs black, pneumonia?
B12–57	s.ad. ?	♀	22 Oct. 1957	Malignant neoplasm of the intestine.[1]
59–48	ad.	♀	4 Mar. 1959	Congenital cystic kidney and edema.[1]

[1] See section on Parasites and Miscellaneous Diseases for a more detailed analysis.

TABLE 58.—*Summary of observations from 83 sea otters found dead at Amchitka Island, Alaska, 1959*

Observation	Number of juveniles	Number of adults
Total animals examined	48	35
Skeletal remains only found [1]	18	14
Field necropsy performed	27	18
Dental malocclusion indicated [2]	24	14
Bone damage to jaw [3]	0	13
Tooth damage (dental attrition): [4]		
None to moderate	44	6
Moderate to severe	0	29
Lesions: [5]		
Hemorrhagic enteritis present	23	11
Stomach parasite (*T. decipiens*) present	2	6
Possible physical injury indicated	12	9
Food in stomach [6]	0	0

[1] Skulls only examined.

[2] In juveniles, malocclusion occurs while the permanent teeth are growing, particularly when deciduous teeth are pushed out of line. In old adults, postcanine teeth may be worn to the gum-line or to the bone.

[3] When teeth of old animals are severely worn, infection of the bone and osteolysis may occur.

[4] See Dental Attrition.

[5] See Parasites and Miscellaneous Diseases.

[6] All carcasses showed signs of emaciation. Body weights (particularly for adults) were abnormally low (see Body Measurements).

hibited a degree of malocclusion caused by the growth of the permanent postcanine teeth. In the early stages of eruption of the permanent teeth, the deciduous teeth are pushed upward, so that occlusion is impaired. When the deciduous teeth are finally lost, the permanent teeth are still below the level of adjacent teeth (see Dentition). Adults having poor teeth comprised 78 percent of the total found dead. The attrition of teeth appears to be another result of the reduction of soft-bodied invertebrates. Hard-shelled organisms are probably eaten to a greater degree by this crowded Amchitka population than in less densely populated areas. Animals having good teeth not only compose a minority (17 percent) of the dead adults on beaches but healthy adults spend less time on shore (as indicated by animals captured there) during periods of storm surf than do emaciated juveniles and old adults.

Weather and sea conditions

In the fall of 1959, the U.S. Weather Bureau began to record weather conditions in the outer Aleutian Islands. Before this time, no such records were available. Thus, during the 21 January to 20 May 1959 study period I kept a daily record of weather conditions. These data demonstrated that the increased mortality coincided with the period of greatest storm activity.

Complete weather records are now available for the years after 1960. These data were recorded at Shemya Island, which is 200 miles west of Amchitka, but radio reports of weather at Shemya received while I was on Amchitka indicated that a few hours after weather conditions were reported at Shemya similar weather reached Amchitka. The annual cycle of weather conditions in the outer Aleutians is quite uniform.

The average seasonal mortality observed on Amchitka from 1955 through 1963 and the mean monthly wind velocities recorded 1960 through 1963 are shown in figure 102. This graph demonstrates that the period of greatest mortality, when 75 percent of the annual mortality occurs, coincide annually with the period of maximum wind velocities in the late-winter, early-spring period. It also shows that the period of least mortality occurs during the summer period of minimum wind velocities. In the fall, when the season of storms begins, a slight increase in mortality occurs. Most animals, however, emerge from the summer, early-fall period in good physical condition and the mortality remains low until after a period of sustained stormy weather reaches a peak in March.

The general coincidence of high mortality and stormy weather

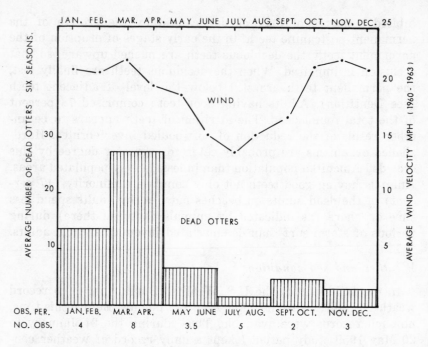

FIGURE 102.—Average seasonal mortality of 311 sea otters found dead on Amchitka beaches 1955–63, and average monthly wind velocities in the outer Aleutian Islands measured by the U. S. Weather Bureau, 1960 through 1963.

or high velocity winds was quite evident. It was also evident, however, that the wind, as such, was only indirectly responsible for precipitating mortality and that more detailed information concerning environmental stresses was needed. Therefore in 1962, between 19 January and 31 March (70 days), I kept a daily record of surf conditions and sea otter mortality for both the Bering Sea and Pacific Ocean coasts of Amchitka. Five surf conditions were recorded: calm (no surf), light surf, moderate surf, heavy surf, and violent surf.

The vast extent and great depth of the Pacific Ocean as compared to the relatively small and shallow Bering Sea creates conditions responsible for differing surf conditions on the coasts exposed respectively to these two bodies of water.

Under the force of storm winds, heavy seas may build up in the Bering Sea, but within a few hours after the passing of a storm the surf may subside and relatively calm or moderate waves may prevail.

In contrast, ground swells in the Pacific Ocean may travel to

Amchitka's shores well ahead of an atmospheric storm. Then they may continue to break violently along the exposed coast for many hours after the storm has passed. In addition, waves created by storms that fail to reach Amchitka, may break on the Pacific coast of the island. Heavy or violent wave action along the Pacific coast was recorded on 43 days during the study period, but similar conditions prevailed on only 12 days along the Bering Sea coast (figs. 103 and 104).

The data indicate that the amount of mortality that occurred in 1962 at Amchitka was related primarily to population size and available habitat. Even though the storm wave action along the Pacific coast was more intense than along the Bering Sea coast, the threshold of stresses sufficient to precipitate mortality was

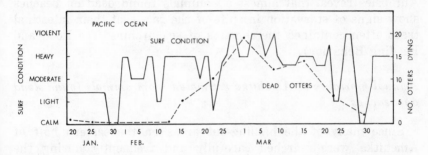

FIGURE 103.—Daily record of surf conditions and of otters found dead on the Pacific Ocean coast of Amchitka from 14 January through 30 April 1962. Partly because ground swells travel long distances in the deep Pacific Ocean, wave activity on that coast is more intense than on the Bering Sea coast (see fig. 104).

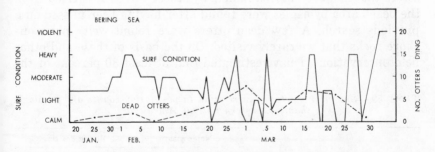

FIGURE 104.—Daily record of observed surf condition and otters found dead on the Bering Sea coast of Amchitka Island from 19 January through 30 March 1962. Surf conditions are more moderate on the Bering Sea coast than on the Pacific coast because in this relatively shallow sea ground swells do not travel ahead of storms and wave action attenuates soon after the passing of wind storms (see also fig. 103).

exceeded on both coasts. Thus, mortality occurred in proportion to the available habitat and population size rather than in proportion to the intensity of storm wave activity. About two-thirds of the available habitat, population, and mortality were found on the Pacific coast (table 59).

Although the period of heavy surf began in late January, the increasing rate of sea otter mortality did not reach a peak until the end of February (figs. 103 and 104). This is explained by the fact that the otters enter the winter with reserves of body fat and in good general physical condition. During weeks of stormy weather, those animals least able to supply their nutritional needs exhaust their physical reserve. After becoming emaciated and being subjected to continuing environmental stress, they die. Autopsies reveal that almost all animals found dead on beaches show signs of starvation in spite of the fact that their intestinal tract often contained the remains of sea urchins (see Food and Feeding Behavior).

Annual mortality at Amchitka estimated from animals found dead on beaches

Since many of the hauling-out areas on the eastern half of Amchitka were searched carefully and frequently during the period of high mortality, probably most of the dead otters in these limited areas were found. The habitually used hauling grounds constitute less than 10 percent of the shoreline on the eastern half of Amchitka. Other areas could not be searched as carefully as the areas of concentration. On several occasions, dead otters that had been buried in kelp by storm waves or carried from the beach area by eagles were found after having been missed on a previous search. A few dead otters were found well up on offshore rocks that we rarely visited. On the basis of these and other field observations, I have estimated that at least 30 percent of the

TABLE 59.—*Sea otter mortality in relation to population counts and available habitat, eastern half of Amchitka*

	Pacific coast		Bering Sea coast	
	Number	Percent	Number	Percent
Dead otters [1]	70	66	36	34
Otter population [2]	766	71	310	29
Available habitat [3]	45	67	22	33

[1] Count, 19 January to 4 April 1962.
[2] Aerial count, 19 May 1959.
[3] Square miles of water 30 fathoms or less in depth, eastern half of Amchitka. Measured from U.S. Coast and Geodetic Survey Chart 8864.

otters dying along the shores of the eastern half of Amchitka in the period of high mortality were not found. A rough estimate of the annual mortality in 1959 and 1962 on Amchitka is presented below:

	Number of dead otters	
	1959	1962
Carcasses found in winter-spring period	84	106
Estimate of carcasses not found (30%)	25	32
Estimated total mortality this period	109	138
Estimated mortality in remainder of the year (25%)	27	35
Estimated annual mortality on eastern half of Amchitka	136	173
Estimated annual mortality on western half of Amchitka (otter population 30% of eastern half, data from aerial surveys)	41	52
Total estimated annual mortality	177	225

The estimated Amchitka otter population in 1959 was about 2,080 (see Distribution and Numbers). Thus, the annual mortality there in at least two seasons was about 9 to 11 percent of the total estimated population. If, instead, the direct counts of living and dead otters are used for the eastern half of Amchitka, then the mortality in 1959 was about 8 percent ($\frac{84}{1076}$) 100 and in 1962 about 10 percent ($\frac{106}{1076}$) 100 of the population as observed in 1959.

Mortality estimates derived from reproductive tracts

The data available from other studies (see Length of stages of reproductive cycle of female sea otter, by D. G. Chapman, and Field counts of sea otters) makes possible an estimate of the mortality that occurred in the transition from the dependent stage to the juvenile stage. Since there are 50 young/100 adult females per year and since the sex ratio among young is 50:50, this implies 25 female young per 100 adult females.

Let the mortality that occurs at the end of the dependent stage be T; then

$$(1-T) \frac{Y}{2} = J_o \text{ if females alone are considered}$$

Also

$$A = \frac{J_o(.915)^n}{.085} \text{ from equation (2) (see "Length of stages of reproductive cycles of female sea otter," by D. G. Chapman, p. 243)}$$

so that
$$J_0 = \frac{.085A}{.766} = .111A$$
$$\therefore (1-T)\frac{Y}{2} = J_0 = .111A$$
or
$$(1-T = 2(.111)\frac{A}{Y} = .222/\frac{Y}{A} = \frac{.222}{.42}$$

from (1) (see Chapman, as above)

whence
$$1-T = .53$$
and
$$T = .47$$

Another way of considering the same problem is as follows: Each 25 female young must survive to replace the 8.5 mortality occurring among the mature females
$$\therefore (25)(1-T).766 = 8.5$$
$$\text{or } (1-T)(19.2) = 8.5$$
$$\text{or } 1-T = .44 \text{ and } T = .56$$

Although these are slightly different, they suggest that the transitional mortality from dependent to juvenile stage is about 50 percent. Some of this may occur during the dependent period.

Also, if the mortality among juveniles is higher than 8.5 percent this would mean the transitional mortality is slightly lower. This could also mean that the estimated length of the independent juvenile period is somewhat less than 3 years.

It should be noted that these estimates of 8.5 percent as an annual mortality, 50 percent mortality at the end of the dependent young stage, and a juvenile period of 3 years apply to females. The data do not provide comparable estimates for males.

MORTALITY ON THE SHUMAGIN ISLANDS

The outer Shumagin Islands provide interesting material for comparison with observations from Amchitka. The outer Shumagins, including Nagai and all islands lying east and west of it, are chosen because (1) A population of about 3,000 sea otters is found there, (2) it appears to offer ideal sea otter habitat, and (3) it was accessible for aerial and surface observations.

The outer Shumagins are surrounded by nearly 700 square miles of water less than 30 fathoms deep. The islands are near enough to each other to allow sea otters to move easily from one to another and near enough to other areas along the southeast coast of the Alaska Peninsula to allow population dispersion.

Between 4 and 14 June 1960, the late Tom O'Brien and I camped on Simeonof and Little Koniuji Islands. We circumnavigated Simeonof and made other dory trips to several beaches on Little Koniuji and Herendeen Islands. Also, we walked more than 15 miles on beaches. At least 80 percent of the beachline that we searched was adjacent to favorite sea otter feeding and resting areas.

We searched beaches carefully but were able to find remains of only one adult male sea otter on Simeonof and fragments of one juvenile skeleton on Little Koniuji. Both animals had been dead for several months. Considering that during aerial surveys of these same areas on 10 April 1962 we counted 549 otters, the observed mortality there was low.

Mortality observations in the Shumagin Islands and data presented in the sections on Body Measurements, Food and Feeding Behavior, and Distribution and Numbers, when compared with similar data from Amchitka, indicate that the Shumagin population (4 otters per square mile of habitat) was not overutilizing food resources as was demonstrated for the Amchitka population (19 otters per square mile of habitat) and that winter-spring starvation and accompanying mortality did not occur.

MORTALITY ON THE SANAK ISLANDS

The Sanak Islands include Sanak, Caton, and a number of small islets and rocks. The population density of this area was estimated to be about two otters per square mile of habitat (see Distribution and Numbers).

In 1960, O'Brien and I spent from 20 to 23 June exploring this area. We landed via dory on Caton Island and seven smaller islets (Leda, Wanda, Elma, Telemitz, Peterson, and Mary Islets, and Princess Rock). We searched more than 10 miles of beach and found the skeletal remains of only one adult female otter, indicating that little winter-spring mortality had occurred.

Discussion

The analysis of data obtained from two classes of populated sea otter habitat were presented. The criterion of population density was the number of otters per square mile of water less than 30 fathoms deep. It was shown that at Amchitka the population was crowded during the study period, having about 19 otters per square mile. The outer Shumagin Islands and Sanak Islands were not crowded, having respectively about four and two otters per square mile. The estimated annual winter-spring mortality at

Amchitka was 8 to 11 percent of the population (perhaps higher in certain seasons). In the areas of uncrowded population, the annual mortality was much lower. It was not calculated because too few dead otters were found.

The natural forces which control the magnitude of the sea otter population at Amchitka were a limited food supply and climate. From his observations on Amchitka, Rausch (1953) suspected that much of the annual mortality was the result of "A population that exceeded the carrying capacity of the habitat." The applicable generalization was aptly stated by Lack (1954):

climatic factors can exert an important modifying influence in the control of animal numbers. Thus, although one may speak loosely of mortality due to climate, the actual cause of death is often starvation, which can be density-dependent.

The data presented here and in the sections on Food and Feeding Behavior and Distribution and Numbers, I believe, support Lack's statement.

The following points are the evidence that lead to the conclusion stated above:

1. The food habits studies of otters at Amchitka indicated that healthy adults, having ample body fat in the late-winter, early-spring period, fed to a large extent on fish and octopus. Sea otters at Amchitka were limited in their search for food to a relatively narrow belt of water surrounding the island where water depths do not exceed 30 fathoms (see Diving). Observations at Amchitka indicated that populations of bottom-inhabiting food species were reduced (see Food and Feeding Behavior).

2. Observations indicated that large juveniles when deserted by mothers were unable to obtain a sufficient quantity of high-calorie food species. Apparently they lacked both the skill and strength to capture and hold most fish and octopus. This may be true also of aging adults.

3. Both of these age groups were forced to obtain what nourishment they could from depleted populations of sedentary and often hard-shelled and low-calorie invertebrates. Because of the hard shells of these organisms the teeth of adult otters in the Amchitka population showed greater attrition than did those of animals from less crowded populations. The teeth of old adults were often worn to the gumline. Evidence of bone infection, which often resulted when tooth attrition was severe, was found in 72 percent of a sample of dead adults. Juveniles in the process of replacing deciduous teeth were unable to eat a sufficient quantity of the available hard-shelled organisms.

4. Both the aging animals and juveniles, forced to utilize poor quality foods, were further hindered in feeding activities by sustained periods of rough seas. Aging adults, and juveniles deserted by mothers, after exhausting accumulated summer and fall reserves of body fat, developed enteritis which is typical of that found in other species of animals under conditions of starvation and stress (see Parasites and Miscellaneous Diseases).

5. Adult otters at Amchitka weighed less than otters from less crowded populations (see Body Measurements).

6. When weakened animals exhibiting symptoms of enteritis (black feces) were captured and placed in a pool of clean water where they were furnished adequate food, some of them regained health. After they were introduced to a diet of fish, all of these captives refused to eat sea urchins and most hard-shelled mollusks. The gastrointestinal tract of similar animals that died on beaches either were empty, or contained only hard-shelled organisms.

PARASITES AND MISCELLANEOUS DISEASES

Both in the wild and in captivity sea otters are afflicted by a variety of pathological conditions. Systematic, long-term studies of pathology were not undertaken, but animals found dead or dying on beaches were examined (Rausch and Locker, 1951; Rausch, 1953) and observations of captives were recorded (Kirkpatrick, et al., 1955; Kenyon, Yunker, and Newell, 1965). Jellison and Neiland (1965, p. 8–9) list the parasites of sea otters. In the following sections these studies are reviewed briefly and additional observations are presented.

Most sea otters found dead on Amchitka Island displayed terminal symptoms of enteritis. Other pathological conditions, such as neoplastic and degenerative changes in the liver, ulceration of the jaws and alveoli of the teeth, and infections of the paws also occurred.

Internal (helminth) parasites

More than 30 sea otters found dead or in moribund condition on Amchitka beaches in 1949, 1951, and 1952 were studied by Rausch (Rausch and Locker, 1951; Rausch, 1953). The helminths recorded from these were: (Cestoda) *Pyramicocephalus phocarum* (Fabricius, 1780); (Trematoda) *Orthosplanchnus fraterculus* Odhner, 1905, *Phocitrema fusiforme* Goto and Ozaki, 1930, *Pricetrema zalophi* (Price, 1932), *Microphallus pirum* (Afanas'ev, 1941); (Nematoda) *Terranova (Porrocaecum) decipiens* (Krabbe, 1873); (Acanthocephala) *Corynosoma strumosum* (Rudolphi, 1802).

R. L. Rausch (letter, 15 Sept. 1967) states:

More recently, *Corynosoma macrosomum* Neiland, 1962, has been described from a sea otter from Prince William Sound, and a single specimen evidently representing this species had been collected earlier from the same host from Simeonof Island (see Neiland, 1962). Cestodes collected by K. W. Kenyon from sea otters from Amchitka Island have been identified provisionally as *Diplogonoporus tetrapterus* (von Siebold, 1848) (Rausch, 1964); this species also was recorded from a sea otter from Prince William Sound.

In general, these helminths probably affect the host little, if at all (Rausch, 1953). However, two species, *Microphallus pirum* and *Terranova decipiens*, were considered to be pathogenic. The cuticular spines of the former evidently cause mechanical injury to the intestinal mucosa, and, when the trematodes are abundant, severe enteritis may result. Immature specimens of *T. decipiens* frequently penetrate the intestinal wall and enter the body cavity, where other organs may be invaded. Peritonitis following such perforations may result in the death of the host.

During the 1955–63 study period, I made gross examinations of about 50 otters believed to have been in good health when killed at Amchitka. Although both *T. decipiens* and *M. pirum* were found, there were no gross lesions in the infested animals. In November of 1957, Dr. Kenneth L. Binkley examined seven adult otters at Amchitka, only one of which appeared to be in "poor" condition when captured. Only the ill animal was infested with an appreciable number of *T. decipiens* (65 worms) and *M. pirum* (many worms), but there was no sure indication that this animal's poor condition was a result of parasite infestation. Problems encountered with *T. decipiens* are discussed under "In Captivity."

In 1959 the stomachs of otters found dead on beaches were examined when possible. Among 27 juveniles, 2 contained *T. decipiens* and among 14 adults, 5 were infested. In none of the animals examined were helminths found in the coelom and no instance of perforation caused by helminths was noted. The animals, in most cases, had been dead for several days before they were examined. Peritonitis caused by perforation of the gastrointestinal tract would probably have been detected. Examination of sample areas of the small intestine revealed moderate to light infestation in some animals, but for *M. pirum* diagnosis was considered unsatisfactory because of decomposition. In addition, this parasite inhabits crypts in the wall of the small intestine and is not easily detected in gross examination.

K. A. Neiland (letter, 9 July 1962) examined the intestinal tracts of 8 adult sea otters chosen at random from 150 animals that were shot in the spring of 1962 at Amchitka. In these he found a total of 271 *Corynosoma* sp. Infestation ranged from 1 to 98 individuals. *T. decipiens,* totaling 40 individuals, occurred in 5 of the tracts and infestation ranged from 1 to 18.

A subadult female sea otter was found dead at Patten Bay, Montague Island, by Theron Smith on 23 April 1962. The animal was estimated to have been dead for 2 or 3 days when it was received for study by Dr. Francis H. Fay. Because death apparently resulted from helminth infestation, his study of this animal (No. 27830) is quoted from his letter of 7 August 1962.

Trematoda: *Orthosplanchnus fraterculus.* Abundant in gall bladder bile ducts. Extreme fibrosis and near-occlusion of bile ducts was noted in several areas of the liver.

Microphallus pirum. Abundant in small intestine.

Cestoda: *Diplogonoporus tetrapterus.* Several large pseudophyllidean cestodes with double genital pores were present in the small intestine. A few smaller cestodes, closely associated with these, were also present and are believed to be aberrant individuals of the same species.

Nematoda: *Terranova decipiens.* Massive infection, mainly of larval worms. These had perforated the stomach in one locality and the duodenum in two. Many were free in the abdominal cavity, together with *M. pirum* and two species of *Corynosoma.* In the abdominal cavity there was about 1,000 ml. of bloody fluid with some remnants of food that evidently had oozed out of the intestine by way of the perforations. A group of nematodes was attached to the greater omentum, and several other groups had penetrated the spleen and liver. Extreme inflammation was evident in these sites even in the then decomposed tissues. All mesenteries in both the abdominal and pleural cavities were granular and inflamed. Adhesions were abundant.

Acanthocephala: *Corynosoma* sp. At least two species of *Corynosoma* were abundant in the small intestine." (These were later identified by K. Neiland as *C. strumosum* and *C. macrosomum.*)

It was apparent from the gross pathology that this animal had died as a result of its dense, infiltrating parasite population, but it was not possible to decide on which of the two most pathogenic organisms (*M. pirum* and *T. decipiens*) was primarily responsible for causing death.

External parasites

Snow (1910, p. 278) examined many sea otters and said of them "Sea-otters are particularly cleanly animals; I have never found a parasite of any description on them."

F. H. Fay (letter, 6 April 1964) said:

We have no records of Anoplura on sea otters, but on the other hand, the number of specimens examined is not great. Both Bob [Rausch] and I feel that Barabash-Nikiforov's record of two specimens of *Proechinophthirus fluctus* (=*Echinophthirus fluctus*) on sea otters probably was fortuitous. Apparently this is a common ectoparasite of *Callorhinus* and *Eumetopias* living in the same area with the otters, and it is not inconceivable that a few would occasionally be picked up by the otters. If it were a common or even uncommon parasite of sea otters, you surely would have noticed it, especially in captive animals.

I have examined many sea otters and found no external parasites other than nasal mites (Halarachnidae). Although these are technically ectoparasites, they are found within the nasal passages. As pointed out previously (Kenyon, Yunker, and Newell, 1965), infestation of the sea otter with *Halarachne miroungae* is probably fortuitous. The only massively infected animal (over 3,000 mites) was a captive that was held under abnormal conditions in a freshwater pool. Infestation in the wild appears to be insignificant.

Enteritis

The following discussion presents observations obtained at Amchitka Island and information contributed by M. C. Keyes, D.V.M., Bureau of Commercial Fisheries.

Enteritis is frequently observed as the terminal symptom at death in sea otters at Amchitka. It is similar to the entero toxemia found in the fur seal, harbor seal, and certain domestic animals. A *Clostridium* organism has been isolated and identified from a fur seal. Keyes (1963) uses the name necrohemorrhagic enteritis. The symptoms observed in the sea otter are quite similar to those observed in lambs and other mammals.

Symptoms exhibited by sea otters found on Amchitka beaches are listed:

1. The animal may be unable to stand or walk.
2. It may appear semicomatose or very lethargic and fearless.
3. It often exhibits hiccup-like convulsions.
4. The vibrissae may be extended rigidly forward.
5. The necropsy reveals intestinal lesions of variable extent.

Young animals may die while lesions are small, affecting 3 to 4 inches of the small intestine. The intestine is inflamed, muscle tone is lost, and affected areas become blackish or greenish black in color. In adult animals, long sections of the small intestine show this condition at death. The colon has not been specifically observed to show the extensive lesions found in the small intestine.

The small intestine and colon often contain the remains of about a dozen small sea urchins. Black tarry feces may or may not be voided before death. In young animals particularly, the progress of enteritis to death may be rapid.

6. Death may occur before the typical black fecal matter is voided. The black condition of the feces is called melena (a combination of the iron found in hemoglobin and hydrogen sulfide to-

gether produce iron sulfide, the putrafactive changes in the intestine produce the H_2S).

7. I have examined the stomachs of more than 200 otters that showed symptoms of enteritis at death. None has contained food. The stomach may contain from 10 to 50 ml. of liquid which may be pinkish, reddish brown, or yellowish. The mucosa may show inflammation.

8. Weight loss, probably caused by dehydration and starvation, characteristically accompanies enteritis. A captive juvenile male (59–159), that died showing symptoms of enteritis, lost 26 percent of its body weight in 3 days.

It appears probable that a *Clostridium* organism is present in all animals and that it becomes active when the animal is subjected to stress, such as starvation or nervous tension. Unsatisfactory conditions in captivity, such as lack of water, may cause such nervous tension. In captivity, I have observed that animals given access to an abundant supply of clear water and abundant food have not been subjected to sufficient stress to develop enteritis. As pointed out elsewhere, animals which show symptoms of enteritis when captured may recover in captivity when given abundant food and water. Stress may be caused in captivity if the fur becomes dirty and the animal is chilled. Extreme anxiety accompanies chilling, a large intake of food may occur but unless the fur condition can be improved the animal experiences stress; enteritis usually develops, and is followed in a few hours by death. In the wild, lack of nourishing food and accompanying rough, stormy seas appear to cause stress that results in enteritis and terminates in death.

Additional laboratory examination of specimen material taken from sick or dying sea otters is needed before we can attain a proper understanding of the relationship between enteritis and the trematode *Microphallus pyrum*, and the bacterium, *Clostridium*, in the sea otter.

Infection and liver degeneration

Dr. Dean Jensen, College of Veterinary Medicine, Colorado State University, kindly made a study of pathological tissues obtained from animals found dead or dying at Amchitka.

An adult female (D7–57), having well-worn teeth, weighed 56 lb. (25.4 kg.) when captured alive on 1 December 1957. Her weight at death, 6 December 1957, was 47 lb. (19 kg.). This animal lacked energy and ate sparingly during the period of captivity.

Fur preening was also inadequate. The animal, in general, appeared to be in poor condition.

Necropsy.—The liver appeared fibrous and spotted with various shades of brown and reddish inflammation. In three places the omentum adhered abnormally to the liver and there were numerous abnormal adhesions between the lobes of the liver. Yellowish scar tissue surrounded the areas of adhesion. The spleen appeared abnormal, exhibiting a somewhat opaque whitish scum over one side. Linear indentations crisscrossed this surface. Specimens were preserved in AFA solution, then transferred to 70 percent alcohol. A large abscess surrounded the root of the lower right canine tooth. Considerable osteolysis of the jaw had occurred around the root of the tooth forming a hole in the bone which measured $10 \times 8 \times 7$ mm. Other organs appeared normal to gross examination.

Dr. Jensen's analysis:

Hemopoietic system: Histopathology: Spleen: Parenchyma is diminished while capsule and trabeculae are abundant. These changes indicate atrophy from unknown cause. The periphery of some central arterioles contain a homogenous acidiphilic substance which may be amyloid [starch-like].

Liver: Many lobules show fatty metamorphosis in central zones. This change is not uniform.

Although Dr. Jensen gave no diagnosis in this case, it was apparent that this animal was moribund. It would appear that toxins from the infected jaw may have caused the fatty degeneration and sclerosis of the liver.

The results of a necropsy of another otter was similar but no localized infection was found: KWK 59–85, adult female, weight 37½ lb. (17 kg.), collected 27 March 1959, found dead well above high-tide line in sleeping position. The liver appeared swollen and fibrous with considerable yellowish discoloration, scar tissue, and abnormal adhesions to the diaphragm and intestines. Peripheral blood vessels of the liver and intestines were turgid. The otter had bled from the rectum before death.

Malignancy

On 22 October 1957, a young adult female sea otter (B–12–57), weighing 42 lb. (19 kg.), was found dead on a rock well above high-tide line at Amchitka. A necropsy revealed abnormal tissue growth in the viscera and a quantity of dark, apparently bloody fluid in the coelom. Externally in other respects the animal appeared normal.

Dr. D. V. Brown, then Associate Professor of Pathology, University of Washington and Chief, Laboratory Service, Veterans Administration Hospital, Seattle, examined the specimen material and gave the following information:

Gross examination: Specimen as received, fixed in formalin, consists of a spleen, stomach, duodenum and what appears to be the greater portion of the small intestine with its mesentery. Tissue preservation appears to be good.

The spleen is firm and rubbery with a roughened, granular capsule which is gray-blue in color. It weighs approximately 60 g. and measures 14.0 × 6.5 × 2.0 cm. in its greatest dimensions. On section it is homogeneous throughout with no focal areas of gross change.

The stomach appears to have a wall of normal thickness. Within the lumen there is a little green pulpy material but no suggestion of old or recent bleeding. The mucosa seems well preserved. The pyloris and duodenum appear normal.

Throughout the small intestine the bowel wall and the adjacent mesentery are irregularly thickened with firm, gray tissue which appears neoplastic [new and abnormal growth]. The bulk of this is in the distal end of the bowel apparently near the cecum. The gray tumorlike tissue infiltrates and thickens the bowel wall in some areas and extends out into the mesentery which is also thickened and gray. Toward the distal end, the mesentery contains a large coarsely nodular mass (8.0 × 6.0 × 4.0 cm.) which on section is solid and gray.

Small solid gray masses scattered through the mesentery are apparently other involved lymph nodes.

Sections for microscopic study are taken as follows: Spleen, stomach, bowel wall, lymph nodes and mesenteric mass.

Microscopic: Sections of spleen are quite well preserved. No abnormalities are recognized.

A portion of pancreas is included and it too does not seem remarkable.

Sections of enlarged lymph nodes show focal areas of apparent neoplastic invasion. The tumor here is partially replacing the nodal substance and is similar to that described below.

M. C. Keyes, D.V.M., who examined Dr. Brown's histological preparations, considers that the condition described may be diagnosed as leiomyoma or a leiomyosarcoma.

Paw infections

Several otters with infected forepaws were captured on Amchitka beaches. It appeared that puncture wounds, perhaps made by sea urchin spines, caused the infections. In captivity, infections developed in all extremities. In at least three cases infections occurred in puncture wounds or cuts originating on sharp ends of hardware cloth, used on the enclosure. Repeated doses of antibiotics successfully cured these infections in some animals.

Blindness

Otherwise healthy sea otters blind in one eye were occasionally seen at Amchitka. No wild otter blind in both eyes was observed. The cornea of the left eye of a yearling otter (Susie) was punctured near the center by a tiny "pinhole" when she was captured at Amchitka in 1955. Within weeks the eye became cloudy and eventually completely blind. About 2 years before her death in 1961 the right eye also became cloudy (presumably affected by the other blind eye) and total blindness resulted. Because she had learned the topography of her enclosure well before losing her sight, she appeared to experience no difficulty in finding her food and her way about her quarters.

Intussusception

Blocking of the small intestine by the intestine "swallowing" itself occurred in three captive otters. These animals were held in unsatisfactory cages without sufficient water for immersion. The animals appeared to experience emotional stress, as evidenced by frequent vocalization for one or more days before death occurred.

Predation

No information exists to indicate that predation by animals (other than man) on the sea otter is an important factor in its population dynamics. Available information on predation is presented below:

SHARKS

It is beyond question that some sea otters are killed by sharks. Snow (1910, p. 278) states:

Wounded otters I have taken on a few occasions, but they had been bitten by sharks, as I know from finding several of the sharks' teeth broken off in wounds.

Orr (1959) discovered the broken tooth of a great white shark *(Carcharadon carcharias)* in the lacerated body of a sea otter found dead at Pebble Beach, Calif. He considered that one other otter he examined definitely died from shark wounds and that several others found dead and bearing lacerations may have died as a result of shark attacks. That skin divers may have inflicted fatal wounds with spears, although a possibility, must be considered an opinion to be carefully weighed, since no proof that this occurred is available. Limbaugh (*in* Gilbert, 1963) says that "white sharks may be threatening" the small sea otter population on the central California coast. The degree to which man or sharks kill sea otters along the California coast still appears to be an unresolved question. In Alaska no deaths attributable to sharks are recorded.

KILLER WHALE *Orcinus orca*

Presumably the killer whale may eat sea otters. I have watched killer whales and otters in the same area and have not seen a whale attack an otter. Nikolaev (1965b, p. 231), however, saw a killer whale catch one sea otter.

On 1 March 1959, near South Bight on the Pacific shore of Amchitka, I watched from the cliff top as five killer whales cruised about outlying reefs. As the whales approached the reefs a harbor seal left the water and climbed onto the rocks. The whales cruised close to the reefs, then proceeded eastward parallel to the shore and into an area where four sea otters were feeding. One otter was eating on the surface when the whales approached and passed only a few feet beneath it. This otter appeared to sense the presence of the whales. It stopped eating and remained motionless while they passed. Otherwise, the otters seemed undisturbed by the whales and the whales exhibited no discernible interest in the otters.

On 9 April 1959, R. D. Jones and I observed killer whales and otters in the same general area off Kirilof Point on the Bering Sea shore of Amchitka. On several occasions between 1345 and 1645 we spent nearly an hour watching two groups of killer whales, one of 9 and the other of 18. They moved parallel to the shore and remained from a quarter to one-half mile from land. Several individuals raised the head and anterior quarter of the body above the surface as if to search the surface visually. Sea otters that were food diving in their vicinity ceased this activity and lay still on the surface or moved slowly toward shore on the surface. We did not see any behavior by the whales which indicated to us that a sea otter was attacked.

A further observation by Jones (letter, 9 July 1961) is similar. At Rat Island he saw six killer whales which remained for some time "from 25 to 100 yards off" shore and in the vicinity of "a large pod (over 200) sea otters." The sea otters exhibited "no alarm" and the whales did not attack them.

Although Barabash-Nikiforov (1947) gives no observation of

a killer whale attack on a sea otter, he lists them as an enemy and presumed "that killer whales terrorize sea otters."

BALD EAGLE *Haliaeetus leucocephalus*

The sea otter population at Amchitka progressed from near extinction at the turn of the century to maximum size in about 40 years. At the same time a large population of eagles occupied Amchitka.

From many months of field observations by a number of observers there is only one authentic observation of an eagle attacking a living sea otter. This occurred on 3 June 1961 at Barr House Cove on Amchitka Island. In a letter of 17 October 1961, R. D. Jones reported what he and Vernon D. Berns observed:

We were on the beach of the cove watching the eagles with binoculars . . . [an eagle] launched and flew . . . to sea losing altitude rapidly and disappearing behind the island. The eagle quickly returned directly to the island . . . carrying a large bulky object . . . [which it] carried . . . to the nest and upon our approach took wing. It was not necessary for us to climb the pinnacle to know there was a sea otter pup in [the nest] for the screaming of the pup was all too clear. We did climb it, however, and observed three eagle nestlings and the still living pup.

Sea otter remains frequently occur in eagle nests (Krog, 1953; Kenyon, 1961, 1964) where the two species occur together. That certain individual eagles may develop a taste for sea otters, while others do not, is indicated by the failure of Murie (1959) and D. C. Hopper (*in* Jones, R. D., unpublished report of 1 January to 31 August 1953) to find sea otter remains in eagle nests they investigated on islands where sea otters were numerous. I obtained many observations at Amchitka of eagles feeding on carcasses of sea otters that died of natural causes and saw them carry parts of these carcasses away in their claws. The otter remains frequently seen in eagle nests undoubtedly include many that were obtained by scavenging rather than predation.

One observation quoted from my field notes is typical of many:

St. Makarius Bay, Amchitka Island, 2 April 1959, 0900. At water's edge an adult eagle was finishing the remains of a large fish (ca. 30 in. (0.75 m.) long, washed ashore dead) while four other eagles (all in subadult plumage) rested on the beach and bluff. In the midst of this group, a young male sea otter—just awakened from the night's sleep—squirmed about on the dry grass (est. wt.=25 lb. (11.3 kg.)). Obviously the eagles were paying no attention to the sea otter and the otter was certainly not alarmed at the eagles' presence.

In places where one or more eagles were near, I frequently saw helpless young sea otters left floating on the surface while the mothers dived for food. Although the young otters would have been easy prey, I never saw an eagle attempt to take one.

My observations indicate that predation by the Bald Eagle on the sea otter is unimportant.

Environmental Pollution

Fur cleanliness is essential to the sea otter's survival. If the fur becomes soiled by foreign matter it loses its water-repellent characteristics, the insulating blanket of air among the dense fur fibers is lost, the animal is chilled, and soon dies.

Pollution of waters by oil and other by-products of industrial development preclude the possibility that the sea otter can today reoccupy all of its former habitat. San Francisco Bay, in early years, "abounded in otters" (Ogden, 1941). Pollution by oil and other wastes today would certainly preclude their survival there or in the vicinity of the Golden Gate. Periodically the outer coast of Washington State, which once supported a thriving sea otter population, is polluted by oil from the many ships which navigate the Strait of Juan de Fuca. That a permanent population of sea otters could today survive in this otherwise ideal coastal habitat is questionable.

Not only is the sea otter affected directly by habitat pollution but where pollution is acute, as in San Francisco Bay, food organisms are also affected and reduced or eliminated.

Poaching

Poaching or illegal killing of sea otters in Alaska is not known to be a serious problem. Holger Larsen of the U.S. Fish and Wildlife Service said "it has been known that illegal furs have moved through Valdez since 1938" (Seattle Times, 2 February 1956). The only arrests in recent years, however, were of a Fairbanks fur dealer in 1944 for the possession of a sea otter and of two men in an Anchorage hotel on 1 February 1956 who had in their possession eight sea otter pelts. Ray Woolford of the U.S. Fish and Wildlife Service said (letter of 18 March 1964):

Probably more sea otters are accidentally shot by inexperienced seal hunters than are deliberately killed with the intent to commercialize on fur. I think the accidental kills by seal hunters and others traveling coastal waters have a potential for increasing so long as seals remain unprotected and a bounty is paid on them.

Various reports of poaching by foreign nationals in the outer Aleutian Islands are not confirmed.

The problem of illegal killing of sea otters may be of more importance in California. Captain Howard Shelby of the California Department of Fish and Game reported that in one period (late 1957 and early 1958) in the Monterey area alone 18 dead otters were found. "Some had a hole clear through them, either spear or bullet wound." He said further that "it's my opinion that there are people and there are groups of people who do definitely shoot this animal. Then there are quite a group that target practice at anything." (California Senate, 1963)

Summary

1. Few sea otters were found dead on Amchitka beaches in the period 1938–40. The first report of significant natural mortality was made in the spring of 1948 when "more than 100" otters were found dead on beaches. Since the late 1940's significant late-winter, early-spring mortality was observed when biologists visited Amchitka. During five study periods from 1956 to 1963, data were obtained from 311 otters found dead or dying on beaches of the eastern half of Amchitka Island.

2. The greatest number of otters usually died in the month of March but considerable mortality also occurred in February, April, and May. In this late-winter, early-spring period about three-quarters of all annual mortality occurred.

3. Approximately 70 percent of the late-winter, early-spring mortality occurred among juveniles deserted by mothers. The other 30 percent of dead animals were predominantly adults showing signs of age.

4. During the period of stress caused by storms, mothers deserted their large juveniles at an earlier age than they did at other seasons. They appeared to do this because it was difficult for a mother to obtain sufficient food to satisfy both herself and the large juvenile. Few very small pups were found dead even though they were present in the population at all seasons.

5. Mortality was usually greater among males than among females. Among juveniles this disparity was greater than among adults. Males in captivity were found to be less hardy than females.

6. Vigorous adults were able to obtain adequate nourishment from high-calorie foods, such as fish and octopus. These organisms were seldom obtained by juveniles and aged animals.

7. A high percentage of juveniles and aged animals found

dead on beaches exhibited malocclusion of the postcanine teeth. In juveniles this condition resulted when deciduous teeth were being replaced by permanent teeth. In adults malocclusion resulted from severe tooth attrition which may have been caused by chewing hard-shelled invertebrates.

8. Prolonged storm conditions precipitated mortality but the amount of mortality was found, in 1962, to be related to the available feeding habitat and population density.

9. The relative intensity of storm wave action was greater on the Pacific Ocean coast than on the Bering Sea coast, but the mortality on each coast was proportional to population density and not to relative intensity of storm conditions, indicating that the threshold of conditions causing mortality was passed on both coasts.

10. The annual mortality of the Amchitka population was estimated in 1959 and 1962 to be about 8 to 11 percent. Two methods of estimating mortality gave similar results.

11. In the Shumagin and Sanak Islands areas, where the sea otter population was about four and two otters per square mile of water less than 30 fathoms deep, respectively, no evidence was found to indicate unusual mortality in the late-winter and early-spring storm periods.

12. The Amchitka population was about 19 otters per square mile of water less than 30 fathoms deep and had overexploited certain food resources. Because of this fact, the population was restricted by relatively high mortality which resulted primarily from malnutrition and was precipitated by environmental stresses during late-winter, early-spring storms.

13. Sea otters are infested by a variety of internal parasites but these rarely appear to be the direct cause of significant mortality. External parasites are limited to fortuitous infestations of nasal mites. Such infestation is unusual in wild otters.

14. The most frequently observed condition at death was emaciation accompanied by hemorrhagic enteritis. Chronic disease conditions and bodily injuries were observed.

15. Sharks, the Bald Eagle, and killer whale are known to kill sea otters. Predation, however, is probably an insignificant source of mortality.

16. Environmental pollution in areas now heavily utilized by man will probably prevent the sea otter from reoccupying all of its former range.

17. No evidence is available to indicate significant illegal killing by man of sea otters in Alaska. In California, however, illegal killing by man may, today, hinder the increase of the sea otter population.

IN CAPTIVITY

The sea otter is highly adaptable to life in captivity. When its environmental and food needs are met, it is hardy and appears contented in air temperatures from about 15° to 85° F. By nature it is placid and tames quickly. Some individuals accept food from the hand within a few minutes of capture.

Certain features of the captive environment are, however, extremely critical. The sea otter in captivity must have free access to an abundant supply of clean water. It also requires access to clean, dry areas but, in warm weather, it may spend entire days without leaving the water. Free air circulation is also a requirement. Cleanliness of the fur is essential; if the fur becomes soiled, the air blanket trapped among its fibers is destroyed, the skin then becomes wet, and death from chilling soon follows.

Its food requirement of about 20 to 25 percent of its body weight per day must be fulfilled. It readily eats a variety of fish, mollusks, and crustaceans but will remain in good health on a monotonous diet.

If clean water is withdrawn for even a short period, as during travel on ship or aircraft, death may occur soon after the animals are allowed to enter cold water. When water is not available, captives are emotionally upset and extremely sensitive to air temperatures. In dry cages, air temperature near 50° F. has caused distress, and animals exposed for a few hours to temperatures near 70° F. died.

The information gained from holding many captive otters is reviewed below.

Capture

Most sea otters taken alive are captured in nets. The historical record indicates that in early times, also, nets were employed. Steller (*in* Jordan, 1898–1899, Vol. 3, p. 214) states that anchored nets were spread on the water's surface and that carved wooden otters were used to attract otters into them. Of the captives he says:

When they are caught in the nets they are so frantic that in their despair they bite off their front feet; but if a male and a female are caught together they both lacerate their skins terribly and knock out their eyes.

After capturing more than 200 sea otters in dip nets, I have concluded that Steller's description is an exaggeration. That a netted otter is frantic is true. One particularly nervous female did chew off the first joint of one hind toe and tore at the skin of her belly with her teeth, but such behavior is unusual. Usually the netted otter bit the netting and with the help of its forepaws attempted to break the strands or attempted to push the strands away from its face and body with the forepaws.

On several occasions a mother and young were taken in the same net. A large juvenile bit its mother repeatedly on the head and body in its frantic efforts to escape. These two animals were quickly separated, tagged, and when released the juvenile joined its mother and the two swam away together. After being placed in a small carrying cage, otters usually rested quietly.

Soviet biologists working in the Kuril and Komandorskie Islands used landing nets and "boundary nets" to capture otters (Barabash-Nikiforov, 1947; Voronov, 1960).

Officials of the Alaska Department of Game successfully captured otters in Prince William Sound in a nylon salmon gillnet set from a boat (J. Vania, personal communication).

At Amchitka, otters haul out at certain times to sleep on beaches. With practice and care we caught these animals in a salmon landing net (fig. 82).

We captured otters most easily during late winter and spring. In this period, prolonged storms caused juveniles and older animals to weaken and come ashore. Healthy young adults were also taken, but less often. In summer, fall, and early winter, when storm periods were of shorter duration, few otters came ashore. In summer months, when calm weather prevailed, otters were particularly difficult to net on beaches. In summer, however, numbers did haul out at night to sleep on kelp-covered rocks close to the water. At this season, we found the best opportunities for netting otters when low tide coincided with dawn.

The reasons that otters may be netted on shore with relative ease are: (1) They often sleep soundly, (2) their sight and hearing are such that unless a moving figure appears above the horizon or unnecessary noises are made, the animals are often unaware of the hunter's presence, (3) they may be easily outrun by a man unless at the water's edge, and (4) they are placid and do not become alarmed easily.

In general, we found that otters may be classified in order of the ease with which they may be captured on shore as (most difficult first): (1) mothers with young, (2) adult females, (3) juveniles, and (4) adult males. Mothers with young were difficult to net because (1) they were alert, slept lightly, and retreated to the water at any hint of danger, and (2) they came ashore in places that were least accessible to enemies.

Because the sea otter has an acute sense of smell, animals of all age and sex classes must be approached upwind. Among rocks and near cliffs, eddy currents may carry enough scent in an upwind direction to alarm and stampede otters before they can be captured.

Captured otters were removed from the landing net either by placing a small carrying cage at its mouth (fig. 105), or by lifting

FIGURE 105.—After a sea otter was netted, a carrying cage was placed horizontally on the rocks and the otter was allowed to move from the net into the cage. After the animal entered, the cage was turned upright and the lid was fastened. The cage was then strapped to a packboard or suspended from a pole for transport to a truck or boat. (KWK 55–8–10)

the animal by its hind legs into a vertically placed cage. An otter held off the ground by its hind legs is unable to bend its body far enough to bite its captor. The caged otter (fig. 106) was then carried to a boat or to the nearest road.

Environmental Needs of Captives

From 1932 to 1937 Soviet biologists experimentally held captive sea otters (Barabash-Nikiforov, 1947). Animals were eventually held successfully in cages built at the edge of a bay where tidal water was used to flush and clean the enclosures (Reshetkin and Shidlovskaya, 1947). The details of this work were unknown to us until 1962. Even so, all coastal areas at Amchitka, where our work was done, were exposed to storm waves, so we could not use enclosures placed directly in sea water. After considerable experimentation, a satisfactory field holding facility was constructed on land.

FIGURE 106.—This 65-lb. male otter was carried for over a mile in this manner. After an initial frantic struggle when netted, it settled down and rode quite calmly in the cage. (KWK 56-3-40)

If sea otters are to survive in captivity, they should, within about 2 hours after capture, be placed in special quarters. The quarters, whether in the field or in a zoo, must essentially simulate the natural environment. If this procedure is not followed, death may occur within a few hours or weeks, depending on which needs are neglected and the degree of neglect. The following brief history of experimental attempts to hold otters in various kinds of enclosures illustrates the requirements for exacting care.

The first modern U.S. attempt to hold captive sea otters was made in March 1951. Refuge Manager Robert D. Jones of the Aleutian Islands National Wildlife Refuge and a crew of men went to Amchitka Island aboard the U.S. Fish and Wildlife Service vessel *Brown Bear*. A camp was established at Crown Reefer Point, and at least 35 otters were captured on tidal rocks. An attempt to hold these animals in shallow, mud-bottomed, fresh-water lakes was unsuccessful. All died within a few hours or a few days after capture.

In February 1954, Drs. Donald Stullken and Charles M. Kirkpatrick, in company with U.S. Fish and Wildlife Service employees, visited Amchitka. Information about the physiology of sea otters and their behavior in captivity was obtained (Stullken and Kirkpatrick, 1955; Kirkpatrick et al., 1955). Otters were kept experimentally in two ways: (1) In a large wooden tank of sea water and (2) in an abandoned house where dry grass was used as bedding. All animals placed in the tank soon showed symptoms of shock and exposure, and died within a few hours or a few days. Of those kept on dry bedding, three were given constant attention and survived. They were brought to Seattle in June 1954 by R. D. Jones. Subsequently, when shipped to the National Zoological Park in Washington, D.C., and placed in a small inside pool, all died within a week.

In March and April 1955, 31 otters were captured at Amchitka, held on bedding of dry straw in a building, then placed aboard ship in small cages having dry bedding (fig. 107). Forty percent (12) of the animals died before leaving Amchitka or aboard ship. The remainder are thought to have died soon after liberation at the Pribilofs (see Transplant Attempts). It became obvious that if the captive sea otters' fur became soiled, the animals could not again clean their fur and survive after liberation in cold water.

My sea otter studies began on 26 July 1955, when one Aleut laborer, Antone Bezezekoff, and I went to Amchitka Island and remained until 5 October. Our primary purpose was to learn how to maintain captive sea otters in good health. We held otters ex-

FIGURE 107.—In 1955, before it was learned that fur of the sea otter quickly lost its waterproof qualities when otters were carried in dry bedding, these animals were transported from Amchitka to the Pribilof Islands as shown. Mortality was high during the trip, and no otters are known to have survived after release. Three that were recaptured within a few minutes after release were soaked to the skin, rigid with cold and near death. (KWK 55-10-2)

perimentally in cages without water for bathing, since the 1954 studies had indicated that the otters survived best when kept dry. A female, "Susie," was given constant care and brought to Seattle where she lived in good health until shortly before her death on 27 October 1961. The pelage of animals held for more than a month in dry bedding became severely worn and matted. The fact that the otter which survived in Seattle did well in a pool demonstrated the need for access to clean water and dry areas.

Between 5 May and 26 July 1956, two experimental enclosures, with pools intermittently filled with water, were built on Amchitka. One of these was inside an abandoned building. Considerable humidity developed, and the fur did not dry properly. All developed enteritis and died within 2 or 3 weeks. Therefore, an outdoor enclosure was built containing a bathing trough through which sea water was pumped for 3 to 4 hours each day. When given only intermittent access to water, however, the waterproof condition of their fur eventually deteriorated. In addition, animals kept with limited access to water frequently developed infections of the paws and flippers which, in combination with eventual wetting of the underfur, contributed to the mortality. Although survival was improved in the outdoor cage, it was evident that caging methods were still inadequate.

In October 1957, an outdoor, cement pool, 15 feet (4.6 m.) long, 8 feet (2.4 m.) wide, and 4 feet (1.2 m.) deep, was built on Amchitka. Surrounding the pool was a wooden platform 7 feet (2.1 m.) wide, and the entire installation was surrounded by a board fence 7 feet (2.1 m.) high (figs. 108 and 109). The enclosure was unroofed. A continuous flow of water was furnished by a clear, fresh-water stream. All healthy animals placed in this enclosure remained healthy, and several that were afflicted with enteritis and apparently starving when captured regained health.

The basic reason for the failure of early experiments with captives became obvious. Under normal conditions in the wild, the

FIGURE 108.—This enclosure around a cement pool satisfactorily prevented escape and furnished ideal conditions where otters could be held indefinitely. Water from a stream was brought to the pool in the wooden pipe, at left. A ramp was constructed (far right) on which a dory, used to obtain fish for otter food, was beached. Storm waves often destroyed the ramp. (KWK 57–27–12)

FIGURE 109.—The cement pool in the enclosure shown in figure 108 where otters were maintained in excellent health. (KWK 57–29–4)

sea otter exists only in clean water and the fur remains water-repellent. The skin is never wet but is protected by a blanket of air trapped in the fur fibers. The waterproof quality of the delicate fur is lost when animals are improperly held.

In shallow lakes (1951), mud and detritus became entangled in fur fibers, admitting water to the skin. In the large wooden tank (1954), an insufficient flow of water allowed suspended food and fecal matter to accumulate and become imbedded in the fur. Also, there was not enough space for the otters to get out of the water to dry themselves. The same results occurred as in the lake. When otters were given intermittent access to water (1956), food scraps and slime became imbedded in the fur during periods when water was not available. The progress of wetting was less rapid under the latter conditions because a degree of cleansing was possible. In addition, humidity developed with inadequate circulation of outdoor air and hindered the drying of fur when otters were held in a building.

Even in the large outdoor pool, built in 1957, care was necessary to limit the number of otters held. If more than five were held simultaneously, the pool had to be drained and cleaned daily to prevent an accumulation of food scraps and feces that affected the water-repellent qualities of the fur. Captive otters were not affected adversely by frigid temperatures (fig. 110) when held in proper enclosures.

No conclusive data are available to demonstrate that fresh water provides a satisfactory permanent environment for captive sea otters. Although no record exists to show that sea otters were ever found in fresh water in nature, captives held in clean fresh water at Amchitka showed no detectable ill effects. One female, Susie, lived for 6 years in a fresh-water pool in Seattle. An autopsy revealed, however, that her reproductive tract had not only failed to mature but had regressed and was less developed than in normal juvenile otters. Could this condition have been related to the fresh-water environment? In addition, severe infestation of nasal mites *(Halarachne miroungae)*, a condition never found in a wild otter, contributed to her death (Kenyon, Yunker, and Newell, 1965). I conclude that fresh water may be temporarily satisfactory for captive animals but that long-term studies of captive otters should be conducted on animals kept in sea water.

FIGURE 110.—Air temperatures down to +15° F. were withstood with no apparent detrimental effects by captive otters in the outdoor pool. Ice which quickly formed during cold spells was removed to provide open water. The otter in the foreground holds up its paws in typical begging posture. (KWK 59–3–1)

When bathing water was withheld, otters were kept in clean, dry litter for periods of several months. Upon reintroduction to water, however, the fur, because it was soiled, immediately became soaked to the skin. The otters shivered and showed distress (Kirkpatrick et al., 1955). With special care, (drying the fur with towels and a warm air heater) or in warm weather, until waterproofness was restored, some captives survived this ordeal. Other harmful effects of dry caging, fur wear and matting, probably cannot be remedied.

It was demonstrated that the sea otter is a hardy animal in captivity if its basic and critical environmental needs are satisfied. It must be kept in clean flowing water that washes away food scraps and body wastes. Free air circulation that aids in drying the fur is also required. The sea otter, having no blubber layer, is dependent for heat retention entirely on the insulation afforded by air trapped within its fur. If the fur becomes soiled, allowing water to reach the skin, chilling will result and if the animal is not artificially and quickly dried, death, often accompanied by enteritis, follows soon. These findings agree with those of Soviet biologists (Reshetkin and Shidlovskaya, 1947; Marakov, 1965).

Food and Feeding of Captives

KINDS OF FOOD OFFERED

Because the sea otter requires a large quantity of food, the feeding of animals held captive in remote, isolated areas, posed problems: (1) A large frozen food supply was seldom available; (2) transportation to replenish dwindling food supplies was not available and commercial facilities from which to obtain food were hundreds of miles distant; and (3) fishing activities to obtain food in Alaskan waters were often interrupted by stormy weather.

For these reasons, experiments were conducted in the hope of developing feeding methods requiring minimum expenditure of time, money, and energy. Table 60 shows foods that were offered and the degree to which they were accepted. Since canned, salted, and dried foods were not readily accepted, the prospect of using foods that are easy to transport and store was abandoned.

Fishing with trammel nets in Constantine Harbor at Amchitka Island was practical. The species taken in greatest number was fringed greenling *(Hexagrammos decagrammus)*. Other species shown in table 60 were taken in lesser quantity.

In 1955 and 1956 no refrigeration was available. Fish that were

TABLE 60.—*Foods offered to captive sea otters*

Food item	Acceptability	Remarks
Crustacea [1] :		
King crab (*Paralithodes*)	Preferred	⎫
Tanner crab (*Chionoecetes*)	do	⎬ A limited amount (2 to 3 lb. per animal) was eaten eagerly. If, however, fish was also available it was eaten and the remaining crab was left uneaten.
Shrimp (misc. sp.)	do	⎭
Mollusca [2] :		
Snails, mussels, limpets	Accepted	Eaten when hungry and nothing else available.
Clams (*Saxidomus, Chione*)	Preferred	Eaten to capacity if sufficient available.
Octopus (*Octopus*)	Highly preferred	Do.
Squid (*Loligo*)	do	Do.
Echinodermata [3] :		
Starfish (*Leptasterias*)	Refused	Sample bitten off then discarded.
Sea urchin (*Strongylocentrotus*)	Accepted	Eaten when gravid; refused when not gravid, and other foods available.
Pisces [4] :		
Herring (*Clupea*)	Accepted	Refused at first but eaten when nothing else available.
Salmon (*Oncorhynchus*)	do	Eaten reluctantly when nothing else available.
Arctic char (*Salvelinus*)	do	Do.
Lancetfish (*Alepisaurus*)	do	Do.
Cod (*Gadus*)	Preferred	Do.
Hake (*Merluccius*)	do	Do.
Rockfish (*Sebastodes*)	Highly preferred	Eaten regularly and consistently— many feedings.
Greenling (*Hexagrammos*)	do	Do.
Lingcod (*Ophiodon*)	do	Do.
Sculpin (*Hemilepidotus*)	do	Do.
Poacher (*Agonus*)	Accepted	Eaten when nothing else available.
Globefish (*Cyclopterichthys*)	do	Do.
Halibut (*Hippoglossus*)	do	Do.
Sole (*Lepidopsetta*)	Preferred	Do.
Canned fish (salmon, mackerel, sardines)	Refused	Refused even when very hungry.
Cooked fresh fish (Greenling, boiled)	do	Do.
Salted and brined (codfish)	Sampled	Small amount eaten reluctantly.[5]
Aves: Goose flesh (*Philacte*)	Taken	Eaten reluctantly when very hungry but passed through tract undigested (Stullken and Kirkpatrick, 1955).
Mammalia: Seal flesh (*Phoca*)	do	Do.
Mink food	Refused	Dried commercial mink food was mixed with fresh fish. Not eaten even when hungry.

[1] Large pieces of shell discarded but many small pieces swallowed. J. Vania found that captive otters took live Dungeness crabs (*Cancer magister*) eagerly and were preferred to the exclusion of other foods during extended periods.

[2] Clam shells discarded but small shells of mussels and snails crushed and swallowed.

[3] Many pieces of shell swallowed.

[4] Viscera and hard bones of head discarded but other bones and skin usually swallowed.

[5] Soviet biologists apparently successfully fed salted cod and haddock after soaking "8–10 days in winter, 4–5 days in summer" (Shidlovskaya, 1947). Our otters might have taken some of the food items that were refused if they had been allowed to become sufficiently hungry.

alive when removed from nets were stored until needed in cages suspended in sea water from Kirilof dock.

Most fish taken at Amchitka were heavily infested with the roundworm *Terranova decipiens*. This parasite was tolerated in small numbers by sea otters but when heavy infestations were accumulated in captive animals they became lethargic and exhibited malaise. On autopsy, intestines of juveniles were found to be perforated by the worms. After 1956, all fish given to captive otters were held frozen (at about $+10°$ F.) for at least 24 hours. Apparently all helminth parasites were killed by this treatment.

A Soviet biologist (Shidlovskaya, 1947) states that fresh fish "is always better than frozen fish." Our experience is not in accord with this statement. During extended periods in captivity, otters were regularly fed fish that had been frozen and health remained excellent.

FOOD QUANTITY REQUIRED

During the period March 1956 through December 1957, records of the food consumed by Susie, a captive female sea otter, were kept on 602 days. Keeper Richard D. Clark used a 25-lb. capacity, Chatillon, platform-spring scale to weigh all food to the nearest ½ lb. (occasionally to ¼ lb.). The otter was fed three times daily (morning, noon, and late afternoon). Food in excess of the otter's daily consumption was offered. Before the morning feeding, the pool was drained and all food scraps from the previous day were removed and weighed. From these data the approximate weight of the food consumed was calculated. A screen over the pool drain minimized loss of remnant food scraps. The data from the daily feeding record are summarized in table 61.

The weight of this female (six weighings) averaged 39 lb. (17.7 kg.). She consumed about (daily average, 1 year, 1957) 8.9 lb. (4.04 kg.) or about 23 percent of her body weight per day, approximately 228 g./day/kg. of body weight. The extremes, using monthly averages were 24 percent (in February) and 20 percent (in April) of body weight consumed per day.

The actual daily consumption of food ranged from a minimum of about 2 lb. (0.9 kg.) to 16 lb. (7.2 kg.). The range in amount

TABLE 61.—*Food consumption of a 39 lb. (17.7 kg.) sea otter (Susie) at the Seattle Zoo*

				Kilograms of food		
					Extremes of average daily intake [1]	
Observation period	Days data kept	Total food offered	Total food consumed	Maximum	Minimum	Average daily intake entire period
1 March–31 December 1956 [2]	261	1,587.3	930.3	4.17	2.95	3.58
1 January–15 December 1957 [3]	341	2,129.6	1,374.7	4.31	3.54	4.04
Total (and mean)	602	3,716.9	2,305.0	4.24	3.24	3.81

[1] The average daily intake during each month was computed.
[2] Except August when no data were kept.
[3] A second otter was placed in the enclosure at the end of this period.

eaten was between 4.5 lb. (2.0 kg.) and 11.5 lb. (5.2 kg.) 94 percent of the time and between 5.5 lb. (2.5 kg.) and 10.5 lb. (4.8 kg.) 78 percent of the time (fig. 111).

Figure 112 demonstrates that in a winter month (February) more food was consumed than in a summer month (August). In February the intake in a 24-hour period ranged from 6 lb. (2.7 kg.) to 14.5 lb. (6.6 kg.) and in August from 5 lb. (2.3 kg.) to 12.5 lb. (5.7 kg.). The average daily consumption in February was 9.5 lb. (4.3 kg.) and in August 8.8 lb. (4.0 kg.). About 3,400 and

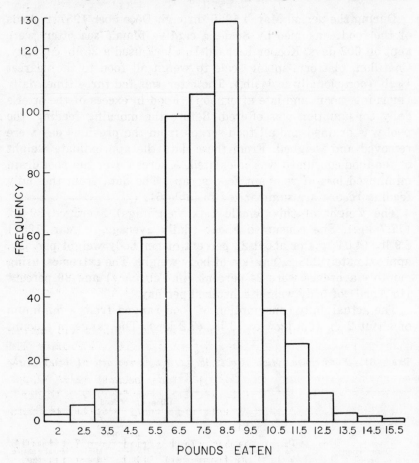

FIGURE 111.—The amount of food consumed by a captive female otter was recorded on 602 days. Food was available in excess of her daily requirement, and the amount consumed in a single day varied from about 2 lb. (1 kg.) to 16.5 lb. (7.5 kg.). Daily consumption was between 4.5 and 11.5 lb. on 567 days (94 percent of the time) and between 5.5 and 10.5 lb. on 470 days (78 percent of the time).

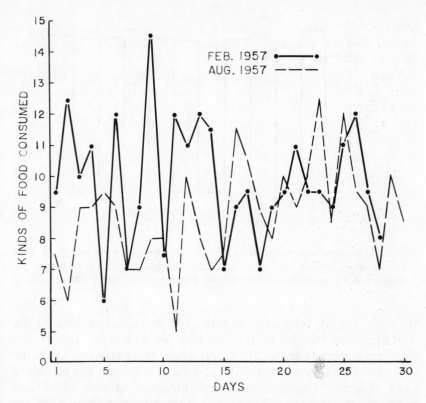

FIGURE 112.—Daily food consumption of a 39-lb. female sea otter (Susie) during a midwinter month (February) and during a midsummer month (August). More food was always available than was consumed. Average consumed in August, 8.8 lb.; average consumed in February, 9.5 lb.

3,200 calories per day were consumed in these winter and summer months, respectively, i.e., about 5 percent more in February than in August. The seasonal variation in consumption of food, however, was inconsistent (fig. 113) probably because water temperatures did not fluctuate greatly (seldom near freezing in winter to about 65° F. in summer), when compared to temperature fluctuations in other environments.

The average daily intake per month varied from 7.2 lb. (3.24 kg.) to 9.3 lb. (4.24 kg.), or from about 183 to 240 g. per kg. of body weight per day. It is interesting to note that dogs of 10 to 20 kg. daily require about 70–80 calories per kg. of body weight and the sea otter requires about 190 calories per kg. per day.

From December 1957 until September 1958, a nearly adult male, Dave, shared Susie's quarters. During the period January

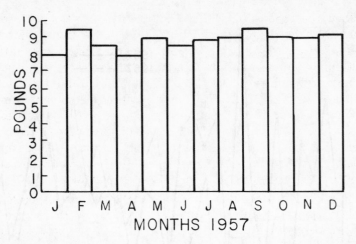

through August, records were kept of their combined food intake. The combined weights of the two animals was about 102 lb. and they consumed (during 212 days when records were kept) an average of 25.1 lb. of food daily, or 24.6 percent of their combined body weights. Unless competition for food stimulated Susie's appetite and increased her intake, this would indicate that the rate of consumption of the male exceeded that of the female.

An adult male, Gus, now (1967) in the Tacoma Aquarium weighs 76 lb. (34.5 kg.) and rarely fails to consume 15 lb. (6.8 kg.), about 20 percent of his body weight, of fish and squid daily. His food is stored frozen in 5 lb. (2.3 kg.) blocks and three of these are offered daily (filleted rockfish morning and evening and squid at noon). From 1 September 1966 through 31 August 1967 he consumed 5,452 lb. (2,473 kg.) of food. During the year period, the otter consumed more than 99 percent of the food offered. When, on several occasions, more than 15 lb. of food was offered the otter either refused it or did not consume the entire ration at a subsequent feeding. On his uniform and regulated diet this otter appeared to remain in excellent condition.

Some captive otters were temperamental about their food. A food that was eaten enthusiastically one day was ignored or eaten reluctantly the next. This behavior was especially evident when an abundant supply of food was available. Days of high consumption might indicate that a fresh supply of particularly desirable food was available.

When the food supply was limited on Amchitka and several otters were held simultaneously in a pool, we found that large juveniles, weighing 20 lb. (9 kg.) to 30 lb. (14 kg.), maintained health and vigor when fed a minimum daily average of about 6 lb. (3 kg.) of food per animal and that adults could subsist on a minimum average of about 8 lb. (4 kg.) fed daily per animal in morning, noon, and evening feedings. Given these quantities, the animals were always hungry and tended to rob food from each other. Stullken and Kirkpatrick (1955) found that when captives held in dry bedding were given only about 12 to 15 percent of their body weight per day enteritis developed.

The northern fur seal which, unlike the sea otter, has a thick blubber layer in addition to its fur, was found to require only about 7 percent of its body weight in food per day (Scheffer, 1950b).

Conclusions

When food was offered daily in excess, the average daily consumption by a female during 602 days was about 23 percent of the body weight. The daily consumption varied greatly. Consumption per day ranged from about 5 percent to 40 percent of the body weight. This animal appeared to be in excellent health during the study period.

When a captive male was offered food that was limited to 20 percent of his body weight each day, he consistently ate the amount offered and remained vigorous and healthy.

At Amchitka when a sufficient number of fish could not be caught, otters were held temporarily in apparent good health on less than the optimum food requirement. Food representing 15 percent of the body weight per day was near the minimum temporary requirement.

COST OF FOOD

Inquiries have been received concerning the economic possibility of operating a sea otter "fur farm." Aside from the high expense of catching and transporting the animals and building suitable quarters for them, the cost of feeding would be an important consideration.

For 1 year a record was kept at the Seattle Zoo of the cost to feed an adult female sea otter (Susie). The information was given to us by Zoo Director Frank Vincenzi (letter, 8 April 1963) and is summarized below:

Clams—20 lb./week at 20 cents/lb. 52 weeks ....$ 208.00
Octopus—346 lb. at 20 cents/lb. _____ 69.20
Fish—11,658 lb. at 10 cents/lb. _____ 1,165.80
    Total cost of food—1 year _____$1,443.00
    $27.75/week or $3.96/day

The cost of food for Gus in 1 year, 1 September 1966 to 1 September 1967, was more than $1,650 (squid at 30 cents per pound and filleted fish varied from 30 cents to 35 cents per pound). Point Defiance Aquarium Director Cecil Brosseau considers that the annual food cost is close to $1,800 or about $5 per day.

FEEDING BEHAVIOR OF CAPTIVES

When captives were kept in ample water they ate readily. Certain individuals consumed food eagerly immediately after capture. Others, in apparent good health, refused to eat for 24 hours or slightly longer. Old and apparently ill animals sometimes refused to eat, or ate too little to survive.

Within 1 or 2 days of capture, captives learned to beg for food and even after storing a quantity under the foreleg would float on their backs, both forepaws upheld in a begging posture (fig. 114). Food was usually tossed to otters individually as they floated on their backs. Pieces of fish were sometimes caught between the forepaws but more usually the food item was allowed to strike the chest before it was grasped by the paws. Often when an attendant entered the enclosure carrying a bucket of fish the more aggressive individuals would rush from the water to take food from the hand (fig. 62). At such times they never attempted to bite and would take food lying flat on an extended hand, avoiding contact between teeth and fingers.

Large adults habitually robbed smaller adults and juveniles, even when the larger ones had all they could carry under the forelegs. The robber would approach the victim from behind or beneath and with one or both forepaws wrench the food from the smaller animal's chest (fig. 115). Certain aggressive adult females growled and snapped at a robbing male, but juveniles and subordinate adults offered no resistance other than to roll away from the robber. Frustration, or perhaps anger, was expressed by the victim at such times by slapping the chest with rapid strokes of both forepaws.

Because food reserves were often low, it was difficult to assure that all captives received sufficient food. To reduce pilferage, a bamboo pole was used to deter food-robbing animals. One adult female, however, became so adept that while diving and projecting

FIGURE 114.—Juvenile otters learned begging behavior within a day or two after capture. The paws were held up and when a piece of fish was thrown (in circle) the otters attempted to catch the food. Sometimes a food item was caught by the paws, but usually it struck the chest. (KWK 59–14–13)

no more than one foreleg above the surface, she could quickly snatch all the food from the chest of a large juvenile floating and eating on the surface. After repeated treatment with the stick, she learned not to rob her pool mates as long as an attendant stood near the pool with the stick.

Kirkpatrick et al. (1955) described how captives ate a variety of food items. During our studies at Amchitka, fishes (head and viscera removed) weighing a pound or less, were the most frequently offered food. Young animals often had difficulty in cutting the fishes' tough skin and reducing the flesh to bite-sized chunks. The fish was held between the forepaws, while the chunks, torn from the body with the canines and incisors, were crushed by the postcanines before swallowing. Bones were often discarded. When whole fish were given, the viscera were not eaten. Sometimes the tail and skin of the fish were eaten. As noted by Stullken and Kirkpatrick (1955), only bones, shells, and calcareous spines passed through undigested.

FIGURE 115.—*A*—A large and unusually light-colored adult female aggressively wrenched a food item from a juvenile otter. After grasping the food tightly to her chest with the forelegs, the adult rolled away and dived. The young otter was unable to retrieve any food after it had been stolen. *B*—The juvenile attempts to retrieve a fish which the adult female had stolen from it. The adult, after rearing back, rolled forward and dived, frustrating the attempts of the juvenile to retrieve its food. (KWK 59–13–3 and 4)

Wild sea otters habitually eat while floating on the surface (see Food and Feeding Behavior). When captives were held in enclosures without sufficient water to swim in, they ate poorly. They refused some foods that were readily eaten by captives held in a pool. They were nervous and distressed. Stullken and Kirkpatrick (1955) noted that three successfully maintained captives kept in dry bedding lost weight, frequently appeared listless, and in weakened condition during the first 10 days in captivity. Digestion was apparently disturbed when animals were kept on dry bedding without a pool. Flatus was observed frequently in otters kept on dry bedding but not in animals kept in a satisfactory pool. Similar food was given to both groups of animals.

Individual animals in apparent good health refused to eat when held on dry bedding without access to a pool. One adult male refused to eat for 4 days and was then released, weakened but still apparently healthy. An adult female kept in similar quarters refused food for 6 days before release. Juveniles, in general, were more adaptable than adults. Sea otters require an abundant supply of clean water in which they can consume food and clean their pelage while eating. Only while in transit for a brief period should they be held in cages without bathing water.

Daily Cycle of Activity

BEHAVIOR DURING THE DAY

Two days, one in midsummer (29 August 1957) and the other in midwinter (21 January 1960) were spent by V. B. Scheffer and me near the enclosure of an adult female sea otter (Susie) in the Seattle Zoo. Her activities as listed below were timed with a stop watch and recorded (table 62). Activities were classified according to four primary categories:

Grooming

Rubbing the fur with the paws, principally the forepaws. It was accomplished while sitting beside the pool or while rolling over and over in the water or lying on the surface of the pool.

Resting

When the eyes were shut the otter was presumed to be sleeping. If the eyes were open while she lay quietly, she was recorded as napping.

[Air temperature: 29 Aug. 1957 at 0515, 52° F. (11° C.); at 1200, 70° F. (21.5° C.); at 1900, 66° F. (19° C.)]

Activity	Minutes						Percent of total	
	In water		On land		Total			
	29 Aug.	21 Jan.	29 Aug.	21 Jan.	29 Aug.	21 Jan.	29 Aug.	21 Jan.
Grooming:								
Energetic	239	86	100	103				
Languid	106	11	0	17				
					445	217	48	40
Resting:								
Sleeping	19	0	63	13				
Napping	84	19	6	38				
					172	70	19	13
Feeding	81	63	0	0	81	63	9	12
Exercise:								
Swimming	190	185	0	0				
Walking	0	0	5	0				
Playing	22	5	0	0				
					217	190	24	35
Total	741 (81%)	369 (68%)	174 (19%)	171 (32%)	915	540	100	100

Feeding

Food was placed in the otter's pool at about 0900, 1230, and again in late afternoon if none remained. Food remaining overnight in the pool was eaten by the otter before her regular feeding time. Feeding activity was most intense shortly after fresh food was placed in the pool. At other times, food items were retrieved from the bottom and eaten.

Exercise (swimming)

Like many zoo animals, the sea otter developed an exercise routine during which she circled her pool. In a certain place she would dive, in another she rose to the surface and turned, swam a short distance on the surface, then dived to complete the circuit. If a number of visitors stood near the fence by her pool, the exercise routine might include a vertical rise with one forepaw on the pool edge while she glanced at the visitors. This was also done before feeding time, when she glanced in the direction from which the keeper would come. Occasionally the otter left the pool to walk briefly about her enclosure. Such short walks did not follow a set pattern similar to the swimming routine. Play was recorded when the otter picked up leaves, peanut shells, or a scrap of paper and with her teeth and forepaws bandied it about; also when small rocks were retrieved from the bottom of the pool and pounded in an apparently aimless way on the edge of the pool. This activity apparently became an exercise routine.

Because of the frequency with which it occurred, the edge of the pool eventually became damaged and zoo officials removed the rocks from the pool.

The primary purpose of these observations was to ascertain whether behavior differed in response to temperature or other environmental seasonal conditions. All conditions, except those associated with season, were similar in the two observation periods.

On 29 August the weather was clear and calm. On 21 January a high overcast persisted until 1300, after which the sky remained clear until sunset.

The summer maximum temperature was 26° F. (18.5° C.) above the winter maximum and the winter minimum was 17° F. (9.5°C.) below the summer minimum on the days of observation. This temperature difference and the difference in hours of daylight (4 hrs., 13 min. less in winter, table 63) apparently did not materially affect the otter's general pattern of daily activity. In spite of the differences in these environmental conditions, the percent of time that the otter spent in the four main activities recorded are similar (table 62).

The amount of time that the otter spent on land, however, showed seasonal differences. On the summer day the otter was in the pool both at sunrise and at sunset. On the winter day she was in her den at both these times. Also, in the winter she spent a greater percent of her time during the day on land, even though her actual time on land was nearly identical (174 and 171 minutes, table 62).

Figure 116 shows the distribution of activity by minutes throughout the summer day. (Because of its similarity, a chart for the winter day is omitted.) This shows that grooming periods were generally distributed through the day, that periods of exercise were concentrated in morning and late afternoon hours, and that periods of rest reached greatest frequency at midday and in the afternoon. There were five prolonged rest periods of relative inactivity on the summer day: from 1126 to 1222, from 1340 to 1430, from 1502 to 1542, from 1733 to 1831, and from 1907 to 1944.

Table 62 demonstrates that the amount of time spent in muscular

TABLE 63.—*Conditions during sea otter observations at the Seattle Zoo*

	29 August 1957	21 January 1960
Sunrise	0527	0740
Sunset	1853	1653
Hours of sunlight	13 hrs. 26 min.	9 hrs. 13 min.
Air temperature (range)	52° to 70° F.	35° to 44° F.
Water temperature (constant)	62° F.	38° F.

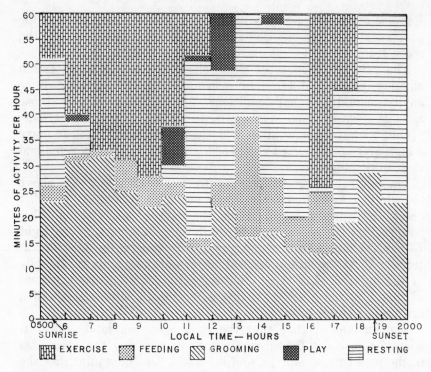

FIGURE 116.—The activities of a captive female sea otter were recorded for each minute from before sunrise to after sunset on 29 August 1957. The minutes spent in five categories of activity are summarized above for each hour of observation.

activity, grooming and exercising combined, was similar (72 percent in summer and 75 percent in winter). Grooming activity, however, consumed more time in summer than in winter.

Daily activity of wild and captive otters

The daily pattern of activity of the captive female and a wild female sea otter (further data are in the section on Breeding Behavior) would be expected to show obvious differences because a wild otter must search for food. Table 64 illustrates the differences. The data (although recorded in the same manner) are not strictly comparable because the captive otter was observed from the time of awakening in the morning until retiring at night. The wild otter was observed only from 1052 until 1820 (local time, Amchitka Island). In general, however, this comparison illustrates the fact that a wild otter must spend more than one-half of its time in feeding while the captive spent less than 10 percent of her

TABLE 64.—*Comparison of daily activities of wild and captive female sea otters in summer*

Activity	Wild otter 21 August 1955 [1]		Captive otter 29 August 1957	
	Minutes	Percent	Minutes	Percent
Feeding	257	55	81	9
Grooming	50	11	445	48
Resting	126	28	172	19
Exercise and play	25	6	217	24
Total	448	100	915	100

[1] See Breeding Behavior for further data.

time in this activity. The wild otter nearly satisfied her need for exercise while diving for food. The captive satisfied this need by swimming and grooming to a greater degree than the wild otter. The percent of time devoted to rest by both animals differed the least.

BEHAVIOR AT NIGHT

From 1 January to 9 September 1958, Mr. Cal Pierce, night watchman at the Seattle Zoo, recorded observations of the behavior of two captive sea otters. The objective was to obtain observations of the time each animal spent in and out of the water and in the den. For a variety of reasons, some nights were missed; substitute watchmen did not always properly record the data. Usable observations were taken on 199 of the 252 nights. Observations were usually made at hourly intervals from 1800 to 2200, and two to four times between 2200 and 0600. Usually the watchman recorded only whether each animal was in the pool, beside the pool, or in the den. Two dens were available, and both sea otters always had free access to all areas within their enclosure. Weather conditions were not recorded during the observation periods, but on several occasions the watchman noted that even during heavy rain the otters remained in the open, sleeping in or beside their pool.

Feeding, grooming, and play were not recorded systematically, but were noted on a number of occasions at various times during the hours of darkness up to about 2200. During late night and early morning hours, however, the animals usually slept quite soundly. Sometimes they awoke with a start in the light of the watchman's flashlight. If beside the pool when awakened, they immediately plunged into the water; if sleeping on the water, they would dive.

Observations made after 9 September are not used. About this time the behavior of the male became abnormal, and he spent increasing amounts of time in the den. His health steadily deteriorated and he died on 22 September.

The general behavior pattern for each animal during the night is indicated in figures 117 and 118. Both animals tended to remain in the water more than out of it during the early evening hours. During late night and early morning hours, the male spent a nearly equal time in and out of the water while the female tended to spend more time out of the water than in it. Both animals preferred to remain out of doors, whether sleeping on the pool edge or in the water, but the female consistently spent more time in the den than did the male.

Even during winter months the sea otters seldom sought shelter in the den (figs. 119 and 120). The amount of time spent in the water at night, however, was greatly reduced in winter months. The male spent only 20 percent of the night in the pool during January. During the spring and summer the amount of time he

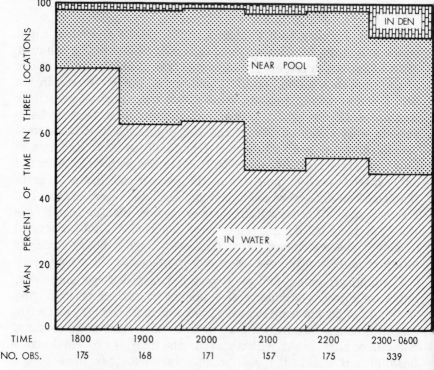

FIGURE 117.—Behavior of an adult male sea otter during a mean or average night. The mean percent of 1,185 observations of the animal in three locations during the night are shown.

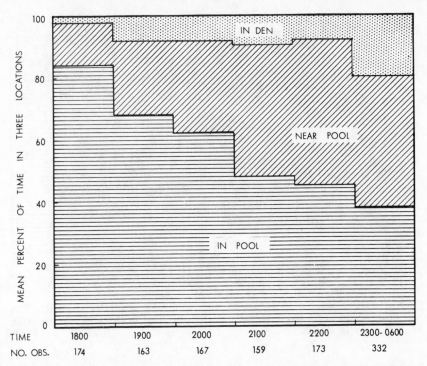

FIGURE 118.—Behavior of an adult female sea otter during a mean or average night. The mean percent of 1,168 observations of the animal in three locations during the night are shown.

spent in the water increased until in June he spent about 90 percent of his time there.

Causes of Death in Captivity

This subject was discussed in the foregoing pages in relation to environmental needs of captive otters.

The terminal symptom noted at death was often the voiding of black, tarry feces. Necropsy revealed enteritis (Stullken and Kirkpatrick, 1955).

K. L. Binkley, D.V.M., described the condition he found in three adult or near adult otters which he transported from Amchitka Island on a commercial, passenger-carrying aircraft (from a typewritten report dated 5 November 1957, in the files of the U.S. Fish and Wildlife Service):

Cause of death; acute pulmonary hemorrhage. Predisposing factors; high altitude flying in a nonpressurized plane, and promazine induced tranquility.

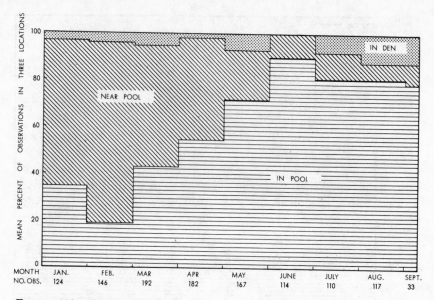

FIGURE 119.—Seasonal behavior of an adult male sea otter at night. The mean percent of 1,185 observations of the animal in three locations during 9 months is shown.

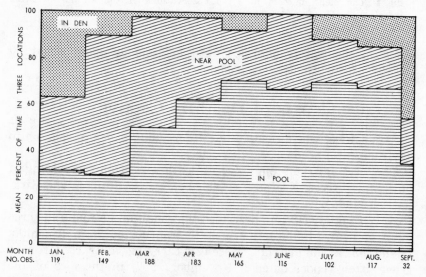

FIGURE 120.—Seasonal behavior of an adult female sea otter at night. The mean percent of 1,170 observations of the animal in three locations during 9 months is shown.

Administered 1.8 cc. Sparine. (Based on a dose of 2 mg. Sparine per lb. body weight, the weight was 43 lb. which resulted in a total dose of 90 mg. Sparine comes 50 mg./cc.) Dose administered approx. 0900 hrs 2 November, the animal died 1230 hrs 2 November. Lungs completely hemorrhagic. Trachea extremely hemorrhagic. Blood dark red, tarlike coagulations. Heart showed compensatory enlargement. Liver pale and anemic looking. Remaining organs normal with some postmortem discoloration. Stomach partially filled with food.

Overheating was probably also an important factor in the deaths of these animals. Post mortem examinations revealed that three captive otters were suffering from intussusceptions of the small intestine. This condition prevents the normal passage of intestinal contents. The reason that it occurred is not known but I suspect that stresses created by unsatisfactory holding facilities and during travel were important factors.

In review, captives died (1) as a result of chilling when the fur became soiled and its insulating air blanket was destroyed, (2) as a result of heat prostration in heated compartments when deprived of bathing water, (3) when infections occurred in the extremities, (4) when old and ill animals failed to eat after capture, (5) when parasitic roundworms *(Terranova)* ingested with fish flesh penetrated the intestine and caused peritonitis, (6) of lung hemorrhages when "tranquilized" otters were carried in small cages aboard a heated, passenger-carrying aircraft, (7) of lung congestion caused by a heavy infestation of nasal mites *(Halarachne)* (Kenyon et al., 1965), and (8) of intussusceptions of the small intestine. Enteritis was a frequent terminal condition. Causes of death are discussed further in the section on Parasites and Miscellaneous Diseases.

In conclusion, when parasite-free food requirements are met and the essential physical features of the sea otter's marine environment are duplicated, it adjusts easily to a healthy life in captivity.

Drug Use

Certain drugs were found useful in the care of captive otters. If drugs had not been used, some captives that survived probably would have died. No attempt was made to use drugs fired from a gun to capture sea otters.

Nembutal

Stullken and Kirkpatrick (1955) found that the normal anesthetic dose for dogs (40 mg. per kg. or 80 mg. per lb. of body weight) injected intraperitoneally caused death in a sea otter in less than 30 minutes. One-half the dog dose gave good anesthesia but thermoregulation was upset. No further experiments with Nembutal were conducted.

Promazine hydrochloride "Sparine" (Wyeth)

The use of this tranquilizer was suggested by K. L. Binkley, D.V.M. It was found to be a useful agent in speeding the adjustment of nervous animals to captive conditions. The dosage of 1 mg. of Sparine per kg. (0.5 mg. per lb.) of body weight was satisfactory. The intramuscular injection took effect within 5 minutes. The animals so treated remained in a relaxed state for about 24 hours. This degree of sedation is, however, usually unnecessary and under certain conditions harmful, since food intake and pelage care were substantially reduced during the tranquilized period. We found that about half this dose or less, i.e., about 0.5 to 1 mg. Sparine per lb. of body weight, induced adequate tranquility and that the otters gave nearly normal attention to their bodily needs. When the effects of the drug wore off, the treated animals in all cases remained tame and well adjusted.

Sparine was particularly useful when mothers with small pups were captured. On one occasion a mother with a newborn pup was placed in the enclosure without receiving an injection. The mother grasped the pup in her mouth and swam frantically about the pool seeking escape (fig. 121), rather than swimming in the normal manner on her back with her pup on her chest. She surely would have drowned the pup if we had not recaptured her, taken the pup from her, and given her the minimum injection. Within 5 minutes we returned the pup and the mother cared for it in the normal way from then on (fig. 122).

Usually when a sea otter pup was taken from its mother it cried almost incessantly, day and night, and accepted little food voluntarily. We found that after a minimum injection of Sparine such orphans became calm and after the effects of the drug had disappeared the pup appeared to have become "imprinted" on the human foster parent. Treated pups readily accepted food and only cried when desiring attention. Unfortunately, time and facilities were not available to maintain helpless captives indefinitely.

No harmful side effects from minimum injections of Sparine were detected in otters kept in a satisfactory enclosure with a pool. Because it was important that sea otters give frequent attention to their pelage and maintain their daily intake of food, it was desirable that use of tranquilizers be kept to a minimum. The

FIGURE 121.—A mother otter was placed in the pool without receiving a tranquilizer. Frantically she searched to escape while swimming about the pool, holding her pup in her mouth, the pup's head under water. Mother and pup were netted and the mother was given a small dose of Sparine ⁻ mg. per lb. of body weight). (KWK 57–29–31)

degree to which the use of Sparine on animals carried aboard an aircraft contributed to their deaths in transit is unknown (see Causes of Death in Captivity).

Propiopromazine hydrochloride "Tranvet" (Diamond)

This tranquilizer was used successfully by biologists of the Alaska Department of Game. Injections were given to captives immediately after capture (about 0.05 to 0.1 mg. per kg. or 0.025 to 0.05 mg. per lb. of estimated body weight). Before placing otters aboard aircraft during transplanting operations, a second dose of the drug, twice the amount of the first, was injected. J. Vania told me that the animals became satisfactorily relaxed and showed

FIGURE 122.—The same female and pup as shown in figure 121 about 10 minutes after the mother had received an injection of Sparine tranquilizer. Although the mother appeared drowsy, she carried the pup on her chest and groomed its fur, not as thoroughly, however, as she normally should have. She also ate, and nursed her pup. After recovering from the effects of the tranquilizer, the mother remained tame and satisfactorily cared for her pup. (KWK 57–29–28)

no harmful side effects. I have used the drug on only two sea otters. It was my general impression that the animals did not regain normal alertness as soon as those given Sparine and gave inadequate attention to feeding and pelage care.

Piperazine citrate

This vermifuge was administered as a precautionary measure to captive sea otters by injecting an aqueous solution into fish before feeding. Before fish were frozen routinely prior to feeding,

314

captives became heavily infested with *Terranova decipiens.* The effectiveness of the vermifuge was difficult to evaluate but it had no ill effect on the sea otters.

Vitamins

Because certain fish contain thiaminase, an enzyme that inhibits the proper utilization of vitamin B (Lee, 1948), thiamine hydrochloride was administered as a prophylactic measure. Pills containing vitamin B complex imbedded in the flesh of fish are readily eaten by otters and are administered daily to otters held permanently in captivity.

Antibiotics

Infections in paws, particularly the front paws, occurred when captive animals apparently scratched or cut these members during capture or in cages. An adult male with a badly infected front paw was given 600,000 units of Benzathine penicillin G "Bicillin" (Wyeth) and the infection disappeared after about 4 days. Two weeks later, however, the paw again began to swell and an additional dose of 600,000 units of Bicillin was administered and the infection disappeared permanently. The life of this animal, as well as those of several additional otherwise healthy animals, were probably saved through the injection of either Crystalline potassium penicillin G "Penicillin" (Wyeth) or Bicillin.

Pentobarbital sodium 3.7 gr. in each cc., isopropyl alcohol 10.5 percent, propylone glycol 10.5 percent, "Lethol" (Haver-Lockhart)

This drug administered intramuscularly was used to kill otters that were captured in nets and for various reasons were needed as specimens. The manufacturer recommended a dose of 1 cc. for every 5 lb. of body weight, but the sea otter was easily affected and we found that a dose of 10 cc. would kill large adults. The immediate effect is similar to other tranquilizers. Death followed injection in about 8 to 10 minutes.

Transportation of Captives

During transit from one location to another, the difficulty of controlling environmental temperatures and of furnishing sufficient bathing water causes severe complications. The longer the period in transit the more critical these factors become.

Sea otters have been transported in automobiles, aircraft, and ships. After many failures, knowledge is now available to assure successful transportation, provided that control of critical conditions is possible.

AUTOMOBILE

Otters were transported only short distances by truck or automobile. They were taken from the place of capture on Amchitka to field headquarters and later between holding facilities and ships or aircraft. Because the trips were short, the animals were conveyed in small carrying cages and no complications were encountered. However, they appeared disturbed, and whined or "whistled" en route. The longest automobile ride, 40 miles, was in 1965 when an adult male, "Gus," was taken from a dock in Seattle to the Tacoma Aquarium at Point Defiance. This animal appeared quite contented throughout the trip.

AIRCRAFT

On several occasions the only air transportation available was that of commercial passenger planes. Here, because of passenger needs, it was not possible to maintain temperatures low enough for sea otters. Distressed otters whined, whistled, and sometimes screamed, and attempted to escape from their cages by tearing at the wire screen cage with their teeth and forepaws. When available, ice was placed in the cages and cold water from bottles was poured on the otters. This they drank eagerly and rubbed into their fur. This treatment did not satisfactorily solve the problem, but several otters survived trips from Seattle to Washington, D.C. in 1954 and from Amchitka to Seattle in 1955 and 1956. The only otters that survived trips on heated, passenger-carrying aircraft were given constant attention, ice, and water during the trip. Of 19 otters taken at Amchitka and carried on commercial, passenger-carrying aircraft, 6 survived to reach Seattle. Of these, only two ultimately recovered from the trip. The time en route was from 36 hours to more than 4 days, and it appeared that few animals could tolerate such prolonged periods of stress.

To avoid self-injury and reduce excitement during air transports, K. L. Binkley, D.V.M., decided to administer a tranquilizer immediately before shipment from Amchitka on 2 November 1957. He wrote:

This was done . . . and the animals shipped. Unfortunately, fatal complications developed when the tranquil animals were exposed to 11,000 feet altitude in a nonpressurized plane. Although it is not known for sure, apparently the drug causes a lowering in metabolism, and also in the animal's ability to compensate for oxygen lack. Some action of the drug might also involve lung tissue permeability. During this attempt to ship 5 otters to the zoo in Seattle, the 4 adult otters were all administered 2 mg. Sparine per pound of body weight. A young 5-week-old pup was also included, although little hope was held for its safe arrival. In 2½ hours the pup was dead—probably from fright and altitude. In 15 more minutes the next youngest otter died, and in 5½ hours from take-off, the 3d otter (mother of the pup) succumbed. The two remaining otters died shortly after arrival in Anchorage, Alaska—or approximately 15 hours from Amchitka. Post mortem findings can be found in "Causes of Death in Captivity."

In the past, otters have been shipped in the same plane at the same altitude with no apparent [in flight] ill effects—although they did die during [delays in] shipment or shortly thereafter from other reasons. The only additional factor in this case was the tranquilizer, and until more work is done with the drug, the use of it under similar circumstances would not be indicated.

The above is from a report of 7 November 1957, by Kenneth L. Binkley, D.V.M., of the Woodland Park Zoo, Seattle, who was temporarily attached to the Sea Otter Project at Amchitka Island from 1 October to 2 November 1957.

After the unfortunate experience described by Binkley, it was decided to make one more transport of otters aboard a commercial passenger aircraft, it being the only available transportation.

In December of 1957 this attempt was made by taking eight otters via Reeve Aleutian Airways from Amchitka to St. Paul Island, Pribilof Islands reservation. No tranquilizer drugs were given. The animals were in excellent condition when they departed Amchitka on the morning of 11 December. A storm, however, caused delay, and unsatisfactory conditions inherent in an unpressurized, heated (to 75° F.), passenger-carrying aircraft caused rapid deterioration and resulted in the death of six animals on the night of 11 December. It appeared that overheating was the primary cause of death. The Pribilofs could not be reached, so two surviving males were taken to Seattle. One, an old adult, failed to recover from the trip and died on 16 December. The other, a young adult, recovered from the trip but subsequently died of unknown causes on 22 September 1958.

No further effort was made to carry sea otters on passenger-carrying commercial aircraft. In 1959, however, a U.S. Fish and Wildlife Service aircraft was available for the specific purpose of transporting sea otters. On 20 May seven otters, each about 1 year old, were placed on the R4D (DC–3) aircraft at Amchitka. On the direct flight of 3.4 hours to St. Paul Island the cabin temperature was maintained at 48° to 49° F., and the maximum altitude attained was 2,000 feet. En route the animals exhibited mild distress but when water from a bottle was poured in their mouths and sprinkled on their fur, they became quiet. It appeared that even at the relatively low cabin temperature they suffered from heat distress when their fur was dry. All arrived at St. Paul Island in excellent condition.

Traveling cages with false wire bottoms were used during all experiments in aerial transportation to reduce fur soiling to a minimum. On the short trip from Amchitka to St. Paul the fur remained clean because the animals were not fed en route. On trips of longer duration (15 to 36 hours) fur soiling could not be avoided. Although body wastes fell through the false cage bottoms, the animals habitually lay on their backs to eat (fig. 123). Fish scraps and slime then accumulated in the fur with resultant loss of waterproof condition.

FIGURE 123.—Captive otters held on dry bedding habitually lay on their back or side. Fish scraps and slime thus fell into the fur while the animals ate. When the otters groomed and rubbed the fur with their paws, it became saturated with filth and particles of bedding material, and its waterproof quality was destroyed. When this animal was placed in water it did not float in the normal manner but sank because the air in its fur was lost. In this condition animals placed in cold water quickly chill and die. (KWK 55–5–1)

SHIP

Otters were carried aboard ship in two ways: (1) in cages with bedding and no water for bathing, and (2) in a cage which included a tank of constantly flowing sea water. Using the first method, when straw bedding could be changed frequently and conditions were such that the animals remained dry and did not chill, they remained in satisfactory condition. The three otters brought successfully from Adak to Seattle aboard a large ship in June of 1954 by R. D. Jones were well protected from the weather. The animals, however, required constant attention and when placed in a Seattle zoo pool the fur became wet to the skin, causing the animals to shiver. In another experiment (April 1955), frigid weather caused chilling and high mortality among the soiled animals resulted.

An experiment to test the second method was conducted in November-December 1965. A young adult male and an aged female were captured on 7 November at Amchitka and placed aboard the MV *Commander*. Their cage included a tank having a flow of about 50 gallons of water per minute. Between capture and arrival at Seattle on 3 December frequent storms were encountered. The female, probably near death when captured, refused to eat and died on 13 November. The male "Gus" survived the 3,000-mile trip and arrived in excellent condition.

It was demonstrated that: (1) sea otters may be transported without food and in small cages aboard unheated aircraft for several hours and arrive at their destination in excellent condition. Delays en route and overheating, however, may result in high mortality. (2) Aboard ship is a satisfactory method of transporting otters over great distances if a pool with an ample flow of clean water is available. (3) For short distances (up to 40 miles, at least) transportation by automobile is satisfactory.

Transplant Attempts

The idea of transplanting sea otters from areas of abundance to unpopulated parts of their former range, from which they were extirpated in the 19th century, has long been popular. Since 1950, six attempts to transplant otters were undertaken, the first five by the U.S. Fish and Wildlife Service and the sixth by the Alaska Department of Fish and Game. A brief resume of these attempts is presented below. Additional information concerning them is given under "Environmental Needs of Captives" and "Transportation of Captives."

A late-winter, early-spring attempt, 1951, to transplant sea otters by ship failed because of insufficient knowledge of the otters' needs in captivity. The 35 animals that were captured on Amchitka Island all died there before any were placed aboard the waiting ship.

Studies of captive otters were conducted in the winter of 1954 on Amchitka and were reported by Kirkpatrick et al. (1955) and Stullken and Kirkpatrick (1955). The knowledge gained through these studies was useful but did not assure survival of captives while awaiting transfer or while in transit to a new location.

Nevertheless, a transplant of 31 otters captured on Amchitka was attempted between 28 March and 4 April 1955. These otters were carried from Amchitka to the Pribilof Islands in cages with bedding of straw aboard the chartered fishing vessel *Paragon*. During the trip their fur became matted with filth, and when the 19 survivors were liberated each animal left a dirty brown trail in the water. Three of these were recaptured by hand within a few minutes of release. They were soaked to the skin, rigid with cold, and near death. None of the animals liberated was subsequently seen at the Pribilofs, and it is reasonably certain that none survived.

In early spring, 1956, Refuge Manager R. D. Jones, with Navy assistance, captured five otters at Amchitka and took them via ship 240 miles to Attu in the Near Islands. Jones told me that the pelage of these animals when they were released was in the usual soiled condition of animals held in dry bedding. No evidence is available to demonstrate whether or not any of these otters survived.

Because these experiences demonstrated the need for a short period of time in transit, the next experimental transplant was an attempt to take otters from Amchitka to the Pribilofs by air 11 December 1957. As described under "Transportation of Captives" none of the eight otters taken aboard a commercial, passenger-carrying airliner at Amchitka reached their destination.

The next experimental aerial transplant was undertaken in 1959 when an aircraft could be devoted exclusively to this undertaking. From 6 to 8 May, during a severe storm, 10 subadult otters were captured and placed in the pool enclosure. Three animals, in weakened condition when captured, soon died. Furthermore, the Amchitka pool was too small for 10 otters. Unless the animals were healthy when captured, their chance of survival was reduced by crowding and competition for food. Therefore, when animals died they were not replaced.

On 20 May, seven otters, including four females and three males, were taken to St. Paul Island by direct flight (see Transportation of Captives, Aircraft). They weighed 26 to 36 lb. and were estimated to be 1 to 1½ years old. They were marked with numbered monel tags on the hind flippers. The animals were liberated at Polovina Point within 20 minutes after landing. All appeared in excellent condition and, except for one, each accepted and ate a fish as it swam from shore. When liberated, the animals scattered.

On 21 May, D. L. Spencer and I watched one otter for some time from the cliffs of Reef Rookery (3 miles from the point of release). This animal was eating a large sea urchin and appeared contented and in good health. A brief aerial survey of a part of the west and south sides of St. Paul was made after takeoff on 21 May. Two additional otters were seen at this time; however, several thousand fur seals in the area made it difficult to distinguish otters.

Subsequent reports indicate that this transplant was partially successful in that the animals survived for a substantial period after liberation. Several observations of them were reported during the remainder of 1959 and in 1960. The last authentic sighting of one otter was by an experienced hunter, Maxim Buterin, in the spring of 1961. He saw it near the same place on two occasions.

Why these transplanted animals did not ultimately survive and reproduce is problematical. Two possible explanations may be considered: (1) Seven immature otters may be too small a nucleus to form a reproducing colony. Before they matured (estimated 2 to 3 years after liberation) too few survived natural attrition to form a colony. (2) The Pribilofs are at the northern limit of the species original range. Hardship caused by winter ice, as described by Nikolaev (1965) might be expected to have caused mortality.

In August 1965, John Vania and Edward Klinkhart, of the Alaska Department of Game, captured 41 and held 35 otters in a floating netted enclosure supported by a wooden frame and styrofoam floats in Constantine Harbor at Hinchinbrook Island in Prince William Sound, Alaska. Free circulation of water and a plentiful supply of food assured excellent survival in the holding facilities. The animals were transported 450 miles in a Grumman Goose Amphibian aircraft after receiving injections of a tranquilizer "Tranvet." During the 3.7-hour flight distress caused by overheating occurred. This problem of overheating was solved by constructing a container for water into the cages but 12 otters died in flight prior to the pen modification. On the last flight, after the cages had been modified, seven otters were transported. All lived and were released in what appeared to be excellent condition. In all, 23 otters survived to be liberated on the west coast of Chichagof Island in Southeastern Alaska. Subsequent reports of sightings indicate that at least some of these animals survived the winter of 1965-66. Further transplants were conducted in 1966 and more are planned.

The knowledge and techniques are now available to hold captive otters in excellent health and to transport and liberate them in condition to survive. Large juveniles weighing about 24 to 35 lb. (11 to 16 kg.), approximately a year or somewhat older, are most adaptable to life in captivity and are hardy and more adjustable to stresses of travel than are older animals. Also, they are of a convenient size to handle. Before being transported in small carrying cages, animals should be held in a satisfactory enclosure for an adjustment period of a week or more.

It is yet to be shown that transplanted otters will form colonies and repopulate vacant habitat. Southeastern Alaska offers hundreds of miles of coastline suitable for sea otters. Will the transplanted otters behave like certain other mammals and scatter after release and therefore fail to form breeding aggregations? Might they also behave like other mammals and seek to return to the home territory where they were captured? These questions can be answered only by continued experimentation.

MANAGEMENT

Management of sea otters depends on knowledge of population size and trend. This knowledge may not become available until a cropping program has been in operation for several years. A tentative management program can, however, be set on the basis of present knowledge.

In the case of the sea otter, incomplete knowledge of population dynamics factors dictates that a flexible management program be initiated. This should be closely coordinated with a continuing program of studies of reproduction, mortality, maturation, aging, optimum population size, movements, and habitat status. Quantitatively these factors will vary in different habitats and according to population density, food availability, etc.

If a wildlife resource is to produce a maximum sustained annual yield, mortality from all causes must not exceed recruitment at an optimum population level. At the present stage of our knowledge of sea otter biology, the following recommendations for a management program appear relevant:

(1) To attain knowledge of the population level of maximum sustainable yield, a relatively isolated study population should be chosen (Amchitka is a possible choice). (2) At the chosen location a sustained annual harvest should be taken without regard to economic yield. (3) Annual population surveys (preferably aerial) should be conducted where harvests take place. (4) Late winter and spring mortality should be monitored. (5) All female reproductive tracts, with carefully gathered field data, should be analyzed. (6) During harvesting operations animals of a size most desired by the fur market should be taken without regard to sex (the sex of an otter in the field is difficult to recognize) except that all females accompanied by young should be spared. (7) If it becomes evident that a kill predominating in males is desired, harvesting operations should be concentrated at or near known male concentration areas.

While a regular annual crop of otters is being taken from the chosen study population, otters should also be taken in other areas where they are now known to be abundant. These areas are (1) the Shumagin Islands, (2) the Bering Sea off Unimak Island and the tip of the Alaska Peninsula, (3) the Sanak Island–Sandman Reefs area, (4) the western Andreanof Islands (including the Delarofs), and (5) the western Rat Islands.

ESTIMATED YIELD

If a harvest is taken from any population annually, the kill should probably be limited initially to about 2.5 percent of the total population (both sexes and all ages older than dependent young).

The total Alaska fur seal population is about 1,200,000 animals, including an annual production of about 350,000 young (Roppel, Johnson, Anas, and Chapman, 1966). The young constitute about 30 percent of the population. In the sea otter it was indicated (see Reproduction in the Female) that 2 years normally elapse between births and that the annual mean number of young in the population is about 14 percent, or approximately one-half that in the fur seal in which 1 year normally elapses between births. It has been found during many years of cropping the fur seal that, on a sustained yield basis, about 5 to 6 percent of the total population may be cropped annually. Under this management system the fur seal herd grew from a population of about 215,000 seals in 1911 to about one and a half million in the late 1940's (Kenyon, Scheffer, and Chapman, 1954) and between 1911 and 1963 yielded 2,761,170 skins (Roppel and Davey, 1965).

Thus, until further experience is gained, it may be concluded that about 2½ to 3 percent of the total sea otter population may be cropped annually on a sustained yield basis.

Further studies of reproduction and of the effect of cropping on populations may modify this preliminary estimate. In spite of the indication that a female sea otter may bear no more than one young in each 2-year interval, it is possible that because maternal care is intensive and prolonged the survival rate of young in a sea otter population might exceed that in the fur seal population.

CLOSED AREAS

Many observations indicate that before sea otters move from a populated area to adjacent vacant habitat, a large local population is formed (see Distribution and Numbers). They apparently move as a result of overutilization of food resources by a crowded population. It follows that if vacant habitat is to be repopulated, large local populations should be allowed to form to create the "population pressure" necessary to cause significant emigration. Thus, it is my opinion that the "spearhead" of population expansion should not be disturbed if nearby but vacant habitat is to be repopulated.

HABITAT STUDIES

Studies of abundance of food species should be undertaken where sea otters are abundant and where they are sparse. It has been observed in several areas that sea otters are capable of overutilizing food resources. In a heavily utilized area, for example Amchitka, underwater exclosures large enough for a diver to enter could be established to evaluate the status of food organisms during a long period in exploited and unexploited areas. During the Amchitka study period (1955–63), it appeared that a large sea otter population was at that time overexploiting its habitat. Body weights of otters were less than those of otters from sparse populations, and the pelage of Amchitka otters appeared "poor" compared to that of otters from a sparse population. Under the condition of a depleted habitat, population manipulation may be necessary for a period of years before habitat recovery occurs and animals having optimum body size and pelage are produced.

TRANSPLANT STUDIES

Capturing, holding, and transporting sea otters is complicated and expensive. The results of experimental transplants are not yet evaluated. Why the transplant of seven healthy, subadult otters to St. Paul Island, Alaska, apparently failed ultimately to survive, in spite of survival after the animals were released, is not known (see Transplant Attempts). Repeated observations of the small Samalga-Umnak population indicate that a small isolated population grows slowly. Studies and transplant experiments undertaken by the State of Alaska and now in progress should yield valuable information. It appears probable that in certain areas and when a significant number of otters may be moved, transplanting may prove to be a valuable management device.

REFERENCES

ABEGGLEN, C. E., A. Y. ROPPEL, and F. WILKE.
1960. Alaska fur seal investigations, Pribilof Islands, Alaska. Report of field activities June-October 1960. U.S. Fish and Wildlife Service, Marine Mammal Biological Laboratory, Seattle, Wash. Unpublished.

ALLANSON, A.
1955. Sea otters on San Miguel. Pacific Discovery, vol. 8, No. 3, p. 24-25.

ANTHONY, A. W.
1925. Expedition to Guadalupe Island, Mexico, in 1922. Proceedings California Academy of Science, 4th series, vol. 14, No. 13, p. 277–320.

BAILEY, V.
1936. The mammals and life zones of Oregon. U.S. Bureau of Biological Survey, North American Fauna No. 55, 416 p.

BARABASH-NIKIFOROV, I. I.
1947. Kalan. [The sea otter, pp. 1–174.] Soviet Ministrov RSFSR. Glavnoe upravlenie po zapovednikam. (In Russian.) [Translated from Russian by Dr. A. Birron and Z. S. Cole. Published for the National Science Foundation by the Israel Program for Scientific Translations, Jerusalem, 1962. 227 p., illus.]

BAUER, RICHARD D., ANCEL M. JOHNSON, and VICTOR B. SCHEFFER.
1964. Eye lens weight and age in the fur seal. Journal of Wildlife Management, vol. 28, No. 2, p. 374–376, April.

BEALS, F. L.
1943. Memorandum to Regional Director, Fish and Wildlife Service, Juneau, Alaska. Sept. 28, 1943. 3 p. 1 map.

BEE, J. W., and E. R. HALL.
1956. Mammals of northern Alaska on the arctic slope. University of Kansas, Miscellaneous Publication No. 8. 309 p.

BELKIN, A. N.
1966. On the population abundance of sea otter on the Kuril Islands. Transactions Pacific Research Institute of Marine Fisheries and Oceanography, vol. 58, p. 3–13.

BENTLEY, W. W.
1959. Sea otter along the California coast. Journal of Mammalogy, vol. 40, No. 1, p. 147.

BOLIN, R. L.
1938. Reappearance of the southern sea otter along the California coast. Journal of Mammalogy, vol. 19, No. 3, p. 301–303.

BOOLOOTIAN, R. A.
1961. The distribution of the California sea otter. California Fish and Game, vol. 47, No. 3, p. 287–292.

BURROUGHS, R. D.
1961. The natural history of the Lewis and Clark Expedition. Michigan State University Press, East Lansing. 340 p.

CALIFORNIA SENATE.

1963. Effect of the sea otter on the abalone resource. Senate Permanent Factfinding Committee on Natural Resources, Subcommittee on sea otters, Hearing, San Luis Obispo, Nov. 19, 1963. 148 p. (Processed.)

1965. The sea otter and its effect upon the abalone resource [Section 1, Chapter 7, pp. 129–144]. *In* Third Progress Report to the Legislature, 1965 Regular Session. Senate Permanent Factfinding Committee on Natural Resources (Sacramento). 144 p.

CHAPSKII, K. K.

1952. Age determination of some mammals according to bone microstructure. (In Russian.) Journal Institute Natural Sciences, Moscow, Izvestiya Estestivennonauchnogo Instituta imeni P.S. Lesgafta, vol. 25, p. 47–66.

COCKS, A. H.

1881. Notes on the breeding of the otter. Proceedings, Zoological Society of London, p. 249–250.

COMMERCIAL FISHERIES REVIEW.

1964a. Sea otter population survey. Vol. 26, No. 4, p. 12–13.

1964b. Sea otter population survey continued. Vol. 26, No. 5, p. 13.

1964c. Sea otter population determined by census. Vol. 26, No. 8, p. 15.

COWAN, I. McT., and C. J. GUIGUET.

1956. The mammals of British Columbia. British Columbia Provincial Museum, Handbook No. 11. 413 p.

COX, K. W.

1962. California abalones, Family Haliotidae. Resources Agency of California Department of Fish and Game, Fish Bulletin No. 118. 133 p.

DALL, W. H.

1870. Alaska and its resources. Sampson Low, Son, and Marston, London. 628 p.

DUKES, H. H.

1943. The physiology of domestic animals. Comstock Publishing Co. Ithaca, N.Y. 5th ed. revised.

EBERT, EARL E.

1968. A food habits study of the southern sea otter, *Enhydra lutris nereis.* California Fish and Game, vol. 54, No. 1, p. 33–42.

ELLIOTT, H. W.

1875. A report upon the condition of affairs in the territory of Alaska. Government Printing Office, Washington, D.C. 277 p.

ESSAPIAN, F. S.

1953. The birth and growth of a porpoise. Natural History, vol. 62, p. 392.

EVERMANN, B. W.

1923. Marine life of the Pacific. Commonwealth Club of California, Transactions, vol. 18, No. 3, p. 109.

EYERDAM, W. J.

1933. Sea otters in the Aleutian Islands. Journal of Mammalogy, vol. 14, No. 1, p. 70–71.

FAY, F. H.

1958. Pacific walrus investigations on St. Lawrence Island, Alaska. Alaska Cooperative Wildlife Research Unit. 54 p. (Processed.)

FISCUS, CLIFFORD H., and HIROSHI KAJIMURA.

1967. Pelagic fur seal investigations, 1965. U.S. Fish and Wildlife Service, Special Scientific Report—Fisheries, No. 537. 42 p.

———— G. BAINES, and F. WILKE.

1964. Pelagic fur seal investigations. U. S. Fish and Wildlife Service, Special Scientific Report—Fisheries No. 475. 59 p.

FISHER, EDNA M.

1939. Habits of the southern sea otter. Journal of Mammalogy, vol. 20, No. 1, p. 21–36.

1940a. Early life of a sea otter pup. Journal of Mammalogy, vol. 21, No. 2, p. 132–137.

1940b. The sea otter past and present. Proceedings Sixth Pacific Science Congress, No. 3, p. 223–236. University of California Press, Berkeley.

1941a. Prices of sea otter pelts. California Fish and Game, vol. 27, No. 4, p. 261–265, October.

1941b. Notes on the teeth of the sea otter. Journal of Mammalogy, vol. 22, No. 4, p. 428–433, November.

1942. Osteology and myology of the California river otter. Stanford University Press. 66 p.

FISHER, H. I.

1957. Footedness in domestic pigeons. Wilson Bulletin, vol. 69, p. 170–177.

FISLER, G. F.

1962. Ingestion of sea water by *Peromyscus maniculatus*. Journal of Mammalogy, vol. 43, No. 3, p. 416–417.

FOX, D. L.

1953. Animal Biochromes. Cambridge University Press, p. 195. [Footnote by Dr. E. M. Scott concerning the purple pigment of sea otter bones, p. 195.]

FRIEDMANN, H., and M. DAVIS.

1938. "Left-handedness" in parrots. Auk, vol. 55, p. 478–480.

GENTRY, R. L., and R. S. PETERSON.

1967. Underwater vision of the sea otter. Nature, vol. 216, p. 435–436.

GILBERT, P. W. (Editor).

1963. Sharks and survival. D.C. Heath, Boston. 578 p.

GOLODOFF, INNOKENTY.

1966. The last days of Attu Village. [As told to Karl W. Kenyon.] Alaska Sportsman, vol. 32, No. 12, p. 8–9.

GRIBKOV, P. F.

1963. O rasprostranenii morskoi vydry po poberezh'yu Kamchatskogo poluostrova. [Dispersion of the sea otter along the coast of the Kamchatka peninsula.] *In* Voprosy geografii Kamchatki. [Problems on the geography of Kamchatka.] Kamchatskaya Pravda, Petropavlovsk-Kamchatskii, vol. 1, p. 68–71.

GULIN, V.

1952. Neobychnyzyver'na chukotka [Unusual mammal in Chukotka]. [Torch] (Moscow), vol. 50, p. 31, illus.

HALL, E. RAYMOND.

1945. Chase Littlejohn, 1854–1943: observations by Littlejohn on hunting sea otters. Journal of Mammalogy, vol. 26, No. 1, p. 89–91.

———— and KEITH R. KELSON.

1959. The mammals of North America, vol. 2, p. 949–950. Ronald Press Co., New York.

HALL, K. R. L.
1965. Tool-using behaviour of the California sea otter. Medical and Biological Illustrations, October, vol. 15, No. 4, p. 216–217.
—— and G. B. SCHALLER.
1964. Tool using behavior of the California sea otter. Journal of Mammalogy, vol. 45, No. 2, p. 287–298.
HAMILTON, W. J., JR., and W. R. EADIE.
1964. Reproduction in the otter, *Lutra canadensis*. Journal of Mammalogy, vol. 45, No. 2, p. 242–252.
HARRIS, C. J.
1968. Otters, a study of the recent Lutrinae. Weidenfeld & Nicolson, London. 397 p.
HILDEBRAND, M.
1954. Incisor tooth wear in the sea otter. Journal of Mammalogy, vol. 35, No. 4, p. 595.
HOOPER, C. L.
1897. A report on the sea-otter banks of Alaska. U.S. Treasury Department, Document No. 1977. 35 p., 2 maps.
HOWELL, A. BRAZIER.
1930. Aquatic mammals. Chas. C. Thomas Co., Springfield.
HUGGETT, A. ST. G., and W. F. WIDDAS.
1951. The relationship between mammalian foetal weight and conception age. Journal of Physiology, No. 144, p. 306–317.
HUTCHINSON, H. B.
1935. Sea otter in the Rat Islands—a report on the existence of. Unpublished memo written aboard the USS *Oglala*, Constantine Harbor, Amchitka Island, 21 June. 6 p.
ICHIHARA, T.
1966. Criterion for determining age of fin whale with reference to ear plug and baleen plate. Scientific Report of Whales Research Institute, No. 20, p. 17–82. Whales Research Institute, Tokyo, Japan.
JELLISON, WILLIAM L., and KENNETH A. NEILAND.
1965. Parasites of Alaskan vertebrates. University of Oklahoma Research Institute, Project 1508. 73 p. (Processed.)
JENSEN, A.
1964. Odderen i Danmark [The otter in Denmark]. Danske Vildtundersøgelser, Heft 11, Kalø Ronde. 48 p. (In Danish with English summary.)
JONES, R. D.
1949–59. Refuge narrative reports. Unpublished, in U.S. Fish and Wildlife Service files.
1951. Present status of the sea otter in Alaska. Transactions of the 16th N. A. Wildlife Conference, March 5, 6, and 7, p. 376–383.
1963. Buldir Islands, site of a remnant breeding population of Aleutian Canada Geese. Wildfowl Trust 14th Annual Report 1961–62, p. 80–84.
1965. Sea otters in the Near Islands, Alaska. Journal of Mammalogy, vol. 46, No. 4, p. 702.
JORDAN, DAVID STARR.
1898–99. The fur seals and fur-seal islands of the North Pacific Ocean. U.S. Treasury Department, Document 2017, 4 parts.
JOYNT, G. T.
1957. Sea otter observations. Unpublished letter of March 1957, U.S. Fish and Wildlife Service files.

KENYON, K. W.

1959. The sea otter. Smithsonian Report for 1958, publication 4364, p. 399–407.

1961. Birds of Amchitka Island, Alaska. Auk, vol. 78, No. 3, p. 304–326.

1964. Wildlife and historical notes on Simeonof Island, Alaska. Murrelet, vol. 45, No. 1, p. 1–8.

1965a. Food of harbor seals at Amchitka Island, Alaska. Journal of Mammalogy, vol. 46, No. 1, p. 103–104.

1965b. Aerial survey of sea otters and other marine mammals, Alaska Peninsula and Aleutian Islands, 19 April to 9 May 1965. U.S. Bureau of Sport Fisheries and Wildlife, Seattle, Wash. 52 p. (Processed.)

—— and D. L. SPENCER.

1960. Sea otter population and transplant studies in Alaska, 1959. U.S. Fish and Wildlife Service, Special Scientific Report—Wildlife, No. 48. 29 p.

—— and V. B. SCHEFFER.

1962. Wildlife surveys along the northwest coast of Washington. Murrelet, vol. 42, No. 3, p. 29–37.

—— C. E. YUNKER, and I. M. NEWELL.

1965. Nasal mites (Halarachnidae) in the sea otter. Journal of Parasitology, vol. 51, No. 6, p. 960.

—— VICTOR B. SCHEFFER, and DOUGLAS G. CHAPMAN.

1954. A population study of the Alaska fur-seal herd. U.S. Fish and Wildlife Service, Special Scientific Report—Wildlife, No. 12. vi + 77 p. (Processed.)

KEYES, MARK C.

1963. Necrotic hemorrhagic enteritis in a seal. Small Animal Clinician, vol. 3, No. 11, p. 627.

KING, JUDITH E.

1964. Seals of the world. British Museum (Natural History), London. 154 p.

KIRKPATRICK, C. M., D. E. STULLKEN, and R. D. JONES, JR.

1955. Notes on captive sea otters. Journal Arctic Institute of North America, vol. 8, No. 1, p. 46–59.

KLUMOV, S. K.

1957. [Breeding places of the fur seal (*Callorhinus ursinus*) and areas inhabited by the sea otter (*Enhydra lutris*) in the Kurils and a tentative estimation of their numbers.] Doklady Akademy Nauk SSSR, vol. 117, No. 1–6, p. 153–156. Translated and published by American Institute of Biological Sciences.

KROG, J.

1953. Notes on the birds of Amchitka Island, Alaska. Condor, vol. 55, p. 299–304.

LACK, D.

1954. The natural regulation of animal numbers. Oxford at the Clarendon Press. 343 p.

LANE, F. W.

1946. Right and left in animals. Zoo Life, vol. 1, p. 30–31.

LANG, T. G., and K. S. NORRIS.

1965. Swimming speed of a Pacific bottlenose porpoise. Science, vol. 151, p. 588–590.

LAUGHLIN, W. S.
1963. The earliest Aleuts. Anthropological papers of the University of Alaska, vol. 10, No. 2, p. 73–136.

LEE, C. F.
1948. Thiaminase in fishery products: a review. Commercial Fisheries Review, vol. 10, No. 4, p. 7–17.

LENSINK, C. J.
1958. Report on sea otter surveys 6 May to 28 September 1957. Unpublished Report, 61 p., in Fish and Wildlife Service Files.
1960. Status and distribution of sea otters in Alaska. Journal of Mammalogy, vol. 41, No. 2, p. 172–182.
1962. The history and status of sea otters in Alaska. A thesis submitted to the Faculty of Purdue University in partial fulfillment of the requirements for the degree of Doctor of Philosophy. Unpublished, copy in Fish and Wildlife Service files.

LIERS, E. E.
1951. Notes on the river otter (Lutra canadensis). Journal of Mammalogy, vol. 32, No. 1, p. 1–9.

LOY, C. L.
1940. Sea otter report of Amchitka Island, Alaska, July 10, 1939 to January 15, 1940. Unpublished report in Fish and Wildlife Service files.
———— and O. A. FRIDEN.
1937. Sea otter survey of Amchitka Island, Alaska, July 11 to September 1, 1937. Unpublished report in Fish and Wildlife Service files.

LUTKE, F.
1835. Voyage autour du monde . . . dans les annees 1826, 1827, 1828, et 1829. Paris, Firmin Didot Freres, 3 vols. and atlas.

MANGEN, J. B., and G. RITTER.
1940. Amchitka Island Report. U.S. Fish and Wildlife Service, unpublished.

MARAKOV, S. V.
1963. Relic of nature or exploitable species?—Fate of the Komandorskii sea otter. Priroda No. 11, p. 79–83, Moscow. [Translated by U.S. Department of Commerce, Office of Technical Services, Joint Publications Research Service, Washington, D.C.]
1965. The present status of the Komandorski population of Enhydra lutris L. and prospects for its practical usage. In Marine Mammals, E. N. Pavlovskii, B. A. Zenkovich, et al., (Editors). [p. 212–220]. Translated by Nancy McRoy, April 1966.

MAYNARD, LT. WASHBURN.
1898 (1874). The sea otter [vol. 3, p. 300–302]. In Seal and salmon fisheries and general resources of Alaska. U.S. Treasury Department, 4 volumes, published 1898; Maynard's contribution dated 1874. (55th Congress, 1st session, House Document 92, pts. 1–4.)

McCANN, CHARLES.
1955. Observations on the polecat (Putorius putorius Linn.) in New Zealand. Records of Dominion Museum, vol. 2, pt. III, p. 151–165.

McCRACKEN, HAROLD.
1957. Hunters of the stormy sea. Doubleday, Garden City, N.Y. 312 p.

McLAREN, I. A.
1960. Are the Pinnipedia byphyletics? Systematic Zoology, vol. 9, No. 1, March, p. 18–28.

McLaughlin, Patsy A.

1963. Survey of the benthic invertebrate fauna of the eastern Bering Sea. U.S. Fish and Wildlife Service, Special Scientific Report—Fisheries, No. 401. 75 p.

McLean, J. H.

1962. Sublittoral ecology of kelp beds of the open coast area near Carmel, California. Biological Bulletin, vol. 122, No. 1, p. 95–144.

Miller, P., and L. G. Miller.

1967. Lost heritage of Alaska: The adventure and art of Alaskan coastal Indians. World Publishing Co., Cleveland, Ohio. 289 p.

Miller, G. S., and R. Kellogg.

1955. List of North American recent mammals. U.S. National Museum, Bulletin 205. 954 p.

Mitchell, Edward.

1966. Northeastern Pacific Pleistocene sea otters. Journal Fisheries Research Board of Canada, vol. 23, No. 12, p. 1897–1911.

Murie, O. J.

1940. Notes on the sea otter. Journal of Mammalogy, vol. 21, No. 2, p. 119–131.

1959. Fauna of the Aleutian Islands and Alaska Peninsula. U.S. Fish and Wildlife Service, North American Fauna, No. 61. 406 p.

Neiland, K. A.

1962. Alaskan species of acanthocephalan genus *Corynosoma* Luehe, 1904. Journal of Parasitology, vol. 48, p. 69–75.

Nikolaev, A. M.

1960. O dinamike chislennosti Kalanov v SSSR [Change in the number of sea otter in the USSR]. Trudy Sakhalinsk, Kompleksn. Nauchn.-Issled. Inst. 9, 108–121. Referat. Zur., Biol., 1962 No. 141256. [Translated abstract seen.]

1961. O. rasprostranenii chislennosti i biologii kalanov. [The biology and population spread of the sea otter.] Trudy Soveshchanii Ikhthiol. Kommiss. Akad. Nauk SSSR 12, p. 214–271.

1965a. The status of the stock of Kurile sea otters and fur seals and measures of their reproduction. *In* Marine Mammals, E. N. Pavlovskii, B. A. Zenkovich, et al., (Editors). [P. 226–230.] Translated by Nancy McRoy, April 1966.

1965b. On the feeding of the Kurile sea otter and some aspects of their behavior during the period of ice. *In* Marine Mammals, E. N. Pavlovskii, B. A. Zenkovich, et al., (Editors). [P. 231–236]. Translated by Nancy McRoy, April, 1966.

——— and V. A. Skalkin.

1963. O pitanii Kuril' skikh kalanov. [The diet of the Kamchatka sea-otter in the Kurile Islands.] Tr. Sakhalinsk. Kompleksnyi Nauchn.-Issled. Inst. 14, p. 54–78.

Novikov, G. A.

1956. Predatory mammals of USSR fauna. (In Russian.) Moscow, Academy of Sciences of USSR. 294 p.

Nozikov, N.

194?. Russian voyages around the world. Hutchinson & Co. Ltd. London. 165 p. [Translated from Russian by E. and M. Lesser.] No publication date is given.

OGDEN, A.
1941. The California sea otter trade 1784–1848. University of California Press, Berkeley and Los Angeles. 251 p.

ORR, R. T.
1959. Sharks as enemies of sea otters. Journal of Mammalogy, vol. 40, No. 4, p. 617.

———— and T. C. POULTER.
1964. Northward movement of the California sea otter. California Fish and Game, vol. 50, No. 2, p. 122–124.

PATCH, C. A.
1922. A biological reconnaissance on Graham Island of the Queen Charlotte Group. Canadian Field Naturalist, vol. 36, p. 101–105, 133–136.

PEDERSEN, R. J., and J. STOUT.
1963. Oregon sea otter sighting. Journal of Mammalogy, vol. 44, No. 3, p. 415.

PETERSON, R. S.
1965. Behavior of the northern fur seal. Doctor of Science Thesis. 214 p. [Unpublished.]

———— and M. W. ODEMAR.
1969. Population growth of the sea otter in California: results of aerial censuses and behavioral studies. A paper read to the 49th Annual Meeting of the American Society of Mammalogists, June 17, 1969. New York. 7 p. + 3 figs. (Processed.)

———— and W. G. REEDER.
1966. Multiple births in the northern fur seal. Zeitschrift fur Saugetierkunde, vol. 31, No. 1, p. 52–56.

POLAND, H.
1892. Fur-bearing animals in nature and in commerce. Burney and Jackson, London. 392 p.

PREBEL, E. A., and W. L. MCATEE.
1923. Birds and mammals of the Pribilof Islands, Alaska. U.S. Bureau of Biological Survey, North American Fauna, No. 46. 255 p.

RAUSCH, R. L.
1953. Studies on the helminth fauna of Alaska. XIII. Disease in the sea otter, with special reference to helminth parasites. Ecology, vol. 34, No. 3, p. 584–604.
1964. Studies on the helminth fauna of Alaska. XLI. Observations on cestodes of the genus *Diplogonoporus* Lonnberg, 1892 (Diphyllobothriidae). Canadian Journal of Zoology, vol. 42, p. 1049–1069.

RAUSCH, ROBERT, and BETTY LOCKER.
1951. Studies on the helminth fauna of Alaska. II. On some helminths parasitic in the sea otter, *Enhydra lutris* (L.). Proceedings of the Helminthological Society of Washington, vol. 18, No. 1, p. 77–81, January.

RESHETKIN, V. V., and N. K. SHIDLOVSKAYA.
1947. [Acclimatization of sea otters, p. 175–224.] *In* Kalan, by I. I. Barabash-Nikiforov, Soviet Ministrov RSFSR. Glavnoe upravlenie po zapovednikam, (In Russian.). [Translated from Russian by Dr. A. Birron and Z. S. Cole. Published for the National Science Foundation by the Israel Program for Scientific Translations, Jerusalem, 1962. 227 p., illus.]

ROPPEL, ALTON Y., and STUART P. DAVEY.
1965. Evolution of fur seal management on the Pribilof Islands. Journal of Wildlife Management, vol. 29, No. 3, p. 448–463.

————ANCEL M. JOHNSON, RAYMOND E. ANAS, and DOUGLAS G. CHAPMAN.

1966. Fur seal investigations, Pribilof Islands, Alaska, 1965. U.S. Fish and Wildlife Service, Special Scientific Report—Fisheries, No. 536. 45 p.

SCAMMON, C. M.

1870. The sea otters. American Naturalist, vol. 4, No. 2, p. 65–74.

SCAPINO, ROBERT P.

1965. The third joint of the canine jaw. Journal of Morphology, vol. 116, No. 1, p. 23–50.

SCHEFFER, V. B.

1940. The sea otter on the Washington coast. Pacific Northwest Quarterly, vol. 3, p. 370–388.

1950a. Growth layers on the teeth of Pinnipedia as an indication of age. Science, September 15, vol. 112, No. 2907, p. 309–311.

1950b. The food of the Alaska fur seal. U.S. Fish and Wildlife Service, Wildlife Leaflet 329. 15 p.

1951. Measurements of sea otters from western Alaska. Journal of Mammalogy, vol. 32, No. 1, p. 10–14.

1955. Body size with relation to population density in mammals. Journal of Mammalogy, vol. 36, No. 4, p. 493–515.

1958. Long life of a river otter. Journal of Mammalogy, vol. 39, No. 4, November, p. 591.

1960. Weights of organs and glands in the northern fur seal. Mammalia, vol. 24, No. 3, p. 476–481.

1962. Pelage and surface topography of the northern fur seal. U.S. Fish and Wildlife Service, North American Fauna, No. 64. 206 p.

1963. Book review: "The natural history of the Lewis and Clark expedition," edited by Raymond Darwin Burroughs. Pacific Northwest Quarterly, vol. 54, No. 2, p. 80–81.

1964. Estimating abundance of pelage fibres on fur seal skin. Proceedings Zoological Society of London, vol. 143, part 1, p. 37–41.

———— and ANCEL M. JOHNSON.

1963. Molt in the northern fur seal. U. S. Fish and Wildlife Service, Special Scientific Report—Fisheries, No. 450. 34 p.

———— and BERTRAM S. KRAUS.

1964. Dentition of the northern fur seal. Fishery Bulletin, vol. 63, No. 2, p. 293–342.

———— and FORD WILKE.

1950. Validity of the subspecies *Enhydra lutris nereis*, the southern sea otter. Journal of the Washington Academy of Sciences, vol. 40, No. 8, p. 269–272, August 15.

SCHUMACHER, G. H.

1961. Funktionelle Morphologie der Kaumuskulatur. Gustav Fisher, Jena.

SHIDLOVSKAYA, N. K.

1947. [Directions for the feeding and care of the male sea otter, p. 225–227.] *In* Kalan, by I. I. Barabash-Nikiforov, Soviet Ministrov RSFSR. Glavnoe upravlenie po zapovednikam, p. 263–266. [Translated from Russian by Dr. A. Birron and Z. S. Cole. Published for National Science Foundation by Israel Program for Scientific Translations, Jerusalem, 1962. 227 p., illus.]

SINHA, A. A.
1965. Morphology of the female reproductive organs of sea otters *Enhydra lutris* L.). University of Missouri, Ph.D., 1965, Zoology (Unpublished).

——— C. H. CONAWAY, and K. W. KENYON.
1966. Reproduction in the female sea otter. Journal of Wildlife Management, vol. 30, No. 1, p. 121–130.

——— and H. W. MOSSMAN.
1966. Placentation of the sea otter. American Journal of Anatomy, vol. 119, No. 3, p. 521–554.

——— and C. H. CONAWAY.
1968. The ovary of the sea otter. Anatomical Record, vol. 160, p. 795–806.

SLIJPER, E. J.
1956. Some remarks on gestation and birth in cetacea and other aquatic mammals. Hvalrådets Skrifter, vol. 41, p. 1–62.

1962. Whales. Basic Books Publishing Co. 475 p. English translation of Walvissen, D. B. Centen's, Uitgeversmaatschappij, Amsterdam.

SNOW, H. J.
1910. In forbidden seas. Edward Arnold, London. 303 p.

STEJNEGER, L.
1936. Georg Wilhelm Steller. Harvard University Press. 623 p.

STELLER, G. W.
1751. De Bestiis marinis. Novi Comm. Acad. Sci. Petropolitanae, vol. 2, p. 289–398, 3 pls. [English translation by Walter Miller and Jennie Emerson Miller (part 3, p. 179–218). *In* The fur seals and fur seal islands . . . see Jordan and Clark, 1898–1899, U. S. Treasury Department, Document 2017.]

STILES, W. B.
1953. The sea otter (*Enhydra marina*). Unpublished manuscript, Fish and Wildlife Service files, Washington, D.C. 19 p.

STULLKEN, DONALD E., and C. M. KIRKPATRICK.
1955. Physiological investigation of captivity mortality in the sea otter (*Enhydra lutris*). Transactions 20th North American Wildlife Conference, p. 476–494.

SVERDRUP, H. U., M. W. JOHNSON, and R. H. FLEMING.
1942. The oceans. Prentice-Hall, Englewood Cliffs, N.J. 1087 p.

SWICEGOOD, Lcdr. S. P.
1936. Amchitka sea otter survey expedition. Unpublished memo from Commanding Officer, U.S. Coast Guard Cutter *Chelan.*, 31 August 1936. 5 p. U.S. Fish and Wildlife Service files.

TAYLOR, WALTER P.
1914. The problem of aquatic adaptation in the Carnivora, as illustrated in the osteology and evolution of the sea-otter. University California Publication, Bulletin Department of Geology, vol. 7, p. 465–495, 15 text figures. (p. 468—drawing of skeleton in standing attitude.)

THENIUS, E., and H. HOFER.
1960. Stammesgeschichte der Säugetiere. Springer, Berlin. 322 p.

U. S. BOARD ON GEOGRAPHIC NAMES.
1963. Decisions on geographic names in the United States. Decision list No. 6302. 81 p.

U. S. BUREAU OF FISHERIES.

1906–11. The commercial fisheries of Alaska in 1905 [. . . 1910]. (Annual reports.)

1912–42. Alaska fisheries and fur-seal industries in 1911 [. . . 1940]. (Annual reports.)

1929. Laws and regulations for the protection of fur seals and sea otters. Department of Commerce Circular 285, 2d ed. Alaska Fisheries Service. 10 p.

VORONOV, V. G.

1960. Opyt otlova kalanov (*Enhydra lutris* L.) na Kuril skikh ostrovakh. [Experimental trapping of sea otters (*Enhydra lutris* L.) in the Kurile Islands.] Trudy Sakhalinsk. Kompleksn. Nauchn.-Issled. Inst. 9, p. 122–129. 1960; Referat. Zhur., Biol. 1962, No. 14 1222. (Abstract of translation only seen.)

1965. Present problems in the study and industrial use of the Kurile sea otter. *In* Marine Mammals, E. N. Pavlovskii, B. A. Zenkovich, et al. (Editors). [p. 221–225.] Translated by Nancy McRoy, April, 1966.

1967. The effect of tsunami on sea otter populations. Priroda (Nature), No. 8, p. 70–72.

WARREN, J. M.

1953. Handedness in the Rhesus monkey. Science, vol. 118, p. 622–623.

WILDMAN, A. B.

1954. The microscopy of animal textile fibres, including methods for the complete analysis of fibre blends. Wool Industries Research Association, Torridon, Headingley, Leeds. 209 p.

WILKE, F.

1957. Food of sea otters and harbor seals at Amchitka Island. Journal of Wildlife Management, vol. 21, No. 2, p. 241–242.

WILLIAMS, C. S.

1937. Notes of the distribution and food habits of the American sea otter, 1936. Unpublished manuscript, Fish and Wildlife Service files.

1938. Notes on food of the sea otter. Journal of Mammalogy, vol. 19, No. 1, p. 105–107.

Appendix 1

FIELD STUDIES OF SEA OTTERS, 1954–66

From 1949 to 1954, Refuge Manager R. D. Jones, Jr., reported sea otter observations. In the winter of 1950–51 he attempted a sea otter transplant. Dr. Robert Rausch and others of the U.S. Public Health Service studied and reported on the helminth parasites of the sea otter. These studies and the reports of other observers are reviewed elsewhere in this report. The purpose of this chronological list is to record the field activities of the U.S. Fish and Wildlife Service under the sea otter study program which actually began in 1954 but was not formally begun until 1955. Appendix 2 summarizes material gathered from 1955 through 1965.

Aleut laborers who participated in various phases of sea otter field work include the late Fred Bezezekoff (Nikolski), Anton Bezezekoff (Nikolski), John Nevzeroff (Atka), Innokenty Golodoff (Atka), and David Zaochni (Atka).

The expeditions listed below include a cumulative time of more than 2 years and 9 months of field work.

1954

10 February to 4 April. Aleutian Islands. At Amchitka Island, field studies of sea otters. (D. Hooper, R. D. Jones, C. M. Kirkpatrick, C. J. Lensink, D. E. Stullken, and F. Wilke.)

1955

15–17 March. Shumagin Islands. Observe sea otters at Simeonof, Little Koniuji, and Herendeen Islands. Transportation aboard M/V *Paragon* (Kenyon, Lensink, and Wilke).

27 March to 4 April. Aleutian Islands. At Amchitka Island capture and hold sea otters for transplant. (Jones, Kenyon, Lensink, and Wilke.)

9–10 April. Transplant attempt. Liberate sea otters at Otter Island, Pribilof Islands.

14–15 April. Shumagin Islands. Attempt to capture sea otters at Simeonof Island. (Kenyon and Wilke.)

26 July to 5 October. Aleutian Islands. At Amchitka Island observe sea otters; experiments with methods of holding otters in captivity and obtaining a food supply for them. (Kenyon.)

10 October. Seattle, Wash. Place two sea otters in Woodland Park Zoo.

1956

5 May to 26 July. Aleutian Islands. At Amchitka Island, field studies of sea otters and further experiments with feeding and holding in captivity. (Kenyon and Lensink.)

30 July. Seattle, Wash. Place two sea otters in Woodland Park Zoo.

1957

6 May to 28 September. Alaska survey. From Kodiak Island to Adak Island, field studies of population size and distribution of sea otters were conducted using boats and aircraft. (C. J. Lensink remained in the field during the entire period. R. D. Jones, R. Lopp, D. L. Spencer, W. Troyer, and Wilke participated with him in different areas.)

1 October to 11 December. Aleutian Islands. Amchitka Island, field studies of otters and further experiments in captive care and feeding of otters. (K. L. Binkley, Kenyon, and H. R. Krear.)

14 December. Seattle, Wash. Place two sea otters in Woodland Park Zoo.

1958

10–21 March. California. Search for sea otters in coastal areas and at Santa Rosa and San Miguel Islands of the Channel Islands group aboard the M/V *Trinity.* (W. J. Barmore and Kenyon.)

1959

14–21 January. Aleutian Islands. Adak Island. Conduct two experimental aerial surveys of sea otters using U.S. Navy UF–1 aircraft. Flight time: 5.6 hours. (Kenyon.)

21 January to 20 May. Aleutian Islands. At Amchitka Island, field studies of sea otters and experiments with otters in captivity were conducted. (Kenyon.)

19 May. Aleutian Islands. Aerial survey of sea otters from Attu to Amchitka Island using DC–3 aircraft. Flight time: 9.1 hours. (Kenyon, T. Smith, D. L. Spencer, and J. Tilford.)

20 May. Pribilof Islands transplant. Fly seven sea otters to St. Paul Island in a DC–3 aircraft and liberate them there. Flight time: 4.3 hours.

21 May. St. Paul Island. Observations of liberated otters.

21–28 May. Aleutian Islands. Aerial survey of sea otters from Semisopochnoi Island eastward to Herbert Island in the Islands of Four Mountains, inclusive, using a DC–3 aircraft. Flight time: 19 hours. Total flight time entire operation: 56.8 hours. (Kenyon, Smith, Spencer, and Tilford.)

13 July. Washington State. Aerial reconnaissance of coastal waters along outer coast of the Olympic Peninsula using a U.S. Coast Guard UF–2 aircraft. Flight time: 3 hours. (G. Eddy, Kenyon, F. Richardson, and V. B. Scheffer.)

14–18 July. Washington State. Boat survey of rocks and islets off the outer coast of the Olympic Peninsula. (Eddy, Kenyon, Richardson, and Scheffer.)

1960

2–5 March. Aleutian Islands. Aerial surveys of sea otters from the Islands of Four Mountains to the Sandman Reefs inclusive, using a DC–3 aircraft. Total flight time: 21.3 hours. (Kenyon, D. W. Rice, Smith, and Spencer.)

30 May to 13 July. Island surveys (surface only) in Alaska. Field studies of sea otters at Simeonof, Little Koniuji, Herendeen, and Nagai in the Shumagin Islands; at Caton and Sanak Islands; at Tigalda Island and in the waters off Unimak Island in the Aleutian Islands, and at Amak Island; transportation between islands was furnished by the M/V *Windward*. (C. H. Fiscus, Kenyon, and the late T. O'Brien.)

1961

3 July to 1 August. Commander Islands. Field observations of sea otters at the Soviet controlled islands of Medny and Bering; transportation aboard the USSR ships *Orel* and *Steregushti* and the U.S. FWS vessel *Penguin II*. (Kenyon, K. Niggol, A. Y. Roppel, and Wilke.)

21 October to 5 November. Aleutian Islands. An attempt to harvest and study sea otters in the outer Aleutians was negated when a U.S. Navy UF–2 aircraft carrying the field party crashed on 27 October at Adak Island during an aerial survey. (L. W. Croxton and Kenyon, and D. Cisney, killed in crash.)

1962

14 January to 4 April. Aleutian Islands. At Amchitka Island conduct field observations of sea otters and collect specimens from State of Alaska kill of 150 sea otters. (Croxton, Jones, and Kenyon.)

29 March and 5–10 April. Aerial surveys in Alaska. Aerial survey of sea otters in the Aleutian Islands from Kiska Island to Amak Island; the Sanak Islands; Sandman Reefs; Shumagin Islands; and areas along the south coast of the Alaska Peninsula to Kuliak Point. Total flight time: 53.6 hours. (J. J. Burns, Kenyon, J. S. Kobza, Smith, and Spencer.)

8–11 September. Washington State. Investigate reports of possible sea otter sightings along the outer coast of the Olympic Peninsula. (Kenyon.)

26–29 October. Alaska State biologists kill 24 sea otters on Amchitka. (Croxton and E. Klinkhart.)

27–28 October. Washington State. Investigate reports of possible sea otter sightings in the San Juan Islands of Puget Sound aboard the M/V *Trinity*. (Kenyon, Rice, and Scheffer.)

1963

4 March to 13 April. Aleutian Islands. At Amchitka Island collect specimens from 303 sea otters taken by State of Alaska biologists. (J. E. Burdick, E. Klinkhart, and J. Vania.)

1–22 July. Aleutian Islands. Field observations of sea otters at Adak Island and Buldir Island in the outer Aleutian Islands. Transportation from Adak to Buldir aboard USCGC *Clover*, return on USCGC *Klamath*. (V. D. Berns, E. L. Boeker, Jones, Kenyon, A. E. Peden, and M. Zhan.)

31 July to 3 August. Aleutian Islands. At Amchitka Island 20 sea otters were taken by State of Alaska biologists and specimens furnished to the Bureau of Sport Fisheries and Wildlife (E. Klinkhart and J. Vania).

1964

In Seattle working on 1963 specimens and analyzing accumulated field data.

1965

23 January to 10 February. Field observations of coastal and island areas of Baja California, Mexico to examine sea otter habitat and search for possible surviving animals. (D. W. Rice, D. Lluch B., and Kenyon.)

18 April to 9 May. Aerial survey of sea otters in the Aleutian Islands, Cold Bay to Attu Island. (E. Klinkhart, D. L. Spencer, T. A. Smith, J. King, and Kenyon.)

23 October to 9 November. At Amchitka Island. Monitor effects of AEC-DOD Long Shot nuclear blast. Aerial surveys and surface observations. (E. Klinkhart, D. L. Spencer, T. A. Smith, R. Tremblay, and Kenyon.)

9 November to 3 December. Transport male sea otter (Gus) aboard M/V *Commander* from Amchitka to Seattle. (Kenyon, Capt. Cliff Andersen.)

1966

Work in Seattle on specimens and accumulated data.

Appendix 2

TABULAR SUMMARY OF SEA OTTERS STUDIED, 1955 THROUGH 1965

Every otter for which any record was kept is included in this table; for some of them the data were inadequate and they are not included in other sections of this report.

Place and time	Number obtained — BD [1]	Shot	Net or club [2]	Number tagged and released ♂	♀	Sex?	Number held captive ♂	♀	Skins taken [2] ADFG	FWS	Total otters studied ♂	♀	Sex?	All
Amchitka Island:														
Mar–Apr 1955	15	—	31	—	—	—	9	19	—	1	20	23	3	46
Aug–Sept 1955	5	—	6	—	—	—	4	2	—	—	4	2	5	11
May–July 1956	58	5	30	5	4	—	10	11	—	7	44	29	20	93
Oct–Dec 1957	31	—	23	2	—	—	10	11	—	12	24	13	17	54
Jan–May 1959	84	—	125	34	52	—	7	7	—	46	104	94	11	209
Various areas: [3]														
June–July 1960	7	14	—	—	—	—	—	—	—	11	10	8	3	21
Amchitka Island:														
Feb–Apr 1962	107	154	122	43	77	—	—	—	155	6	141	234	8	383
October 1962 [4]	3	24	—	—	—	—	—	—	24	—	6	19	2	27
Mar–Apr 1963 [5]	42	285	13	4	2	1	—	—	303	3	126	199	15	340
Aug–Sept 1963	—	20	—	—	—	—	—	—	20	—	1	19	—	20
Nov. 7, 1965	—	—	2	—	—	—	1	1	—	—	1	1	—	2
Total	352	502	352	88	135	1	41	51	502	86	481	641	84	1,206

[1] BD = beach dead, i.e., remains of sea otters found on beaches; 41 of the remains listed were so fragmentary that no use was made of them.
[2] Most of these were netted on beaches; several were clubbed in 1962 and 1963 during the Alaska Department of Fish and Game cropping operations in which the U.S. Fish and Wildlife Service (FWS) cooperated.
[3] Specimens were collected in the Shumagin and Sanak Islands and in the Bering Sea off the north coast of Unimak Island.
[4] Specimens and data collected by L. W. Croxton and E. Klinkhart, Alaska Department of Fish and Game.
[5] Specimens and data collected by J. E. Burdick.

INDEX

Many geographic locations (islands, points, passes, etc.) mentioned in the text are omitted from the index. They may be found in the text under the island groups (Andreanof Islands, Fox Islands, etc.) or adjacent geographic areas (such as Alaska Peninsula), which are included in the index. In general, scientific names of organisms are omitted from the index but are included in the text. An attempt was made to avoid repeating in the index what may be found in the table of contents.

measurements, iv.
  body weight, adult, 20.
  intestine length, 26.
  length (see Body Measurements), 19.
  miscellaneous, 26.
  organ weights, 27.
  skin length (compared with body length) 26.
  weight loss at death, 25.
  weight, pregnant female, 230.
  weight (see Body Measurements). 19.
Medny Island, U.S.S.R., 188.
Mexico, 5, 187.
midden, 129, 179, 184, 185.
Middle Reef, Alaska, 69.
migration, 6.
mile, nautical and statute, iv.
military, at Amchitka, 250.
Miller, G. S., 4, 332.
Miller, P. and L. G., 1, 332.
mink, 43.
Mitchell, E. D., iii, 4, 332.
mite, nasal, 103, 274, 292.
mollusks, 110.
molt, 37–39.
monia, pearly (see oyster, rock).
Monterey, Calif., 130.
Morro Hermoso, Baja California, Mexico, 133, 187.
mortality:
  age-specific, 253, 258.
  body fat, 261.
  body weight, 271.
  defective teeth, 50, 261, 263.
  during flight, 317.
  emaciation, 261.
  enteritis, 261, 271.
  estimated, Amchitka, 266, 268.
  factors, 261.
  food depletion, 270.
  juveniles, desertion of, 270.
  peak period, 266.
  rate, 245.
  Sanak Island, 269.
  sex-specific, 258.
  Shumagin Islands, 268.
  starvation, 261, 271.
  storm waves, 264, 266.
  studies, 1955–63, 250, 251.
  study methods, 251, 252.

mortality—Cont.
  time of, 252, 253.
  tooth attrition, 270.
  weather related, 263.
Mossman, H. W., iii, 232, 335.
Murie, O. J., 1, 123, 150, 157, 159, 165, 175, 218, 221, 238, 280, 332.
muscle:
  masseter, 42.
  masticatory, 42.
  temporal, 42.
musculature of jaw, 42–43.
Musculus, 118.
mussels, blue, 52, 83, 106.
Mustelidae, 4.

Naknek River, Alaska, 175.
Natividad Island, Mexico, 187.
Nazan Bay, Alaska, 166.
Near Islands, Alaska, 147–149, 188.
Neiland, K. A., iii, 271, 272, 329, 332.
Nelson, U. C., iii.
nembutal, 311.
Nereocystis (see also kelp), 57.
Nesterov, G. A., 188.
netting, 284–286.
Nevzoroff, J., 129, 337.
Newell, I. M., iii, 271, 292, 330.
Niggol, K., 339.
Nikolaev, A. M., 65, 105, 135, 149, 189, 204, 279, 321, 332.
Nikolski Village, Alaska, 146, 170, 171.
Norris, K. S., 63, 330.
Novikov, G. A., 39, 332.
Nozikov, N., 181, 332.

O'Brien, T. P., iii, 339.
octopus, 102, 118.
Ogden, A., 1, 133, 187, 281, 333.
Oglala Pass, Alaska, 154.
Ogliuga Island, Alaska, 159.
Oregon, 185.
orphan, 243.
Orr, R. T., iii, 187, 278, 333.
Osmeridae (smelt), 83.
otter:
  American river, 4, 9–13, 43, 55, 184, 236.
  European river, 39, 236, 238.
oyster, rock (pearly monia), 43, 109, 118.
oystercatcher, black, 103.

349

A CATALOGUE OF SELECTED DOVER BOOKS
IN ALL FIELDS OF INTEREST

A CATALOGUE OF SELECTED DOVER BOOKS
IN ALL FIELDS OF INTEREST

AMERICA'S OLD MASTERS, James T. Flexner. Four men emerged unexpectedly from provincial 18th century America to leadership in European art: Benjamin West, J. S. Copley, C. R. Peale, Gilbert Stuart. Brilliant coverage of lives and contributions. Revised, 1967 edition. 69 plates. 365pp. of text.

21806-6 Paperbound $3.00

FIRST FLOWERS OF OUR WILDERNESS: AMERICAN PAINTING, THE COLONIAL PERIOD, James T. Flexner. Painters, and regional painting traditions from earliest Colonial times up to the emergence of Copley, West and Peale Sr., Foster, Gustavus Hesselius, Feke, John Smibert and many anonymous painters in the primitive manner. Engaging presentation, with 162 illustrations. xxii + 368pp.

22180-6 Paperbound $3.50

THE LIGHT OF DISTANT SKIES: AMERICAN PAINTING, 1760-1835, James T. Flexner. The great generation of early American painters goes to Europe to learn and to teach: West, Copley, Gilbert Stuart and others. Allston, Trumbull, Morse; also contemporary American painters—primitives, derivatives, academics—who remained in America. 102 illustrations. xiii + 306pp.

22179-2 Paperbound $3.50

A HISTORY OF THE RISE AND PROGRESS OF THE ARTS OF DESIGN IN THE UNITED STATES, William Dunlap. Much the richest mine of information on early American painters, sculptors, architects, engravers, miniaturists, etc. The only source of information for scores of artists, the major primary source for many others. Unabridged reprint of rare original 1834 edition, with new introduction by James T. Flexner, and 394 new illustrations. Edited by Rita Weiss. 6⅝ x 9⅝.

21695-0, 21696-9, 21697-7 Three volumes, Paperbound $15.00

EPOCHS OF CHINESE AND JAPANESE ART, Ernest F. Fenollosa. From primitive Chinese art to the 20th century, thorough history, explanation of every important art period and form, including Japanese woodcuts; main stress on China and Japan, but Tibet, Korea also included. Still unexcelled for its detailed, rich coverage of cultural background, aesthetic elements, diffusion studies, particularly of the historical period. 2nd, 1913 edition. 242 illustrations. lii + 439pp. of text.

20364-6, 20365-4 Two volumes, Paperbound $6.00

THE GENTLE ART OF MAKING ENEMIES, James A. M. Whistler. Greatest wit of his day deflates Oscar Wilde, Ruskin, Swinburne; strikes back at inane critics, exhibitions, art journalism; aesthetics of impressionist revolution in most striking form. Highly readable classic by great painter. Reproduction of edition designed by Whistler. Introduction by Alfred Werner. xxxvi + 334pp.

21875-9 Paperbound $3.00

VISUAL ILLUSIONS: THEIR CAUSES, CHARACTERISTICS, AND APPLICATIONS, Matthew Luckiesh. Thorough description and discussion of optical illusion, geometric and perspective, particularly; size and shape distortions, illusions of color, of motion; natural illusions; use of illusion in art and magic, industry, etc. Most useful today with op art, also for classical art. Scores of effects illustrated. Introduction by William H. Ittleson. 100 illustrations. xxi + 252pp.
21530-X Paperbound $2.00

A HANDBOOK OF ANATOMY FOR ART STUDENTS, Arthur Thomson. Thorough, virtually exhaustive coverage of skeletal structure, musculature, etc. Full text, supplemented by anatomical diagrams and drawings and by photographs of undraped figures. Unique in its comparison of male and female forms, pointing out differences of contour, texture, form. 211 figures, 40 drawings, 86 photographs. xx + 459pp. 5⅜ x 8⅜.
21163-0 Paperbound $3.50

150 MASTERPIECES OF DRAWING, Selected by Anthony Toney. Full page reproductions of drawings from the early 16th to the end of the 18th century, all beautifully reproduced: Rembrandt, Michelangelo, Dürer, Fragonard, Urs, Graf, Wouwerman, many others. First-rate browsing book, model book for artists. xviii + 150pp. 8⅜ x 11¼.
21032-4 Paperbound $2.50

THE LATER WORK OF AUBREY BEARDSLEY, Aubrey Beardsley. Exotic, erotic, ironic masterpieces in full maturity: Comedy Ballet, Venus and Tannhauser, Pierrot, Lysistrata, Rape of the Lock, Savoy material, Ali Baba, Volpone, etc. This material revolutionized the art world, and is still powerful, fresh, brilliant. With *The Early Work,* all Beardsley's finest work. 174 plates, 2 in color. xiv + 176pp. 8⅛ x 11.
21817-1 Paperbound $3.75

DRAWINGS OF REMBRANDT, Rembrandt van Rijn. Complete reproduction of fabulously rare edition by Lippmann and Hofstede de Groot, completely reedited, updated, improved by Prof. Seymour Slive, Fogg Museum. Portraits, Biblical sketches, landscapes, Oriental types, nudes, episodes from classical mythology—All Rembrandt's fertile genius. Also selection of drawings by his pupils and followers. "Stunning volumes," *Saturday Review.* 550 illustrations. lxxviii + 552pp. 9⅛ x 12¼.
21485-0, 21486-9 Two volumes, Paperbound $10.00

THE DISASTERS OF WAR, Francisco Goya. One of the masterpieces of Western civilization—83 etchings that record Goya's shattering, bitter reaction to the Napoleonic war that swept through Spain after the insurrection of 1808 and to war in general. Reprint of the first edition, with three additional plates from Boston's Museum of Fine Arts. All plates facsimile size. Introduction by Philip Hofer, Fogg Museum. v + 97pp. 9⅜ x 8¼.
21872-4 Paperbound $2.50

GRAPHIC WORKS OF ODILON REDON. Largest collection of Redon's graphic works ever assembled: 172 lithographs, 28 etchings and engravings, 9 drawings. These include some of his most famous works. All the plates from *Odilon Redon: oeuvre graphique complet,* plus additional plates. New introduction and caption translations by Alfred Werner. 209 illustrations. xxvii + 209pp. 9⅛ x 12¼.
21966-8 Paperbound $4.50

DESIGN BY ACCIDENT; A BOOK OF "ACCIDENTAL EFFECTS" FOR ARTISTS AND DESIGNERS, James F. O'Brien. Create your own unique, striking, imaginative effects by "controlled accident" interaction of materials: paints and lacquers, oil and water based paints, splatter, crackling materials, shatter, similar items. Everything you do will be different; first book on this limitless art, so useful to both fine artist and commercial artist. Full instructions. 192 plates showing "accidents," 8 in color. viii + 215pp. 8⅜ x 11¼. 21942-9 Paperbound $3.75

THE BOOK OF SIGNS, Rudolf Koch. Famed German type designer draws 493 beautiful symbols: religious, mystical, alchemical, imperial, property marks, runes, etc. Remarkable fusion of traditional and modern. Good for suggestions of timelessness, smartness, modernity. Text. vi + 104pp. 6⅛ x 9¼. 20162-7 Paperbound $1.50

HISTORY OF INDIAN AND INDONESIAN ART, Ananda K. Coomaraswamy. An unabridged republication of one of the finest books by a great scholar in Eastern art. Rich in descriptive material, history, social backgrounds; Sunga reliefs, Rajput paintings, Gupta temples, Burmese frescoes, textiles, jewelry, sculpture, etc. 400 photos. viii + 423pp. 6⅜ x 9¾. 21436-2 Paperbound $5.00

PRIMITIVE ART, Franz Boas. America's foremost anthropologist surveys textiles, ceramics, woodcarving, basketry, metalwork, etc.; patterns, technology, creation of symbols, style origins. All areas of world, but very full on Northwest Coast Indians. More than 350 illustrations of baskets, boxes, totem poles, weapons, etc. 378 pp. 20025-6 Paperbound $3.00

THE GENTLEMAN AND CABINET MAKER'S DIRECTOR, Thomas Chippendale. Full reprint (third edition, 1762) of most influential furniture book of all time, by master cabinetmaker. 200 plates, illustrating chairs, sofas, mirrors, tables, cabinets, plus 24 photographs of surviving pieces. Biographical introduction by N. Bienenstock. vi + 249pp. 9⅞ x 12¾. 21601-2 Paperbound $5.00

AMERICAN ANTIQUE FURNITURE, Edgar G. Miller, Jr. The basic coverage of all American furniture before 1840. Individual chapters cover type of furniture—clocks, tables, sideboards, etc.—chronologically, with inexhaustible wealth of data. More than 2100 photographs, all identified, commented on. Essential to all early American collectors. Introduction by H. E. Keyes. vi + 1106pp. 7⅞ x 10¾. 21599-7, 21600-4 Two volumes, Paperbound $11.00

PENNSYLVANIA DUTCH AMERICAN FOLK ART, Henry J. Kauffman. 279 photos, 28 drawings of tulipware, Fraktur script, painted tinware, toys, flowered furniture, quilts, samplers, hex signs, house interiors, etc. Full descriptive text. Excellent for tourist, rewarding for designer, collector. Map. 146pp. 7⅞ x 10¾. 21205-X Paperbound $3.00

EARLY NEW ENGLAND GRAVESTONE RUBBINGS, Edmund V. Gillon, Jr. 43 photographs, 226 carefully reproduced rubbings show heavily symbolic, sometimes macabre early gravestones, up to early 19th century. Remarkable early American primitive art, occasionally strikingly beautiful; always powerful. Text. xxvi + 207pp. 8⅜ x 11¼. 21380-3 Paperbound $4.00

ALPHABETS AND ORNAMENTS, Ernst Lehner. Well-known pictorial source for decorative alphabets, script examples, cartouches, frames, decorative title pages, calligraphic initials, borders, similar material. 14th to 19th century, mostly European. Useful in almost any graphic arts designing, varied styles. 750 illustrations. 256pp. 7 x 10.   21905-4 Paperbound $4.00

PAINTING: A CREATIVE APPROACH, Norman Colquhoun. For the beginner simple guide provides an instructive approach to painting: major stumbling blocks for beginner; overcoming them, technical points; paints and pigments; oil painting; watercolor and other media and color. New section on "plastic" paints. Glossary. Formerly *Paint Your Own Pictures.* 221pp.   22000-1 Paperbound $1.75

THE ENJOYMENT AND USE OF COLOR, Walter Sargent. Explanation of the relations between colors themselves and between colors in nature and art, including hundreds of little-known facts about color values, intensities, effects of high and low illumination, complementary colors. Many practical hints for painters, references to great masters. 7 color plates, 29 illustrations. x + 274pp.
20944-X Paperbound $3.00

THE NOTEBOOKS OF LEONARDO DA VINCI, compiled and edited by Jean Paul Richter. 1566 extracts from original manuscripts reveal the full range of Leonardo's versatile genius: all his writings on painting, sculpture, architecture, anatomy, astronomy, geography, topography, physiology, mining, music, etc., in both Italian and English, with 186 plates of manuscript pages and more than 500 additional drawings. Includes studies for the Last Supper, the lost Sforza monument, and other works. Total of xlvii + 866pp. 7⅞ x 10¾.
22572-0, 22573-9 Two volumes, Paperbound $12.00

MONTGOMERY WARD CATALOGUE OF 1895. Tea gowns, yards of flannel and pillow-case lace, stereoscopes, books of gospel hymns, the New Improved Singer Sewing Machine, side saddles, milk skimmers, straight-edged razors, high-button shoes, spittoons, and on and on . . . listing some 25,000 items, practically all illustrated. Essential to the shoppers of the 1890's, it is our truest record of the spirit of the period. Unaltered reprint of Issue No. 57, Spring and Summer 1895. Introduction by Boris Emmet. Innumerable illustrations. xiii + 624pp. 8½ x 11⅝.
22377-9 Paperbound $8.50

THE CRYSTAL PALACE EXHIBITION ILLUSTRATED CATALOGUE (LONDON, 1851). One of the wonders of the modern world—the Crystal Palace Exhibition in which all the nations of the civilized world exhibited their achievements in the arts and sciences—presented in an equally important illustrated catalogue. More than 1700 items pictured with accompanying text—ceramics, textiles, cast-iron work, carpets, pianos, sleds, razors, wall-papers, billiard tables, beehives, silverware and hundreds of other artifacts—represent the focal point of Victorian culture in the Western World. Probably the largest collection of Victorian decorative art ever assembled—indispensable for antiquarians and designers. Unabridged republication of the Art-Journal Catalogue of the Great Exhibition of 1851, with all terminal essays. New introduction by John Gloag, F.S.A. xxxiv + 426pp. 9 x 12.
22503-8 Paperbound $5.00

A HISTORY OF COSTUME, Carl Köhler. Definitive history, based on surviving pieces of clothing primarily, and paintings, statues, etc. secondarily. Highly readable text, supplemented by 594 illustrations of costumes of the ancient Mediterranean peoples, Greece and Rome, the Teutonic prehistoric period; costumes of the Middle Ages, Renaissance, Baroque, 18th and 19th centuries. Clear, measured patterns are provided for many clothing articles. Approach is practical throughout. Enlarged by Emma von Sichart. 464pp. 21030-8 Paperbound $3.50

ORIENTAL RUGS, ANTIQUE AND MODERN, Walter A. Hawley. A complete and authoritative treatise on the Oriental rug—where they are made, by whom and how, designs and symbols, characteristics in detail of the six major groups, how to distinguish them and how to buy them. Detailed technical data is provided on periods, weaves, warps, wefts, textures, sides, ends and knots, although no technical background is required for an understanding. 11 color plates, 80 halftones, 4 maps. vi + 320pp. 6⅛ x 9⅛. 22366-3 Paperbound $5.00

TEN BOOKS ON ARCHITECTURE, Vitruvius. By any standards the most important book on architecture ever written. Early Roman discussion of aesthetics of building, construction methods, orders, sites, and every other aspect of architecture has inspired, instructed architecture for about 2,000 years. Stands behind Palladio, Michelangelo, Bramante, Wren, countless others. Definitive Morris H. Morgan translation. 68 illustrations. xii + 331pp. 20645-9 Paperbound . $3.00

THE FOUR BOOKS OF ARCHITECTURE, Andrea Palladio. Translated into every major Western European language in the two centuries following its publication in 1570, this has been one of the most influential books in the history of architecture. Complete reprint of the 1738 Isaac Ware edition. New introduction by Adolf Placzek, Columbia Univ. 216 plates. xxii + 110pp. of text. 9½ x 12¾. 21308-0 Clothbound $12.50

STICKS AND STONES: A STUDY OF AMERICAN ARCHITECTURE AND CIVILIZATION, Lewis Mumford.One of the great classics of American cultural history. American architecture from the medieval-inspired earliest forms to the early 20th century; evolution of structure and style, and reciprocal influences on environment. 21 photographic illustrations. 238pp. 20202-X Paperbound $2.00

THE AMERICAN BUILDER'S COMPANION, Asher Benjamin. The most widely used early 19th century architectural style and source book, for colonial up into Greek Revival periods. Extensive development of geometry of carpentering, construction of sashes, frames, doors, stairs; plans and elevations of domestic and other buildings. Hundreds of thousands of houses were built according to this book, now invaluable to historians, architects, restorers, etc. 1827 edition. 59 plates. 114pp. 7⅞ x 10¾. 22236-5 Paperbound $4.00

DUTCH HOUSES IN THE HUDSON VALLEY BEFORE 1776, Helen Wilkinson Reynolds. The standard survey of the Dutch colonial house and outbuildings, with constructional features, decoration, and local history associated with individual homesteads. Introduction by Franklin D. Roosevelt. Map. 150 illustrations. 469pp. 6⅝ x 9¼. 21469-9 Paperbound $5.00

THE ARCHITECTURE OF COUNTRY HOUSES, Andrew J. Downing. Together with Vaux's *Villas and Cottages* this is the basic book for Hudson River Gothic architecture of the middle Victorian period. Full, sound discussions of general aspects of housing, architecture, style, decoration, furnishing, together with scores of detailed house plans, illustrations of specific buildings, accompanied by full text. Perhaps the most influential single American architectural book. 1850 edition. Introduction by J. Stewart Johnson. 321 figures, 34 architectural designs. xvi + 560pp.
22003-6 Paperbound $5.00

LOST EXAMPLES OF COLONIAL ARCHITECTURE, John Mead Howells. Full-page photographs of buildings that have disappeared or been so altered as to be denatured, including many designed by major early American architects. 245 plates. xvii + 248pp. 7⅞ x 10¾.
21143-6 Paperbound $3.50

DOMESTIC ARCHITECTURE OF THE AMERICAN COLONIES AND OF THE EARLY REPUBLIC, Fiske Kimball. Foremost architect and restorer of Williamsburg and Monticello covers nearly 200 homes between 1620-1825. Architectural details, construction, style features, special fixtures, floor plans, etc. Generally considered finest work in its area. 219 illustrations of houses, doorways, windows, capital mantels. xx + 314pp. 7⅞ x 10¾.
21743-4 Paperbound $4.00

EARLY AMERICAN ROOMS: 1650-1858, edited by Russell Hawes Kettell. Tour of 12 rooms, each representative of a different era in American history and each furnished, decorated, designed and occupied in the style of the era. 72 plans and elevations, 8-page color section, etc., show fabrics, wall papers, arrangements, etc. Full descriptive text. xvii + 200pp. of text. 8⅜ x 11¼.
21633-0 Paperbound $5.00

THE FITZWILLIAM VIRGINAL BOOK, edited by J. Fuller Maitland and W. B. Squire. Full modern printing of famous early 17th-century ms. volume of 300 works by Morley, Byrd, Bull, Gibbons, etc. For piano or other modern keyboard instrument; easy to read format. xxxvi + 938pp. 8⅜ x 11.
21068-5, 21069-3 Two volumes, Paperbound $12.00

KEYBOARD MUSIC, Johann Sebastian Bach. Bach Gesellschaft edition. A rich selection of Bach's masterpieces for the harpsichord: the six English Suites, six French Suites, the six Partitas (Clavierübung part I), the Goldberg Variations (Clavierübung part IV), the fifteen Two-Part Inventions and the fifteen Three-Part Sinfonias. Clearly reproduced on large sheets with ample margins; eminently playable. vi + 312pp. 8⅛ x 11.
22360-4 Paperbound $5.00

THE MUSIC OF BACH: AN INTRODUCTION, Charles Sanford Terry. A fine, nontechnical introduction to Bach's music, both instrumental and vocal. Covers organ music, chamber music, passion music, other types. Analyzes themes, developments, innovations. x + 114pp.
21075-8 Paperbound $1.95

BEETHOVEN AND HIS NINE SYMPHONIES, Sir George Grove. Noted British musicologist provides best history, analysis, commentary on symphonies. Very thorough, rigorously accurate; necessary to both advanced student and amateur music lover. 436 musical passages. vii + 407 pp.
20334-4 Paperbound $4.00

JOHANN SEBASTIAN BACH, Philipp Spitta. One of the great classics of musicology, this definitive analysis of Bach's music (and life) has never been surpassed. Lucid, nontechnical analyses of hundreds of pieces (30 pages devoted to St. Matthew Passion, 26 to B Minor Mass). Also includes major analysis of 18th-century music. 450 musical examples. 40-page musical supplement. Total of xx + 1799pp.
(EUK) 22278-0, 22279-9 Two volumes, Clothbound $25.00

MOZART AND HIS PIANO CONCERTOS, Cuthbert Girdlestone. The only full-length study of an important area of Mozart's creativity. Provides detailed analyses of all 23 concertos, traces inspirational sources. 417 musical examples. Second edition. 509pp.
21271-8 Paperbound $4.50

THE PERFECT WAGNERITE: A COMMENTARY ON THE NIBLUNG'S RING, George Bernard Shaw. Brilliant and still relevant criticism in remarkable essays on Wagner's Ring cycle, Shaw's ideas on political and social ideology behind the plots, role of Leitmotifs, vocal requisites, etc. Prefaces. xxi + 136pp.
(USO) 21707-8 Paperbound $1.75

DON GIOVANNI, W. A. Mozart. Complete libretto, modern English translation; biographies of composer and librettist; accounts of early performances and critical reaction. Lavishly illustrated. All the material you need to understand and appreciate this great work. Dover Opera Guide and Libretto Series; translated and introduced by Ellen Bleiler. 92 illustrations. 209pp.
21134-7 Paperbound $2.00

BASIC ELECTRICITY, U. S. Bureau of Naval Personel. Originally a training course, best non-technical coverage of basic theory of electricity and its applications. Fundamental concepts, batteries, circuits, conductors and wiring techniques, AC and DC, inductance and capacitance, generators, motors, transformers, magnetic amplifiers, synchros, servomechanisms, etc. Also covers blue-prints, electrical diagrams, etc. Many questions, with answers. 349 illustrations. x + 448pp. $6\frac{1}{2}$ x $9\frac{1}{4}$.
20973-3 Paperbound $3.50

REPRODUCTION OF SOUND, Edgar Villchur. Thorough coverage for laymen of high fidelity systems, reproducing systems in general, needles, amplifiers, preamps, loudspeakers, feedback, explaining physical background. "A rare talent for making technicalities vividly comprehensible," R. Darrell, *High Fidelity*. 69 figures. iv + 92pp.
21515-6 Paperbound $1.35

HEAR ME TALKIN' TO YA: THE STORY OF JAZZ AS TOLD BY THE MEN WHO MADE IT, Nat Shapiro and Nat Hentoff. Louis Armstrong, Fats Waller, Jo Jones, Clarence Williams, Billy Holiday, Duke Ellington, Jelly Roll Morton and dozens of other jazz greats tell how it was in Chicago's South Side, New Orleans, depression Harlem and the modern West Coast as jazz was born and grew. xvi + 429pp.
21726-4 Paperbound $3.95

FABLES OF AESOP, translated by Sir Roger L'Estrange. A reproduction of the very rare 1931 Paris edition; a selection of the most interesting fables, together with 50 imaginative drawings by Alexander Calder. v + 128pp. $6\frac{1}{2}$x$9\frac{1}{4}$.
21780-9 Paperbound $1.50

AGAINST THE GRAIN (A REBOURS), Joris K. Huysmans. Filled with weird images, evidences of a bizarre imagination, exotic experiments with hallucinatory drugs, rich tastes and smells and the diversions of its sybarite hero Duc Jean des Esseintes, this classic novel pushed 19th-century literary decadence to its limits. Full unabridged edition. Do not confuse this with abridged editions generally sold. Introduction by Havelock Ellis. xlix + 206pp. 22190-3 Paperbound $2.50

VARIORUM SHAKESPEARE: HAMLET. Edited by Horace H. Furness; a landmark of American scholarship. Exhaustive footnotes and appendices treat all doubtful words and phrases, as well as suggested critical emendations throughout the play's history. First volume contains editor's own text, collated with all Quartos and Folios. Second volume contains full first Quarto, translations of Shakespeare's sources (Belleforest, and Saxo Grammaticus), Der Bestrafte Brudermord, and many essays on critical and historical points of interest by major authorities of past and present. Includes details of staging and costuming over the years. By far the best edition available for serious students of Shakespeare. Total of xx + 905pp. 21004-9, 21005-7, 2 volumes, Paperbound $7.00

A LIFE OF WILLIAM SHAKESPEARE, Sir Sidney Lee. This is the standard life of Shakespeare, summarizing everything known about Shakespeare and his plays. Incredibly rich in material, broad in coverage, clear and judicious, it has served thousands as the best introduction to Shakespeare. 1931 edition. 9 plates. xxix + 792pp. 21967-4 Paperbound $4.50

MASTERS OF THE DRAMA, John Gassner. Most comprehensive history of the drama in print, covering every tradition from Greeks to modern Europe and America, including India, Far East, etc. Covers more than 800 dramatists, 2000 plays, with biographical material, plot summaries, theatre history, criticism, etc. "Best of its kind in English," New Republic. 77 illustrations. xxii + 890pp. 20100-7 Clothbound $10.00

THE EVOLUTION OF THE ENGLISH LANGUAGE, George McKnight. The growth of English, from the 14th century to the present. Unusual, non-technical account presents basic information in very interesting form: sound shifts, change in grammar and syntax, vocabulary growth, similar topics. Abundantly illustrated with quotations. Formerly Modern English in the Making. xii + 590pp. 21932-1 Paperbound $3.50

AN ETYMOLOGICAL DICTIONARY OF MODERN ENGLISH, Ernest Weekley. Fullest, richest work of its sort, by foremost British lexicographer. Detailed word histories, including many colloquial and archaic words; extensive quotations. Do not confuse this with the Concise Etymological Dictionary, which is much abridged. Total of xxvii + 830pp. 6½ x 9¼. 21873-2, 21874-0 Two volumes, Paperbound $7.90

FLATLAND: A ROMANCE OF MANY DIMENSIONS, E. A. Abbott. Classic of science-fiction explores ramifications of life in a two-dimensional world, and what happens when a three-dimensional being intrudes. Amusing reading, but also useful as introduction to thought about hyperspace. Introduction by Banesh Hoffmann. 16 illustrations. xx + 103pp. 20001-9 Paperbound $1.00

POEMS OF ANNE BRADSTREET, edited with an introduction by Robert Hutchinson. A new selection of poems by America's first poet and perhaps the first significant woman poet in the English language. 48 poems display her development in works of considerable variety—love poems, domestic poems, religious meditations, formal elegies, "quaternions," etc. Notes, bibliography. viii + 222pp.
22160-1 Paperbound $2.50

THREE GOTHIC NOVELS: THE CASTLE OF OTRANTO BY HORACE WALPOLE; VATHEK BY WILLIAM BECKFORD; THE VAMPYRE BY JOHN POLIDORI, WITH FRAGMENT OF A NOVEL BY LORD BYRON, edited by E. F. Bleiler. The first Gothic novel, by Walpole; the finest Oriental tale in English, by Beckford; powerful Romantic supernatural story in versions by Polidori and Byron. All extremely important in history of literature; all still exciting, packed with supernatural thrills, ghosts, haunted castles, magic, etc. xl + 291pp.
21232-7 Paperbound $3.00

THE BEST TALES OF HOFFMANN, E. T. A. Hoffmann. 10 of Hoffmann's most important stories, in modern re-editings of standard translations: Nutcracker and the King of Mice, Signor Formica, Automata, The Sandman, Rath Krespel, The Golden Flowerpot, Master Martin the Cooper, The Mines of Falun, The King's Betrothed, A New Year's Eve Adventure. 7 illustrations by Hoffmann. Edited by E. F. Bleiler. xxxix + 419pp.
21793-0 Paperbound $3.00

GHOST AND HORROR STORIES OF AMBROSE BIERCE, Ambrose Bierce. 23 strikingly modern stories of the horrors latent in the human mind: The Eyes of the Panther, The Damned Thing, An Occurrence at Owl Creek Bridge, An Inhabitant of Carcosa, etc., plus the dream-essay, Visions of the Night. Edited by E. F. Bleiler. xxii + 199pp.
20767-6 Paperbound $2.00

BEST GHOST STORIES OF J. S. LEFANU, J. Sheridan LeFanu. Finest stories by Victorian master often considered greatest supernatural writer of all. Carmilla, Green Tea, The Haunted Baronet, The Familiar, and 12 others. Most never before available in the U. S. A. Edited by E. F. Bleiler. 8 illustrations from Victorian publications. xvii + 467pp.
20415-4 Paperbound $3.00

MATHEMATICAL FOUNDATIONS OF INFORMATION THEORY, A. I. Khinchin. Comprehensive introduction to work of Shannon, McMillan, Feinstein and Khinchin, placing these investigations on a rigorous mathematical basis. Covers entropy concept in probability theory, uniqueness theorem, Shannon's inequality, ergodic sources, the E property, martingale concept, noise, Feinstein's fundamental lemma, Shanon's first and second theorems. Translated by R. A. Silverman and M. D. Friedman. iii + 120pp.
60434-9 Paperbound $2.00

SEVEN SCIENCE FICTION NOVELS, H. G. Wells. The standard collection of the great novels. Complete, unabridged. *First Men in the Moon, Island of Dr. Moreau, War of the Worlds, Food of the Gods, Invisible Man, Time Machine, In the Days of the Comet.* Not only science fiction fans, but every educated person owes it to himself to read these novels. 1015pp. (USO) 20264-X Clothbound $6.00

MATHEMATICAL PUZZLES FOR BEGINNERS AND ENTHUSIASTS, Geoffrey Mott-Smith. 189 puzzles from easy to difficult—involving arithmetic, logic, algebra, properties of digits, probability, etc.—for enjoyment and mental stimulus. Explanation of mathematical principles behind the puzzles. 135 illustrations. viii + 248pp.

20198-8 Paperbound $2.00

PAPER FOLDING FOR BEGINNERS, William D. Murray and Francis J. Rigney. Easiest book on the market, clearest instructions on making interesting, beautiful origami. Sail boats, cups, roosters, frogs that move legs, bonbon boxes, standing birds, etc. 40 projects; more than 275 diagrams and photographs. 94pp.

20713-7 Paperbound $1.00

TRICKS AND GAMES ON THE POOL TABLE, Fred Herrmann. 79 tricks and games— some solitaires, some for two or more players, some competitive games—to entertain you between formal games. Mystifying shots and throws, unusual caroms, tricks involving such props as cork, coins, a hat, etc. Formerly *Fun on the Pool Table*. 77 figures. 95pp.

21814-7 Paperbound $1.25

HAND SHADOWS TO BE THROWN UPON THE WALL: A SERIES OF NOVEL AND AMUSING FIGURES FORMED BY THE HAND, Henry Bursill. Delightful picturebook from great-grandfather's day shows how to make 18 different hand shadows: a bird that flies, duck that quacks, dog that wags his tail, camel, goose, deer, boy, turtle, etc. Only book of its sort. vi + 33pp. 6½ x 9¼. 21779-5 Paperbound $1.00

WHITTLING AND WOODCARVING, E. J. Tangerman. 18th printing of best book on market. "If you can cut a potato you can carve" toys and puzzles, chains, chessmen, caricatures, masks, frames, woodcut blocks, surface patterns, much more. Information on tools, woods, techniques. Also goes into serious wood sculpture from Middle Ages to present, East and West. 464 photos, figures. x + 293pp.

20965-2 Paperbound $2.50

HISTORY OF PHILOSOPHY, Julián Marias. Possibly the clearest, most easily followed, best planned, most useful one-volume history of philosophy on the market; neither skimpy nor overfull. Full details on system of every major philosopher and dozens of less important thinkers from pre-Socratics up to Existentialism and later. Strong on many European figures usually omitted. Has gone through dozens of editions in Europe. 1966 edition, translated by Stanley Appelbaum and Clarence Strowbridge. xviii + 505pp. 21739-6 Paperbound $3.50

YOGA: A SCIENTIFIC EVALUATION, Kovoor T. Behanan. Scientific but non-technical study of physiological results of yoga exercises; done under auspices of Yale U. Relations to Indian thought, to psychoanalysis, etc. 16 photos. xxiii + 270pp.

20505-3 Paperbound $2.50

Prices subject to change without notice.
Available at your book dealer or write for free catalogue to Dept. GI, Dover Publications, Inc., 180 Varick St., N. Y., N. Y. 10014. Dover publishes more than 150 books each year on science, elementary and advanced mathematics, biology, music, art, literary history, social sciences and other areas.